Software Portability
with imake

Software Portability
with imake

Paul DuBois

O'Reilly & Associates, Inc.
103 Morris Street, Suite A
Sebastopol, CA 95472

Software Portability with imake

by Paul DuBois

Copyright © 1993 O'Reilly & Associates, Inc. All rights reserved.
Printed in the United States of America.

Editor: Adrian Nye

Printing History:

July 1993:	First Edition.
December 1993:	Minor corrections.
August 1994:	Minor corrections. Appendix J, X11R6, added.

ISBN: 1-56592-055-4

Table of Contents

Preface   xxii

Why Read This Handbook? xviii
Scope of This Handbook xix
    Part I xix
    Part II xx
    Part III xxi
Conventions Used in This Book xxii
Comments and Corrections xxiii
Acknowledgments xxiii

1: Introduction   1

The Nature of Nonportability 5
    Why Not Just Use make? 6
The Nature of Configurability 7
How Does imake Work? 8
What Can imake Do for You? 11
Slaying the Beast 12

2: A Tour of imake   15

Getting Started—The Essential Toolkit 16
The Exercises 16
    Exercise 1. Write an Imakefile and Generate the Makefile 17
    Exercise 2. Build a Program 19
    Exercise 3. Examine the Makefile 21
    Exercise 4. Compare Makefiles on Different Systems 24
    Exercise 5. Generate Header File Dependencies 25
    Exercise 6. Add a Default Target 27
    Exercise 7. Check Source Files 29
    Exercise 8. Install the Program 30
What Have You Learned? 31

3: Understanding Configuration Files   *33*

Two Principles 34
Use Machine-Independent Description Files 35
    Recognize Target-building Patterns 35
    Invent a Rule Macro Syntax 38
Organize the Structure of imake Input 41
Parameterize Variation 44
Select Parameters by System Type 47
Allow Conditional Parameter Assignments 52
Allow for Local Convention 55
Write Rules to be Replaceable 57
Final Architecture 57

4: The X11 Configuration Files   *61*

The X11 Template 62
Default Configuration Information 64
    General System Parameters—Imake.tmpl 64
    Project-Specific Parameters—Project.tmpl 65
    How To Build Things—Imake.rules 68
Machine-Specific Configuration Information 68
    Vendor Block Selection 69
    Vendor-Specific Configuration Information—vendor.cf 72
    Site-Specific Configuration Information—site.def 74
What To Build 75
    Directory-Specific Targets—Imakefile 75
    Default Makefile Target Entries 75
Miscellaneous Topics 76
    Token Concatenation 76
    Commenting 79

5: Writing Imakefiles   *83*

General Strategy 84
Invoking Rules 86
Building One Program 87
    Building a Single Program (One Source File) 87
    Building a Single Program (Multiple Source Files) 88
Specifying Libraries 90
    Link Libraries 90
    Dependency Libraries 91

Within-project Libraries 92
System Libraries 92
X Libraries 93
Mixing Library Types 95
Building Multiple Programs 95
Building Two or Three Programs 96
Building an Arbitrary Number of Programs 99
linting Multiple Programs 102
Organizing Source and Object File Lists 102
Building Libraries 103
Other Kinds of Libraries 104
Compiling Object Files Specially 105
Installing Files 106
Managing Multiple Directory Projects 107
Restricting the Scope of Recursive Operations 110
Adding a New Directory to an Existing Project 110
Constraints on the Value of SUBDIRS 110
Specifying Debugging Flags 111
Combination Branch/Leaf Directories 111
Other Useful make Variables 111
Questions 114

6: Imakefile Troubleshooting   121

Diagnosing Errors 122
General Disaster Recovery 123
Extraneous Spaces in Rule Invocations 124
Misspelled Rules and Macros 125
Recursive Rules and Spelling Errors 126
Broken Comments 126
Incorrect Library Dependency Specifications 128
Malformed Variable Assignments 129
Incorrect Value Assignments 129
Errors of Omission 130

7: A Closer Look at Makefile Generation   131

What imake Needs to Know 132
Configuration File Location 132
Project Root Location 134
Running imake From a Makefile 136
Where Are the Configuration Files? 137

Building Makefiles Recursively 139

Makefile Generation in X11 141

8: A Configuration Starter Project   *145*

Creating the Starter Project 146

    Changes To Imake.tmpl 150

    Changes To Project.tmpl 151

    Changes to Imake.rules 152

Testing the Starter Project 152

Using the Starter Project 153

    Installing Your Project's Configuration Files 153

9: Coordinating Sets of Configuration Files   *157*

Designing a General Purpose Bootstrapper 158

Implementing imboot 161

Cooperating with imboot 163

Backward Compatibility 164

    The X11 Configuration Files 164

    Multiple X11 Releases 165

    Kerberos V5 166

    Motif and Open Windows 167

    Incompatible Projects 169

Using imboot in Makefiles 169

10: Introduction to Configuration File Writing   *173*

Setting Up 174

Deleting Information 175

    FORTRAN Support 176

    X Support 176

    Shared Library Support 176

    Miscellaneous Symbol Deleting Guidelines 177

    A Shocking Fact 179

Retaining Information 179

    Modifying Retained Information 180

    Simplifying Retained Information 181

Adding Information 182

    Adding Macros and Parameter Variables 182

    Choosing Default Macro Values 183

    Subdirectory Support 186

11: Writing Rule Macros 189

Rule Syntax 190
Building the Basic Rule 190
    Parameterizing the Rule 191
    Link Libraries 192
    Passing Information to Rules 193
    Libraries as Dependencies 194
    Implications of Parameterization 195
    Special Linker Information 196
Making the Rule Work Harder 198
    The clean Target 198
    The all Target 201
    The lint Target 202
Refining the Scope of a Target 204
Documenting Rules 205
Building Libraries 206
Installation Rules 207
    Should BuildProgram( ) Generate an install Target? 213
    Refining the Scope of Installation Rules 214

12: Configuration Problems and Solutions 215

Describing Project Layout 216
Specifying Library Names 218
Handling Newly Discovered Nonportabilities 219
Conditionals in Imakefiles 220
    Selecting Targets to Build 220
    Selecting Files or Directories to Process 221
    Selecting Flags For Commands 224
Configuring Source Files 225
    Configuring Source Files with msub 228
    Configuring Macro Values into Source Files 231
    Configuring Header Files 232
Using make Suffix Rules 233
    Defining New Target Types 236
Shell Programming in Rules 236
    Multiple Line Constructs 237
    Directory Changes 238
    Command Echoing 239
    Error Processing in Rules 239
Writing a World Target 240

13: Troubleshooting Configuration Files 243

Three Simple Rule Syntax Errors 243
Extraneous Spaces in Rule Definitions 244
Unbalanced Conditionals 245
Malformed Conditionals 246
Missing Default Values 247
Troublemaker make Comments 248
Incorrect Version Number Tests 249
Missing Template 249
Nonportable cpp or make Constructs 250
Insufficient Wariness of cpp 250

14: Designing Extensible Configuration Files 253

Reusing Configuration Files 254
Are the X11 Configuration Files Reusable? 255
Methods of Reusing Configuration Files 258
    Method 1: Copy and Modify Existing Configuration Files 258
    Method 2: Share Comprehensive Configuration Files 259
    Method 3: Share Extensible Configuration Files 260
Implementing Extensible Configuration Files 262
    Step 1: Modify Imake.tmpl 263
    Step 2: Determine Configuration File Directory Locations 267
    Step 3: Modify Makefile Building Commands 268
Does This Architecture Really Work? 271

15: Creating Extensible Configuration Files 273

Preliminaries 273
Setting Up 274
Modify the Architecture 274
Make the Files Self-aware 276
Generalize File Contents 278
Install the Files 281

16: Using Extensible Configuration Files 283

Starting Your Project 284
Override and Extension Principles 284
Project Layout 285
Installation Directories 287
Project-specific Rules 288

Libraries 288
System Characteristics 288
The Site-specific File 289
Configuration File Experimentation 290
Distributing Software Configured with Extensible Files 290
Creating a New Set of Extensible Files 290

A: Obtaining Configuration Software   293

Obtaining the Distributions 294
    FTP 294
    GOPHER 295
    FTPMAIL 295
    BITFTP 296
    UUCP 297

B: Installing Configuration Software   299

Distribution Layout 300
Find Out What You Already Have 301
Prepare to Install the Distribution 302
    Installing with Limited Privileges 303
Build the Distribution— Quick Instructions 303
Install the Software 305
Detailed Instructions 306
    Write the Vendor File 308
    Write the Vendor Block 309
    Configure imake 310
    Build imake 314
    Build the Rest of the Distribution 315
imake versus Open Windows 316

C: Configuration Programs: A Quick Reference   319

D: Generating Makefiles: A Quick Reference   329

E: Writing Imakefiles: A Quick Reference   331

Subdirectory Support 332

F: Writing Configuration Files: A Quick Reference   *343*
Parameter Settings and Feature Symbols 344
Rule Syntax 344

G: Basics of make and cpp   *349*
Basics of make 349
Basics of cpp 351

H: A Little History   *355*

I: Related Documents   *357*

J: X11R6   *359*

Index   *371*

Figures

1: Introduction   *1*

1-1   Producing software with make alone   8
1-2   Producing software with make and imake   9
1-3   Software development and porting with make alone   9
1-4   Software development and porting with imake and make   10

2: A Tour of imake   *15*

2-1   Location of complexities   23

3: Understanding Configuration Files   *33*

3-1   Schematic configuration file template architecture   42
3-2   Final template architecture   58

4: The X11 Configuration Files   *61*

4-1   X11 configuration file template architecture   62
4-2   Section of Imake.tmpl specifying configuration defaults   64
4-3   Section of Imake.tmpl specifying machine-specifics   68
4-4   Section of Imake.tmpl specifying site-specifics   74
4-5   Section of Imake.tmpl specifying target entries   75

5: Writing Imakefiles   *83*

5-1   Sample multiple directory project   108
5-2   xblob project   112

7: A Closer Look at Makefile Generation   *131*

7-1   Sample project layout   133

8: A Configuration Starter Project   *145*

8-1   Project that builds programs in project root   146
8-2   Project that builds programs in subdirectories   147
8-3   Minimal configuration-related parts of project tree   147

10: Introduction to Configuration File Writing   *173*

10-1   DP configuration file ancestry   175

12: Configuration Problems and Solutions   *215*

12-1   Simple project tree   216
12-2   Directory-selecting Imakefile   222

14: Designing Extensible Configuration Files   *253*

14-1   X11R5/SP template architecture   263
14-2   Extensible architecture (EA) template   264

15: Creating Extensible Configuration Files   *273*

15-1   EA template architecture   275

16: Using Extensible Configuration Files   *283*

16-1   Prototype project layout   286
16-2   Project with layout differing from prototype   287

B: Installing Configuration Software   *299*

B-1   imake distribution project tree   300

J: X11R6   *359*

J-1   Architecture of X11 configuration file template Imake.tmpl   363

Tables

5: Writing Imakefiles   83
5-1   make Variables for X Libraries   93
5-2   Link and Dependency Library Specifier Summary   95

7: A Closer Look at Makefile Generation   131
7-1   Specifying Confdir for Within-project Configuration Files   133

11: Writing Rule Macros   189
11-1 A Set of Installation Parameters   211

12: Configuration Problems and Solutions   215
12-1 Directory Locations Expressed Using Relative Pathnames   216
12-2 Directory Locations Expressed Using Parameters   217
12-3 System CPU-time Interface Differences   222

13: Troubleshooting Configuration Files   243
13-1 Macro Types   246

16: Using Extensible Configuration Files   283
16-1 Defining Feature Symbol Default and Override Values   289

B: Installing Configuration Software   299
B-1   Bootstrap Flags for Various Systems   304

J: X11R6   359
J-1   R5 and R6 Install Directories   360

Preface

The hungry sheep look up, and are not fed...
—John Milton, *Lycidas*

This book is about *imake*, a UNIX tool that helps you write portable programs.

Most program development under UNIX is done with *make*, using a *Makefile* to direct the build and install processes. But Makefiles aren't portable, and it's often difficult to rewrite them by hand to accommodate machine dependencies for different systems. *imake* provides an alternative based on a simple idea: describe the dependencies for various systems in a set of configuration files and let *imake* generate the *Makefile* for you after selecting the dependencies appropriate for your machine. This frees you from writing and rewriting Makefiles by hand and helps you produce portable software that can be built and installed easily on any of the systems described in the configuration files.

imake has been used successfully to configure software such as the X Window System, the Kerberos authentication system, and the Khoros software development environment. X in particular is a large project that, despite its size and complexity, is remarkable in its portability. Much of this portability is due to the use of *imake*, which is thus arguably one of the reasons X has been so successful.

Nevertheless, despite the fact that it's freely available and runs on a variety of systems, *imake* isn't as widely exploited as it could be. There are at least two reasons for this:

- *imake* itself is a simple program, but the configuration files it uses sometimes are not. In particular, most people first encounter *imake* through the configuration files distributed with X. The X files are powerful and flexible, but they're also complicated and forbidding, and don't provide a very accessible entry point into the world of *imake*.

- *imake* hasn't been well documented. Normally when you don't understand how to use a program, you turn to the documentation. But for *imake* there hasn't been much available, which compounds the difficulty of learning it. Consequently, *imake* remains a mystery, leaving potential *imake* users in the predicament of Milton's sheep—seeking help in vain.

I freely acknowledge that *imake* can be difficult to make sense of. But it doesn't *need* to be so, nor should you have to become an initiate into the Eleusinian mysteries to be granted an understanding of how *imake* works.

Why Read This Handbook?

The goal of this book is to show how *imake* can help you write portable software and to make it easier for you to use *imake* on a daily basis. Then you'll be able to see it as a tool to be used, not a stumbling block to trip over.

If you don't know how to use *imake* at all, this book will teach you. If you already use *imake*, you'll learn how to use it more effectively. The book provides assistance on a number of levels, and you'll find it useful if you're in any of the situations below:

- You wonder what *imake* is and how it works.

- You couldn't care less what *imake* is or how it works. (As in, "I just got this program off the net. What do I do with this *Imakefile* thing? I'm not interested in *imake*, I just want to get the program built!")

- You're curious about the relationship between an *Imakefile* and a *Makefile*.

- You're faced with the task of using *imake* for the first time and are finding it less than obvious.

- You're trying to use *imake* but you need help diagnosing problems that occur. For example: "I just generated my *Makefile*, but *make* says it contains a syntax error; what do I do now?"

- You're tired of editing your Makefiles every time you move your programs from one machine to another.

- You've inherited projects that were developed using *imake* and you need to understand how they're configured so you can maintain them.

- You've been able to use *imake* to configure, build, and install the X Window System on your workstation using the instructions provided with the X source distribution, but it all seemed like magic. You want to better understand what goes on during that process.

- You're planning to write X-based software. It's best to do this using an *Imakefile* (since X itself is *imake*-configured), and you'll be required to provide one anyway if you plan to submit your software to the X Consortium for inclusion in the X *contrib* distribution.

- You admire the portability of X and want to achieve the same for your own software, but you've found it difficult to use *imake* without a copy of X nearby. You suspect it's possible for *imake* to stand on its own, but you're not sure how.

- You're looking for a general purpose tool for long-term software development and are considering using *imake* to that end.

Scope of This Handbook

This book is divided into three parts. Part I provides an overview of *imake* and how to use it, a basic description of the operation of configuration files, and how to write and troubleshoot Imakefiles. Part II describes how to write your own configuration files. Part III comprises appendices for your reference. Each chapter and appendix is described briefly below: use this information to navigate to those of most interest to you.

Part I

Chapter 1, *Introduction*, describes what *imake* is and what it does. It also discusses why *make* is inadequate for achieving software portability. Read this to find out what problems *imake* attempts to solve.

Chapter 2, *A Tour of imake*, is an *imake* tutorial. In this chapter, I assume that you're not particularly interested in details about how *imake* works, you just want to know how to use it to do specific things: how to write a simple *Imakefile* to specify programs you want to build, how to generate the *Makefile* from the *Imakefile*, etc. Instead of starting from "first principles," you use *imake* to run through some basic exercises to get a feel for what it does and how to make it do what you want.

Chapter 3, *Understanding Configuration Files*, describes the principles governing the design of configuration files that you need to know to understand their structure and content—what's in them and how they work together. You don't need to read this chapter if you're a casual *imake* user, but you should if you want to employ *imake* more effectively or if you plan on writing your own configuration files. In this chapter I assume you want to understand *imake*'s workings in more detail—not just what it does, but how and why.

Chapter 4, *The X11 Configuration Files*, discusses the configuration files from the X Window System, relating them to the general principles described in Chapter 3 and pointing out some of their unique features. This isn't an X book, but the X11 configuration files are the most well known instance of the use of *imake* to date. As such, they provide a fertile source of examples and discussion. It would be unwise not to take advantage of the lessons they provide.

Chapter 5, *Writing Imakefiles*, describes how to write Imakefiles for programs configured with the X11 configuration files. This chapter provides simple examples that require little or no knowledge of the X11 files, as well as detailed discussion to increase your practical understanding of how the X11 files work.

Chapter 6, *Imakefile Troubleshooting*, discusses things that can go wrong when you write Imakefiles and how to fix them.

Part II

Chapter 7, *A Closer Look at Makefile Generation*, examines the process by which *imake* builds Makefiles, including a discussion of how `Makefile` and `Makefiles` target entries work.

Chapter 8, *A Configuration Starter Project*, shows how to convert the X11 configuration files into a starter project you can use as a jumping-off point for developing new projects or new sets of configuration files.

Chapter 9, *Coordinating Sets of Configuration Files*, discusses the problems that arise in a world populated by multiple sets of configuration files and how to solve the problems so you can manage those files easily.

Chapter 10, *Introduction to Configuration File Writing*, shows by example how to write a set of configuration files. It describes in general the various ways you can modify the contents of configuration files.

Chapter 11, *Writing Rule Macros*, continues the discussion begun in Chapter 10, focusing on the design and implementation of *imake* rules.

Chapter 12, *Configuration Problems and Solutions*, discusses several configuration problems and shows how to solve them using the principles and techniques described in Chapters 10 and 11.

Chapter 13, *Troubleshooting Configuration Files*, discusses things that can go wrong when you write configuration files and how to fix them. It complements Chapter 6, *Imakefile Troubleshooting*.

Chapter 14, *Designing Extensible Configuration Files*, discusses how to design configuration files to be shared easily among projects, while allowing individual projects to specify their own particular requirements by extending or overriding the information in the shared files. This extensible architecture reduces the need to write new configuration files for a project when existing files don't quite match a project's configuration requirements.

Chapter 15, *Creating Extensible Configuration Files*, describes a procedure you can use to convert existing project specific configuration files to the extensible architecture.

Chapter 16, *Using Extensible Configuration Files*, shows how to develop new projects that take advantage of the flexibility afforded by the extensible architecture.

Part III

Appendix A, *Obtaining Configuration Software*, describes how to get the software described in this book. *imake* is owned and copyrighted by MIT but may be freely redistributed. So although *imake* isn't usually included as part of the software distributed with the UNIX operating system, anyone with FTP or GOPHER access on the Internet can get it. *imake* is also available by electronic mail.

Appendix B, *Installing Configuration Software*, discusses how to build and install the software described in this book.

Appendix C, *Configuration Programs: A Quick Reference*, documents the software described in this book in "abbreviated manpage" format.

Appendix D, *Generating Makefiles: A Quick Reference*, briefly describes how to build a *Makefile* from an *Imakefile*.

Appendix E, *Writing Imakefiles: A Quick Reference*, briefly describes how to write an *Imakefile*.

Appendix F, *Writing Configuration Files: A Quick Reference*, briefly describes how to write configuration files.

Appendix G, *Basics of make and cpp*, provides brief overviews of *make* and *cpp*. Since *imake* produces Makefiles, you need to understand a little about *make*. You should also understand something about *cpp*, because *imake* uses *cpp* to do most of its work.

Appendix H, *A Little History*, describes how *imake* came into being.

Appendix I, *Related Documents*, lists some other useful sources of information.

Appendix J, *X11R6*, describes configuration-related differences between the X11R5 and X11R6 distributions.

Conventions Used in This Book

The following conventions are used in this book:

Bold   is used to emphasize new terms and concepts when they are introduced.

Italic   is used for options to commands, for file and directory names when they appear in the body of a paragraph, and for program and command names.

`Constant`   is used in examples to show the contents of files or the output
`Width`   from commands; and to indicate environment variables, rules, entries, and targets.

Constant
Bold
is used in examples to show commands or other text that should be typed literally by the user. For example, **rm foo** means to type "rm foo" exactly as it appears in the text or example.

Constant
Italic
is used in code fragments and examples to show variables for which a context-specific substitution should be made. The variable *filename*, for example, would be replaced by some actual filename.

Comments and Corrections

If you have comments on this book or suggestions for improvement, or if you find errors, please feel free to contact me by sending electronic mail to *dubois@primate.wisc.edu.*

Acknowledgments

Many people contributed in various ways to this book; those listed here were especially helpful.

Thanks are due to Todd Brunhoff, Jim Fulton, Bob Scheifler, and Stephen Gildea for their willingness to answer my myriad questions about *imake* and the X11 configuration files.

Mary Kay Sherer waded through early drafts and refused to be nice to them. But faithful are the wounds of a friend; her criticisms helped weed out many incomprehensiblenesses.

The staff of O'Reilly & Associates was a pleasure to work with. Adrian Nye provided editorial guidance and oversight and is really the one to whom *Software Portability with imake* owes its existence (the book was his idea; I just wrote it). Laura Parker Roerden copyedited what must have seemed an intractable thicket of words and managed final production with the indispensable help of Clairemarie Fisher O'Leary. Lenny Muellner fielded a constant stream of *troff* questions. Ellie Cutler wrote the index. Jennifer Niederst provided design support. Jeff Robbins produced the figures. And Edie Freedman designed the book and the cover with that marvelous snake. David Brooks, Gary Keim, David Lewis, Andy Oram, and Tom Sauer provided helpful review comments. For the reprint of this handbook, Nicole Gipson entered new edits, Chris Reilly designed the figure for the new appendix, and Chris Tong prepared the index.

Most of all I'd like to thank my wife Karen, who endured author's-widow tribulations with considerable grace and understanding. And patience: she listened while I rehearsed often and at length my thoughts about the topics in this book, even though she "cared for none of those things." This was invaluable in helping me sort out what I was trying to write. Her contribution was significant, and greatly appreciated.

In this chapter:
- *The Nature of Nonportability*
- *The Nature of Configurability*
- *How Does imake Work?*
- *What Can imake Do for You?*
- *Slaying the Beast*

1

Introduction

> *There is no such thing as portable software,*
> *only software that has been ported.*
> —Unknown

The problem of how to write portable software confronts a broad spectrum of developers—from the lone programmer seeking to move a single program from one machine to another, to commercial enterprises seeking to port large, complex projects to run on several systems to maximize the market for their product. In each case, the common aim is to move software from one system to another without a substantial burden in time and effort for code revision.

In the UNIX world, software development typically involves *make*, using a *Makefile* describing how to build and install the programs in which we're interested.* The *Makefile* lists **targets** (e.g., programs to be built) and associates each with the commands that build it. When you invoke *make*, it determines which targets you're interested in, and for each one that's out of date, rebuilds it by executing the commands associated with it. This process is recursive; if a target depends on other prerequisite targets being up to date, *make* first executes the commands associated with the prerequisites as necessary.

In essence, *make* functions as a command-generating engine, and the *Makefile* controls which commands to generate for specific targets. This is a tremendous convenience for the programmer, since it eliminates the need

---

*If you're unfamiliar with *make* and Makefiles, see Appendix G, *Basics of make and cpp*.

to type out a bunch of commands each time you want to build something. The *Makefile* serves as a repository for your knowledge, encoded in such a way that arbitrarily complex command sequences can be called forth and reenacted at will simply by naming targets.

Unfortunately, Makefiles aren't portable. The commands that *make* so conveniently generates at the drop of a hat are subject to variation from system to system, so a *Makefile* that works on my system may not work on yours. Ideally, we'd be able to take a software project, plop it on another machine, compile and install it, and it would run. But it doesn't always work that way.

Suppose we're writing a small C program, *myname*, consisting of a single source file *myname.c*:

```
#include <stdio.h>
int main ()
{
char    *getenv ();
char    *p;
    p = getenv ("USER");
    if (p == (char *) NULL)
        printf ("cannot tell your user name\n");
    else
        printf ("your user name is %s\n", p);
    exit (0);
}
```

The *Makefile* for the program might look like this:

```
myname: myname.o
    cc -o myname myname.o
install: myname
    install myname /usr/local
```

To build and install *myname*, we'd use these commands:

```
% make myname
cc -c myname.c
cc -o myname myname.o
% make install
install myname /usr/local
```

The first *make* command does two things: it compiles *myname.o* from *myname.c* (*make* has built-in intelligence about producing .o files from .c files), and it links *myname.o* to produce an executable *myname*. The second *make* command installs *myname* in the */usr/local* directory.

All our friends are astonished at the usefulness of this program and immediately begin hectoring us mercilessly for the source code. We give it to one of them, together with the *Makefile*, and he lopes off to install it on his machine. The next day he sends back the following report:

- We don't have any *install* program, so I used *cp*.
- Our local installation directory is */usr/local/bin* rather than */usr/local*.

He sends back a revised *Makefile*, having made the necessary changes, and also having conveniently parameterized the things he found to be different on his system, using the *make* variables* INSTALL and BINDIR at the beginning of the *Makefile*:

```
# set following variables appropriately for your machine
INSTALL = cp
 BINDIR = /usr/local/bin
myname: myname.o
    cc -o myname myname.o
install: myname
    $(INSTALL) myname $(BINDIR)
```

This is a step forward. The installation program and directory as specified in this *Makefile* are no longer correct for our machine, but now they're parameterized and thus easily located and modified. We change the values back to *install* and */usr/local* so they'll work on our machine, and both we and our friend are happy.

Alas, our idyllic state of mind doesn't last long. We give the program to another friend. She builds it and reports back her changes:

- I prefer to use *gcc*, not *cc*.
- Our C library is broken and doesn't contain *getenv()*; I have to link in *–lc_aux* as well.
- The environment variable USER isn't used on our system, but LOGNAME is, so I used that instead.

She, too, sends back a revised *Makefile*, further parameterized:

```
# set following variables appropriately for your machine
        CC = gcc
EXTRA_LIBS = -lc_aux
    BINDIR = /usr/local
    INSTALL = install
```

---

*What I'm calling *make* **variables** are sometimes referred to as *make* **macros**. In this book, the word "macro" always means a *cpp* macro, not a *make* macro.

```
myname: myname.o
    $(CC) -o myname myname.o $(EXTRA_LIBS)
install: myname
    $(INSTALL) myname $(BINDIR)
```

The *Makefile* solves her first two problems, as they involve variations in building and installing the program. The third problem involves a non-portability in the program source itself. Our friend took the easy way out and simply edited *myname.c*, changing the parameter passed to the *getenv()* call from USER to LOGNAME. However, that's a bad idea, since she'll have to remember to edit the source every time we release a new, latest-and-greatest version of *myname*. It would be better to use the *Makefile* to make the nonportability explicit.

It's easy to solve the problem using some of *make*'s built-in intelligence. The default command that *make* executes to produce an object file *x.o* from a C source file *x.c* looks something like this:

```
$(CC) $(CFLAGS) -c x.c
```

The default command may vary somewhat from system to system, but will include $(CFLAGS) in it somewhere. We can use CFLAGS to control whether *myname* attempts to reference USER or LOGNAME at run time. First, we change the line in *myname.c* where the *getenv()* call occurs from this:

```
p = getenv ("USER");
```

to this:

```
#ifdef USE_LOGNAME
    p = getenv ("LOGNAME");
#else
    p = getenv ("USER");
#endif
```

Then we define CFLAGS appropriately in the *Makefile*. To select LOG-NAME, write this:

```
CFLAGS = -DUSE_LOGNAME
```

To select USER, write this instead:

```
CFLAGS =
```

Now, with a simple change to the *Makefile*, *myname* can be compiled on machines that use either environment variable. This is encouraging. Using our vast-and-ever-increasing porting experience, *myname* now works on more machines—three! And the revised *Makefile* is better than the original:

- It parameterizes all the nonportabilities we've encountered so far.
- Nonportabilities are identified explicitly at the beginning of the *Makefile*.
- They're easily modified by editing the *Makefile*.

However, we begin to notice uneasily that the number of things that might need changing from machine to machine is increasing. There were only two differences between machines when we built *myname* on two systems. Now we can build it on three systems, but the number of differences has increased to five. How many differences will we find when we attempt to port *myname* to additional systems? As the *Makefile* editing job gets bigger, it becomes more difficult. Each nonportability adds another increment to the burden incurred each time *myname* is built on a different machine.

Also, we'd better keep a list of parameters appropriate for each type of machine on which the program is known to run, or we'll forget them. And we need to distribute the list to other people who want to build the program, so they can consult it to see how they might need to modify the *Makefile* on their systems.

The Nature of Nonportability

The preceding example illustrates that even simple programs must be adapted to variation, both in the way their source code is written and in the way they're built and installed. *myname* is by no means an exotic program, but we encountered several nonportabilities during its development. There are variations in:

- User environment (USER vs. LOGNAME)
- Program building tools (*cc* vs. *gcc*)
- System library contents (presence/absence of *getenv()* in the C library)
- Installation tools (*install* vs. *cp*)
- Installation locations (*/usr/local* vs. */usr/local/bin*)

If we encounter this many variations with such an utterly trivial program, you can imagine (and probably know from experience!) how much worse the problem is for larger projects. For a project with a *Makefile* and one source file in a single directory, it might be no more than an annoyance to make the necessary changes. But if it has dozens or hundreds of source files distributed throughout five, 10, or 50 directories, we have a much more difficult problem on our hands.

Software portability is sometimes discussed from the perspective of eliminating machine dependencies from source code. That's worthwhile but insufficient, because many nonportabilities involve factors other than the program source itself. This was shown by our experience of porting *myname* to various systems: only one of the nonportabilities had anything to do with *myname*'s source code. The others involved variations in the build and install process, and the tools used during that process had to be selected and adapted for each system. This means the notion of "portable programs" must include a portable development process that allows us to select those tools easily.

Why Not Just Use make?

It would be advantageous to ensure portability with *make*, since we're already using it. But *make* alone isn't up to the task:

- **There are no conditionals.**

  If we could assign values to *make* variables conditionally, we could parameterize machine dependencies by assigning variable values appropriate to a given machine type. This would be a useful way of setting CFLAGS when building *myname*.

  If we could define target entries conditionally, we could build targets in the most appropriate way. For example, on machines with *ranlib*, we'd run it after building a library. On machines without it, we wouldn't. To some extent we can use the shell's *if*-statement syntax to get around lack of conditionals in target entries, but it's clunky to do so.

- **There is no flow control.**

  Loops and iterators must be done using shell commands to simulate them.

- **It's difficult to make global changes.**

  For example, suppose you use BINDIR to name your installation directory. You can assign it the proper value in each *Makefile* in your project. But if you decide to change it, you must find and change every *Makefile*. Alternatively, you can assign BINDIR once in the top-level *Makefile* and pass the value to *make* commands in subdirectories using suitable recursive rules. But then you can't run *make* directly in a subdirectory because BINDIR won't have the proper value. Recursive rules are difficult to write correctly, anyway.

If *make* had a mechanism for file inclusion, global information could be split out into a separate file and included from within each *Makefile*. Then the information would need to be specified in only one file and would be easier to change. Some versions of *make* have in fact been extended to allow file inclusion, but the extension isn't universal and thus is nonportable itself. So we can't rely on it.

- **Header file dependencies for C source files are inherently nonportable.**

  Different systems organize header files differently. You might even have multiple sets on systems that support development under more than one environment (BSD, System V, POSIX, etc.). This makes it impossible to list header file dependencies statically in the *Makefile*. They must be computed on the target machine at build time.

The *Makefile* is a terrific vehicle for expressing knowledge about building a target on a given system, but it's not especially good for adapting to variation between systems. *make* variables allow the variation to be parameterized, but that makes the Makefiles easier to configure only if you have a mechanism for changing them—and *make* doesn't provide one. In order to adapt to variation, the Makefiles must be changed by some external configuration process.

The Nature of Configurability

Perhaps the simplest configuration process is the brute force approach: "the person installing the software will edit the *Makefile* as necessary." Using this "method," we distribute a *README* file with the program indicating how to manually edit the *Makefile*. The *README* clearly and explicitly expresses what needs to be changed. However, the mechanism for translating that knowledge into a properly configured *Makefile* (i.e., hand editing) leaves something to be desired, especially as a project becomes more complex and subject to variation in a larger number of parameters. "Aren't these computers supposed to do the dirty work for us?" becomes the plaintive cry of despair of anyone who tries to configure software this way.

It would be better if we could express what we know about building a project on various systems so that a program could use our knowledge to reparameterize Makefiles automatically. Then we'd just say *poof!* and the Makefiles would be reconfigured for the machine we're using.

Our difficulties in writing and porting *myname* provide valuable instruction from which we can formulate two principles for portable software development:

- **Our knowledge of configuration requirements must be explicit.**

  We need to leave a trail by writing down what we know. If we carry our knowledge in our heads it will be lost.

- **Our knowledge must be machine-readable.**

  If configuration information isn't in a form a program can use, we'll still end up editing it ourselves each time a project is moved to a different machine. Also, we want to specify the information once, not replicate it manually in every *Makefile*. If any replication is necessary, a program should do it for us.

imake helps us follow these principles. It provides the means to avoid extensive manual *Makefile* rewriting by giving you a method for expressing your knowledge about configuration requirements for various systems in explicit, machine-usable form. When the software is moved to different machines, *imake* automatically uses your knowledge to rebuild Makefiles without manual intervention.

How Does imake Work?

When you're producing software using *make* alone, you write machine dependencies directly into your *Makefile*, using an editor such as *vi* or *emacs*. Then you run *make* to build your programs (Figure 1-1).

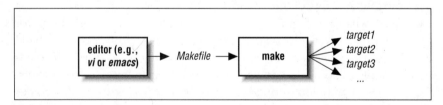

Figure 1-1: Producing software with make alone

With *imake*, you don't write a *Makefile*. Instead you write an *Imakefile*-a machine-independent description of the targets you want built. Machine dependencies are centralized into a set of configuration files isolated in their own directory, so they don't appear in the *Imakefile*. This makes the differing requirements for various systems explicit in a well known place and keeps them out of your target descriptions. *imake* reads the *Imakefile* and generates a properly configured *Makefile* by selecting from the configuration files those dependencies appropriate for your system. Then you run *make* to build your programs (Figure 1-2).

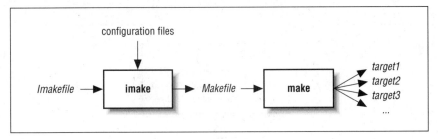

Figure 1-2: Producing software with make and imake

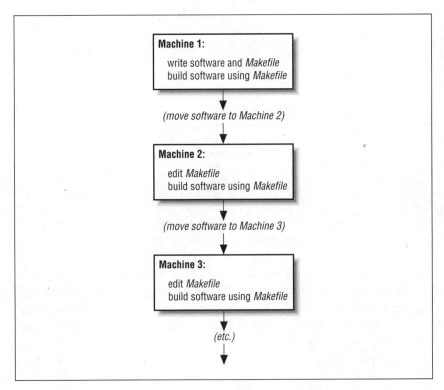

Figure 1-3: Software development and porting with make alone

When we move the software to another system, we need to factor porting activities into the development process. In particular, a different set of machine dependencies apply, so the *Makefile* is no longer correct. If you're using *make* alone, you edit the *Makefile* by hand again (Figure 1-3). By contrast, if you're using *imake*, you just run it again to generate a new *Makefile* (Figure 1-4).

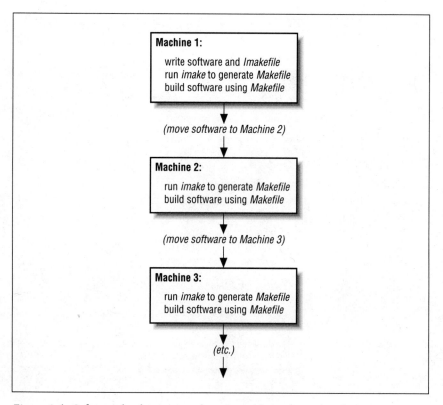

Figure 1-4: Software development and porting with imake and make

Figures 1-3 and 1-4 are similar, but there's a big difference between editing a *Makefile* manually and running *imake* to generate the *Makefile* for you, especially for multiple directory projects involving several Makefiles. When you specify configuration information by hand directly in your Makefiles, you have to find and edit information splattered all over your project every time you build it on a different machine. With *imake*, you localize machine dependencies in the configuration files and run *imake* to replicate that information into the Makefiles automatically.

What Can imake Do for You?

imake isn't a magic bullet that instantly and effortlessly solves all your porting woes. But it can reduce project development and maintenance tasks considerably. Here are some examples of what *imake* does for you:

- *imake* provides a notational convenience. It's easier to write an *Imakefile* than a *Makefile* because it's shorter and simpler.

- If you develop projects in collaboration with people who work on various types of machines, *imake* helps you work cooperatively by making it easier to build the software on the machines involved.

- If you work on a heterogeneous network composed of systems from several different vendors, *imake* helps you cope with your mix of machines by making it easier to build your software on various platforms. This allows you to move your software around to make it more uniformly available.

- If you want to make projects you've written available to others, *imake* helps you configure it to run on many systems, increasing the potential audience for your work.

- When you want to port an *imake*-configured project to a new platform, *imake* facilitates the process by providing an open-ended mechanism that allows you to incorporate new information into the configuration files. The information is explicitly represented in the configuration files, and, once it's specified, *imake* uses it automatically.

The rest of this book shows how to use *imake* by providing extensive documentation, as well as exercises you can do to gain hands-on experience. You'll be able to get started without digesting a lot of details first. The details are available when you want them, but presented in the context of principles that will help you organize your understanding of them.

For instance, *imake*'s configuration files can seem fairly impenetrable, but there are really only two basic principles you need to know in order to decipher them. One is to understand the purpose of each file and how different files relate to each other; the other is to understand the idioms by which their contents are specified. All configuration files consist mainly of the repetition of these idioms in their proper context. When you know how to speak this idiomatic language, you'll be able to exploit it to good purpose and use *imake* to its full potential.

You'll also be able to use *imake* for a variety of projects, and in doing so break free of one of the common misperceptions about *imake*: it's just an X tool. *imake* first received extensive exposure as part of the X Window

System, so it's often seen as a special purpose program limited to that environment. Nevertheless, *imake* isn't tied to X, it's a tool that can be used for general software development. My own experience illustrates this.

Slaying the Beast

Like many people, I first met *imake* through X. I had obtained a copy of the X11 distribution sometime during the tenure of Release 1 (X11R1), but I just wanted to read the documentation and poke through the source code a bit to see what X was all about. I wasn't actually interested in building or using it. Of course, it's difficult to get very far into the X distribution before encountering *imake*. For one thing, I was confronted with this thing called an *Imakefile* at every turn. So I decided to investigate *imake* in more detail.

My curiosity was short-lived. As I began to examine the configuration files used by *imake*, I realized I was unable to make the slightest sense of any of them. Sure, there were familiar words like CFLAGS, BINDIR, and INCLUDES scattered here and there, but there were also arcana like this:

```
#define InstallMultiple(list,dest)                        @@\
install:: list                                            @@\
    @case '${MFLAGS}' in *[i]*) set +e;; esac; \          @@\
    for i in list; do \                                   @@\
        (set -x; $(INSTALL) -c $(INSTALLFLAGS) $$i dest); \ @@\
    done
```

I don't know what that does for you, but my brain recoiled from it. The general sense is somewhat discernible (it installs programs), but how to use it was a mystery. *imake* seemed a gorgon, turning my thoughts to stone, and I put it aside, horrified. Nevertheless, there remained the suspicion in the back of my mind that a tool capable of configuring a project as large and complex as X must have some merit, and that perhaps *imake* would be useful for configuring my own software—if only I could figure out how to use it.

As new releases of X11 became available (R2, R3), I looked them over in turn, reexamining the configuration files each time. These repeated exposures had their effect, and I began to have some slight comprehension. My suspicions about the potential usefulness of *imake* for configuring my own software increased, but I was as yet unable to realize them since my understanding of how it worked was still quite rudimentary.

Sometime between X11R3 and X11R4 I was faced with the need to transport software frequently between two very dissimilar versions of UNIX (a VAX running Ultrix and a Mips M/120 running RISC/os). The difficulty of accommodating the differences between the machines proved to be extremely frustrating, so I finally decided to force myself to understand *imake*. To that end, I sat down with the X11R3 configuration files (several times!), determined to wrest from them their closely guarded secrets.

Eventually, I was able to configure some of my own projects using heavily modified copies of the X files. The result was that I could move those projects back and forth between my machines without concern for rewriting the Makefiles. *imake* took care of that for me. The effort expended had paid off.

Shortly thereafter, X11R4 became available. As before, I obtained a copy of the distribution. As before, I began to examine the configuration files (now with heightened interest) to see if they had changed, and, if so, how. And I found that although they had changed in some significant and important ways, it was a relatively straightforward task to make sense of them—a welcome and pleasant discovery.

I now consider *imake* indispensible and use it for virtually everything I write: program libraries, network client-server applications, bibliographic utilities, data analysis programs, mail servers, graphics generators. I also use it to develop documentation—including *Software Portability with imake*.

This road was long and difficult, but you need not travel it. In a sense this book is a distillation of my own experience, rearranged and presented in a form suited to easier understanding so you can short-circuit the learning process and begin to use *imake* quickly. I hope the book succeeds in making *imake* accessible and helps you in your own development efforts. I've found *imake* an extraordinarily useful tool. I think you will, too.

In this chapter:
- *Getting Started—*
  The Essential Toolkit
- *The Exercises*
- *What Have You*
  Learned?

2

A Tour of imake

> *Does the road wind uphill all the way?*
> —Christina Georgina Rosetti,
> *Uphill*

This chapter discusses how to run *imake* and how to write a simple *Imakefile*. It also describes *xmkmf, makedepend*, and *mkdirhier*, three programs that are useful in conjunction with *imake*. The discussion isn't an explanation of how *imake* works internally, it's a set of exercises forming a brief "do this, this, and this, and this is what should happen" walk-through. If you've used *imake* before, you may want to skip this chapter. If you haven't used it, or if you're one of those for whom *imake* seems an impenetrable riddle, you'll find it helpful to go through the exercises to get a feel for what *imake* does without wading through a nuts-and-bolts explanation of how it works.

Using *imake* is very much a learn-by-doing experience, so you really should do the exercises. They give you a chance to observe yourself actually surviving the experience of using *imake* to do something. This is similar to the way new UNIX users can type:

```
% who
```

to see that the computer doesn't blow up when they touch it.

Getting Started—The Essential Toolkit

To use *imake*, there are certain crucial ingredients:

- *imake* itself
- *cpp* and *make*; *imake* uses the former to produce Makefiles for the latter
- A set of configuration files
- *xmkmf* or another program to bootstrap a *Makefile* from an *Imakefile*

A couple of other programs are particularly useful in conjunction with *imake*:

makedepend   Generates header file dependencies from C source files

mkdirhier   Creates directories during file installation operations

I'm going to assume that the programs listed above and a set of configuration files are installed and available to you so you can try out the examples. However, with the exceptions of *cpp* and *make*, the elements of this toolkit aren't part of the software usually distributed with UNIX and you may need to obtain some of them first. In that case, see Appendix A, *Obtaining Configuration Software*, and Appendix B, *Installing Configuration Software*.

The Exercises

The exercises in this chapter are based on the configuration files from the X Window System, Version 11, Release 5. A likely spot to look for the files on your machine is */usr/lib/X11/config*; that's also where they're assumed to be installed here. If your files are installed somewhere else, you should simply substitute the directory they're in for */usr/lib/X11/config* whenever you see the latter in the examples throughout this book.*

If you like, you can use the TOUR configuration files described in Appendix A instead. They're equivalent to the X files for trying out the examples, but they're simpler. Should you get an irresistible urge to study configuration files directly as you're going through the chapter, you'll find them easier to understand than the X11 files. The TOUR distribution also contains the Imakefiles and source files described here, if you don't want to type them in yourself.

---

*For instance, if you're using Open Windows, the configuration files might be installed in */usr/openwin/lib/config*.

Okay, let's see how *imake* works. First, create a directory to use for a work area and move into it:

```
% mkdir TOUR
% cd TOUR
```

All the exercises should be carried out in the *TOUR* directory.

Exercise 1. Write an Imakefile and Generate the Makefile

To use *imake*, you need an *Imakefile*. An empty file will do for now. Create it like this:

```
% touch Imakefile
```

Or, if you don't have *touch*, use one of these commands:

```
% cp /dev/null Imakefile or
% echo > Imakefile
```

Once you have an *Imakefile*, you generate a *Makefile* from it. Normally, you do this with the command *make Makefile*, which tells *make* to generate the *imake* command needed to rebuild the *Makefile*. That is, you use the *Makefile* to recreate itself. But you don't have a *Makefile* yet!

There is a paradox here: you want to use the *Makefile* to run *imake* for you, but you need to run *imake* to get the *Makefile* in the first place. To get around this circularity, you need to know either how to run *imake* manually or how to use a *Makefile*-bootstrapping program. The bootstrapper associated with the X files is *xmkmf*, which you use as follows:

```
% xmkmf
imake -DUseInstalled -I/usr/lib/X11/config
```

Notice that *xmkmf* shows you the *imake* command it generates before it executes it. The important argument here is *–I/usr/lib/X11/config*, which tells *imake* where to look for the configuration files used to build the *Makefile*.

After running *xmkmf*, you should have a *Makefile* generated from your empty *Imakefile*. Use it to try out a few *make* commands: ·

```
% make clean
rm -f *.CKP *.ln *.BAK *.bak *.o core errs ,* *~ *.a .emacs_* \
    tags TAGS make.log MakeOut "#"*
```

```
% make
(no output)
% make Makefile
+ rm -f Makefile.bak
+ mv Makefile Makefile.bak
imake -DUseInstalled -I/usr/lib/X11/config -DTOPDIR=. -DCURDIR=.
```

The first *make* command runs *rm* to remove various kinds of "garbage" files, such as *.o* files from compiler operations. (This command isn't very useful at the moment. We haven't built anything, so there's nothing to remove.) The second command produces no output (there's nothing to build yet, either). The third regenerates the *Makefile*, after saving the current one as *Makefile.bak*.

Perhaps it seems a little strange that anything at all happens when you run these commands. The *Imakefile* was empty—how could it have contained any information to tell *make* what to do? Why doesn't *make* just spit out error messages?

The reason is that the *Imakefile* isn't the only source of information *imake* uses to generate the *Makefile*. It also uses the configuration files, which supply a number of target entries automatically. Among these are a `clean` entry, a `Makefile` entry, and a default target entry named `emptytarget` that does nothing (the latter target is why *make* with no arguments silently does nothing instead of producing an error message). The amount of information supplied automatically by configuration files can be surprising, even imposing. For example, on the machine I'm using to write this book, the *Makefile* built from an empty *Imakefile* and the X11 configuration files is about 300 lines long and includes entries for 10 default targets.

You should consider it a given that *imake* generates Makefiles that will be larger than those you'd write by hand. If you find yourself horrified at the difference between the size of an *Imakefile* and that of the resulting *Makefile*, you needn't think, "Oh, no! I've created a monster!": don't assume that the *Makefile's* size indicates you've done something wrong. The size reflects only that the configuration files supply a lot of structure in the *Makefile* for you. Besides, when you're using *imake*, you usually don't look at the *Makefile* anyway. You write the *Imakefile* and leave the *Makefile* to *make*, which can digest large Makefiles more easily than you can.

Exercise 2. Build a Program

Now let's use *imake* to do some serious software development—the "hello, world" program known and loved by C programmers the world over. Create a file *hello.c* that contains the following program:

```
#include <stdio.h>
main ()
{
    printf ("hello, world\n");
}
```

If you were writing a *Makefile* by hand to build the *hello* program, it might look like this:

```
hello: hello.o
        cc -o hello hello.o
```

Then you'd run *make* to generate the commands that build the program:

```
% make
cc -c hello.c
cc -o hello hello.o
```

To use *imake* instead, edit *Imakefile* so that it looks like this:*

```
NormalProgramTarget(hello,hello.o,NullParameter,NullParameter,▶▶▶
▶▶▶NullParameter)
```

This is a **target description**, i.e., a specification indicating something to be built. You may find it unedifying at this point. That's okay; with *imake*, nothing is obvious at first. `NormalProgramTarget()` is what's called a **rule**.† When you need a target entry to build a program, you invoke a rule in your *Imakefile*. When you generate the *Makefile* from the *Imakefile*, the invocation is turned into the entry that specifies how to build the target.

Rules often take arguments; `NormalProgramTarget()` in particular takes five. The first specifies the name of the program to build. The second specifies the object files from which to build it. The third, fourth, and fifth arguments are used when you have more complicated targets that require special information. *hello* is a pretty simple program, so no more information is necessary. The last three arguments are specified as

---

*This example contains a line that's too wide for the page but must be entered as a single line in the *Imakefile*. Such lines are indicated throughout this chapter by "▶▶▶", which means that the line ending with "▶▶▶" should be joined to the next line beginning with "▶▶▶", with no intervening space.

†*imake* rules are defined in the configuration files, but we won't look at any rule definitions until Chapter 3, *Understanding Configuration Files*.

`NullParameter` (a placeholder with a null value) because empty arguments aren't allowed.

You've specified the target you're interested in by invoking `Normal-`
`ProgramTarget()` in the *Imakefile*, so build the program:

```
% make
```

Hmm. Nothing happened, did it? Try being more specific:

```
% make hello
make: Fatal error: Don't know how to make target "hello"
```

Nope. That didn't work, either.

"What a wretched program," you think to yourself. Don't be so hasty. The
problem is that you changed the *Imakefile* but haven't yet regenerated the
Makefile to reflect those changes. This is a fact of *imake* life: you must
rebuild the *Makefile* after each change to the *Imakefile*. Do that now:

```
% make Makefile
```

xmkmf isn't necessary now because you've got a *Makefile* generated by
imake, and *imake* will have put the proper *Makefile*-regenerating entry into
it.*

Okay, try again to build the program. This time when you run *make*, it
should produce the commands necessary to compile and link *hello*:

```
% make
cc -O -c hello.c
rm -f hello
cc -o hello hello.o
```

Run the program and you should see a familar refrain:

```
% hello
hello, world
```

Your mission is now accomplished, so you can clean up:

```
% make clean
rm -f hello
rm -f *.CKP *.ln *.BAK *.bak *.o core errs ,* *~ *.a .emacs_* \
    tags TAGS make.log MakeOut "#"*
```

make generates one *rm* command to remove the executable *hello*, and
another to remove general left over rubble (such as *hello.o*).

---

*If you make a typo when you edit a *Imakefile*, you'll often find that the resulting *Makefile* is
unusable and *make Makefile* won't work! In that case, type *xmkmf* again to bootstrap the
Makefile—after you fix the typo in the *Imakefile*.

`NormalProgramTarget()` produces the `clean` target entry that generates the first *rm* command, and the configuration files automatically produce a default `clean` entry that generates the second.

By going through the preceding exercises, you've done several of the activities common with *imake*:

* Written an *Imakefile*
* Bootstrapped the initial *Makefile* with *xmkmf*
* Used the *Makefile* to regenerate itself
* Used the *Makefile* to build a program
* Used the *Makefile* to remove debris

Exercise 3. Examine the Makefile

Gird your loins and prepare for combat: I want you to take a look through the *Makefile*. You'll find that it can be divided into three sections:

* Several million lines of *make* variable assignments
* The target entries generated by your *Imakefile*
* The entries supplied for you automatically by the configuration files

To find the section of the *Makefile* that corresponds to your *Imakefile*, search for a `hello` target entry. You should discover five lines that look like this:

```
hello: hello.o
    $(RM) $@
    $(CC) -o $@ hello.o $(LDOPTIONS) $(LDLIBS) $(EXTRA_LOAD_FLAGS)
clean::
    $(RM) hello
```

To better understand this, ignore all the stuff about LDOPTIONS, LDLIBS, etc. In essence, you have two target entries here: a `hello` entry to build your program, and a `clean` entry to get rid of it. That's all. These two entries resulted from your invocation of `NormalProgramTarget()` in the *Imakefile*. Everything else in the *Makefile* was put there by *imake* automatically.

And it certainly does put a lot there. If you examine an *imake*-generated *Makefile* for anything but the briefest period of time, its contents may prompt you to cry in anguish, "Why is the *Makefile* so complicated?" Attempts to explain this generally derive from one of two schools of thought. One is that *imake* wants to scare you off so you'll leave it alone. The other is that *imake* is trying to knock you insensate by subjecting you to information overload. The effectiveness of both strategies in discouraging developers from using *imake* on any regular basis must be admitted, and it's difficult to choose either of these hypotheses over the other because each seems to account for about half of *imake*'s victims.

The truth is that *imake* deserves neither fear nor stupor from you. The complexity has another purpose: flexibility. It's unfortunate that flexibility is attained by sacrificing simplicity of the *Makefile*, but that's the way it is. If the complexity tempts you to toss *imake* out the window, consider these two things first:

- The complexity allows the configuration file writer a lot of latitude to parameterize how particular kinds of targets are built on different types of machines. But the complexity in the *Makefile* comes from the configuration files, not from the Imakefiles. If you don't write configuration files (and most *imake* users don't), you don't need to deal directly with the complexity that's in them.

- You don't often deal with the complexity in the *Makefile*, either, since you don't usually need to look at it. I'm only having you do so here so you can see the connection between what you've written in the *Imakefile* and what ends up in the *Makefile*. Normally, when you use *imake*, you work with the *Imakefile* to express what you want to do, and let *make* worry about processing the *Makefile*. *imake*-generated Makefiles are like PostScript files: people can read them, but they're really intended for machine processors.

The difference in the complexity of the *Imakefile* and the *Makefile* reflects a difference in the nature of their contents.

The *Imakefile* contains the "what" details: what you want to build, and what to build it from. That kind of information doesn't vary from machine to machine, so the *Imakefile* is machine-independent. (For instance, you usually don't change the name of a program or the set of source files you build it from as you build it on different machines.)

The *Makefile* contains "what" information, but it also contains the "how" details that come from the configuration files. Those files supply the commands necessary to build the targets in which you're interested, parameterized specifically for your particular machine. The *Makefile* is thus very machine-dependent.

In a sense, *imake* takes your simple generic target description file and adds to it all the ugly machine-specific complexity necessary to generate the correct *Makefile* for your system (Figure 2–1). That complexity ends up in the

Makefile, so it's machine-specific and ugly, too. But since you work with the *Imakefile*, you don't care.

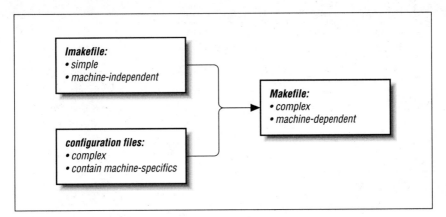

Figure 2-1: Location of complexities

imake generates Makefiles that heavily use *make* variables. Look again at the `hello` and `clean` entries generated by `NormalProgramTarget()`. You'll notice that practically the only things referenced literally in these two entries are the arguments you passed to `NormalProgramTarget()`, namely *hello* and *hello.o.* Everything else is specified using *make* variables: `CC`, `RM`, `LDLIBS`, etc. If you look at the first section of the *Makefile* (the part containing all the *make* variable assignments), you should be able to find the lines where each of these *make* variables get their values. On my machine the lines look like this (they'll be similar on yours, though perhaps not identical):

```
            CC = cc
            RM = rm -f
     LDOPTIONS = $(CDEBUGFLAGS) $(CCOPTIONS) $(LOCAL_LDFLAGS)
        LDLIBS = $(SYS_LIBRARIES) $(EXTRA_LIBRARIES)
EXTRA_LOAD_FLAGS =
```

These variables express the **parameters** of your machine's configuration. Their values may vary from system to system, but *imake* figures out from the configuration files which values are appropriate for your system before it dumps them into your Makefiles. (Of course, someone has to put the correct parameter values in the configuration files initially. We'll discuss how this is done in Chapter 3, *Understanding Configuration Files.*)

Exercise 4. Compare Makefiles on Different Systems

If you have an account on another machine running a different version of UNIX, I suggest you move *hello.c* and *Imakefile* to that machine and build *hello* again by repeating Exercises 2 and 3. (You'll also need *imake*, *xmkmf*, and the configuration files on the second machine, of course.)

By comparing the two Makefiles, you'll see how *imake* individualizes a *Makefile* to the machine on which it's running, even though the *Imakefile* remains the same. You'll also see differences in the commands *make* generates when you run it. For example, when I build *hello* on three machines to which I have access, these are the commands that result:

Ultrix 3.1:

```
% make
cc -O -c hello.c
rm -f hello
cc -o hello hello.o -O
```

SunOS 4.1.1:

```
% make
cc -O -pipe -target sun4 -c hello.c
rm -f hello
cc -o hello hello.o -O -pipe
```

Mips RISC/os 4.01:

```
% make
cc -O -signed -systype bsd43 -Olimit 2000 \
    -Wf,-XNd8400,-XNp12000 -DMips -DBSD43 -c hello.c
rm -f hello
cc -o hello hello.o -O -signed -systype bsd43 -Olimit 2000 \
    -Wf,-XNd8400,-XNp12000 -lmld
```

The first two sets of commands are similar, but the last one is dramatically different. This demonstates that the same *Imakefile* can be used on different systems (so you don't have to think as much about machine dependencies), and that the resulting *Makefile* on different systems can be very different (because *imake* does a lot of thinking about machine dependencies).

The *Makefile* can even vary on the same machine if the machine supports multiple development environments. For example, RISC/os supports both the BSD and System V environments. The commands shown for RISC/os above are those for the BSD environment. If the configuration files were set up to select the System V environment instead, the commands would be different. Again, the *Imakefile* wouldn't need to change since the configuration files would take care of the necessary adjustments.

Exercise 5. Generate Header File Dependencies

In the next several exercises, we'll elaborate the *Imakefile* a bit to handle some other common targets: `depend`, `all`, `lint`, and `install`. Let's add the `depend` target first.

If you're building C programs, you need to indicate which targets are dependent on header files: when a header file changes, object files compiled from source files that include that header file must be rebuilt. The problem with this kind of dependency is that it can't be statically specified in the *Makefile* due to differences in the way different systems organize header files. For instance, *hello.c* contains the following `#include` directive:

```
#include <stdio.h>
```

This means *hello.o* must be recompiled whenever *stdio.h* changes. If *stdio.h* is located in */usr/include*, the dependency line in the *Makefile* looks like this:

```
hello.o: /usr/include/stdio.h
```

If *stdio.h* is located in */usr/sysv/include* instead, the dependency is different:

```
hello.o: /usr/sysv/include/stdio.h
```

The implication is that header file dependencies must be generated dynamically. That's the job of the tool *makedepend*:*

- It searches your source files to find `#include` directives.
- It looks through header file directories to determine where the included files are located.
- It adds the appropriate dependency lines to the end of the *Makefile*.

Of course, you don't want to run *makedepend* by hand, you want *make* to do it for you. That involves two additions to the *Imakefile*:

1. Invoke the `DependTarget()` rule to generate a `depend` entry.
2. Add an assignment for the *make* variable `SRCS`. `DependTarget()` has no idea what files you're interested in, so it assumes that `SRCS` names all the source files to be processed and leaves it to you to supply the proper value.

---

*There are several programs named *makedepend* floating around. You need the one written for use with *imake*. It's available as part of the *imake.tar.Z* distribution (see Appendix A, *Obtaining Configuration Software*).

After you make these changes to your *Imakefile*, it should look like this:

```
SRCS = hello.c
NormalProgramTarget(hello,hello.o,NullParameter,NullParameter,▶▶▶
▶▶▶NullParameter)
DependTarget()
```

Rebuild the *Makefile* to reflect the changes you just made, and run *make-depend* to generate the dependencies:

```
% make Makefile
+ rm -f Makefile.bak
+ mv Makefile Makefile.bak
imake -DUseInstalled -I/usr/lib/X11/config -DTOPDIR=. -DCURDIR=.
% make depend
makedepend -s "# DO NOT DELETE" --  -- hello.c
```

Notice that *hello.c* appears in the *makedepend* command generated by the depend target. That's a good sign; it tells you that the value of SRCS was correctly substituted into the command.

The object file *hello.o* is dependent on the header file *stdio.h*, since the latter is #include'd by *hello.c*. So the end of the *Makefile* should look like this when *makedepend* gets done with it:

```
# ------------------------------------------------------------
# dependencies generated by makedepend
# DO NOT DELETE
hello.o: /usr/include/stdio.h
```

If you build a more sophisticated program that consists of multiple source files, or if you build multiple programs using the same *Imakefile*, set SRCS to the names of all the source files for all the programs. However, you still invoke DependTarget() just once in the *Imakefile*. For example, suppose you have another program *goodbye* compiled from *good.c* and *bye.c*:

good.c:

```
main ()
{
    bye ();
}
```

bye.c:

```
#include <stdio.h>
bye ()
{
    printf ("goodbye, cruel world\n");
}
```

To modify the *Imakefile* to know about the second program, invoke `NormalProgramTarget()` again and add the source files *good.c* and *bye.c* to the value of SRCS:

```
SRCS = hello.c good.c bye.c
NormalProgramTarget(hello,hello.o,NullParameter,NullParameter,▶▶▶
▶▶▶NullParameter)
NormalProgramTarget(goodbye,good.o bye.o,NullParameter,▶▶▶
▶▶▶NullParameter,NullParameter)
DependTarget()
```

You've changed the *Imakefile* again, so rebuild the *Makefile*:

```
% make Makefile
```

After you do this, take another look through your *Makefile*. You'll discover that it has additional entries to build and remove *goodbye* now, but that the header file dependency information at the end has disappeared into thin air! *imake* doesn't carry it from one *Makefile* to another, so rebuilding the *Makefile* destroys any dependencies you've generated before. This is another fact of *imake* life: when you change the *Imakefile*, you must not only recreate the *Makefile*, you must regenerate header file dependencies. Therefore, your standard procedure should always be:

```
% make Makefile
% make depend
```

Exercise 6. Add a Default Target

Typically, when you have multiple programs listed in a *Makefile*, you want to be able to build all of them with a single command, usually one of the following:

```
% make all
% make
```

If you try these commands using the *Makefile* resulting from the previous exercise, you'll find that they don't work properly. The first gives you an error message ("don't know how to make all"), and the second builds *hello* but not *goodbye*.

To understand why, consider what's in the *Makefile*. The first instance of `NormalProgramTarget()` in the *Imakefile* generates `hello` and `clean` targets. The second instance generates `goodbye` and `clean` targets. That's why the commands above don't work:

- *make all* fails because there's no `all` target.

- *make* (with no argument) builds only *hello* because when you don't specify any target, *make* builds the target associated with the first entry in the *Makefile*. In this case, that's the `hello` entry.

After adding the "`SRCS=hello.c`" line to the *Imakefile* in Exercise 5, you rebuilt the *Makefile* and regenerated the dependency lines in two steps:

```
% make Makefile
% make depend
```

If instead you tried to combine the steps into one command:

```
% make Makefile depend
```

you'd find it wouldn't work; no dependencies would be generated. However, if you then ran that same command a second time, it would work. Why?

When you first assign a value to SRCS in the *Imakefile*, the *Makefile* doesn't yet know about it. Thus, the first time you run:

```
% make Makefile depend
```

the command is processed using a *Makefile* that contains no value for SRCS. The depend target is processed using an empty source file list, and no dependencies are generated.

This is non-intuitive, because it's easy to assume that since the Makefile target is processed first, the *Makefile* built by it is used to process the depend target. But it isn't. *make* reads the *Makefile* into memory and processes all targets named on the command line using the in-memory copy, regardless of what happens to the *Makefile* in the meantime.

The command does rebuild the *Makefile*, though, and it puts the SRCS assignment into it. So the second time you run the command, the depend target is processed with the correct (non empty) source file list and dependencies are generated correctly.

Lesson: If you need to rebuild the *Makefile* and process other targets as well, it's better to recreate the *Makefile* first by itself, and then process any other targets in a separate *make* command:

```
% make Makefile
% make other-targets
```

It's easy to fix the problem. Invoke `AllTarget()` in the *Imakefile* before each invocation of `NormalProgramTarget()`:

```
SRCS = hello.c good.c bye.c
AllTarget(hello)
NormalProgramTarget(hello,hello.o,NullParameter,NullParameter,▶▶▶
▶▶▶NullParameter)
AllTarget(goodbye)
NormalProgramTarget(goodbye,good.o bye.o,NullParameter,▶▶▶
▶▶▶NullParameter,NullParameter)
DependTarget()
```

This generates `all` entries for each program in the *Makefile*, which has two effects:

- *make all* causes both programs to be built because each is associated with an `all` entry.
- `all` becomes the default target because the first `all` entry becomes the first entry in the *Makefile*. Thus, *make* is equivalent to *make all*.

Exercise 7. Check Source Files

If you want to improve your programs by using *lint* to find problems in your source code, invoke `LintTarget()` in your *Imakefile* to generate a lint entry. `LintTarget()` is like `DependTarget()` in that it assumes SRCS is set to the list of all source files of interest, and it should be invoked only once per *Imakefile*.

You've already specified the value of SRCS for use with `Depend-Target()`, so you needn't do so again. Just add `LintTarget()` to the *Imakefile*:

```
SRCS = hello.c good.c bye.c
AllTarget(hello)
NormalProgramTarget(hello,hello.o,NullParameter,NullParameter,▶▶▶
▶▶▶NullParameter)
AllTarget(goodbye)
NormalProgramTarget(goodbye,good.o bye.o,NullParameter,▶▶▶
▶▶▶NullParameter,NullParameter)
DependTarget()
LintTarget()
```

After you rebuild the *Makefile* (don't forget to regenerate the dependencies, too!), you can use the `lint` entry to run your sources through the *lint* program:

```
% make lint
lint -axz -DLINT hello.c good.c bye.c
```

One problem here is that some of *lint*'s output is superfluous. For example, it will tell you that `main` is multiply defined. This is because the source for multiple programs passes through a single invocation of *lint* and illustrates a shortcoming of the X11 rules. With a little practice, you'll learn to distinguish useful from nonuseful *lint* output.

Exercise 8. Install the Program

When you write a program, you usually intend to install it somewhere. Your *Imakefile* doesn't help you do that yet because it generates no `install` entries. To add them, use `InstallProgram()`. It takes two arguments:

```
InstallProgram(program, directory)
```

program is the program to install and *directory* is the directory in which to install it.

Modify your *Imakefile* by invoking `InstallProgram()` once for each program:

```
SRCS = hello.c good.c bye.c
AllTarget(hello)
NormalProgramTarget(hello,hello.o,NullParameter,NullParameter,▶▶▶
▶▶▶NullParameter)
InstallProgram(hello,$(BINDIR))
AllTarget(goodbye)
NormalProgramTarget(goodbye,good.o bye.o,NullParameter,▶▶▶
▶▶▶NullParameter,NullParameter)
InstallProgram(goodbye,$(BINDIR))
DependTarget()
LintTarget()
```

BINDIR is defined in the configuration files as some public installation directory on your system. By default its value is */usr/bin/X11*.

After you rebuild the *Makefile* (and the dependencies), it will have an `install` target entry for each program. Of course, *hello* and *goodbye* are just toy programs, so we don't really want to install them. But we can see what *make* would do if we were to try. The *–n* flag tells *make* to show us the commands it would generate without actually executing them:

```
% make -n install
if [ -d /usr/bin/X11 ]; then set +x; \
else (set -x; /bin/sh /usr/bin/X11/mkdirhier /usr/bin/X11); fi
install -c hello /usr/bin/X11
if [ -d /usr/bin/X11 ]; then set +x; \
else (set -x; /bin/sh /usr/bin/X11/mkdirhier /usr/bin/X11); fi
install -c goodbye /usr/bin/X11
```

The *Makefile* generates a sequence of installation commands for each program. As part of the sequence, the installation directory is created if it's missing. *imake* uses *mkdirhier* for directory creation instead of *mkdir* because *mkdirhier* creates intermediate directories if they're missing. Consider the following command:

```
% mkdirhier /usr/bin/X11
```

If */usr* exists but */usr/bin* does not, *mkdirhier* creates */usr/bin* before creating */usr/bin/X11*. *mkdir* doesn't, it just fails. (Actually, some versions of *mkdir* can create intermediate directories, but that behavior is nonstandard and we can't rely on it.)

Your *Imakefile* is now complete. It can build, depend, *lint*, install, and clean up your programs—in just nine lines of instructions. Not bad.

What Have You Learned?

This chapter provides an overview of how to use *imake* and an *Imakefile* to develop programs. Here are some points to remember:

- *Imakefile* writing is primarily an exercise in rule invocation.
- Rebuild the *Makefile* after you modify the *Imakefile*.
- Regenerate header-file dependencies after you rebuild the *Makefile*.
- *imake*-generated Makefiles are larger than those you'd write by hand, but normally you don't need to look at them.

Now that you have some experience with *imake*, where do you go from here? To understand how configuration files do their job, read Chapter 3, *Understanding Configuration Files*. To learn about the X11 files in particular, read Chapter 4, *The X11 Configuration Files*. For further discussion about using the X11 files to write Imakefiles, read Chapter 5, *Writing Imakefiles*. If you're anxious to learn more about writing Imakefiles right away, you can read much of Chapter 5 without having read Chapters 3 or 4.

In this chapter:
- *Two Principles*
- *Use Machine-
  Independent
  Description Files*
- *Organize the
  Structure of imake
  Input*
- *Parameterize
  Variation*
- *Select Parameters
  by System Type*
- *Allow Conditional
  Parameter
  Assignments*
- *Allow for Local
  Convention*
- *Write Rules to be
  Replaceable*
- *Final Architecture*

3

Understanding Configuration Files

*The thing which I greatly
feared is come upon me.*
—Job 3:25

Now it's time to send you fleeing in terror. In this chapter we tackle the Dread Configuration Files to see what's in them and how they work together. It's possible to write Imakefiles by looking at existing ones and copying the forms you find there, and you can get by this way for a while. However, to write Imakefiles effectively, at some point you'll need to bite the bullet and look at the configuration files you're using and understand how they work.

The more you know about the files, the better you'll know what you can do with them. Sooner or later you'll find yourself trying to use them to develop software having configuration requirements very different from those of the project for which the files were written. When that happens, you'll need to be able to determine whether you can continue to use them and work around their limitations, or whether you'd be better off to write your own. To make a realistic evaluation of the files you're using, you'll need to be able to understand them. There'll be much wailing and gnashing of teeth if they seem like gibberish when you look them over.

This chapter explains how to understand configuration files by showing what goes on behind the scenes as *imake* turns your *Imakefile* into a *Makefile*. I'm not going to start with a set of files used to configure some existing project and explain how they work. Instead I'll use a progressive approach, starting from scratch and showing the process you might go through if you tried to design configuration files yourself. Then you can see how certain design issues come up and how to resolve them. This will give you a better feel not just for what configuration files do, but why they do things a particular way.

I'll start with some primitive ways of organizing configuration information. Then I'll point out problems—how simple structures fail to increase portability as much as they might. This will lead us into more sophisticated organizations which address the problems one by one, until finally we end up with a reasonably capable configuration file architecture.

This is a relatively difficult chapter, and it may not be painless. But by the end, you'll understand the general ideas and concepts used in *imake* configuration files. You should then be able to apply your knowledge to configuration files from any project that's configured using *imake* and determine how they work—because despite differences in the way projects use *imake* configuration files, there are usually broad areas of agreement.

Two Principles

The key aspects of the configuration files used by *imake* are the kinds of information in them and the way the files are organized. You should keep in mind two fundamental principles whenever you approach any set of configuration files:

- The way configuration files are organized defines their **architecture**. Files have specific purposes that you need to determine.

- Configuration files consist of a few constructs that are used over and over—the peculiaries of *imake*-speak which are its **idioms**. To understand the contents of configuration files, you must understand these idioms.

I will proceed to develop several configuration file architectures, introducing the idioms along the way as they become necessary.

Use Machine-Independent Description Files

When you use *make*, you write a target description file called a *Makefile*. However, Makefiles are not portable because the commands needed to build targets vary from system to system. Thus, our first step is to develop an alternative form of description file that doesn't change when you move your software around to different machines.

If we examine *Makefile* target entries, we find that some things remain the same when we port programs to different machines, whereas other things vary. For example, you normally build a program from the same set of source files no matter what system you build it on. On the other hand, the commands to generate the object files and link them together are extremely likely to vary from system to system: special compiler flags, link options, system libraries, and so forth may be needed.

This tells us that a machine-independent description file will specify what to build and what to build it from. It will not specify the details about how to build it; those are machine-dependent. To put this observation into practice, we need a way to abstract target-building instructions out of our target descriptions.

Recognize Target-building Patterns

Suppose we want to build two programs. The *Makefile* entries might look like this:*

```
proga: proga.o
    cc -o proga proga.o -lm
install:: proga
    install proga /usr/local/bin
```

---

*Double colons are used in the `install` target entries, which allows multiple entries to be associated with the target name. The double colon mechanism is not a widely appreciated feature of *make*, but it's essential for writing configuration files. We'll use it frequently in this book.

```
progb: progb.o parse.o
    cc -o progb progb.o parse.o -ly
install:: progb
    install progb /usr/local/bin
```

Observe that the programs are built according to one pattern and installed according to another. This is typical of Makefiles. Entries tend to be written using highly redundant patterns. We can exploit those redundancies by using prototypes so that we only need to specify information that varies between entries. For example, the general form of the program building entry is this:

```
PROGRAM: OBJECT-FILES
    cc -o PROGRAM OBJECT-FILES LIBRARIES
```

This prototype specifies several things: the entry target is the program name, the program's dependencies are its object files, it's built by running the C compiler, etc. The prototype doesn't specify the program name, object files, or libraries for particular targets, although it shows where they should be placed in the entry. Those pieces of information must be supplied on a per-target basis. If we want to generate a target entry, we can copy the prototype into the *Makefile* and substitute the appropriate information into the correct places. For instance, to produce entries for *proga* and *progb*, we'd make the following substitutions:

proga:
PROGRAM → proga
OBJECT-FILES → proga.o
LIBRARIES → -lm

progb:
PROGRAM → progb
OBJECT-FILES → progb.o parse.o
LIBRARIES → -ly

In a similar way, the program installation entries follow a pattern like this:

```
install:: PROGRAM
    install PROGRAM DIRECTORY
```

This prototype indicates the general form of the entry; to produce entries for particular targets, we'd need to give specific program names and installation directories:

proga:
PROGRAM → proga
DIRECTORY → /usr/local/bin

progb:
PROGRAM → progb
DIRECTORY → /usr/local/bin

Naturally, we don't want to do any of this prototype copying and substitution by hand. The mere thought is enough to make us gag. We want to write specifications that *imake* can process automatically, so we can tell it something like this: "Take these prototypes and generate *Makefile* entries for such-and-such targets, using the following pieces of information." Then we'd expect *imake* to turn our target specifications into full-blown *Makefile* entries for us.

You may have noticed that what we're asking *imake* to do here bears a suspicious resemblance to macro processing. Prototypes are like macro definitions; "build such-and-such an entry" is like invoking a macro; substituting target-specific information into a prototype is like performing macro parameter substitution.

Indeed, that's just how *imake* works, although in typical UNIX fashion, *imake* avoids as much work as possible by calling on an existing program to do the work. In *imake*'s case, the choice is *cpp*. (Another macro processor such as *m4* could have been used. *cpp* was a more expedient choice simply because *imake* is often used to write C programs and C programmers are already familiar with *cpp*.* *m4* isn't nearly as well known or widely used.)

Macros describing how to generate *Makefile* entries are called **rules**. A macro's name describes what kind of entry to generate, the body provides the entry prototype, and the arguments indicate the per-target information to substitute into the prototype.

cpp macros with arguments are invoked like this:

> *MacroName(arg_1,arg_2, . . . ,arg_***n***)

If we take the entries in the *Makefile* for *proga* and *progb* and express them using macro notation, they'll look something like this:

```
BuildProgramTarget(proga,proga.o,-lm)
InstallProgramTarget(proga,/usr/local/bin)

BuildProgramTarget(progb,progb.o parse.o,-ly)
InstallProgramTarget(progb,/usr/local/bin)
```

These invocations comprise the target description file for *imake*—the *Imakefile*. Notice that it's smaller than the corresponding *Makefile*. By taking advantage of the patterns in the way we tend to do things, our target descriptions become more concise.

The rule invocations also contain information only about what we want done. They don't say anything about how to do it, i.e., they don't indicate what commands need to be run to build targets. Since machine

---

*If you're unfamiliar with *cpp*, see Appendix G, *Basics of make and cpp*.

dependencies tend to be concentrated in those commands, moving the commands into the macro definitions has the effect of making our target specifications more machine-independent. (They aren't completely so; the installation directory is hardwired into them, for instance. We'll deal with that problem in the section "Parameterize Variation," later in this chapter.)

To produce a *Makefile*, we feed the rule definitions and the *Imakefile* into *imake*, which runs *cpp* to do all the macro processing for it. *cpp* reads the definitions and replaces each invocation with its proper expansion, substituting arguments as necessary. When it's all done, out pops our *Makefile*. That was easy.

Except we haven't written the macros yet. Oops! We'd better do that now.

Invent a Rule Macro Syntax

Let's consider how to write rules, using the target specifications for *proga* as an example. We want the following rule invocations:

```
BuildProgramTarget(proga,proga.o,-lm)
InstallProgramTarget(proga,/usr/local/bin)
```

to turn into these *Makefile* entries:

```
proga: proga.o
    cc -o proga proga.o -lm
install:: proga
    install proga /usr/local/bin
```

cpp macros are specified using #define, so our rules should look something like this:

```
#define BuildProgramTarget(program,objects,libraries)
program: objects
    cc -o program objects libraries

#define InstallProgramTarget(program,destdir)
install:: program
    install program destdir
```

The first line of a rule gives the invocation sequence, i.e., the name of the rule and the arguments we must pass to it. The other lines specify the body of the definition, which is what invocations of the rule should expand to. However, these definitions won't work without modification, because *cpp* macro definitions only extend to the end of the #define line unless you put a backslash at the end of lines that should continue to the next. To fix the definitions so they can be spread over multiple lines, we add continuation indicators to all lines of each but the last:

```
#define BuildProgramTarget(program,objects,libraries)        \
program: objects                                             \
     cc -o program objects libraries
#define InstallProgramTarget(program,destdir)                \
install:: program                                           \
     install program destdir
```

This allows us to write multiple-line input. However, the rules don't produce multiple-line output, because *cpp* collapses all definitions to a single line internally! The resulting macro expansions would look like this:

```
proga: proga.o     cc -o proga proga.o -lm
install:: proga    install proga /usr/local/bin
```

That kind of thing would give *make* indigestion since the entries have target and command lines glued together.

This problem is serious enough that *imake* agrees, grudgingly, to do a little work itself. But it exacts revenge on us by introducing a hideous construction. Instead of using "\" to indicate line continuation, we must use "@@\":

```
#define BuildProgramTarget(program,objects,libraries)        @@\
program: objects                                             @@\
     cc -o program objects libraries
#define InstallProgramTarget(program,destdir)                @@\
install:: program                                           @@\
     install program destdir
```

I know what you're thinking, and I agree: this syntax is U-G-L-Y. But it's effective. Here's how the @@\ trick works. When *cpp* reads a rule definition, it removes the backslashes and collapses the definition to a single line. Occurrences of @@ are left alone, since as far as *cpp* is concerned they have no special meaning. Any invocations of the rule occurring later in the input are expanded normally (including the @@'s). *imake* examines the *cpp* output for @@ sequences and replaces them with line breaks to restore the multiple lines we want.

Let's follow our sample *Imakefile* as it winds its way through this process. *imake* takes the rules and the *Imakefile* and feeds them into *cpp*. *cpp* processes them and disgorges something like this:

```
@@proga: proga.o @@    cc -o proga proga.o -lm
@@install:: proga @@    install proga /usr/local/bin
@@progb: progb.o parse.o @@    cc -o progb progb.o parse.o -ly
@@install:: progb @@    install progb /usr/local/bin
```

imake takes this result and breaks the lines where it sees instances of @@ to produce the intended final output:

```
proga: proga.o
    cc -o proga proga.o -lm
install:: proga
    install proga /usr/local/bin

progb: progb.o parse.o
    cc -o progb progb.o parse.o -ly
install:: progb
    install progb /usr/local/bin
```

Voilà!

In short, the purpose of the strange syntax of *imake* rules is to keep *cpp* from totally destroying the usefulness of its own output for *make* purposes. Thus, although *imake* relies heavily on *cpp*, one of *imake's* jobs is to undo some of the damage done by *cpp*—an uneasy alliance indeed.

There is nothing inherently special about @@ except that it's not treated specially by *cpp*, and it's unlikely to be used in a *Makefile*. This makes it a pretty safe choice for a symbol whose only role in life is to serve as a transient placemarker.

Of all the dramas played out in *imake*, the role of @@ is surely among the saddest—a tragedy in miniature. Dutifully taking its place in the process of *Makefile*-creation, the @@-symbol serves faithfully and steadfastly without complaint when thrown into the maelstrom of *cpp* processing. Yet its reward at the last is to be thrown out and discarded unceremoniously— refuse cast on the slag heap, unacknowledged and forgotten. Ignominious fate!

imake rules are simultaneously awful and wonderful: awful because the syntax is so bizarre when you're trying to write them, wonderful because once they're written, you can invoke them in your *Imakefile* to concisely express what you want to do without concern for how to do it. If it's any consolation, I assure you that my own eyes glazed over the first few times I tried to understand a set of rules. Take heart; immunity to *imake* rules develops eventually through repeated exposure; the syntax that at first seems deadly becomes second nature.

imake rules can draw on all the power of *cpp's* macro-processing capabilities, so they're extremely powerful for generating *Makefile* entries. Despite the difficulties of their syntax, rules are the first idiom of the language of *imake*.

Specify targets in an *Imakefile* using rules defined as *cpp* macros. This lets you specify what you want to do without getting bogged down in the details of how to do it.

What do we gain by using rule macros?

- Rules provide a target description shorthand; it's easier to specify a target to build by invoking a rule in an *Imakefile* than by writing out a full entry in a *Makefile*. Since writing *Makefile* entries can be tedious and error prone, especially for complex targets, specifying targets by invoking rules simplifies the software developer's task.

- Rules help hide machine-dependencies by placing the mechanics of target building in the rule definitions rather than in the description file. The definitions can be placed in a configuration file that's located elsewhere (see the next section). As a result, an *Imakefile*, unlike a *Makefile*, contains machine-independent target descriptions, allowing us to concentrate on goal rather than process.

Organize the Structure of imake Input

I've been making vague statements about how "*imake* takes the rules and the *Imakefile* and does such-and-such with them." Such statements gloss over certain details. Just how is *imake* invoked? What are its arguments? What is its input? These questions bring us to the topic of configuration file architecture—how to organize the information *imake* uses.

imake assumes you have an *Imakefile* describing the targets you want built. Other than that, it imposes little constraint on the structure of the input you give it. *imake* requires only that you use a template file that describes the input, but lets you specify its contents as you like. This gives you a lot of latitude to decide how to organize your information.

imake accomplishes this by sending into *cpp* the following three line input, which acts as a "wrapper" around your template. The wrapper tells *cpp* to read the template, after first defining its name and that of the description file symbolically:

```
#define IMAKE_TEMPLATE "template-name"
#define INCLUDE_IMAKEFILE <Imakefile-name>
#include IMAKE_TEMPLATE
```

The default names of the template file and target description file are *Imake.tmpl* and *Imakefile*. These can be overridden with the *-Tfile* and *-ffile* command-line options.*

The wrapper gives you both responsibility and freedom. Your responsibility is to put the following line somewhere in the template if you want your description file to be processed:

```
#include INCLUDE_IMAKEFILE
```

This line is needed because *imake* provides a symbolic name by which to refer to the *Imakefile*, but doesn't actually cause its contents to be inserted into the input stream anywhere. Your template must do that.

The wrapper gives you freedom by minimizing *imake*'s need to know anything about your configuration files. The only file *imake* tells *cpp* to read directly is the template. *imake* doesn't know anything about any other files the template might reference—not their names or even whether there are any. This means you can organize the template using any architecture that suits the requirements of your project.

Schematically, templates break down as shown in Figure 3-1. The `#include` line must be present somewhere in the template, so you implement your configuration file architecture by deciding what the template does before and after the *Imakefile* is processed.

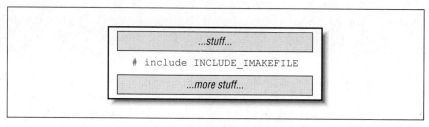

Figure 3-1: Schematic configuration file template architecture

We need to translate the general layout shown in Figure 3-1 into specifics. We have two kinds of information so far: rule definitions that specify how to build targets, and rule invocations that specify which targets to build. The invocations are the basic content of the *Imakefile*. What about the definitions? Where do they go?

---

*Note that line 3 of the wrapper is an `#include` directive that uses a macro to specify the name of the file. Some older *cpp*'s cannot handle this. If yours is one of them, see Appendix A, *Obtaining Configuration Software*, for information on alternate *cpp*'s.

If we adopt a modular approach we can separate rule definitions into their own file, *Imake.rules*. Our first version of the template, *Imake.tmpl*, is then quite simple, needing only to refer to the rules file *Imake.rules* and to the *Imakefile*:

```
#include <Imake.rules>          Rule macro definitions
#include INCLUDE_IMAKEFILE      Target descriptions
```

Now that we actually have a template, we need to deal with the question of where it (and the files `#include`'d by it) should be located. The question can be decided as a matter of how widely the files are used.

Each directory in a project is used for a particular purpose, so each *Imakefile* is different. When we're building a *Makefile* in a particular directory, we want to build it from the *Imakefile* in that same directory. By contrast, the template and rules files are the same no matter which directory of a project we're in. They should be placed in a well known location and shared among all the Imakefiles with which they're used. Let's assume this configuration file directory is */usr/lib/myconfdir*.

In order that *cpp* be able to find all the files, *imake* would start it up like this:

```
cpp -I. -I/usr/lib/myconfdir
```

cpp's *-Ipath* option means "look in the directory *path* when searching for files referenced by `#include` directives." *imake* passes *-I.*, so *cpp* can find the *Imakefile* in the current directory, and *-I/usr/lib/myconfdir*, so it can find the template and rules files in the configuration file directory.

It's a given that the *Imakefile* comes from the current directory, so *imake* knows to pass *-I.* to *cpp* automatically. But *imake* doesn't know where the configuration file directory is and must find that out from its own command line. That implies *imake* must understand *-Ipath* itself and pass it along to *cpp*. Thus, you invoke *imake* like this:

```
imake -I/usr/lib/myconfdir
```

An alternative architecture is to put rule definitions directly in the *Imakefile* rather than in their own file. There are good reasons not to do so, all of which hinge on the distinction between the *Imakefile* as directory-specific and rule definitions as shared. Suppose we put the definitions in an *Imakefile*. If we ever wanted to use them in another *Imakefile*, we'd have to copy them from one to the other. Worse yet, suppose we copy them into several Imakefiles and then find a bug in one of our rules—we'd have to fix it everywhere we've used it.

Keeping the rules in their own file and putting them in a separate directory is a much better policy. The file can be shared, so a rule only needs to be defined in one place, even if it's used by a number of Imakefiles. Should we later find a bug in it, or think of a way to make it better, we edit the definition (once), then use *imake* to rebuild Makefiles automatically. We don't have to edit zillions of Makefiles by hand.

This principle applies more widely, not just to rules, but to any sort of configuration information that needs to be available more generally than in a single directory. The mechanism for sharing information is:

- Reference the information from the template. The easiest way to do this is to put it in its own file and `#include` the file from the template.

- Put the file in a well known directory.

- Tell *imake* where the directory is, using *–Ipath*.

Parameterize Variation

Thus far we've developed three files:

- A machine-independent form of target description file—the *Imakefile*

- A notation for expressing target entry prototypes—rule macros in *Imake.rules*

- A simple configuration file architecture—the template *Imake.tmpl*

These give us a way to move machine dependencies out of our description files, but don't really do much to enhance portability.

Rules are a case in point. Rules allow us to generate target entries more easily, but as we've written them so far, they don't in themselves give us much help in porting our software. We need only ask what happens if we want to use our rules to build software on another machine. We have to figure out how each of the rules might need changing, because they refer literally to machine-dependent aspects of the development process. Consider the present definition of `InstallProgramTarget()`:

```
#define InstallProgramTarget(program,destdir)      @@\
install:: program                                  @@\
     install program destdir
```

If we want to build software on a machine with a missing or broken *install* program, we have to modify this rule, perhaps to use *cp* instead. Now we have an ugly job. How can we know what needs to be changed? We can't just go into the editor and globally replace "install" with "cp", because "install" is used both as a target name on the dependency line and as a program name on the command line. It should be changed only where it's used as a program name. This means we must understand each rule that contains "install" and determine from context whether or not to change it.

That's a fairly trivial task for the rules we've been using here, since only one of them is an installation rule. But the rules file for any real world project is likely to have several such rules. For example, X11 has installation rules for programs, scripts, header files, manual pages, libraries, etc.—more than 25 of them!

Understanding that many rules is a sizable job. It's not one we'd willingly take on ourselves if we had obtained a rules file from someone else. It's not reasonable to expect that anyone else will want to do so with rules we write, either.

The basic problem here is that while nonportabilities are localized in the rules file, they're not explicitly identified in any obvious way (so they're hard to find), and they're written using literal values (so we have to change each instance).

We can identify nonportabilities explicitly and make them easier to change if we express them as parameters. This is easy to do because *make* has a facility for parameterization—it allows us to use variables. A value is assigned once to a variable, which can then be used any number of times in a *Makefile*. By changing the assignment, every use is affected.

make variables are extremely important. Variable references are visually distinctive, so they're easy to spot. More significant, by changing variable assignments, we can easily effect change throughout the entire *Makefile*. This is one of *make's* strengths and the second *imake* idiom takes advantage of it:

Idiom 3-2

Any aspect of the software development process that can vary between machines should be a parameter in the configuration files, expressed using a *make* variable.

To use this idiom, we can rewrite our rules in terms of *make* variables. First we choose variables for things likely to be machine-dependent and assign them appropriate values:

```
    CC = cc
INSTALL = install
```

For modularity, we can keep variable assignments in their own file, *Imake.params*. (It should be placed in the configuration file directory so any *Imakefile* can use it.) Then, instead of writing cc and install literally into our rule definitions in *Imake.rules*, we write rules so they refer to CC and INSTALL:

```
#define BuildProgramTarget(program,objects,libraries)        @@\
program: objects                                             @@\
    $(CC) -o program objects libraries

#define InstallProgramTarget(program,destdir)                @@\
install:: program                                            @@\
    $(INSTALL) program destdir
```

The template needs to refer to the parameter file now, so we change its architecture slightly:

```
#include <Imake.params>         Default parameter values
#include <Imake.rules>          Rule macro definitions
#include INCLUDE_IMAKEFILE      Target descriptions
```

When we tell *imake* to build the *Makefile* from the *Imakefile* and our current set of configuration files, this is what we get:

```
    CC = cc
INSTALL = install
proga: proga.o
    $(CC) -o proga proga.o -lm
install:: proga
    $(INSTALL) proga /usr/local/bin

progb: progb.o parse.o
    $(CC) -o progb progb.o parse.o -ly
install:: progb
    $(INSTALL) progb /usr/local/bin
```

What do we gain by parameterization?

- We can completely reconfigure a project by changing the parameter variable assignments and rebuilding the Makefiles.
- When we know something varies among machines, we can use parameter variables to make our knowledge explicit. That can be helpful when we want to configure software on a machine to which it's not yet been

ported, because by looking at the variable assignments, we get an idea of what's already known to vary.

- The editing job for configuring software on another machine becomes a lot easier. For instance, instead of changing literal instances of "install" in the rules file several times, we change the "INSTALL=install" variable assignment in *Imake.params* once.

- The rules file becomes more stable. If we write rules in terms of *make* variables, we don't need to change them when configuration information changes; we edit the parameter assignments instead. Stability of the rules file is a good thing. Rules have to obey *cpp* syntax as well as the additional @@\ syntax layered on top of that. They have such a highly constrained format that it's quite easy to make mistakes while writing or revising them.

Parameterization also helps us complete the job of making our Imakefiles machine-independent. So far we've been generating `install` target entries for our programs, *proga* and *progb*, by invoking these rules in our *Imakefile*:

```
InstallProgramTarget(proga,/usr/local/bin)
InstallProgramTarget(progb,/usr/local/bin)
```

However, we can't really assume that everybody can or wants to install the programs in */usr/local/bin*—that's a machine-dependent thing. To fix this, we can parameterize the installation directory in *Imake.params*:

```
BINDIR = /usr/local/bin
```

Then we write *Imakefile* entries in terms of that parameter:

```
InstallProgramTarget(proga,$(BINDIR))
InstallProgramTarget(progb,$(BINDIR))
```

This makes it easy to change the installation directory: just modify the value of `BINDIR` and rebuild the *Makefile*. Now there's no messing with the *Imakefile* at all. It's completely machine-independent.

Select Parameters by System Type

Parameterization of variation is a big step forward, but the use of a single parameter file is deficient. It makes configuration requirements explicit for only one machine. This causes two problems:

- It still involves hand editing. The parameter file needs to be changed appropriately each time we move the configuration files to a different machine.

- We know that to configure a project on another machine, we change the parameter file, but we can't tell from looking at it what the appropriate values should be. We could distribute a *README* file containing that kind of information (e.g., "CC is normally *cc*, but you'll get better results with the GNU C compiler if you have it; in that case, set CC to *gcc*"). However, we want the information in a form that *imake* can use for itself.

Both of these problems can be solved with a simple conceptual change. Right now we have a single parameter file that we edit to the requirements of different machines when we move the software around. Instead, we can keep a separate parameter file for each type of machine on which we want to build software (one for SunOS, one for Ultrix, etc.). Then we select the proper file when we build our Makefiles. On a Sun, we use SunOS parameters; on a DECstation, we use Ultrix parameters, etc.

To illustrate how this works, let's consider once again the program *myname* from Chapter 1, *Introduction*. There we used a *Makefile* to configure *myname* for three different machines. Now we'll configure it using *imake*.

We need to express target rules as macro definitions, but that's done already, because we can use `BuildProgramTarget()` and `Install-ProgramTarget()`. We also need to identify machine dependencies—things that differ between systems. We already did that in Chapter 1, where we found five sources of variation. These should be expressed as parameters using *make* variables:

CC	*C compiler*
CFLAGS	*Flags for compilation commands*
EXTRA_LIBRARIES	*Extra libraries needed for linking*
INSTALL	*Installation program*
BINDIR	*Installation directory*

Instead of using a single parameter file *Imake.params* and editing it each time we move the configuration files to another machine, we'll use separate parameter files, each tailored for a single machine. So we tell *Imake.params* it's no longer welcome in our architecture, invite it to leave, and create three machine-specific parameter files to take its place.

Suppose we're using a machine from Vendor A, and our two friends who also built *myname* are using machines from Vendors B and C. The parameter files for these systems look like this:

VendorA.cf:

```
            CC = cc
        CFLAGS =
EXTRA_LIBRARIES =
       INSTALL = install
        BINDIR = /usr/local
```

VendorB.cf:

```
            CC = cc
        CFLAGS =
EXTRA_LIBRARIES =
       INSTALL = cp
        BINDIR = /usr/local/bin
```

VendorC.cf:

```
            CC = gcc
        CFLAGS = -DUSE_LOGNAME
EXTRA_LIBRARIES = -lc_aux
       INSTALL = install
        BINDIR = /usr/local
```

The template architecture changes a little, since we're replacing the reference to *Imake.params* with a reference to a vendor-specific parameter file:

```
#include <vendor.cf>          Vendor-specific parameter values
#include <Imake.rules>        Rule macro definitions
#include INCLUDE_IMAKEFILE    Target descriptions
```

vendor.cf will be *VendorA.cf, VendorB.cf,* or *VendorC.cf,* according to the type of machine the configuration files are being used on.

This architecture solves one problem: how to specify parameters on a vendor-specific basis. It also creates another: how to select the right version of *vendor.cf.* *imake* handles this by passing to *cpp* a definition for a symbol that uniquely identifies the type of system on which it's being used. That is, in addition to any other arguments *imake* passes to *cpp*, it also passes *–Dvendor*:

```
cpp -I. -I/usr/lib/myconfdir -Dvendor
```

When you build *imake*, you teach it the symbol to use for your machine. (See Appendix B, *Installing Configuration Software*, for further details.)

Normally, system-identifying symbols are vendor-OS oriented (`ultrix`, `sun`, `hpux`, `ibm`, etc.). I'm going to use fake symbols for purposes of illustration: `VendorA`, `VendorB`, `VendorC`. On a system from vendor C, for instance, *imake* invokes *cpp* like this:

```
cpp -I. -I/usr/lib/myconfdir -DVendorC
```

In this way, *cpp* knows the vendor symbol, and we can take advantage of that knowledge in the configuration files by using *cpp*'s conditional construct to select the vendor file:

```
#ifdef VendorA
#define VendorFile <VendorA.cf>
#endif

#ifdef VendorB
#define VendorFile <VendorB.cf>
#endif

#ifdef VendorC
#define VendorFile <VendorC.cf>
#endif
```

These are **vendor blocks**; each block defines `VendorFile` as the name of the parameter file for a particular vendor. The file can then be processed with:

```
#include VendorFile
```

When *imake* is invoked on any of our three machines, it passes *–DVendorA*, *–DVendorB*, or *–DVendorC*, according to which machine it's running on. On a Vendor A system, *imake* passes *–DVendorA*, *cpp* selects the vendor block for Vendor A, `VendorFile` is defined as `<VendorA.cf>`, and the directive to include `VendorFile` effectively becomes the following:

```
#include <VendorA.cf>
```

On a Vendor B system, *imake* passes *–DVendorB* and the directive becomes:

```
#include <VendorB.cf>
```

imake responds similarly for a Vendor C system.

In each case, *cpp* receives from *imake* the information it needs for selecting the proper machine-specific parameter file, and the *Makefile* is built using the parameters appropriate to that machine.

If we put the vendor blocks in a file *Imake.vb*, the template architecture becomes:

```
#include <Imake.vb>          Vendor blocks
#include VendorFile          Vendor-specific parameter values
#include <Imake.rules>       Rule macro definitions
#include INCLUDE_IMAKEFILE   Target descriptions
```

Only one of the vendor files *VendorA.cf, VendorB.cf,* or *VendorC.cf* is selected for any given system. However, in order to make sure that the correct one is available when the configuration files are shipped around to different systems, all vendor files should be distributed together.

What do we gain by vendor-specific parameterization?

- Machine dependencies are more obvious because they are explicitly isolated into files organized according to vendor differences. With a single parameter file, machine dependencies are explicit for only one vendor's systems.

- Parameter information is encoded so that *imake* can use it without human intervention. Using a single parameter file, it's possible to distribute a *README* file indicating what the parameter values should be for other systems, but you still have to do the editing yourself. Vendor files represent that same information in a form that's usable by the configuration process automatically. This makes parameter files more stable because the parameters on one Vendor A machine won't need to change much (if at all) when we move the configuration files to another Vendor A machine.

- It becomes easier to port the configuration files (and thus the configuration process) to a new machine; we write a `vendor.cf` file for it and add another vendor block to *Imake.vb*. None of the existing configuration files change except *Imake.vb*, and that's a simple change that need be done only once, when we first port the configuration files to the new machine.

Now we have a great deal of flexibility in selecting configuration parameters for various machines and an open-ended mechanism allowing new machines to be included in the porting process. Naturally, we're buoyed by this *fait accompli*—but not so much that we cease to cast a critical eye on our configuration files, searching out yet another occasion for improvement. And indeed, under scrutiny, they soon reveal another flaw: the parameter files are still written in a way that requires a lot of work—we're specifying every parameter in every machine-specific file. This has two implications, neither appealing:

- If we port the configuration files to a new machine, we must list every parameter in the new vendor file.

- If we want to define a new configuration parameter, we must add an assignment for it to every vendor file.

This harsh reality quickly dissipates our initial flush of success and causes us to ask whether there isn't a better way to represent parameters in the configuration files.

Allow Conditional Parameter Assignments

Instead of listing every parameter in every vendor file, it would be more economical to assign a default value to each parameter. Then the machine-specific files would need to list only the parameters that differ from the defaults. So we apologize profusely to *Imake.params* for our imprudence in dismissing it so hastily and invite it back in to take its rightful place in the architecture—that of holding the default parameter values:

```
#include <Imake.vb>              Vendor blocks
#include VendorFile              Vendor-specific parameter values
#include <Imake.params>          Default parameter values
#include <Imake.rules>           Rule macro definitions
#include INCLUDE_IMAKEFILE       Target descriptions
```

The intent here is to allow parameter values to be picked up from the machine-specific vendor file first, and then from the defaults file for any parameters that remain unassigned. Conceptually, the contents of the defaults file are as follows:

```
if CC has not been specified yet
    CC = cc
if CFLAGS has not been specified yet
    CFLAGS =
if EXTRA_LIBRARIES has not been specified yet
    EXTRA_LIBRARIES =
if INSTALL has not been specified yet
    INSTALL = install
if BINDIR has not been specified yet
    BINDIR = /usr/local
```

Unfortunately, *make* doesn't have any conditional construct, so we can't write anything into the *Makefile* that would instruct it, "if this variable has not been assigned a value yet, give it such-and-such a value."

cpp has conditionals (#ifdef, #ifndef), but we can't use those to test whether a *make* variable has been assigned a value. *cpp* understands very little even about C, the language for which it was designed; it certainly knows nothing at all about *make*. However, the difficulty is not insuperable, and we can solve the problem by adding an intermediate step.

For each *make* parameter variable, we invent a corresponding *cpp* macro. Then, instead of assigning a value to the variable directly, we assign to it the macro value. The macro is given a default value, but only if it has not been set earlier. Thus any definition encountered earlier takes precedence over the default.

Example: If we expect that *cc* will be the most usual C compiler, we use the following construct to set the default value in *Imake.params*:

```
#ifndef CcCmd
#define CcCmd cc
#endif
CC = CcCmd
```

In the absence of any prior definition of CcCmd, CC is assigned the value *cc*. This can be overridden by providing a different definition in the vendor file, since that's processed before *Imake.params*. For example, if *gcc* should be used instead of *cc*, the vendor file should contain a line like this:

```
#define CcCmd gcc
```

Then when *Imake.params* is processed, CcCmd already has a value, the #define line that sets the default value is not processed, and CC is assigned the value *gcc* instead.

This mechanism allows default parameter values to be overridden on a vendor-specific basis. Another important advantage is that we need to provide values in vendor files for only those parameters that differ from the defaults.

Combining conditionally-defined *cpp* macros with *make* variables provides a simple but powerful construct. The idea it expresses is central to effective use of *imake*:

Idiom 3-3

Provide a default value for each configuration parameter, but allow the default to be overridden. Assign the parameter to a *make* variable using a *cpp* macro which is given a default value; put the macro definition inside #ifndef/#endif to allow its value to be overridden.

Let's see how we use the macro/variable idiom in practice. Suppose the defaults file *Imake.params* looks like this:

```
#ifndef CcCmd
#define CcCmd cc
#endif
#ifndef CFlags
#define CFlags /* as nothing */
#endif
#ifndef ExtraLibraries
#define ExtraLibraries /* as nothing */
#endif
#ifndef InstallCmd
#define InstallCmd install
#endif
#ifndef BinDir
#define BinDir /usr/local
#endif

              CC = CcCmd
          CFLAGS = CFlags
 EXTRA_LIBRARIES = ExtraLibraries
         INSTALL = InstallCmd
          BINDIR = BinDir
```

Then the vendor files *VendorA.cf, VendorB.cf*, and *VendorC.cf* need to specify values only for parameters that differ from the defaults. They look like this:

VendorA.cf:

```
/* empty -- defaults are all correct */
```

VendorB.cf:

```
#define InstallCmd cp
#define BinDir /usr/local/bin
```

VendorC.cf:

```
#define CcCmd gcc
#define CFlags -DUSE_LOGNAME
#define ExtraLibraries -lc_aux
```

The default values are all correct for Vendor A, but *vendorA.cf* must still exist (even if only as an empty file), to prevent *cpp* from issuing file-not-found file inclusion errors.

What do we gain by the override mechanism?

- The override idiom allows *imake* to use *cpp*'s strengths to compensate for *make*'s weaknesses. You cannot test whether or not a variable already has a value in a *Makefile*. But you can test *cpp* macros and define them conditionally. By assigning *make* variables to conditionally-defined macro values you achieve the effect of conditional variable assignment.

- Much of the work of configuring a *Makefile* for a given system consists of determining the proper values for *make* variables. The override idiom provides a lot of flexibility in setting those variables.

- Since any parameter which gets its value using the override idiom is assigned a default value, it's not necessary to provide a value for the parameter in every single vendor file. The default need be overridden only for those systems for which the default is incorrect. This minimizes the information that needs to be contained in the vendor file. That, in turn, makes it easier to create new vendor files when *imake* is ported to a different system.

Allow for Local Convention

The *vendor.cf* files allow us to accommodate the particular requirements of systems from different vendors. However, they're still a bit ill-conceived: a single file holds all machine dependencies for a system. That's parsimonious, but not ideal. There are really *two* kinds of machine specifics. Some are vendor-oriented (such as which environment variable a system supplies, or extra libraries required to compensate for C library deficiencies), but others are user-oriented. For instance, the particular kind of system you're using doesn't really have much to do with whether locally installed programs should go in */usr/local* or */usr/local/bin.* Those issues pertain to the local conventions you like to use (or those your system administration ogre imposes on you).

The parameters for *myname* break down this way:

Vendor-specific:	*Site-specific*:
EXTRA_LIBRARIES	CC
ENV_VAR_NAME	BINDIR
INSTALL	

The distinction between vendor- and site-specific parameters can be realized by providing a site-specific file *site.def* and placing in it those machine-specifics that aren't vendor-oriented. For *myname,* the definitions for CcCmd and BinDir belong in the site file, not the vendor file. When we shuffle the definitions around properly, the vendor files for our three machines look like this:

VendorA.cf:

```
/* empty -- defaults are all correct */
```

VendorB.cf:

```
#define InstallCmd cp
```

VendorC.cf:

```
#define CFlags -DUSE_LOGNAME
#define ExtraLibraries -lc_aux
```

The site file *site.def* changes from machine to machine. You edit it to reflect local convention when you install the configuration files. On the three machines in question, *site.def* looks like this:

Our machine:

```
/* empty -- defaults are all correct */
```

First friend's machine:

```
#define BinDir /usr/local/bin
```

Second friend's machine:

```
#define CcCmd gcc
```

The architecture of *Imake.tmpl* must now incorporate the site file:

```
#include <Imake.vb>              Vendor blocks
#include VendorFile              Vendor-specific parameter values
#include <site.def>              Site-specific parameter values
#include <Imake.params>          Default parameter values
#include <Imake.rules>           Rule macro definitions
#include INCLUDE_IMAKEFILE       Target descriptions
```

What do we gain by splitting site-specifics out of the vendor file?

- Configuration parameters vary from vendor to vendor, but many of those parameters tend to be stable among the group of machines running a given vendor's system. Within that group, most of the things that change relate to local convention, so by removing site-related machine specifics and putting them in a separate file, the vendor file becomes more stable.

- We also further isolate (to *site.def,* a single, small file) the values likely to need editing when we move the configuration files from machine to machine. The vast majority of the configuration information is now instantiated in a form that the configuration process can use automatically—and in files that don't need editing. Aside from the site-specifics in *site.def*, the configuration files should be pretty usable right out of the box on any machine for which a vendor file exists.

Write Rules to be Replaceable

Parameter macros are defined so they can be overridden, using this conditional construct:

```
#ifndef ParamMacro
#define ParamMacro DefaultValue
#endif
```

But rules are defined as macros, too. For maximum flexibility, it's best to enclose rule definitions within #ifndef/#endif so that rules can be overridden as necessary. The two rules we've used in this chapter should therefore be written like this:

```
#ifndef BuildProgramTarget
#define BuildProgramTarget(program,objects,libraries)          @@\
program: objects                                               @@\
    $(CC) -o program objects libraries
#endif

#ifndef InstallProgramTarget
#define InstallProgramTarget(program,destdir)                  @@\
install:: program                                              @@\
    $(INSTALL) program destdir
#endif
```

Note that you don't put @@\ on the ends of the #ifndef or #endif lines because they aren't part of the definitions.

In practice, occasions when you need to replace a rule are rare, but by using the override construct, you can do so easily, should it become necessary. For instance, if a rule doesn't work on a particular platform for some reason, you can redefine it in the vendor file for that platform so it does work.

Final Architecture

This chapter describes a step-by-step plan for constructing configuration files. In practice, the process of writing files is not so linear; you'd be using the concepts from each step simultaneously because they interrelate.

We've looked piecemeal at each of the configuration files used in this chapter. Now let's look at them together in their final form. For the architecture we've developed, the final form of the template, *Imake.tmpl*, is shown in Figure 3–2.

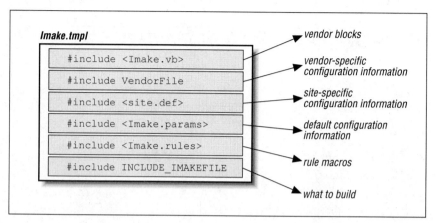

Figure 3-2: Final template architecture

The configuration files to which *Imake.tmpl* refers are shown below.

Imake.vb (vendor blocks):

```
#ifdef VendorA
#define VendorFile <VendorA.cf>
#endif
#ifdef VendorB
#define VendorFile <VendorB.cf>
#endif
#ifdef VendorC
#define VendorFile <VendorC.cf>
#endif
```

Imake.params (default parameter values):

```
#ifndef CcCmd
#define CcCmd cc
#endif
#ifndef CFlags
#define CFlags /* as nothing */
#endif
#ifndef ExtraLibraries
#define ExtraLibraries /* as nothing */
#endif
#ifndef InstallCmd
#define InstallCmd install
#endif
#ifndef BinDir
#define BinDir /usr/local
#endif
```

```
            CC = CcCmd
         CFLAGS = CFlags
EXTRA_LIBRARIES = ExtraLibraries
        INSTALL = InstallCmd
         BINDIR = BinDir
```

Imake.rules (rule macro definitions):

```
#ifndef BuildProgramTarget
#define BuildProgramTarget(program,objects,libraries)          @@\
program: objects                                               @@\
    $(CC) -o program objects libraries
#endif

#ifndef InstallProgramTarget
#define InstallProgramTarget(program,destdir)                  @@\
install:: program                                              @@\
    $(INSTALL) program destdir
#endif
```

VendorFile (vendor-specific files):

VendorA.cf:

```
/* empty -- defaults are all correct */
```

VendorB.cf:

```
#define InstallCmd cp
```

VendorC.cf:

```
#define CFlags -DUSE_LOGNAME
#define ExtraLibraries -lc_aux
```

site.def (site-specific file; contents vary by site):

Our machine:

```
/* empty -- defaults are all correct */
```

First friend's machine:

```
#define BinDir /usr/local/bin
```

Second friend's machine:

```
#define CcCmd gcc
```

Note that there really isn't much to these files, which is in itself instructive. It's not necessary for configuration files to form a huge, monstrously complex entity. This may surprise you, especially if your exposure to *imake* is primarily through the X11 configuration files.

In Chapter 1, I said that a portable configuration process should be characterized by explictly-represented configuration information in program-readable form. That is exactly what *imake* provides. Our configuration knowledge is represented in the configuration files (not in our heads), and all the configuration files are processed by *imake* or *cpp* without manual intervention.

In this chapter:
- *The X11 Template*
- *Default Configuration Information*
- *Machine-Specific Configuration Information*
- *What To Build*
- *Miscellaneous Topics*

4

The X11 Configuration Files

> *Abandon hope, all ye who enter here.*
> —Dante, *Inferno*

Chapter 3, *Understanding Configuration Files*, lays out general principles of configuration file design. In this chapter we'll apply those principles to the configuration files from the X Window System. They take some effort to understand, but it's worth it because they're more widely distributed than any other configuration files and exert a considerable influence in the *imake* world.

Many other sets of configuration files in existence today seem to trace their ancestry back to the files from some release of X11 or another. Certain aspects of the X files are particularly widespread, among them the vendor block, commenting, token concatenation, and recursive rule conventions. Knowledge of these conventions can be useful if you plan on designing your own configuration files sometime. The many vendor files included with the X files are also useful. They provide a measure of the idiosyncrasies of various systems, which can be helpful in assessing and anticipating portability problems you may need to deal with in your own configuration files.

The X11 configuration files are worth studying because they successfully solve an extremely difficult and complex configuration task. You should read this chapter if you're interested in understanding them better. Because they provide many valuable lessons for those who aspire to design configuration files, you should also read this chapter if you plan on writing your own set of files sometime.

You'll find it useful to have copies of the X configuration files on hand to examine as you work through the narrative. (The files described in this chapter are from X Version 11, Release 5, patchlevel 24. I don't expect much of the discussion here or elsewhere in the book to be invalidated when Release 6 comes out.)

The X11 Template

To analyze a set of configuration files you should go straight to the template, since it determines the architecture—how the other configuration files and the *Imakefile* are referenced during the configuration process. The X11 template *Imake.tmpl* is illustrated in Figure 4–1.

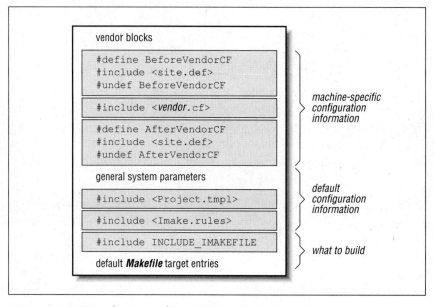

Figure 4-1: X11 configuration file template architecture

The template contains some configuration information itself (vendor blocks, system description, default *make* targets), and it tells *cpp* to draw the rest from several other sources using #include.

The information contained directly in *Imake.tmpl* or referenced by it falls into three categories:

Default configuration information

This is made up of the system and project parameters sections and the rules file. The system and project sections specify the most likely defaults for most configuration parameters (taken together, they correspond to the use of *Imake.params* in the previous chapter). The rules indicate how to build particular types of targets.

Configuration information for your machine

This consists of the particulars for your machine's operating system (OS) in *vendor.cf* and for your site in *site.def.* Values in these files take precedence over values in the generic configuration sections.

What to build   Information in the first two categories is worthless alone; it says how to do things (what C compiler to use, where to find header files, etc.), but provides no direction as to what to do (what programs should be built, where they should be installed, etc.). That direction is provided by the *Imakefile* and the default *Makefile* target entries, which specify what to build in the current directory.

I'll discuss the pieces of the template that make up these three categories in more detail below. At the beginning of each section, a diagram of the relevant part of the template is repeated for reference.

A few miscellaneous symbols defined near the beginning of *Imake.tmpl* don't fit into any of the three categories. They appear in some of the examples, so I'll note them briefly here:

```
#ifndef XCOMM
#define XCOMM #
#endif

#define YES 1
#define NO  0
```

XCOMM is used for writing comments that should end up in the *Makefile*. YES and NO are used for true and false, respectively. References to these symbols are legion throughout the configuration files.

Default Configuration Information

The system and project parameters sections of the template define the default configuration parameter values (Figure 4–2). The X files split the configuration information into two sections, one for general system-related parameters and another for parameters related specifically to X. The rules file defines the default target-building instructions.

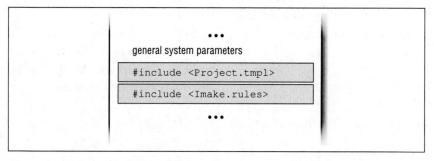

Figure 4-2: Section of Imake.tmpl specifying configuration defaults

General System Parameters—Imake.tmpl

This section of the template contains lots of definitions. Some of them describe system characteristics, such as:

- Does it have the *putenv()* library function?
- Does it have sockets?
- Does it have shared memory?
- Can it execute scripts that begin with # ! ?

These characteristics are usually represented by macros that take on one of the values YES or NO.

Other definitions are related to management of software building and installation, such as:

- What is the name of the C compiler?
- What special flags does the loader need?
- How do you make a link to a file?
- What flags are used to install executable or non-executable files?

This kind of information is usually represented by parameters specified using the macro/variable idiom.

Project-Specific Parameters—Project.tmpl

The system parameters section of *Imake.tmpl* describes the tools used to build and install the X software distribution, but says nothing about X itself. X-related parameters are found in *Project.tmpl*, which contains definitions for things like this:

- What is the screen resolution?
- What sorts of connections should the server accept (e.g., UNIX, TCP, or DECnet)?
- Should debugging, profiling, or shared versions of libraries be built?
- Where should programs and libraries be installed?

Directory locations

One especially important kind of information in *Project.tmpl* is directory locations. Most location parameter variables are named in one of two ways, *DIR or *SRC.

Variables named using the *DIR form specify installation directories. Since you might wish to change these on a system- or site-dependent basis, they're defined via the usual idiom of equating them to the values of *cpp* macros that can be overridden:

```
   LIBDIR = LibDir
  FONTDIR = FontDir
   XDMDIR = XdmDir
   TWMDIR = TwmDir
        etc.
```

Variables named using the *SRC form indicate the layout of various source directories within the X11 distribution. These variables are assigned values directly without using *cpp* macros:

```
 CLIENTSRC = $(TOP)/clients
    LIBSRC = $(TOP)/lib
INCLUDESRC = $(TOP)/X11
 SERVERSRC = $(TOP)/server
    DOCSRC = $(TOP)/doc
        etc.
```

There is no provision for overriding the values of the *SRC variables because the internal structure of the X distribution remains constant. The only project location parameter that might legitimately change when the project is put onto different machines is TOP, which indicates the top, or root, of the project tree.

The variable TOP

The *make* variable TOP is important as a reference point because other locations within the project can be specified in relation to it. For instance, if the library *libX11.a* is located in the *lib* directory under the project root, we can refer to it as $(TOP)*/lib/libX11.a.* By anchoring the reference to TOP, we need not be concerned where the project is located within the file system. Nor need we be concerned where our current directory is within the project.

In Chapter 7, *A Closer Look at Makefile Generation*, we'll discuss in more detail how TOP is used and how it gets its value. For now, suffice it to say that it's set to the correct value for you by *imake* when the *Makefile* is generated.

A separation of powers

For the most part, information in the system and project sections doesn't overlap. In theory, if you're using the X files, you could use them to configure a different project by plugging in a different *Project.tmpl* file. (This would also be true for any other set of files that splits parameters into system and project sections.)

In practice, it's not always easy to achieve a clean separation of configuration information into system and project components, so the breakdown is sometimes imperfect. For instance, the structure of the system's manual page hierarchy doesn't vary according to the project you're developing, so you might reasonably suppose that parameters relating to installation of manual pages into that hierarchy would go in the general system description section of the template.

That's not always true in the X11 files. For instance, two symbols related to manual page installation are InstManFlags (which specifies flags to use for the *install* command) and ManDirectoryRoot (which specifies the root of the manual page hierarchy). InstManFlags is in the system parameters section of template, as you'd expect. But ManDirectory-Root is tied to an X-related symbol XmanLocalSearchPath (indentation added):

```
#ifndef ManDirectoryRoot
#  ifdef ProjectRoot
#    define ManDirectoryRoot Concat(ProjectRoot,/man)
#    ifndef XmanLocalSearchPath
#      define XmanLocalSearchPath ManDirectoryRoot
#    endif
#  else
```

```
#    if SystemV4
#       define ManDirectoryRoot /usr/share/man
#    else
#       define ManDirectoryRoot /usr/man
#    endif
#  endif
#endif
```

Due to this entanglement with an X-specific symbol, the definition of `Man-DirectoryRoot` occurs in *Project.tmpl*.

A more convoluted example involves the specification of the *imake* command used to build a *Makefile*. In *Project.tmpl* the variable `IMAKE` is assigned a value to specify the name of the *imake* program. Where is `IMAKE` used? In `IMAKE_CMD`, which specifies the command line used to run *imake*. To find `IMAKE_CMD`, you go to *Imake.tmpl*. If you look at the definition of `IMAKE_CMD` there, you find it uses `IRULESRC` to indicate the directory in which the configuration files should be found. Where is `IRULESRC`? Back in *Project.tmpl*!

Initially, you might view these excursions back and forth between the various configuration files with some sense of adventure. But as you trace through their turnings and begin to wind your way further and further into their passageways, the true nature of the situation begins to dawn on you. What you thought was a quest to unlock the mysteries of the configuration files, is now revealed with frightful clarity as a trap for the unwary. The true secret of the files is this: they are the Labyrinth of Daedalus. Trapped inside, you can only await the approach of the menacing inhabitant concealed within: the Minotaur—in body half-man, half-bull; in spirit unbridled fury throughout. And now, because none escape the Labyrinth alive, only dread and despair lie before you—the fate of all who dare explore the X11 configuration files.

Well, actually, purple prose aside (or whatever my editors left of it), things aren't quite so bad as that. You're still here alive and reading, after all. But the sometimes maze-like interaction between the various X11 configuration files does take its toll on ease of comprehension. For the case just described (the definition of `IMAKE_CMD`), the difficulty in cleanly partitioning the information in the files comes about because they not only use a version of *imake* distributed with and located within the X project tree, they provide a way to install *imake* on your system for public use as well. This is a nice convenience because then you can use *imake* for other projects. However, it makes it more difficult to decide whether *imake*-related information is properly classified as a property of the X project or of the system at large. When you're using the version of *imake* located within the source tree, its location is clearly a project parameter. But after *imake* is installed in a public directory, it isn't part of the X project per se, and the location can be considered a system parameter.

How To Build Things—Imake.rules

The system and project sections describe the parameters needed to build and install programs, but don't say how to use them to do anything. That's the purpose of the file *Imake.rules*—it contains *cpp* rule macros that indicate how to use these tools to build and install particular types of targets, i.e., how to compile a C program, how to install a manual page, how to build a library, how to compress and uncompress a font file, etc.

The X rules are far too numerous to discuss here in any detail (there are about a hundred of them). General rule syntax is described in Chapter 3, *Understanding Configuration Files*, and we'll look at function, use, and implementation of several of the more commonly used rules in Chapter 5, *Writing Imakefiles*. If you're looking for an extensive catalog of the X rules and what they're used for, see Appendix I, *Related Documents*.

Machine-Specific Configuration Information

Now let's go back to the beginning of the template *Imake.tmpl* (Figure 4–3).

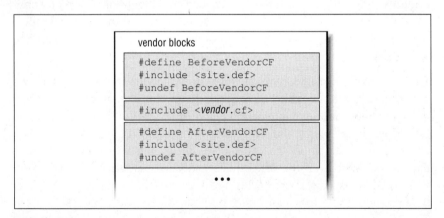

Figure 4-3: Section of Imake.tmpl specifying machine-specifics

If X were configured using only the information given by the system and project sections of the architecture, its Makefiles would look pretty much the same no matter what machine they were built on. Those two sections specify generic defaults only and provide little in the way of tailoring the configuration to a given machine. That kind of tailoring is the function of the machine-specific information, which is given in three places:

- The vendor block section, which determines your system type
- The vendor-specific file, *vendor.cf,* which adapts to peculiarities of your system type
- The site-specific file, *site.def,* which adapts to local conventions you use

The ability to specify machine-specific parameters and select them automatically is what makes it possible for X's developers to configure X quite closely to the requirements of different machines using the same set of configuration files.

Note that *site.def* is processed twice, once before and once after the vendor file is processed. I'll explain this shortly.

Vendor Block Selection

Vendor-specific files have names like *sun.cf, ultrix.cf, hp.cf, sgi.cf,* etc. There's one vendor file for each type of system on which the configuration files may be used.

The vendor file is referenced in two stages. First, the name of the file is determined and used to define the macro `MacroIncludeFile`. Then the template inserts the contents of the file into the input stream using the following directive:

```
#include MacroIncludeFile
```

In effect, this becomes:

```
#include <vendor.cf>
```

Once the name of the file is known, reading it is easy. The problem is figuring out the correct value of *vendor.cf.* To do that, *imake* needs to determine what type of system you're running (actually, *cpp* needs to make the determination, since it's the one that reads the configuration files). That's what the vendor block section of *Imake.tmpl* is for. The X11 architecture differs from the architecture discussed in Chapter 3, *Understanding Configuration Files,* where the vendor blocks were placed in the file *Imake.vb.* In the X11 architecture, the vendor blocks are placed directly in the template.

The system type is determined by looking for a **trigger**—a *cpp* macro that uniquely and unambiguously indicates a given platform. For instance, "sun", "apollo", and "ultrix" indicate Sun systems, Apollo systems, and Ultrix systems. The blocks for these vendors are shown below:

Sun:
```
#ifdef sun
#define MacroIncludeFile <sun.cf>
#define MacroFile sun.cf
#undef sun
#define SunArchitecture
#endif /* sun */
```

Apollo:
```
#ifdef apollo
#define MacroIncludeFile <apollo.cf>
#define MacroFile apollo.cf
#undef apollo
#define ApolloArchitecture
#endif /* apollo */
```

Ultrix:
```
#ifdef ultrix
#define MacroIncludeFile <ultrix.cf>
#define MacroFile ultrix.cf
#ifdef vax
#undef vax
#define VaxArchitecture
#endif
#ifdef mips
#undef mips
#define MipsArchitecture
#endif
#undef ultrix
#define UltrixArchitecture
#endif
```

Each vendor block is written so that if its trigger symbol isn't defined, the whole thing is skipped. When *cpp* processes the vendor block section of the template, it looks at each block in turn, examines it, and ignores it if the trigger symbol isn't the right one. Once *cpp* finds the block with the correct symbol, it processes it and three things happen:

- The name of the associated vendor-specific *vendor.cf* file is defined, for later inclusion by the template.

- One or more architecture indicator symbols are defined. These symbols are unambiguous and can be used elsewhere in the configuration files to test for particular software or hardware platforms.

- The trigger symbol is undefined to avoid problems with file and directory names. For example, if you have a Sun machine, the symbol sun will be defined (as 1), but it isn't good for sun to remain defined as a macro during the configuration process since references in the configuration files to directories like *mit/server/ddx/sun* and files like *sun.h* and *sun.c* become *mit/server/ddx/1, 1.h,* and *1.c,* respectively. The vendor block undefines sun to circumvent these problems.

If *cpp* doesn't find the proper trigger symbol defined, it might be that you're trying to use the configuration files on a system for which no vendor block exists (i.e., to which X has not been ported). If that's true, you'll need to write a vendor file and add a vendor block to *Imake.tmpl* so that your vendor file is selected properly.

Since the trigger symbol selects the vendor block and the vendor block specifies the vendor file name, it's pretty important that the proper trigger be defined. Where does this symbol come from?

It depends. On some systems, *cpp* predefines a system-specific symbol that can be used as a trigger. That was the situation for X11R1, when X11 was in its infancy and life was simple; every system on which X ran had a *cpp* that predefined a unique symbol. Sun *cpp* predefined sun, Apollo *cpp* predefined apollo, etc. *imake* could assume that *cpp* would select the proper vendor block without any help.

That's no longer true. Triggers must be chosen with care, because it's now more difficult to find symbols that are unique to a single system type. For instance, mips might be defined on any version of UNIX that's based on Mips hardware. There are several of these now, so the mips symbol doesn't unambiguously indicate system type.

Worse yet, symbols are disappearing right out from under us. The ANSI standard deprecates predefinition of all but a very few symbols, none of which are for distingushing system types. As we fall further and further into the ANSI trance, the trend in preprocessors seems to be to predefine fewer and fewer symbols, so your *cpp* may not predefine anything useful at all. This was already starting to happen back in the days of X11R4, and it will probably become more common as time goes by.

To work around the problems posed by the lack of a unique predefined symbol, *imake* can be built so it passes an explicit trigger definition to *cpp* (using *–Dtrigger*). The problem of choosing an appropriate symbol is dealt with further in Appendix B, *Installing Configuration Software*.

If there is a vendor block for your system and *imake* still fails, then *imake* probably wasn't built correctly, i.e., it doesn't pass a usable trigger symbol definition to *cpp*.

Architecture indicator symbols defined in vendor blocks take the form *System*Architecture. An architecture symbol may refer both to the software and hardware, or separate indicators may be defined. Often both kinds of symbols are necessary to properly describe a given system, since the relationship between hardware and software isn't one-to-one. A given OS may run on multiple hardware types (e.g., Ultrix runs on either VAX or Mips chips). Conversely, a given hardware type may be used by several different OS's (e.g., `MipsArchitecture` can be defined for Ultrix, SGI, or Sony systems; `VaxArchitecture` can be defined for Ultrix or BSD systems).

Anything past the vendor block section of the template that depends on the system type (including the *Imakefile*) should test the architecture indicator symbols defined in the vendor block, rather than trigger symbols. The former are more reliable because they're unambiguous, and the latter are undefined by the vendor block, anyway.

Vendor-Specific Configuration Information—vendor.cf

Each vendor file contains definitions needed to make X (or other software configured with the X files) build and install correctly on systems from a particular manufacturer. Vendor files are often a hodgepodge, because it might be necessary to override defaults of all sorts (system or project parameters, or perhaps even some of the rules). Some of the types of infor mation you might find in the vendor files are listed below.

- **Version numbers**

    If you're using version *xx.yy* of your operating system, this is indicated in the vendor file as:

    ```
    #define OSMajorVersion xx
    #define OSMinorVersion yy
    ```

    Some symbol values may be contingent upon the OS version, to accommodate system changes, deficiencies, or bugs. For example, *sgi.cf* contains the following to handle versions of the OS from release 3.2 up:

    ```
    #if OSMajorVersion>3 || (OSMajorVersion==3 && OSMinorVersion>2)
    #define NeedVarargsPrototypes    YES
    #define NeedConstPrototypes      YES
    #define NeedWidePrototypes       NO
    #endif
    ```

    For this kind of test to select information correctly, it's important that version numbers in the vendor file accurately reflect your system. You may need to change them if your version of the OS is different than that for which the file was originally set up.

    Version numbers are also defined for C compilers in some vendor files and used in ways similar to OS version numbers. If necessary, you should change the C compiler version numbers to those used on your system.

- **Overall system type**

  If your system is based on SVR3 (System V Release 3) or SVR4 (Release 4), the vendor file should contain one (not both!) of the following definitions:

  ```
  #define SystemV  YES /* SVR3-based */
  #define SystemV4 YES /* SVR4-based */
  ```

  This is important because many of the default parameter values in later parts of the template depend on the value of `SystemV` or `SystemV4`. *lint* is a good example of this. It often behaves differently on BSD-based systems than on System V-based systems, so the flags passed to it need to be different. For instance, to create a *lint* library, BSD *lint* uses −*C*, whereas System V *lint* uses −*o*, so the following (from *Imake.tmpl*) depends on `SystemV` and `SystemV4` being set correctly:

  ```
  #ifndef LintLibFlag
  #if SystemV || SystemV4
  #define LintLibFlag -o
  #else
  #define LintLibFlag -C
  #endif
  #endif
  ```

- **Command workarounds**.

  Vendor files often contain workarounds for commands that are missing, broken, or located in non standard places. For instance, *cray.cf* defines `InstallCmd` with the value of an installation command that emulates BSD *install* properly on Cray machines. *DGUX.cf* defines UNCOM-PRESSPATH because *uncompress* is found in a non standard location. *Mips.cf* defines `InstallCmd` for the same reason.

- **Rules**.

  Sometimes a rule doesn't work correctly on a given platform. This can be fixed by placing a working definition in the vendor file. For example, the default definitions of `ObjectCompile()` and `LibObj-Compile()` are overridden in *sgi.cf*.

- **Vendor-specific symbols**.

  You can't use the trigger symbol in a vendor file to test for the presence of a given system type (recall that the trigger is undefined by the vendor block). However, inside the vendor file, you do know something about the OS you're using—the file wouldn't be processed otherwise. This means that in the vendor-specific file only, you may find it useful to test for particular vendor-supplied predefined *cpp* symbols. For example, *sun.cf* does some checking to see whether or not `sparc` or `sun386` are defined.

Site-Specific Configuration Information—site.def

This file contains site-specific definitions pertaining to local conventions you use that may require different parameter values than those provided by the system, project, or vendor defaults. If you want to override the defaults for parameters such as installation directories, special versions of programs to use during the build, whether to build the server, etc., this is the place to do so.

There is a peculiar relationship between *site.def* and the vendor file. The relevant part of the template is shown in Figure 4–4.

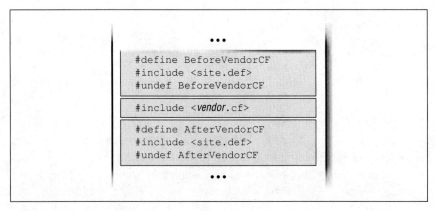

Figure 4-4: Section of Imake.tmpl specifying site-specifics

site.def is included twice, once before and once after the vendor-specific file, because it's possible that vendor-specific information will depend on a site-specific parameter. The contents of *site.def* are constructed so that only the correct part is processed each time it's included:

```
#ifdef BeforeVendorCF
    /* site-dependent parameters the vendor file needs to know about */
#endif /* BeforeVendorCF */

#ifdef AfterVendorCF
    /* all other site-dependent stuff */
#endif /* AfterVendorCF */
```

Most site-specific settings typically go in the `AfterVendorCF` part, but not all. In particular, if `HasGcc` is `YES`, some systems require special flags for *gcc* (or it won't compile things properly), but the vendor files for those systems can't determine whether to use those flags unless they know your (site-specific) preference for using *gcc* or not.

Note that you cannot rely on the values of `SystemV` or `SystemV4` in the `BeforeVendorCF` part of *site.def*, because they don't have any meaningful values until after the vendor file has been processed.

What To Build

The final section of the template specifies the target entries to generate (Figure 4–5).

Figure 4-5: Section of Imake.tmpl specifying target entries

Directory-Specific Targets—Imakefile

The last file referenced by the X11 template is the *Imakefile* from the current directory. An *Imakefile* usually invokes rules defined in *Imake.rules* to specify target entries to generate in the *Makefile*. If the *Imakefile* invokes rules that rely implicitly on the values of *make* variables, it must also assign values to those variables. Chapter 5, *Writing Imakefiles*, explores these issues further.

Default Makefile Target Entries

The last section of *Imake.tmpl* adds some common entries to the *Makefile*, such as a `Makefile` target entry to regenerate the *Makefile* itself, and default `tags` and `clean` entries.

If the directory has subdirectories, recursive `install`, `install.man`, `clean`, `tags`, `Makefiles`, and `includes` target entries are generated. These recursive entries are added if the *Imakefile* contains these lines:

```
#define IHaveSubdirs
#define PassCDebugFlags
SUBDIRS = subdirectory-list
```

The *make* variable `SUBDIRS` lists subdirectories in the current directory to which recursive rules should apply, e.g.:

```
SUBDIRS = include lib apps man doc
```

This mechanism is extremely important because it makes it possible to issue commands such as:

```
% make clean
% make depend
% make install
```

from any directory within the X source tree and have them apply to the entire subtree from that point down. This makes it relatively effortless to apply far-reaching operations to extensive portions of the X distribution. Multiple directory project management using the X configuration files is discussed further in Chapter 5, *Writing Imakefiles.*

Miscellaneous Topics

This section discusses token-concatenation and commenting conventions as implemented in the X11 configuration files. These aren't part of the architecture as such, but their use is pervasive throughout the files, so it's useful to know how they work.

Token Concatenation

It's often necessary to construct a token or token sequence by concatenating other tokens (this is also known as token pasting). As an example, you might have a macro `LibBaseName` defined as the basename of a library you're working with:

```
#define LibBaseName mylib
```

If you want to construct the full name of a library (*libmylib.a*) by concatenating the basename, the prefix "lib", and the suffix "a", how would you do it?

It's easy enough to concatenate the basename and the suffix, since you can put a "." between them:

```
LibBaseName.a
```

The value of the concatenation is `mylib.a`. However, to concatenate the prefix "lib" onto this to complete the name, we can't simply write this:

```
libLibBaseName.a
```

The preprocessor does not recognize `libLibBaseName` as two separate tokens because there's nothing between them. One way to separate tokens in this situation is by putting an empty comment between them as a "fake" token:

```
lib/**/LibBaseName.a
```

This works for preprocessors that process comments by deleting them entirely (e.g., most older versions of *cpp*). *cpp* recognizes `lib` and `LibBaseName` as separate tokens, deletes the empty comment, and performs the desired substitutions to produce the value `libmylib.a`.

However, empty comments don't work for token pasting under the preprocessing rules defined by the ANSI standard, because each comment is replaced by a space instead of being completely deleted. If we define the library name as shown above, its value becomes "`lib mylib.a`." The ANSI standard does provide a concatenation operator `##`, though, so we can construct the library name like this instead:

```
lib##LibBaseName.a
```

This gives us two different methods for token-pasting, but since only one works on any given system, we need a way to choose between them appropriately. The X11 files select the method by defining a macro `Concat()` in *Imake.tmpl* as follows:

```
#if __STDC__ && !defined(UnixCpp)
#define Concat(a,b)a##b
#else
#define Concat(a,b)a/**/b
#endif
```

Using `Concat()`, we can construct the name `libmylib.a` easily:

```
Concat(lib,LibBaseName.a)
```

NOTE

Don't put any spaces in the arguments to `Concat()`, because they'll be propagated into the macro result, defeating the intent of the macro.

The definition of `Concat()` that's chosen depends on `__STDC__` (forget about `UnixCpp` for a moment). The ANSI standard says `__STDC__` should be defined as 1 if an implementation conforms to the ANSI standard, so the ANSI token-pasting method is selected for ANSI preprocessors, and the empty-comment method is selected otherwise.

However, the construct sometimes selects the wrong method.* When that happens, you'll see one of two symptoms:

- If pasted tokens end up with `##` between them, the ANSI method was selected when it shouldn't have been. This is where `UnixCpp` comes in. You define it to force the empty-comment method to be used. Place this definition in your vendor file:

  ```
  #ifndef UnixCpp
  #define UnixCpp /* as nothing */
  #endif
  ```

- If pasted tokens end up with a space between them, the empty-comment method was selected when it shouldn't have been. The X11R6 configuration files will provide an `AnsiCpp` symbol (analogous to `UnixCpp`) to correct this problem. But in R5 there's no way to force use of the ANSI method, so you need to override `Concat()` by placing the following in your vendor file:

  ```
  #ifndef Concat
  #define Concat(a,b)a##b
  #endif
  ```

---

*This can happen, for instance, due to the ambiguity of `__STDC__`. The ANSI standard says that an implementation claiming to follow ANSI rules should define `__STDC__` as 1. But of course, non-conforming implementations aren't bound by the standard and can do anything they want with `__STDC__`. If an implementation defines it as 0, for example, to indicate partial conformance, the empty-comment method is selected. This will be incorrect if `##` token-pasting is included in the preprocessor's level of conformance.

In addition to `Concat()`, the X configuration files provide a `Concat3()` macro for pasting three tokens together:

```
#if __STDC__ && !defined(UnixCpp)
#define Concat3(a,b,c)a##b##c
#else
#define Concat3(a,b,c)a/**/b/**/c
#endif
```

`Concat3()` provides an alternative to `Concat(Concat(a,b),c)`, which is excessively ugly and doesn't work under ANSI rules, anyway, due to vagaries in the way ANSI token-pasting behavior interacts with macro expansion. (As Kernighan and Ritchie say of the ANSI standard, "Some of the new rules, especially those involving concatenation, are bizarre.")

Commenting

Since *imake* accepts input files in C preprocessor format and produces output files in *Makefile* format, there are two kinds of comments you can use in configuration files and Imakefiles: C comments and *make* comments. Each has a different syntax and a different use.

C comments

C comments consist of text bracketed by `/*` and `*/`. They're deleted from the input by *cpp* and don't appear in the final output (the *Makefile*). However, they're useful for documenting the contents of the configuration files and the *Imakefile*, as in the following fragment:

```
#ifndef StripInstalledPrograms
#define StripInstalledPrograms NO /* leave symbol table just in case */
#endif
```

The comment explains the `#if/#endif` construct. Since the construct itself is deleted by *cpp* and doesn't appear in the *Makefile*, there's no reason for the comment to appear in the *Makefile* either, and a C comment is appropriate in such cases.

C comments are also suitable for commenting out large blocks of text when the need arises, since they can span multiple lines. This allows you to disable a portion of an *Imakefile* temporarily without deleting it, for instance.

make comments

make comments begin with a # and continue to the end of the line. They're useful for documenting the contents of Makefiles. Of course, since you don't write the *Makefile* directly, the comments must be present in the configuration files or the *Imakefile*, and they must survive the configuration process.

We can't just write *make* comments directly into the configuration files, though. The # character that begins them also introduces *cpp* preprocessing directives, so it's ambiguous.

To avoid the ambiguity, a # that begins a *make* comment must be "protected" from *cpp* somehow. There are three ways to do this. All of them fail under certain circumstances, but the last is reasonably robust:

- Indent the # character. For older versions of *cpp*, # indicates a preprocessor directive only when it occurs in the first column, so you can indent the # by a space to fool *cpp* into ignoring it. That doesn't work if you have an ANSI preprocessor, because # can be preceded by whitespace under ANSI rules.

- Hide the # with an empty C comment:

  ```
  /**/# this is a comment for the Makefile
  ```

  The intent is for *cpp* to strip off the C comment and pass the line through without interpreting it as a directive. You'll see this construct quite often in older configuration files written before ANSI preprocessors became prevalent. It doesn't work under ANSI rules because comments are processed (replaced by a single space) before preprocessor directive recognition occurs. Since the # is then recognized as the first non-whitespace character, the line is treated as a directive.

- Hide the # in a macro and use the macro to write comments:

  ```
  #define XCOMM #
  XCOMM this is a comment for the Makefile
  ```

  This is the approach adopted by the X11 configuration files starting with Release 5. XCOMM effectively decouples the sense that # has in *cpp* from the sense it has in *make*, in that it makes clear that the line is intended as a *make* comment and not a preprocessor directive, and it keeps *cpp* from tampering with it.*

---

* It's somewhat unfortunate that the name XCOMM was chosen, since the "X" in the symbol name connotes an X-specific function, whereas the need to generate *make* comments from within configuration files isn't restricted to X. The name ICOMM might be better since it's more clearly *imake*-related.

The only problem with this method is that certain preprocessors that claim to be ANSI don't like the definition of XCOMM. For instance, recent versions of GNU *cpp* interpret the # as the ANSI "convert to string" operator and the definition fails. In such cases, you need to edit *Imake.tmpl* to change the definition of XCOMM slightly:*

```
#define XCOMM \#
```

A "feature" of *imake* is that it tries to shield *Imakefile* writers from the need to protect *make* comments. If it finds a line in the *Imakefile* that begins with a #, *imake* examines the line to see if it appears to be a true preprocessor directive (beginning with #if, #ifdef, #define, etc.). If not, it prepends an empty C comment /**/ to the line before passing it to *cpp*. This is supposed to cause *cpp* not to process the line as a directive.

That used to work reliably, but not any more, since you can't hide # from ANSI preprocessors with an empty comment. Therefore, XCOMM should be used to write *make* comments not just in configuration files, but in Imakefiles as well.

---

*Alternatively, you can tell *imake* to pass the *–traditional* flag to GNU *cpp*.

In this chapter:
- *General Strategy*
- *Invoking Rules*
- *Building One Program*
- *Specifying Libraries*
- *Building Multiple Programs*
- *Organizing Source and Object File Lists*
- *Building Libraries*
- *Compiling Object Files Specially*
- *Installing Files*
- *Managing Multiple Directory Projects*
- *Other Useful make Variables*
- *Questions*

5

Writing Imakefiles

The easiest way to write an Imakefile is to find another one that does something similar and copy/modify it.

—mit/config/README

This chapter describes how to write Imakefiles using the X11 configuration files. If you're not interested in X, don't be deterred from reading the chapter. You can use the X configuration files to write Imakefiles for non-X programs, and many of the concepts and ideas presented here apply to any set of configuration files.

Most of the chapter centers around how to use the rule macros in the X11 *Imake.rules* file. There are about a hundred such rules; the discussion here covers just a few. But once you understand those few, you should be able to look at *Imake.rules* and understand many of the other rules, too.

When I discuss a given rule, I give some basic information (the purpose of the rule, how to use it), and some detailed information (how the rule is defined, how it works). If you don't know or care how rules work and you just want to get your programs built, read only the basic information. This might be the situation if you've skipped directly to this chapter from Chapter 2, *A Tour of imake*, for example.

If you've read Chapter 3, *Understanding Configuration Files*, and Chapter 4, *The X11 Configuration Files*, you should be familiar with rule syntax and X files structure. If you want to gain a greater understanding of the X11 configuration files, learn to choose between rules in situations where more than one seems applicable, or write your own configuration files, read about how rules work and are defined.

To begin, I'll discuss the general strategy to build your project once you've already written your *Imakefile*. The rest of the chapter shows how to select and use the rules you invoke in your *Imakefile* for the targets you want to build. The discussion covers several common situations:

- Building a single program from a single source file
- Building a single program from multiple source files
- Building two or three programs
- Building an arbitrary number of programs
- Building a library
- Installing files

I'll also discuss some related issues such as how to refer to libraries, commonly used *make* variables, and management of multiple directory projects.

NOTE

Some of the rule definitions shown here have been reformatted to fit the page. They're slightly different than the original definitions in *Imake.rules*, but functionally they are the same.

General Strategy

To write an *Imakefile*, you invoke rules: concise specifications of the types of targets you want to build, such as executable programs, shell scripts, libraries, or font files. *imake* reads your *Imakefile* and expands the rules into *Makefile* target entries. Then you run *make* to build your targets.

The advice given in the epigraph illustrates the spirit of *Imakefile* writing. It's almost always true with *imake* that it's easier to copy something that works and modify it to suit your own purposes than to write it from scratch. Consider the Imakefiles in this chapter as working examples, select one that's close to what you want, copy it, modify it, and use it as a basis for your own work. Another way to apply the advice is to search through Imakefiles from existing projects until you find one that looks like you might be able to use it.

Once your *Imakefile* is written, a typical sequence of commands to build and install a project looks like this:

```
% xmkmf            Generate the Makefile (xmkmf calls imake)
% make clean       Remove any leftover debris
% make depend      Generate header file dependencies
% make             Build the software
% make install     Install the software
```

If the project consists of multiple directories, the sequence is similar except that the initial *Makefile*-generating step is followed by:

```
% make Makefiles
```

A shortcut is to use *xmkmf -a*, which does most of the above steps for you including:

```
xmkmf
make Makefiles
make includes
make depend
```

Remember that if you change an *Imakefile*, you must rebuild the *Makefile* and regenerate header file dependencies:

```
% make Makefile
% make depend
```

You can test whether your intentions in the *Imakefile* are realized in the *Makefile* by using the *-n* option. This causes *make* to show what commands it would generate to build a particular target, without actually executing them:

```
% make -n target
```

For the preceding commands to work, the X11 configuration files must be available on your machine, as well as the programs *imake, xmkmf, makedepend*, and *mkdirhier*. If you need to install any of these, see Appendix A, *Obtaining Configuration Software*, and Appendix B, *Installing Configuration Software*.

Invoking Rules

To invoke a rule, you name it and pass it any arguments necessary:

> *RuleName*(*arguments*)

RuleName is the name of the rule and *arguments* is the argument list.

There are a few guidelines you should follow when you invoke rules in an *Imakefile*:

- The argument list may be empty or consist of one or more arguments. When there are multiple arguments, separate them by commas, as show in the following examples:

```
DependTarget()
SimpleProgramTarget(myprog)
InstallLibrary(mylib,$(BINDIR))
NormalProgramTarget(myprog,$(OBJS),$(DEPXLIB),$(XLIB),-lm)
```

- When a rule has a non-empty argument list, you must specify something for each argument. Missing arguments are not allowed. However, it's sufficient to pass an argument that has no value. The X11 configuration files provide the symbol `NullParameter` for that purpose:

```
ComplexProgramTarget_1(myprog,,-lm)                /* incorrect */
ComplexProgramTarget_1(myprog,NullParameter,-lm)   /* correct */
```

- A cosmetic reason to use `NullParameter` is that it makes invocations more readable. Compare the following instances of `CppScript-Target()`. Without some close inspection, it may not be apparent that the last argument in the first instance is empty:

```
CppScriptTarget(x,x.cpp,-'DDIRS="/a/b,/g/h"',)
CppScriptTarget(x,x.cpp,-'DDIRS="/a/b,/g/h"',NullParameter)
```

- Do not add extra whitespace around arguments:

```
NormalLibraryTarget(mylib,$(OBJS))      /* correct */
NormalLibraryTarget(mylib ,$(OBJS))     /* incorrect */
NormalLibraryTarget(mylib, $(OBJS))     /* incorrect */
NormalLibraryTarget( mylib , $(OBJS) )  /* VERY incorrect */
```

The whitespace may end up as a part of your target entries in an unpleasant way (this is discussed further in Chapter 6, *Imakefile Troubleshooting*).

- Whitespace within an argument is allowable when it comprises a list of items such as file names, libraries, or flags:

```
NormalLibraryTarget(mylib,a.o b.o c.o)
ComplexProgramTarget_1(myprog,$(XMULIB) $(XLIB),-ly -lm)
SpecialObjectRule(file.o,file.c,-DFLAG1 -DFLAG2)
```

- You cannot split a rule invocation across lines:

```
/* incorrect */
NormalProgramTarget(prog1,$(OBJS1),$(DEPXLIB),$(XLIB),\
    NullParameter)
/* correct */
NormalProgramTarget(prog1,$(OBJS1),$(DEPXLIB),$(XLIB),NullParameter)
```

Now let's look at some specific rules and how to use them.

Building One Program

When you want to build a single program in your *Imakefile*, you have a choice of two rules. If the program is built from a single source file, use `SimpleProgramTarget()`. If it's not, use `ComplexProgram-Target()`.

Building a Single Program (One Source File)

The simplest case of all is when you're building one program from one source file. If your program fits the bill, use `SimpleProgramTarget()` and your *Imakefile* will be easy to write:

```
SimpleProgramTarget(prog)
```

prog is the name of the program. The source file must be named *prog.c*.

`SimpleProgramTarget()` generates targets for all the following commands:

```
% make all
% make prog
% make install
% make install.man
% make depend
% make lint
% make clean
```

You can also specify libraries to link into the final executable; this topic is discussed in the section "Specifying Libraries," later in this chapter.

The definition of `SimpleProgramTarget()` looks like this:

```
/*
 * SimpleProgramTarget - generate rules for compiling and linking
 * programs that only have one C source file.  It should only be
 * used in Imakefiles that describe a single program.
 */
#ifndef SimpleProgramTarget
#define SimpleProgramTarget(prog)                           @@\
            OBJS = prog.o                                   @@\
            SRCS = prog.c                                   @@\
                                                            @@\

ComplexProgramTarget(prog)
#endif /* SimpleProgramTarget */
```

`SimpleProgramTarget()` is actually quite lazy: it foists off onto `ComplexProgramTarget()` most of the work of generating entries to build and install the program. `SimpleProgramTarget()` deigns only to assign to SRCS the name of the program's source file and to OBJS the program's object file, because `ComplexProgramTarget()` expects those values to be set. `SimpleProgramTarget()` automatically determines SRCS and OBJS on the basis of the fixed relationship assumed between the name of the program and the names of its source and object files.

Building a Single Program (Multiple Source Files)

If you're building a single program from more than one source file, you can't use `SimpleProgramTarget()`. Use `ComplexProgram-Target()` instead, which makes no assumptions about how many files your program is built from or what they're named. This gives you the freedom to use an arbitrary set of files. However, SRCS and OBJS still need to be set, and their values cannot be determined from the program name. You must assign them yourself.

For example, if you want to build a program *myprog* from *main.c, connect.c,* and *display.c,* the *Imakefile* looks like this:

```
SRCS = main.c connect.c display.c
OBJS = main.o connect.o display.o
ComplexProgramTarget(myprog)
```

`ComplexProgramTarget()` generates the same targets as `Simple-ProgramTarget()`.

If your program needs to be built with libraries, see the section "Specifying Libraries."

The definition of `ComplexProgramTarget()` is quite a bit more elaborate than that of `SimpleProgramTarget()`:

```
/*
 * ComplexProgramTarget - generate rules for compiling and
 * linking the program specified by $(OBJS) and $(SRCS),
 * installing the program and its man page, and generating
 * dependencies.  It should only be used in Imakefiles that
 * describe a single program.
 */
#ifndef ComplexProgramTarget
#define ComplexProgramTarget(prog)                              @@\
        PROGRAM = prog                                          @@\
                                                                @@\
AllTarget(prog)                                                 @@\
                                                                @@\
prog: $(OBJS) $(DEPLIBS)                                        @@\
    RemoveTargetProgram($@)                                     @@\
    $(CC) -o $@ $(OBJS) $(LDOPTIONS) $(LOCAL_LIBRARIES) \       @@\
                    $(LDLIBS) $(EXTRA_LOAD_FLAGS)               @@\
                                                                @@\
InstallProgram(prog,$(BINDIR))                                  @@\
InstallManPage(prog,$(MANDIR))                                  @@\
DependTarget()                                                  @@\
LintTarget()                                                    @@\
                                                                @@\
clean::                                                         @@\
    $(RM) $(PROGRAM)
#endif /* ComplexProgramTarget */
```

`ComplexProgramTarget()` expands to several entries in the *Makefile*. A few of them are generated directly; most are produced by invoking other rules:

- `AllTarget()` generates an `all` entry so that *make all* compiles the program. The `all` entry is first in the resulting *Makefile*, so `all` becomes the default target and *make* with no arguments is equivalent to *make all*.

- The `prog` entry specifies that the target program depends on its object files and libraries and indicates how to link it. (The name of the entry is the name of the program, not "prog".) `LOCAL_LIBRARIES` and `DEPLIBS` specify link and dependency libraries; they're discussed in the next section, "Specifying Libraries."

- `InstallProgram()` and `InstallManPage()` generate `install` and `install.man` entries for installing the target program and its manual page in their respective directories.

- `DependTarget()` produces a `depend` entry for running *makedepend* to generate header file dependencies. This rule expects that `SRCS` names all of the program's source files.

- LintTarget() generates a lint entry for checking the program's source files. It, too, uses SRCS implicitly.

- The clean entry clobbers the compiled program. The configuration files automatically produce a default clean entry that removes .o files, but that entry doesn't know the name of the program built by ComplexProgramTarget(). So ComplexProgramTarget() provides a clean entry to remove the executable explicitly.

Besides SRCS and OBJS, which we've already discussed, Complex-ProgramTarget() uses a number of other *make* variables: CC, LD-OPTIONS, LDLIBS, EXTRA_LOAD_FLAGS, BINDIR, MANDIR, and RM. You can ignore all of them. PROGRAM is set by ComplexProgram-Target() itself; the others are assigned values as necessary by the configuration files.

Specifying Libraries

Programs often use functions contained in libraries, in which case *make* must link in those libraries when it produces the final executables. This section describes what to put in your *Imakefile* so that happens correctly.

SimpleProgramTarget() and ComplexProgramTarget() don't provide any way of specifying libraries in the argument list when you invoke them. Instead, you specify libraries using a trio of *make* variables: LOCAL_LIBRARIES, SYS_LIBRARIES, and DEPLIBS. The first two variables name the libraries in a form the linker can use. The third names them in a form *make* can use for dependency checking.

Link Libraries

LOCAL_LIBRARIES and SYS_LIBRARIES name libraries that need to be linked in when the final executable is created. The X configuration files don't give either variable any default value, so if libraries are needed, you must assign values yourself or the link step will fail.

Libraries can be specified for the linker either by pathname or by using –*l* notation. Typically, you use a pathname when you know the location of a library, e.g., when it's built within your project. You assign this kind of library to LOCAL_LIBRARIES. Use –*l* notation when you want the linker to find the library for you, e.g., for a system library. Libraries specified like this are assigned to SYS_LIBRARIES.

Dependency Libraries

The third variable, DEPLIBS, names the libraries your program needs, but in dependency form. This addresses a common *Makefile* deficiency: program building entries that list the program's object files as dependencies, but not the libraries necessary for the success of the final link step. DEP-LIBS allows you to characterize your program's dependencies more completely. Then, when a library changes, *make* knows that the program must be relinked.

make understands only filenames for purposes of dependency checking, so libraries must be assigned to DEPLIBS in pathname, not *–l* form. The following doesn't work:

```
/* incorrect */
DEPLIBS = -lm
```

If you assign such a value to DEPLIBS, *make* complains when you use the resulting *Makefile*:

```
make: Fatal error: Don't know how to make target "-lm"
```

The default value of DEPLIBS refers to the Xlib, Xext, Xt, Xmu, and Xaw libraries. You should reassign it if your program uses a different set of libraries. For instance, if your program uses no libraries at all, turn DEP-LIBS off by assigning it an empty value:

```
DEPLIBS =
```

In fact, even if your program does use libraries, you can cheat and turn DEPLIBS off. If all the libraries are present, your program will still link correctly. (And if the libraries are missing, you have more pressing concerns than writing an *Imakefile*!)

Now we know how library variables are used in general; let's look at some specific examples.

For a program that requires no libraries, the variables all have empty values:

```
LOCAL_LIBRARIES =
  SYS_LIBRARIES =
        DEPLIBS =
```

Since the first two variables aren't assigned any default value by the configuration files, the following is equivalent and simpler to write:

```
DEPLIBS =
```

For a program that does need libraries, we must consider three cases:

- Libraries built within the project
- System libraries
- X libraries

Within-project Libraries

If a library is built within your project, you refer to it by pathname, usually relative to the project root, which is specified by the *make* variable TOP. *imake* sets TOP for you when you build the *Makefile*. It provides a stable point of reference to use when specifying within-project paths, no matter what directory of your project you happen to be in.

Within-project library assignments are written using the *make* variable LOCAL_LIBRARIES. For example, if a program uses a library *libmylib.a* located in the *lib* directory under the project root, specify it using the pathname $(TOP)/*lib/libmylib.a.* Since pathnames are suitable for dependency lines, too, specify the library the same way for dependency purposes and assign it to the variable DEPLIBS. Thus, you set the variables like this:

```
LOCAL_LIBRARIES = $(TOP)/lib/libmylib.a
        DEPLIBS = $(TOP)/lib/libmylib.a
```

System Libraries

If you need a library that isn't built within your project, chances are it's a system library accessed using *–l* syntax for linking purposes. This kind of library is typically assigned to the variable SYS_LIBRARIES. The math library is a good example. If your program needs it, write this:

```
SYS_LIBRARIES = -lm
```

So far, so good. Now, how do we specify the library in dependency form for DEPLIBS?

You don't: DEPLIBS requires a pathname and *–lm* isn't one. You could figure out where a given system library is located on your machine and write its pathname into your *Imakefile*, but that's system-specific. (You might know that the math library is in */usr/lib/libm.a* on your machine, but not all machines are like yours. One of the machines I use has the math library in */bsd43/usr/lib/libm.a.*) In the absence of a portable mechanism for specifying the locations of arbitrary system libraries, we just leave them out of `DEPLIBS`:

```
SYS_LIBRARIES = -lm
      DEPLIBS =
```

X Libraries

When you're building X programs, you'll need X libraries (Xlib at minimum, possibly others). You can refer to these literally as *–lX11*, *–lXt*, etc. for linking, but the X configuration files provide a set of *make* variables for the same purpose, as well as a set for use in dependencies. Table 5–1 lists the most common ones; consult *Project.tmpl* for the full list.

Table 5-1: make Variables for X Libraries

X Library	Link Name	Dependency Name
Xlib	XLIB	DEPXLIB
Xmu	XMULIB	DEPXMULIB
X Toolkit	XTOOLLIB	DEPXTOOLLIB
Athena Widgets	XAWLIB	DEPXAWLIB
X Input Extension	XILIB	DEPXILIB
PHIGS	PHIGSLIB	DEPPHIGSLIB
PEX Library	PEXLIB	DEPPEXLIB

Suppose a program needs the Xlib and X Toolkit libraries. Consulting the table, we find that the names suitable for the linker are `XLIB` and `XTOOL-LIB`. Similarly, `DEPXLIB` and `DEPXTOOLLIB` are the names to use for dependency checking. So we write:

```
LOCAL_LIBRARIES = $(XTOOLLIB) $(XLIB)
        DEPLIBS = $(DEPXTOOLLIB) $(DEPXLIB)
```

The order is important here. The X Toolkit uses routines from Xlib, so Xt must precede Xlib in the link command. Otherwise, the linker doesn't know which Xlib routines to extract from the library and put into the executable, and you'll get "undefined symbol" errors.

X libraries: are they local or system libraries?

I assigned the link libraries to LOCAL_LIBRARIES in the preceding example. Actually, the X libraries are ambiguous, because they can be considered system libraries in some circumstances. If you're writing an application within the source tree of the X distribution, you'll probably use versions of the libraries found within that tree. Those libraries are local to the distribution. If you're writing an application outside the X source tree, you'll probably use versions of the X libraries installed in a public directory such as */usr/lib*. Those libraries are system libraries.

In practice, this distinction isn't a problem. As long as you use the *make* variables to refer to X libraries, you can treat them either as local or system libraries and expect your program to link properly. Thus, these two sets of *make* variable assignments are equivalent:

```
LOCAL_LIBRARIES = $(XMULIB) $(XLIB)
  SYS_LIBRARIES =
         DEPLIBS = $(DEPXMULIB) $(DEPXLIB)
LOCAL_LIBRARIES =
  SYS_LIBRARIES = $(XMULIB) $(XLIB)
        DEPLIBS = $(DEPXMULIB) $(DEPXLIB)
```

If you're skeptical about this, take a look at the programs in the X *contrib* (user-contributed) distribution. They aren't built within the X source tree, but by and large their Imakefiles treat the X libraries as local libraries.

Athena client libraries

If a client program uses the Athena widgets, it uses Xaw, the Athena Widget library. Xaw in turn requires the Xlib, Xmu, and Xt libraries. You could write this in your *Imakefile*:

```
LOCAL_LIBRARIES = $(XAWLIB) $(XMULIB) $(XTOOLLIB) $(XLIB)
        DEPLIBS = $(DEPXAWLIB) $(DEPXMULIB) $(DEPXTOOLLIB) $(DEPXLIB)
```

However, it's a lot more convenient to use the *cpp* symbols XawClient-Libs and XawClientDepLibs instead:

```
LOCAL_LIBRARIES = XawClientLibs
        DEPLIBS = XawClientDepLibs
```

The X configuration files define these two symbols as shorthand to achieve the same effect as the previous set of assignments. They're easier to write and they make sure the libraries are specified in the correct order for you.

The X extensions library

Xext, the X extensions library, contains routines for locally available extensions such as those for non-rectangular window shapes, multi-buffering, and shared memory. If your program uses extensions, you don't need to write anything special in the *Imakefile* beyond including the Xlib variables XLIB and DEPXLIB in the link and dependency library lists. XLIB and DEPXLIB automatically include references to the extensions library.

Mixing Library Types

When you need several types of libraries (within-project, system, X libraries), specify the combination as the concatenation of the way you'd specify them individually. For a program that uses the local library $(TOP)/lib/libmylib.a, the X libraries Xlib and Xmu, and the system library −*lm*, set the variables like this:

```
LOCAL_LIBRARIES = $(TOP)/lib/libmylib.a $(XMULIB) $(XLIB)
  SYS_LIBRARIES = -lm
        DEPLIBS = $(TOP)/lib/libmylib.a $(DEPXMULIB) $(DEPXLIB)
```

Table 5–2 summarizes the use of link and dependency specifiers for different library types. *pathname* represents the path to a library starting from the project root. *libname* represents the basename of a system library.

Table 5-2: Link and Dependency Library Specifier Summary

Type of library	Link form	Dependency form
Within-project	$(TOP)/*pathname*	$(TOP)/*pathname*
System	−l*libname*	none
X library (e.g., Xlib)	$(XLIB)	$(DEPXLIB)
Athena client libraries	XawClientLibs	XawClientDepLibs

Building Multiple Programs

You cannot use SimpleProgramTarget() or ComplexProgram-Target() when you want to build more than one program in your *Imakefile*. To handle this, the X configuration files provide rules for building exactly two or three programs, and a rule for building an arbitrary number of programs.

Building Two or Three Programs

To build two or three programs in an *Imakefile*, you can use `Complex-ProgramTarget_1()`, `ComplexProgramTarget_2()`, and `Complex-ProgramTarget_3()`. The invocation sequence for each of the `ComplexProgramTarget_n()` rules is:

```
ComplexProgramTarget_n(prog,loclibs,syslibs)
```

prog is the name of your program. The other two arguments specify libraries needed to get *prog* to link correctly: *loclibs* is for libraries local to your project, and *syslibs* is for libraries provided by the system. Their values are specified just like the `LOCAL_LIBRARIES` and `SYS_LIBRARIES` variables used with `ComplexProgramTarget()`. The difference is that you specify the values in the rule argument list rather than by setting *make* variables.

If you don't need libraries of a particular kind, pass `NullParameter` for *loclibs*, *syslibs*, or both.

While you don't use `LOCAL_LIBRARIES`, `SYS_LIBRARIES`, or `DEPLIBS` with the `ComplexProgramTarget_n()` rules, You're expected to assign values to other *make* variables in the *Imakefile*:

- Set the variable `PROGRAMS` to the names of the programs you're building:

  ```
  PROGRAMS = prog1 prog2 prog3
  ```

  If you do not do this, *make all* and *make depend* won't work correctly.

- Set `SRCSn` and `OBJSn` to the source and object file lists for program *n*:

  ```
  SRCS1 = file1a.c file1b.c
  OBJS1 = file1a.o file1b.o

  SRCS2 = file2a.c file2b.c file2c.c file2d.c
  OBJS2 = file2a.o file2b.o file2c.o file2d.o

  SRCS3 = file3a.c
  OBJS3 = file3a.o
  ```

  `SRCSn` is needed for depending and *lint*-ing the sources. `OBJSn` is needed for compiling and linking the program.

- `DEPLIBSn` names the libraries that program *n* depends on. The default value is the same as `DEPLIBS`, but you might wish to assign a different value. If a program uses no libraries, assign the empty value to `DEP-LIBSn` to clear it. Otherwise, the value of `DEPLIBSn` should contain the dependency forms of the link libraries you use for the *loclibs* and *syslibs* arguments for program *n*. Let's assume you're invoking `ComplexProgramTarget_2()` like this:

```
ComplexProgramTarget_2(prog2,$(TOP)/lib/libmylib.a $(XLIB),-lm)
```

Here, *loclibs* names $ (TOP) */lib/libmylib.a* and $ (XLIB), and *syslibs* names -lm. To specify the value of DEPLIBS2, assign it the dependency forms of these three libraries: the reference to the local library *libmylib.a* is repeated without modification, XLIB becomes DEPXLIB, and *−lm* has no dependency form, so it's left out. Here's the result:

```
DEPLIBS2 = $(TOP)/lib/libmylib.a $(DEPXLIB)
```

An *Imakefile* using the `ComplexProgramTarget_n()` rules to build two programs, *prog1* and *prog2*, might look like this:

```
PROGRAMS = prog1 prog2
   SRCS1 = file1a.c file1b.c
   OBJS1 = file1a.o file1b.o
DEPLIBS1 = $(DEPXLIB)
   SRCS2 = file2a.c file2b.c file2c.c file2d.c
   OBJS2 = file2a.o file2b.o file2c.o file2d.o
DEPLIBS2 = $(DEPXTOOLLIB) $(DEPXLIB)
ComplexProgramTarget_1(prog1,$(XLIB),NullParameter)
ComplexProgramTarget_2(prog2,$(XTOOLLIB) $(XLIB),NullParameter)
```

To add a third program, *prog3*, append its name to PROGRAMS; set SRCS3, OBJS3, and DEPLIBS3; and invoke `ComplexProgramTarget_3()`:

```
PROGRAMS = prog1 prog2 prog3
   SRCS1 = file1a.c file1b.c
   OBJS1 = file1a.o file1b.o
DEPLIBS1 = $(DEPXLIB)
   SRCS2 = file2a.c file2b.c file2c.c file2d.c
   OBJS2 = file2a.o file2b.o file2c.o file2d.o
DEPLIBS2 = $(DEPXTOOLLIB) $(DEPXLIB)
   SRCS3 = file3a.c
   OBJS3 = file3a.o
DEPLIBS3 = $(TOP)/lib/libutil.a $(DEPXLIB)
ComplexProgramTarget_1(prog1,$(XLIB),NullParameter)
ComplexProgramTarget_2(prog2,$(XTOOLLIB) $(XLIB),NullParameter)
ComplexProgramTarget_3(prog3,$(TOP)/lib/libutil.a $(XLIB),-lm)
```

If you want to add a fourth program, *prog4*, you, uh ... can't. Not without rewriting the *Imakefile*, anyway. Sorry. (See the discussion of Normal-ProgramTarget() in the next section.)

The definitions of ComplexProgramTarget_1() and Complex-ProgramTarget_2() are shown in the example below. Complex-ProgramTarget_3() isn't shown because it's essentially identical to ComplexProgramTarget_2().

```
/*
 * ComplexProgramTarget_1 - generate rules for compiling and
 * linking the program specified by $(OBJS1) and $(SRCS1),
 * installing the program and its man page, and generating
 * dependencies for it and any programs described by $(SRCS2)
 * and $(SRCS3).  It should be used to build the primary program
 * in Imakefiles that describe multiple programs.
 */
#ifndef ComplexProgramTarget_1
#define ComplexProgramTarget_1(prog,loclibs,syslibs)            @@\
            OBJS = $(OBJS1) $(OBJS2) $(OBJS3)                    @@\
            SRCS = $(SRCS1) $(SRCS2) $(SRCS3)                    @@\
                                                                @@\
AllTarget($(PROGRAMS))                                          @@\
                                                                @@\
prog: $(OBJS1) $(DEPLIBS1)                                      @@\
    RemoveTargetProgram($@)                                     @@\
    $(CC) -o $@ $(LDOPTIONS) $(OBJS1) loclibs $(LDLIBS) \       @@\
                        syslibs $(EXTRA_LOAD_FLAGS)             @@\
                                                                @@\
InstallProgram(prog,$(BINDIR))                                  @@\
InstallManPage(prog,$(MANDIR))                                  @@\
                                                                @@\
DependTarget()                                                  @@\
LintTarget()                                                    @@\
                                                                @@\
clean::                                                         @@\
    $(RM) $(PROGRAMS)
#endif /* ComplexProgramTarget_1 */


/*
 * ComplexProgramTarget_2 - generate rules for compiling and
 * linking the program specified by $(OBJS2) and $(SRCS2) and
 * installing the program and man page.  It should be used to
 * build the second program in Imakefiles describing more than
 * one program.
 */
#ifndef ComplexProgramTarget_2
#define ComplexProgramTarget_2(prog,loclibs,syslibs)            @@\
prog: $(OBJS2) $(DEPLIBS2)                                      @@\
    RemoveTargetProgram($@)                                     @@\
    $(CC) -o $@ $(LDOPTIONS) $(OBJS2) loclibs $(LDLIBS) \       @@\
                        syslibs $(EXTRA_LOAD_FLAGS)             @@\
                                                                @@\
InstallProgram(prog,$(BINDIR))                                  @@\
InstallManPage(prog,$(MANDIR))
#endif /* ComplexProgramTarget_2 */
```

Of the three rules, `ComplexProgramTarget_1()` does the most work. It does everything the other two rules do along with setting `SRCS` and `OBJS`, and producing `depend`, `lint`, and `clean` entries. Because of the way the rules work, these additional things need only be done once, not repeated three times.

I mentioned earlier that failure to set `PROGRAMS` causes two commands to work incorrectly:

```
% make all
% make clean
```

If you examine the definition of `ComplexProgramTarget_1()`, you can see that this is because `PROGRAMS` is used to generate the `all` and `clean` entries. When you set `PROGRAMS` properly, the `all` entry causes your programs to be built and the `clean` entry removes the executables. But when you don't set it, the value of `PROGRAMS` is empty, and the two entries effectively end up looking like this in your *Makefile*:

```
all::

clean::
    $(RM)
```

As a result, neither entry does anything—not quite the intended effect.

Building an Arbitrary Number of Programs

To build an arbitrary number of programs, invoke `NormalProgram-Target()` for each one:

```
NormalProgramTarget(prog, objs, deplibs, loclibs, syslibs)
```

You don't need to set any *make* variables to use `NormalProgram-Target()`. All the information it needs is passed in through the argument list. *prog* is the name of your program and *objs* is the set of object files from which it's built. *loclibs* and *syslibs* name the local and system link libraries your program needs. *deplibs* names those libraries in a form suitable for dependency checking.

Here's an *Imakefile* that uses `NormalProgramTarget()` to build four programs. (The *make* variables `OBJS1` through `OBJS4` are used to improve readability. You could just as well put the object lists in the rule invocations.)

```
OBJS1 = prog1a.o prog1b.o
OBJS2 = prog2a.o prog2b.o prog2c.o prog2d.o
OBJS3 = prog3a.o
OBJS4 = prog4a.o prog4b.o
```

```
NormalProgramTarget(prog1,$(OBJS1),$(DEPXLIB),$(XLIB),NullParameter)
NormalProgramTarget(prog2,$(OBJS2),$(DEPXLIB),$(XLIB),NullParameter)
NormalProgramTarget(prog3,$(OBJS3),$(DEPXLIB),$(XLIB),NullParameter)
NormalProgramTarget(prog4,$(OBJS4),$(DEPXLIB),$(XLIB),NullParameter)
```

This *Imakefile* is incomplete because it produces a *Makefile* without `all`, `install`, `depend`, or `lint` entries. To see why, take a look at the definition of `NormalProgramTarget()`:

```
/*
 * NormalProgramTarget - generate rules to compile and link the
 * indicated program; since it does not use any default object
 * files, it may be used for multiple programs in the same
 * Imakefile.
 */
#ifndef NormalProgramTarget
#define NormalProgramTarget(prog,objs,deplibs,loclibs,syslibs) @@\
prog: objs deplibs                                             @@\
        RemoveTargetProgram($@)                                @@\
        $(CC) -o $@ objs $(LDOPTIONS) loclibs $(LDLIBS) syslibs \  @@\
                        $(EXTRA_LOAD_FLAGS)                    @@\
                                                               @@\
clean::                                                        @@\
        $(RM) prog
#endif /* NormalProgramTarget */
```

`NormalProgramTarget()` generates only two entries, a *prog* entry to build the executable program and a `clean` entry to remove it. This contrasts with the `ComplexProgramTarget_n()` rules, which epitomize the cradle-to-grave approach of producing entries for every target you need, and then some. `NormalProgramTarget()` is the entrepreneur's rule—it presumes you have more initiative. You must invoke the appropriate rules yourself if you want entries for any of the following targets:

`all` Invoke `AllTarget(`*prog*`)` before each invocation of `NormalProgramTarget(`*prog*`)`.

`install` Invoke an installation rule for each program you want installed. You have a choice of several installation rules; the simplest is `InstallProgram()`. It takes two arguments, the name of the program and the directory in which to install it:

```
InstallProgram(prog,dir)
```

`depend` and `lint`

Invoke `DependTarget()` and `LintTarget()` once each per *Imakefile*. To use either of these rules you must set `SRCS` to the list of all source files used by all the programs in the *Imakefile*.

install.man

> If you provide any manual pages, you should also invoke
> InstallManPage() for each one:
>
> InstallManPage(*prog*,$(MANDIR))
>
> MANDIR is the manual page installation directory. Note that
> the rule takes the program name in the argument list, but the
> manual page itself should be named *prog.man*.

To fix the preceding *Imakefile* so it includes all, install,
install.man, depend, and lint targets, write it like this:

```
SRCS1 = prog1a.c prog1b.c
OBJS1 = prog1a.o prog1b.o

SRCS2 = prog2a.c prog2b.c prog2c.c prog2d.c
OBJS2 = prog2a.o prog2b.o prog2c.o prog2d.o

SRCS3 = prog3a.c
OBJS3 = prog3a.o

SRCS4 = prog4a.c prog4b.c
OBJS4 = prog4a.o prog4b.o

 SRCS = $(SRCS1) $(SRCS2) $(SRCS3) $(SRCS4)

AllTarget(prog1)
NormalProgramTarget(prog1,$(OBJS1),$(DEPXLIB),$(XLIB),NullParameter)
InstallProgram(prog1,$(BINDIR))
InstallManPage(prog1,$(MANDIR))

AllTarget(prog2)
NormalProgramTarget(prog2,$(OBJS2),$(DEPXLIB),$(XLIB),NullParameter)
InstallProgram(prog2,$(BINDIR))
InstallManPage(prog2,$(MANDIR))

AllTarget(prog3)
NormalProgramTarget(prog3,$(OBJS3),$(DEPXLIB),$(XLIB),NullParameter)
InstallProgram(prog3,$(BINDIR))
InstallManPage(prog3,$(MANDIR))

AllTarget(prog4)
NormalProgramTarget(prog4,$(OBJS4),$(DEPXLIB),$(XLIB),NullParameter)
InstallProgram(prog4,$(BINDIR))
InstallManPage(prog4,$(MANDIR))

DependTarget()
LintTarget()
```

When you use NormalProgramTarget() to write an *Imakefile*, you
have to do more work than when you use the ComplexProgram-
Target_*n*() rules. In return, NormalProgramTarget() gives you a
broader range of choices in determining what ends up in the *Makefile*. It's
also more general since you can use it to build any number of programs
without a separate rule *n* for every *n*-th program.

linting Multiple Programs

The `ComplexProgramTarget_n()` rules automatically generate a `lint` target entry for you. `NormalProgramTarget()` does not, but you can invoke `LintTarget()` yourself to generate one. In both cases, you can use the `lint` entry to run your sources through the *lint* program. However, you must interpret the output with some caution. *lint* expects to be fed the source files for a single program, but the `lint` entry passes the sources for all your programs. The result is output that contains spurious warnings, such as that *main()* is multiply defined.

In Chapter 11, *Writing Rule Macros*, we'll see an alternative way of generating `lint` entries that doesn't have this problem.

Organizing Source and Object File Lists

The *Imakefile* just shown illustrates an important organizational technique: judicious use of *make* variables to improve the readability of the *Imakefile*. If we had written object file lists directly in the rule invocations, the invocations would be more opaque, particularly for targets built from lots of files. Instead of writing object file lists directly in invocations of `Normal-ProgramTarget()`, we assign them to variables and refer to the variables when we invoke the rules.

Similarly, variables make it easier to use `DependTarget()` and `Lint-Target()`, which expect the *make* variable `SRCS` to name all source files used in the *Imakefile*. If you use a variable to specify the source list for each of your programs, you can set `SRCS` to their concatenation:

```
SRCS1 = prog1a.c prog1b.c
SRCS2 = prog2a.c prog2b.c prog2c.c prog2d.c
SRCS3 = prog3a.c
SRCS4 = prog4a.c prog4b.c
 SRCS = $(SRCS1) $(SRCS2) $(SRCS3) $(SRCS4)
```

Using variables for lists of source and object files adds more lines to the *Imakefile*. However, the *Imakefile* is better structured, easier to read, and less prone to error:

- It's more obvious which files make up a given program because they're explicitly specified on their own line, not buried in an invocation of `NormalProgramTarget()`.

- When a new file is added to the source file list, it's harder to forget to add the corresponding object file to the object file list if the two lists are located together, because their contents are completely parallel:

```
SRCS1 = progla.c proglb.c
OBJS1 = progla.o proglb.o
```

In the assignments above, it's not likely you'll add a file to SRCS1 but forget to add the corresponding file to OBJS1.

- When SRCS is defined as the concatenation of individual program source list variables, changes to an individual program's source list automatically propagate into SRCS, so that *make lint* and *make depend* continue to work properly without special attention.

Building Libraries

The X rules allow you to build normal, shared, debugging, or profiling libraries. I'll describe how to build normal libraries first, then the other kinds.

The most common rule for creating a library is NormalLibrary-Target(). It takes two arguments: the "basename" of the library, and a list of the object files comprising it. The basename of library *libxyz.a* is *xyz*.

Here's a sample library-building *Imakefile*:

```
SRCS = a.c b.c c.c
OBJS = a.o b.o c.o
NormalLibraryObjectRule()
NormalLibraryTarget(xyz,$(OBJS))
InstallLibrary(xyz,$(USRLIBDIR))
DependTarget()
```

Notice that you don't use NormalLibraryTarget() in isolation:

- Precede NormalLibraryTarget() with an invocation of Normal-LibraryObjectRule(), which provides some machinery telling *make* how to compile object files that are intended to be combined into libraries.
- Use InstallLibrary() to generate an install entry, because NormalLibraryTarget() does not provide one.
- Invoke DependTarget(). This requires that you set SRCS.
- NormalLibraryTarget() doesn't generate a clean entry; there is no need because *.a* files are automatically removed by the default clean entry provided by the configuration files.

Other Kinds of Libraries

When you want to compile shared, profiled, or debugging libraries in addition to or instead of a normal library, things become more interesting.

Your *Imakefile* should begin with this prolog:

```
#define DoNormalLib BoolVal
#define DoSharedLib BoolVal
#define DoDebugLib BoolVal
#define DoProfileLib BoolVal

#include <Library.tmpl>

SRCS = file1.c file2.c file3.c ...
OBJS = file1.o file2.o file3.o ...

LibraryObjectRule()
```

The first four lines define library-related, boolean-valued macros that indicate what types of libraries you want to create. *BoolVal* is either YES or NO (it need not be the same on all four lines).

Library.tmpl is a special library template file. When processed, it triggers a flurry of activity that sets up special definitions and rules that enable the right kinds of object files to be built for the types of libraries you're building. (The stuff in *Library.tmpl* is wondrously complex; take a look at it sometime when you're feeling intrepid.)

SRCS and OBJS name the source and object files, just as for normal libraries.

LibraryObjectRule() is defined in *Library.tmpl*. When invoked, among other things, it makes sure that you have *shared*, *debugger*, and *profiled* subdirectories for building special object files.

Following the prolog just shown, you invoke rules for building each kind of library, surrounding each by the appropriate conditional construct. For normal, debugging, and profiled libraries, write this:

```
#if DoNormalLib
NormalLibraryTarget(xyz,$(OBJS))
InstallLibrary(xyz,$(USRLIBDIR))
#endif

#if DoDebugLib
DebuggedLibraryTarget(xyz,$(OBJS))
InstallLibrary(xyz_d,$(USRLIBDIR))
#endif
```

```
#if DoProfileLib
ProfiledLibraryTarget(xyz,$(OBJS))
InstallLibrary(xyz_p,$(USRLIBDIR))
#endif
    .
    .
    .
```

Note that for debugging or profiling libraries, the library name in the installation rules should be followed by _d or _p.

For a shared library, you specify a revision number (denoted *rev* below) in addition to the library name. Also, the creation of shared libraries depends on whether or not you're building normal libraries:

```
#if DoSharedLib
#if DoNormalLib
SharedLibraryTarget(xyz,rev,$(OBJS),shared,..)
#else
SharedLibraryTarget(xyz,rev,$(OBJS),.,.)
#endif
InstallSharedLibrary(xyz,rev,$(USRLIBDIR))
#endif
```

After you finish writing your *Imakefile*, build the *Makefile* from it, type *make* and then sit back and watch the fireworks.

This brief summary doesn't do justice to a complex topic. If you intend to build libraries other than normal libraries, examine the Imakefiles for the libraries under *mit/lib* in the X source distribution; this will give you an idea of special cases that may arise and how to handle them.

Compiling Object Files Specially

Sometimes you need to compile a particular object file specially, i.e., to pass it special flags. To do this, invoke `SpecialObjectRule()`. It takes three arguments:

```
SpecialObjectRule(obj,depends,options)
```

This generates an entry to compile *obj*. The *depends* argument names dependencies for *obj*, and *options* names any special options needed to compile *obj*.

For example, you might have a file *src.c* that uses the *vfork()* system call if it's available and *fork()* otherwise. The X11 configuration files provide a macro `HasVFork` indicating the availability of *vfork()*, but you can't directly test `HasVFork` in your source file—the configuration files aren't accessed when your program is compiled. However, you can indirectly use

`HasVFork` to pass a flag to the compiler, by putting the following in your *Imakefile*:

```
#if HasVFork
    VFORK_FLAGS = -DVFORK
#endif
SpecialObjectRule(src.o,src.c,$(VFORK_FLAGS))
```

In the resulting *Makefile*, VFORK_FLAGS is –DVFORK if *vfork()* is otherwise available and undefined, i.e., empty. This allows you to test VFORK in *src.c* like this:

```
#ifndef VFORK
#define vfork() fork()  /* vfork() unavailable, use fork() */
#endif
```

Installing Files

Some rules, such as `ComplexProgramTarget()`, generate their own `install` entries. For those that do not, such as `NormalProgram-Target()` and `NormalLibraryTarget()`, you need to invoke installation rules yourself. In general, they take this form:

InstallRuleName(what,where)

`what` is the file you want to install; `where` is the destination directory in which to install it.

X11 has more than 25 rules for installing various kinds of targets. Many of them are for unusual cases; the list below describes rules for some of the more common target types. You don't need to check whether the installation directory exists—all the rules shown create the directory if it's missing by invoking `MakeDir()`.

`InstallProgram(prog,dir)`

> Generates an `install` entry to install the executable program *prog* into *dir/prog*. `InstallProgram()` can also be used to install executable scripts.

`InstallManPage(prog,dir)`

> Generates an `install.man` entry to install the manual page *prog.man* into *dir/prog*.$(MANSUFFIX). The *dir* argument is normally $(MANDIR), and $(MANSUFFIX) is n by default.

InstallAppDefaults(*prog*)

> Generates an install entry to install the application defaults file *prog.ad* into $(XAPPLOADDIR)/*prog*. Don't specify the *.ad* suffix when you invoke InstallApp-Defaults(). This rule differs from the others in assuming a default installation directory XAPPLOADDIR, the value of which is set by the configuration files. Consequently, the rule only takes one argument.

InstallLibrary(*xyz*,*dir*)

> Generates an install entry to install the library *libxyz.a* into *dir/libxyz.a.*

InstallNonExecFile (*file*, *dir*)

> Generates an install entry to install *file* into *dir/file* as a read-only file.

Managing Multiple Directory Projects

When you have a project made up of multiple directories, it's convenient to have *make* operate on the entire project tree (or on the entire subtree below your current position within the project) for commands such as these:

```
% make
% make Makefiles
% make clean
% make depend
% make install
```

The alternative to having *make* process the project tree for you is to move into each directory individually and run *make* yourself. Ugh. Fortunately, that's not necessary. The X configuration files provide rules you can invoke in your *Imakefile* to generate recursive target entries in your *Makefile*. This reduces to a relatively simple process the otherwise difficult project management task of creating Makefiles that allow you to perform directory-traversing *make* operations throughout your entire project tree.

I'll show how to do this using the sample multiple directory project organized as shown in Figure 5–1.

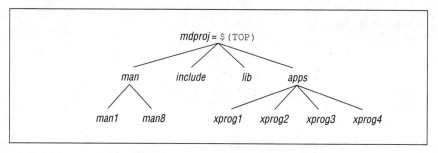

Figure 5-1: Sample multiple directory project

First create a project directory tree and populate it with empty Imakefiles:

```
% mkdir mdproj
% cd mdproj
% mkdir man include lib apps \
    man/man1 man/man8 \
    apps/xprog1 apps/xprog2 apps/xprog3 apps/xprog4
% touch `find . -type d -print | sed 's:$:/Imakefile:'`
```

To be a good citizen in a multiple directory project, each *Imakefile* needs certain minimal content. The nature of that content depends on whether or not the directory in which the *Imakefile* is located has subdirectories in which *make* should be run. I'll call a directory with subdirectories a **branch** directory, and a directory without subdirectories a **leaf** directory. The sample project contains three branch directories: $(TOP), *man*, and *apps*. The others are leaf directories.

In a branch directory, the *Imakefile* must trigger the recursive rules and specify which subdirectories they apply to. You do this by beginning the *Imakefile* with the following three lines:

```
#define IHaveSubdirs
#define PassCDebugFlags
SUBDIRS = subdirectory-list
    ⋮
    ⋮
```

When the *Makefile* is built, the configuration files see that `IHaveSubdirs` is defined and they generate entries that perform recursive *make* operations. `SUBDIRS` names the subdirectories those entries operate on, in the order you want them processed. (`PassCDebugFlags` is used for specifying debugging flags when you build your project; we'll discuss it shortly.)

In addition, you should invoke `MakeSubdirs()` and `DependSubdirs()` to generate recursive `all` and `depend` target entries, so the pattern for a minimal branch *Imakefile* looks like this:

```
#define IHaveSubdirs
#define PassCDebugFlags
SUBDIRS = subdirectory-list
MakeSubdirs($(SUBDIRS))
DependSubdirs($(SUBDIRS))
```

These two rules must be invoked because the X configuration files produce `clean`, `install`, `includes`, and `Makefile` entries automatically, but not `all` or `depend` entries. `MakeSubdirs()` should be invoked first so that `all` becomes the default target.

For the sample project, create the branch directory Imakefiles according to the preceding pattern, using the values of `SUBDIRS` shown below.

`$(TOP)`/*Imakefile*:

```
SUBDIRS = man include lib apps
```

man/Imakefile:

```
SUBDIRS = man1 man8
```

apps/Imakefile:

```
SUBDIRS = xprog1 xprog2 xprog3 xprog4
```

We haven't written very much so far (the leaf directory Imakefiles are still empty). Nevertheless, we've already got enough to allow the Makefiles to be built. Execute the following commands in the project root directory. The first command bootstraps the root-level *Makefile* and the second causes *make* to traverse the rest of the project tree to create the other Makefiles:

```
% xmkmf
% make Makefiles
```

However, if you try *make all* after building the Makefiles, you'll find that the command works only partially. *make* descends properly into subdirectories, but when it reaches a leaf directory, it fails: none of the leaf directory Imakefiles contain an `all` target. (*make depend* fails for similar reasons.)

To fix this, each leaf *Imakefile* must produce at least an `all` entry and a depend entry. The minimum leaf *Imakefile* we can get away with is this:

```
all::
depend::
```

Put this minimal *Imakefile* in each of the sample project's leaf directories.

Then build all subdirectory Makefiles:

```
% make Makefiles
```

Now *make all* and *make depend* will properly traverse the project tree.

The minimal leaf *Imakefile* shown here contains just enough to keep the `all` and `depend` *make* operations from generating errors. However, when you get around to building programs in a leaf directory, you should generate an `all` entry for each program by invoking `AllTarget()` or by using rules that invoke `AllTarget()` themselves. Don't forget to set `SRCS` and invoke `DependTarget()` if your program building rules don't do so for you.

Restricting the Scope of Recursive Operations

If you want to perform a recursive *make* operation on some subdirectories but not others, you can override any value `SUBDIRS` might have in the *Makefile* by specifying a value for `SUBDIRS` directly on the *make* command line. For example, in the *apps* directory, this command installs programs only in the subdirectories *xprog1* and *xprog4*:

```
% make install "SUBDIRS=xprog1 xprog4"
```

Adding a New Directory to an Existing Project

To add a new directory to an existing project, you must create it and put an *Imakefile* in it. Then, in the parent directory's *Imakefile*, add the subdirectory's name to the value of `SUBDIRS`. Finally, rebuild the parent directory's *Makefile* so it knows about the new subdirectory, and use that *Makefile* to rebuild the subdirectory's *Makefile*:

```
% make Makefile
% make Makefiles "SUBDIRS=subdir"
```

Once this is done, recursive operations invoked from the parent will include the new subdirectory.

Constraints on the Value of SUBDIRS

You cannot assign an empty value to `SUBDIRS`. Nor can `SUBDIRS` name the current directory or any directories above the current directory:

```
/* these are all incorrect */
SUBDIRS =
SUBDIRS = .
SUBDIRS = ..
```

If you assign SUBDIRS an empty value (perhaps thinking recursive operations will be null operations), you'll get syntax errors when you run *make*. If you assign the current or parent directory to SUBDIRS, *make* will either go into a loop, or crash and burn.

Specifying Debugging Flags

If you anticipate a need to specify debugging flags when you build a project, don't define PassCDebugFlags with an empty value in branch Imakefiles. Define it like this instead:

```
#define PassCDebugFlags 'CDEBUGFLAGS=$(CDEBUGFLAGS)'
```

Then you can specify debugging flags from the *make* command line:

```
% make "CDEBUGFLAGS=-g"
```

Combination Branch/Leaf Directories

A directory can be a branch directory and a leaf directory at the same time. That is, it can contain subdirectories, and you can also build targets in it. If you use a directory this way, though, it's difficult to process targets in just that directory without processing all the subdirectories, too.

Other Useful make Variables

DEFINES and INCLUDES are useful in Imakefiles for compiling programs, no matter which rules you're using:

- Use DEFINES to pass special *–D* or *–U* flags to the C compiler.
- Use INCLUDES to pass special *–I* flags to the C compiler.

These variables allow you to specify information on a per-*Imakefile* basis. Their values are incorporated by the X configuration files into the CFLAGS variable and passed automatically to compilation commands and to invocations of *makedepend* and *lint*.

NOTE

This means you should never set CFLAGS directly in the *Imakefile*!

To demonstrate how to use DEFINES and INCLUDES (as well as some of the other variables discussed earlier), suppose we have a project to build a program, *xblob*, composed of a root directory and three subdirectories (Figure 5–2).

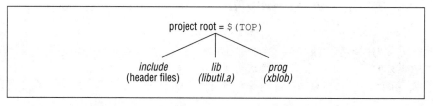

Figure 5-2: xblob project

We want to build *xblob* in the *prog* directory with the following considerations in mind:

- *xblob* is the only program in the *prog* directory.
- *xblob* is built from two source files: *main.c* and *funcs.c.*
- The *xblob* source files use the X multi-buffer extension if possible, by bracketing sections of code like this:

```
#ifdef MULTIBUFFER
    /* multi-buffer code */
#endif
```

This means we need to compile *xblob* with *–DMULTIBUFFER* when the extension is available.

- *xblob* source files include header files from the project's *include* directory.
- The *xblob* executable needs routines from the *util* library (found in the *lib* directory), Xlib, Xext, and the math library.

How shall we write the *Imakefile* in the *prog* directory?

The two rules most suited for building a single program are `Simple-ProgramTarget()` and `ComplexProgramTarget()`. We can't use `SimpleProgramTarget()` because that's only for programs built from a single source file. That leaves `ComplexProgramTarget()`.

Having decided which rule to use, we can set the relevant *make* variables in the *Imakefile* as follows:

- DEFINES is the natural way to specify the *MULTIBUFFER* flag. The X11 symbol `ExtensionDefines` contains the value *–DMULTIBUFFER* if the multi-buffer extension is available, so we assign a value to DEFINES like this:

```
DEFINES = ExtensionDefines
```

- We can use INCLUDES to pass directories in which to look for header files. TOP always indicates the project root directory, so we can refer to *include* as $(TOP)/*include* and set INCLUDES like this:

```
INCLUDES = -I$(TOP)/include
```

- For ComplexProgramTarget(), use LOCAL_LIBRARIES and SYS_LIBRARIES to specify the link forms of any libraries needed. The *util* library is specified relative to TOP, Xlib is given by XLIB, and the math library is given as *–lm*:

```
LOCAL_LIBRARIES = $(TOP)/lib/libutil.a $(XLIB)
  SYS_LIBRARIES = -lm
```

It's not necessary to explicitly list the Xext library because the value of XLIB automatically refers to it.

- Use DEPLIBS to specify the dependency forms of any libraries needed. The *util* library is specified relative to TOP, the dependency-checking form of Xlib is DEPXLIB, and the math library is a system library that has no dependency form, so we omit it:

```
DEPLIBS = $(TOP)/lib/libutil.a $(DEPXLIB)
```

As with XLIB, DEPXLIB includes a reference to the Xext library automatically.

- ComplexProgramTarget() requires SRCS and OBJS to be set. It's straightforward to do so:

```
SRCS = main.c funcs.c
OBJS = main.o funcs.o
```

Putting all this together, we write the *Imakefile* to build *xblob* like so:

```
          DEFINES = ExtensionDefines
         INCLUDES = -I$(TOP)/include
  LOCAL_LIBRARIES = $(TOP)/lib/libutil.a $(XLIB)
    SYS_LIBRARIES = -lm
          DEPLIBS = $(TOP)/lib/libutil.a $(DEPXLIB)

             SRCS = main.c funcs.c
             OBJS = main.o funcs.o

ComplexProgramTarget(xblob)
```

Questions

These questions are intended to provoke further thought about how the X rules work, to illustrate some of their properties not discussed in the main chapter text, and to ask you how you might rewrite rules to fix problems.

They're not for beginners, so if you can't figure out the answers now and you don't understand the answers given, you might want to look at the questions again after reading Chapter 10, *Introduction to Configuration File Writing*, and Chapter 11, *Writing Rule Macros*.

1) The ComplexProgramTarget_*n*() rules require you to set the *make* variable PROGRAMS because they don't do it themselves. Unfortunately, if you forget to set PROGRAMS, *make* doesn't do what you want for either of these commands:

```
% make all
% make clean
```

There are at least two ways to rewrite these rules to fix the problem. What are they?

Answer: The approach you take depends on whether you want to continue to use PROGRAMS or not. (Only ComplexProgramTarget_1() and ComplexProgramTarget_2() are shown in the answers following. ComplexProgramTarget_3() is essentially identical to Complex-ProgramTarget_2(); just substitute "3" for "2".)

If you continue to use PROGRAMS, each rule can define a PROGRAM*n* variable and ComplexProgramTarget_1() can set PROGRAMS to the concatenation of the three PROGRAM*n* variables, in the same way that SRCS and OBJS are set to the concatenations of SRCS*n* and OBJS*n*:

```
#define ComplexProgramTarget_1(prog,loclibs,syslibs)    @@\
        PROGRAM1 = prog                                 @@\
        PROGRAMS = $(PROGRAM1) $(PROGRAM2) $(PROGRAM3)  @@\
           OBJS = $(OBJS1) $(OBJS2) $(OBJS3)            @@\
           SRCS = $(SRCS1) $(SRCS2) $(SRCS3)            @@\
    :
#endif /* ComplexProgramTarget_1 */

#define ComplexProgramTarget_2(prog,loclibs,syslibs)    @@\
        PROGRAM2 = prog                                 @@\
    :
#endif /* ComplexProgramTarget_2 */
```

```
#define ComplexProgramTarget_3(prog,loclibs,syslibs)          @@\
        PROGRAM3 = prog                                        @@\
 .
 .
 .
#endif /* ComplexProgramTarget_3 */
```

If you want to eliminate PROGRAMS entirely, the three rules should each be
written to generate `all` and `clean` entries for their respective individual
programs. The effect would be the same as setting PROGRAMS, but *make
all* and *make clean* would work automatically without programmer intervention, and PROGRAMS becomes superfluous:

```
#define ComplexProgramTarget_1(prog,loclibs,syslibs)          @@\
            OBJS = $(OBJS1) $(OBJS2) $(OBJS3)                  @@\
            SRCS = $(SRCS1) $(SRCS2) $(SRCS3)                  @@\
AllTarget(prog)                                                @@\
 .
 .
 .
clean::                                                        @@\
    $(RM) prog
#endif /* ComplexProgramTarget_1 */
#define ComplexProgramTarget_2(prog,loclibs,syslibs)          @@\
AllTarget(prog)                                                @@\
 .
 .
 .
clean::                                                        @@\
    $(RM) prog
#endif
#define ComplexProgramTarget_3(prog,loclibs,syslibs)          @@\
AllTarget(prog)                                                @@\
 .
 .
 .
clean::                                                        @@\
    $(RM) prog
#endif
```

Using either method, the `ComplexProgramTarget_n()` rules would be
a little easier to use because there'd be one less thing to remember.

2) Will your rewritten `ComplexProgramTarget_n()` rules work with an
Imakefile in which PROGRAMS does happen to be set properly? That is, are
they backward compatible with the current implementation?

Answer: If your rewritten rules continue to use PROGRAMS, an *Imakefile*
will work as long as the *Imakefile* assigns a value to PROGRAMS prior to the
invocation of the `ComplexProgramTarget_1()` rule. Then the assignment in the rule will take priority.

If you rewrite the rules to make PROGRAMS irrelevant, they'll work no matter what the *Imakefile* does with PROGRAMS.

3) Suppose you're building a single program consisting of multiple source files. Why might you choose to use `NormalProgramTarget()` instead of `ComplexProgramTarget()`?

Answer: You gain more control over what happens in the *Makefile*. For example, `ComplexProgramTarget()` decides for you that the installation directory is BINDIR (by default */usr/bin/X11*). When you install the program, the following commands are generated:

```
% make install
if [ -d /usr/bin/X11 ]; then set +x; \
else (set -x; /bin/sh /usr/bin/X11/mkdirhier /usr/bin/X11); fi
install -c prog /usr/bin/X11
```

You can try to change the installation directory */usr/bin/X11* by reassigning BINDIR in your *Imakefile*:

```
BINDIR = /usr/local/bin
```

But when you rebuild your *Makefile* and try to use it, the installation will fail:

```
% make install
if [ -d /usr/local/bin ]; then set +x; \
else (set -x; /bin/sh /usr/local/bin/mkdirhier /usr/local/bin); fi
install -c prog /usr/local/bin
```

Notice that the pathname of *mkdirhier* has changed; this happens because the parameter MKDIRHIER is defined in terms of BINDIR! By changing BINDIR, you mess up that definition—an unwanted and unfortunate side effect.

In this sense, `ComplexProgramTarget()` makes too many choices for you. `NormalProgramTarget()` puts the burden on you to invoke a rule to generate an `install` target, but then you can specify any installation directory you want.

4) Suppose you're building three programs. Why might you choose to use three instances of `NormalProgramTarget()` rather than the `Complex-ProgramTarget_n()` rules?

Answer: The `ComplexProgramTarget_n()` rules are easier to use if you're building just three programs. But if you decide to add another one, you have to rewrite most of your *Imakefile*. If you start with `Normal-ProgramTarget()`, you have to do more work to write your initial three-program *Imakefile*, but you can continue to use what you've already written in your *Imakefile* (rather than replace it) as you add more programs to it. Thus, `NormalProgramTarget()` might be a better choice if you're building three programs initially, but anticipate you'll build more than that eventually.

5) Suppose you build *prog1*, *prog2*, and *prog3* using the Complex-ProgramTarget_*n*() rules. Later you decide *prog1* is useless, so you delete its name from the value of PROGRAMS and delete the SRCS1 and OBJS1 assignments and the invocation of ComplexProgram-Target_1() from your *Imakefile*. After rebuilding your *Makefile*, you discover some problems:

```
% make all
make: Fatal error: Don't know how to make target "all"
% make depend
make: Fatal error: Don't know how to make target "depend"
% make lint
make: Fatal error: Don't know how to make target "lint"
```

How do you explain this? What else do you need to change in your *Imakefile*?

Answer: Remember that ComplexProgramTarget_1() does more work than ComplexProgramTarget_2() or ComplexProgram-Target_3(). In particular, it sets the value of SRCS and generates all, depend, lint, and clean entries. By deleting the rule from your *Imakefile*, you remove a number of useful things from the *Makefile*.

To fix the problem, you need to do some renaming in your *Imakefile*:

$$\text{SRCS2} \rightarrow \text{SRCS1}$$
$$\text{OBJS2} \rightarrow \text{OBJS1}$$

$$\text{SRCS3} \rightarrow \text{SRCS2}$$
$$\text{OBJS3} \rightarrow \text{OBJS2}$$

$$\text{ComplexProgramTarget\_2()} \rightarrow \text{ComplexProgramTarget\_1()}$$
$$\text{ComplexProgramTarget\_3()} \rightarrow \text{ComplexProgramTarget\_2()}$$

By the way, this illustrates another reason why you might prefer to use NormalProgramTarget() rather than ComplexProgramTarget_*n*() right from the start; it's not only easier to add new programs to your *Imakefile*, it's easier to get rid of them.

6) The Motif 1.2 rules extend the X rules by adding ComplexProgram-Target_*n*() rules for *n* from 4 through 10. (They look essentially like ComplexProgramTarget_3() with instances of "3" changed to the appropriate number.) However, the Motif extension isn't quite correct: SRCS only knows about SRCS1 through SRCS3, which means the depend

and `lint` targets generated by `ComplexProgramTarget_1()` don't operate on the sources for programs 4 through 10. How would you fix this by rewriting the Motif rules?

Answer: One way is to reassign `SRCS`. `ComplexProgramTarget_1()` assigns `SRCS` like this:

```
SRCS = $(SRCS1) $(SRCS2) $(SRCS3)
```

`ComplexProgramTarget_4()` can include a reassignment that looks like this:

```
SRCS = $(SRCS1) $(SRCS2) $(SRCS3) $(SRCS4) $(SRCS5) \
       $(SRCS6) $(SRCS7) $(SRCS8) $(SRCS9) $(SRCS10)
```

The reassigned `SRCS` will take precedence over the initial assignment as long as the invocation of `ComplexProgramTarget_4()` in the *Imakefile* follows that of `ComplexProgramTarget_1()`.

7) When you invoke `ComplexProgramTarget()`, use `DEPLIBS` to specify libraries the program depends on. That variable already has a default value assigned to it by the X configuration files, so if you assign a value to `DEPLIBS` in your *Imakefile*, the resulting *Makefile* has two `DEPLIBS` assignments (one provided by the X configuration files and one from your *Imakefile* later). If you want to check which value of `DEPLIBS` *make* actually uses, how do you make sure you find the correct assignment?

Answer: Multiple assignments to a given variable name are not a problem as far as *make* is concerned; it simply uses the last one. However, if you read the *Makefile* into an editor and simply start searching from the top downward for the variable's definition, you'll likely find the first assignment. Instead, start at the bottom of the file and search upward to find the last instance. Alternatively, use *make -p*, which prints out the variable values that *make* actually uses:

```
% make -p | grep DEPLIBS
DEPLIBS3= $(DEPLIBS)
DEPLIBS2= $(DEPLIBS)
DEPLIBS1= $(DEPLIBS)
DEPLIBS= $(DEPXAWLIB) $(DEPXMULIB) $(DEPXTOOLLIB) $(DEPXLIB)
```

The last line of the output is the one you're looking for.

8) Why should you assign `DEPLIBS` an empty value to clear it if your program uses no libraries?

Answer: The default value of `DEPLIBS` refers to several X11 libraries. This makes your program dependent on them. On a machine with X installed, that's not a problem. *make* finds the libraries and silently passes over the dependency. But on a machine without the X libraries, the dependencies fail and *make* refuses to link your program even if all of its object files have been compiled:

```
% make
make: Don't know how to make "/usr/lib/libXaw.a". Stop.
```

Explicitly assigning an empty value to DEPLIBS eliminates the problem because then your program isn't dependent on the X libraries.

9) The MakefileSubdirs() rule generates the Makefiles entry to do *Makefile*-building in subdirectories. It uses MakeMakeSubdirs() and MakeNsubdirMakefiles() to do its work. But these rules are way too complicated. How would you rewrite them?

Answer: Heh. See me after class.

In this chapter:
- *Diagnosing Errors*
- *General Disaster Recovery*
- *Extraneous Spaces in Rule Invocations*
- *Misspelled Rules and Macros*
- *Broken Comments*
- *Incorrect Library Dependency Specifications*
- *Malformed Variable Assignments*
- *Incorrect Value Assignments*
- *Errors of Omission*

6

Imakefile Troubleshooting

> *Even if it can't go wrong, it will.*
> —Corollary to "Murphy's Law"

imake helps you create software that's portable to and easily configurable on a variety of machines—when your configuration files and Imakefiles are set up properly. However, when you make changes to those files, it's quite possible to introduce all sorts of errors that cause the careful planning to go awry. The result is Makefiles that are unusable.

For some errors, it's easy to determine their cause. Others are more subtle. It may not be immediately obvious, for example, that the source of the following error is an extra space in the argument list of a rule invocation in your *Imakefile*:

```
make: Warning: Infinite loop: Target "lib" depends on itself
```

Compounding the difficulty of tracking down the causes of errors is the fact that a problem may originate at a location far from its actual cause. An #endif that's missing from the early part of *Imake.tmpl* isn't detected until the end of the input stream—far away from the error.

The preceding counsel of despair notwithstanding, many of the problems you'll enounter are easily fixed, if you know what causes them. You should be at a point where you can write Imakefiles; in this chapter I'll discuss problems likely to occur in Imakefiles and possible solutions. That's not to ignore the fact that problems can also occur in your configuration files, but we're not ready to tackle those yet. We've seen something of how configuration files work, but errors in those files are better discussed after we've dealt more fully with the issues involved in writing them. Thus, the second half of this topic is deferred until Chapter 13, *Configuration File Troubleshooting*.

This chapter often refers to the X11 configuration files since those are the ones we've looked at most closely. If you're writing Imakefiles for use with another set of configuration files, there's no need to feel left out: you can make the mistakes described here just as easily, with equally lamentable results.

Diagnosing Errors

You'll discover on occasion, when rebuilding a *Makefile* and trying to use it, that it's not usable due to some mistake you made while editing the *Imakefile*. The phenomenon occurs less frequently as you gain experience with *imake*, but it never disappears entirely.

The error messages *make* produces can help you figure out where a problem occurs. Often *make* tells you which line of the *Makefile* it didn't like:

```
% make
make: line nnn: syntax error
```

Other times *make* lets you know which target it's having trouble with:

```
% make
make: don't know how to make "target". Stop.
```

Either way, the information given helps narrow your focus when you search through the *Makefile* looking for the source of the problem. Locating the faulty part of the *Makefile* often allows you to relate the error back to the part of the *Imakefile* from which it's generated.

When *make* tells you there's an error on line *nnn*, you should view that as an approximation. The error might actually occur a line or two earlier, since *make* sometimes doesn't detect or announce an error until a bit later than its actual location. Also, the squawks emitted by *make* on your system might differ somewhat from those shown in this chapter; different versions of *make* sometimes produce different messages for a given *Makefile* problem.

General Disaster Recovery

When you find yourself faced with a *Makefile* that's been turned into a pile of rubble, you need to regenerate it—after fixing your *Imakefile*, naturally. Of course, since the *Makefile* has been destroyed you can no longer use it to rebuild itself. That is, the following command no longer works:

```
% make Makefile
```

You can run *imake* manually, but that's a last resort because of all the command-line options required. There are other alternatives:

- Use a bootstrapping program such as *xmkmf*. *xmkmf* works best in the root directory of a project. Fortunately, many projects consist of only one directory anyway.

- Use the backup *Makefile* if you have one. Rules that generate a *Makefile* typically rename any existing *Makefile* to *Makefile.bak*, so even if you've just generated a *Makefile* that's garbage, you may have a backup that isn't. If so, save it and use it to generate a new *Makefile*:

  ```
  % mv Makefile.bak Makefile.sav
  % make -f Makefile.sav Makefile
  ```

- If the *Makefile* in the parent of your current directory works, change directory into the parent and use the `Makefiles` target entry. You can set `SUBDIRS` on the command line to limit the effect of the *make* command to only the directory you're interested in:

  ```
  % make Makefiles "SUBDIRS=subdir"
  ```

  The command uses the parent *Makefile*'s knowledge about how to build child directory Makefiles.

- Use the general purpose bootstrapper *imboot* developed in Chapter 9, *Coordinating Sets of Configuration Files*. *imboot* can be used anywhere in the project tree.

Now that we know how to recover from disaster, let's have a look at some of the ways we can invite it to happen.

Extraneous Spaces in Rule Invocations

When you invoke a rule, an argument may contain spaces internally if it comprises a list of items such as filenames, libraries, or flags. However, you shouldn't put spaces at either end of the argument. This may take some getting used to if your programming style for writing macro calls is to separate arguments by spaces like this:

```
Macro(arg1, arg2, arg3)      /* incorrect */
```

For *imake*, you should invoke the macro like this:

```
Macro(arg1,arg2,arg3)        /* correct */
```

If you put extraneous spaces in an argument list, you'll often find that the invocation expands to a malformed *Makefile* entry, particularly if the rule constructs tokens from its arguments. Consider the X11 rule `Aliased-LibaryTarget()`, which looks like this:

```
#define AliasedLibraryTarget(name,alias)        @@\
AllTarget(Concat(lib,alias.a)                    @@\
                                                 @@\
Concat(lib,alias.a): Concat(lib,name.a)          @@\
    $(RM) $@                                      @@\
    $(LN) Concat(lib,name.a) $@
```

Consider also the following two invocations of the rule and the corresponding entries to which they expand in the *Makefile* (the `all` entries generated by `AllTarget()` are not shown):

```
AliasedLibraryTarget(abc,xyz)   →   libxyz.a: libabc.a
                                        $(RM) $@
                                        $(LN) libabc.a $@
AliasedLibraryTarget( abc, xyz) →   lib xyz.a: lib abc.a
                                        $(RM) $@
                                        $(LN) lib abc.a $@
```

The invocations are only slightly different, but the difference between the resulting *Makefile* entries is significant. The extra spaces in the second rule invocation propagate directly into the rule expansion and are incorporated into the entry's target name and dependency. Consequently, the entry appears to have two target names and dependencies, and one of the names (`lib`) is dependent on itself! Thus, you have an entry with a dependency loop. This results in the "infinite loop" error message mentioned at the beginning of the chapter.

Misspelled Rules and Macros

Suppose you're using the X11 configuration files and you include the following line in an *Imakefile* you're using to build a library:

```
NormalLibraryObjectrule()
```

After you regenerate *Makefile*, it's broken:

```
% make
make: Must be a separator on rules line nnn.  Stop.
```

You look at line *nnn* of your *Makefile*, only to find:

```
NormalLibraryObjectrule()
```

In other words, the rule wasn't expanded. This error is symptomatic of a spelling mistake (the rule name is actually `NormalLibraryObjectRule`, as you'll see if you look closely at *Imake.rules*). By misspelling a rule name, you effectively invoke a rule that doesn't exist. The result is macro expansion failure and typically an unusable *Makefile*.

The same phenomenon occurs with non-rule macros. Suppose you write the following in your *Imakefile* to indicate that your program uses the Athena Widget client libraries:

```
LOCAL_LIBRARIES = XawClientLibs
        DEPLIBS = XawClientDeplibs
```

You'd expect these to turn into properly expanded library lists in the *Makefile*:

```
LOCAL_LIBRARIES = $(XAWLIB) $(XMULIB) $(XTOOLLIB) $(XLIB)
        DEPLIBS = $(DEPXAWLIB) $(DEPXMULIB) $(DEPXTOOLLIB) $(DEPXLIB)
```

But to throw you into the slough of despond, *cpp* turns them into the following instead:

```
LOCAL_LIBRARIES = $(XAWLIB) $(XMULIB) $(XTOOLLIB) $(XLIB)
        DEPLIBS = XawClientDeplibs
```

This happens because `XawClientLibs` is spelled correctly in the *Imakefile*, but `XawClientDepLibs` is not. The resulting *Makefile* isn't syntactically malformed, but it won't work either:

```
% make
make: Don't know how to make "XawClientDeplibs".  Stop.
```

Recursive Rules and Spelling Errors

The final section of the X11 template *Imake.tmpl* generates several important recursive target entries for you automatically when `IHaveSubdirs` is defined. If you misspell that macro in your *Imakefile*, e.g., as `IHave-SubDirs`, the section of the template that generates those entries is not triggered and they'll be missing from your *Makefile*. Result: operations such as *make Makefiles, make clean, make install,* etc., don't process subdirectories like they should.

Broken Comments

The X11 configuration files use the `XCOMM` macro for generating *Makefile* comments, so that a line like this in an *Imakefile*:

```
XCOMM This is a comment
```

turns into this in the *Makefile*:

```
# This is a comment
```

An easy way to destroy a perfectly good comment is to invoke a rule in it. *cpp* doesn't know anything about *make*, so it doesn't understand you intend the `XCOMM` line to be a *Makefile* comment and it merrily expands the rule anyway. If the rule expands to more than one line, goodbye *Makefile*.

For example, suppose you have a rule named `TouchTarget()` that expands to entries of this form:

```
target::
        touch target
        echo target touched.
```

Then suppose you put a comment like this in your *Imakefile*:

```
XCOMM Update modification time by invoking TouchTarget(xyz)
```

The reference to `TouchTarget()` is processed by *cpp* and your comment ends up looking like this:

```
# Update modification time by invoking xyz:
        touch xyz
        echo xyz touched.
```

The *Makefile* is malformed because it appears to contain an entry with no dependency line preceding the command lines. As a result, it's useless:

```
% make
make: line nnn: Unexpected end of line seen
```

You can fix the problem by quoting the invocation:

```
XCOMM Update modification time by invoking "TouchTarget(xyz)"
```

Note that leaving the parentheses out doesn't work:

```
XCOMM It does not work to refer to TouchTarget this way
```

cpp issues an "argument mismatch" error, expands the macro as well as it can without the arguments, and still usually succeeds in decimating your *Makefile*.

Another form of *make* comment error occurs when you assume you can write arbitrary punctuation in them. You can't. Some versions of *cpp* complain about invalid C tokens, so if you write this:

```
XCOMM Don't use contractions in your comments
```

cpp may tell you:

```
unterminated string or character constant
```

Write this instead:

```
XCOMM Do not use contractions in your comments
```

Such errors aren't necessarily fatal since *cpp* may generate complaints but continue to process the input and generate the *Makefile* correctly. Nevertheless, it can be disconcerting to see the error messages during *Makefile*-generation, so avoid contractions in comments. This will relieve others who use your software of the burden of figuring out whether such errors can be ignored or whether the errors must be attended to.

I suppose as an alternative to avoiding contractions you could go in the other direction and use them to the extreme:

```
XCOMM I'd've thought that this'd've been illegal; it is not.
```

This type of comment doesn't contain any illegal tokens, but it's hardly an aid to understanding, either.

Incorrect Library Dependency Specifications

Libraries on dependency lines must be specified using pathnames, not using −*l* linker syntax. If you see an error like this:

```
make: Fatal error: Don't know how to make target "-lX11"
```

you probably have a target entry that uses −*l* to list Xlib as a library dependency, e.g.:

```
prog:: prog.o -lX11
    $(CC) -o prog prog.o -lX11
```

This kind of error is sometimes difficult to relate back to its cause. You typically indicate a library by referring to a *make* variable rather than by writing it out literally, whereas error messages from *make* write out the literal value, not the variable name. Also, *imake* rules usually don't look much like the target entries they produce, so the part of the *Makefile* in which the error occurs may bear little resemblance to the part of the *Imakefile* from which it's generated.

The following invocation is syntactically legal but semantically incorrect because it generates a target entry with an −*l* name in the dependency list:

```
NormalProgramTarget(xprog,$(OBJS),$(XLIB),NullParameter,$(XLIB))
```

The error doesn't exactly leap off the page at you, does it? Hint: look at the third argument. For `NormalProgramTarget()` that argument indicates dependency libraries, but `XLIB` isn't a dependency symbol. The invocation should use `DEPXLIB` instead:

```
NormalProgramTarget(xprog,$(OBJS),$(DEPXLIB),NullParameter,$(XLIB))
```

The same considerations apply when you're assigning a value to `DEPLIBS` in your *Imakefile*. Make sure the values on the right-hand side of the assignment represent pathnames, not −*l* names:

```
/* these are correct */
DEPLIBS = $(DEPXTOOLLIB) $(DEPXLIB)
DEPLIBS = XawClientDepLibs
/* these are incorrect */
DEPLIBS = $(XTOOLLIB) $(XLIB)
DEPLIBS = XawClientLibs
```

Malformed Variable Assignments

Multiple-line *make* variable definitions need the "\" continuation character at the end of all lines but the last. Suppose you mess up and write an assignment like this in your *Imakefile*:

```
VAR = a b \
      c d \
      e f           ← missing backslash
      g
```

When you use the resulting *Makefile*, you'll be rewarded for your efforts with a message like one of these:

```
make: line nnn: Unexpected end of line seen
make: line nnn: syntax error
```

Once you take a look at line *nnn* in the *Makefile*, you'll probably realize a backslash is missing.

Another related error is to put spaces after a backslash. In this case, *make* won't consider the next line a continuation of the line with the backslash, and the variable value will be incomplete. You can find such lines with this command:

```
% grep '\\  *$' Imakefile
```

There are two spaces before the `*`, and you should use single quotes, not double quotes, to prevent the shell from interpreting the $ as the beginning of a variable reference.

make variable assignments in Imakefiles are often indented to make the = signs line up:

```
         DEPLIBS = XawClientDepLibs
 LOCAL_LIBRARIES = XawClientLibs
            SRCS = xclock.c
            OBJS = xclock.o
```

This improves readability, but make sure to indent assignments using spaces; some versions of *make* report an error if you use tabs.

Incorrect Value Assignments

cpp macros are given values with `#define` directives:

```
#define MacroName value
```

make variables are given values with assignment statements:

```
VARNAME = value
```

Do not reverse these or you won't get the right results. That is, do not use #define to set a *make* variable, and do not use = to set a macro value. One helpful rule of thumb is that macro names are ususally written in mixed case, whereas variable names are usually uppercase (e.g., LibDir is a macro and LIBDIR is a variable). This guideline isn't infallible (e.g., TOPDIR, CURRENT_DIR, YES, and NO are macros, not variables), but it's true far more often than not.

Errors of Omission

If you use INCLUDES in an *Imakefile* to specify header file directories to be searched, don't leave out the *–I* before each directory. The following isn't correct:

```
INCLUDES = $(TOP)/include
```

Write it like this instead:

```
INCLUDES = -I$(TOP)/include
```

Regenerating a *Makefile* has the side effect of wiping out header file dependencies, so remember to regenerate those too:

```
% make Makefile
% make depend
```

It's not actually an error to omit the second command, but if you do, you'll find your programs not being rebuilt properly after you make modifications to header files.

Make sure you have a newline at the end of your *Imakefile*. Some versions of *cpp* generate an incorrect *Imakefile* if you don't.

In this chapter:
- *What imake Needs to Know*
- *Running imake From a Makefile*
- *Makefile Generation in X11*

7

A Closer Look at Makefile Generation

Know thyself.
—Oracle of Delphi
(Plutarch, *Morals*)

This chapter takes a detailed look at the *Makefile* generation process, focusing on the construction of *imake* commands, rather than on the function of individual configuration files. In particular, we'll examine how these two commands work:

```
% make Makefile
% make Makefiles
```

The first command causes the *Makefile* to regenerate itself, and the second builds the Makefiles in any subdirectories.

The `Makefile` and `Makefiles` target entries are available in the *Makefile* because the configuration files put them there. The entries help you produce new Makefiles by relieving you of the burden of typing *imake* commands manually, and they can be issued in any directory of your project, which lends consistency to the *Makefile* generating process. (Both commands presuppose you have a *Makefile* in the first place, of course. You generate the initial *Makefile* from your *Imakefile* using a bootstrapper such as *xmkmf.*)

Being able to use Makefiles to rebuild themselves is something that normally proceeds without incident when we're using an existing set of configuration files. We tend to take that process for granted without thinking about it much. But you need to understand how the process works if you plan to write your own configuration files, since their usefulness will be severely compromised if they can't produce self-regenerating Makefiles.

What imake Needs to Know

imake needs two pieces of information to build a properly configured *Makefile*:

- It must know where the configuration files are located or it will fail to build any *Makefile* at all.
- It must know the location of the project root so that parameters defined relative to the root can be given their proper values.

Configuration File Location

The first thing *imake* needs to know is the location of the configuration file directory. If `confdir` denotes that directory, the *Makefile*-building command looks like this:

```
% imake -Iconfdir
```

When we're using configuration files installed in some public directory outside the project we're working on, `confdir` is normally specified using an absolute path. For instance, to use the X11 configuration files stored in */usr/lib/X11/config*, the *imake* command is:

```
% imake -I/usr/lib/X11/config
```

When the configuration files are located within the project, `confdir` can be specified in either of two ways. To illustrate, suppose we have a project with the directory layout shown in Figure 7–1. The project is rooted at */usr/src/proj* and the configuration files are located in the *config* directory under the project root.*

---

*You can put the configuration files anywhere within the project you like. However, I strongly recommend that you always put within-project configuration files in a directory named *config* under the project root if you have any thought of making your files participate as good citizens in a world where multiple sets of configuration files are the norm (see Chapters 9, 14, and 15).

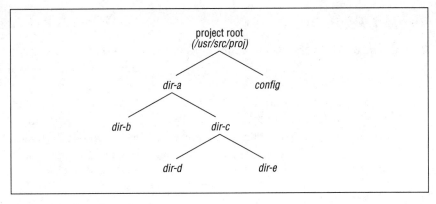

Figure 7-1: Sample project layout

For configuration files located inside the project tree, `confdir` can be specified using either an absolute path or a path relative to the current directory (Table 7–1).

Table 7-1: Specifying Confdir for Within-project Configuration Files

Location of current directory within project	`confdir` specified as an absolute path	`confdir` specified as a relative path
Project root	*/usr/src/proj/config*	*./config*
One level down	*/usr/src/proj/config*	*../config*
Two levels down	*/usr/src/proj/config*	*../../config*
Three levels down	*/usr/src/proj/config*	*../../../config*

When we use an absolute path, the value of `confdir` doesn't vary, so the command to build a *Makefile* is the same in any of the project's directories:

```
% imake -I/usr/src/proj/config
```

On the other hand, when we specify `confdir` relative to the current directory, its value changes as we change directories within the project. Thus, if we begin at the project root directory and descend through different levels of the project tree, the *imake* command varies accordingly:

```
% imake -I./config
% cd dir-a
% imake -I../config
% cd dir-c
% imake -I../../config
% cd dir-d
% imake -I../../../config
```

Project Root Location

Telling *imake* where the configuration files are located is sufficient to build a *Makefile*, but not sufficient to build a correctly configured one. *imake* also needs to know where the project root is, because configuration files often define parameters specified relative to the project root. For instance, we might use DOCSRC, LIBSRC, and INCLUDESRC to denote the locations of project directories that contain documentation, libraries, and header files. The project root is a convenient anchor point against which to specify such parameters.

Configuration files typically use the *make* variable TOP to signify the top (or root) of the project tree. That's why you see lines like these when you examine Makefiles generated by *imake*:

```
     DOCSRC = $(TOP)/doc
     LIBSRC = $(TOP)/lib
 INCLUDESRC = $(TOP)/include
```

This notation is easy to conceptually grasp because it reflects how we think about the location of project directories in relation to the project root. The hard part is figuring out how to specify TOP. The obvious way to set its value is with an assignment statement in one of the configuration files, e.g., like this:

```
TOP = /usr/src/proj
```

But it's not as simple as that. Suppose we're using publicly installed configuration files:

- We can't set TOP to an absolute path. Different projects have different root directories, and a fixed value of TOP cannot be correct for all of them simultaneously.

- If we specify TOP using a relative path instead, we get some consistency across projects. That is, TOP is always "." in the project root (no matter where the project is located), ".." in directories one level down, "../.." in directories two levels down, etc. However, by using relative paths, TOP becomes a dynamic quantity, and only fixed values can be specified in the configuration files.

If we're using configuration files located within the project tree, we still encounter problems:

- We can set TOP to the project root location using an absolute path because we need not be concerned with whether or not it's correct for any other project. But the value needs editing when the project is built on different machines, since other people will put the project tree wherever they like in their file systems. We might even need to edit TOP ourselves, e.g., if we move a large project elsewhere on our own machine to put it on a file system with more free space.

- If we use relative values for TOP, again we run into the problem that TOP becomes a dynamic value.

The way around these difficulties is to set TOP's value at *Makefile* generation time, when we run *imake*. Here the idiom of setting a *make* variable using an associated *cpp* macro is useful. Since it doesn't work to set TOP directly to a fixed value in the configuration files, we can set it to the value of a *cpp* macro instead and specify the macro value on the *imake* command line.

First, we set up (in *Imake.tmpl*) some machinery for TOP to get its value from a macro, TOPDIR:

```
#ifndef TOPDIR
#define TOPDIR .
#endif
TOP = TOPDIR
```

We give TOPDIR a default value of ".” (the value that's correct in the project root) but that can be overridden by defining TOPDIR on the *imake* command line. Thus, we can set TOP on the fly to any value we like without editing the configuration files. The general form of the *imake* command now looks like this:

```
% imake -Iconfdir -DTOPDIR=topdir
```

As an example, suppose we're building Makefiles in the project shown in Figure 7–1, using relative paths for *confdir* and *topdir*. Starting in the project root and descending through the project tree, the *imake* commands are as follows:

```
% imake -I./config -DTOPDIR=.
% cd dir-a
% imake -I../config -DTOPDIR=..
% cd dir-c
% imake -I../../config -DTOPDIR=../..
% cd dir-d
% imake -I../../../config -DTOPDIR=../../..
```

In each case, *imake* can find the configuration files properly and can give TOP the correct value for the directory in which the *Makefile* is generated.

Now we know how to construct an *imake* command. Of course, our interest in knowing how to do this isn't so we can run *imake* manually. We want our Makefiles to generate the commands for us.

Running imake From a Makefile

Configuration files should provide a rule that expands to a `Makefile` target entry allowing us to use an existing *Makefile* to build a new one:

```
% make Makefile
```

The way configuration files write Makefiles with the ability to regenerate themselves is one of the areas of *imake* most shrouded in mystery—not quite deep magic from the dawn of time, but not obvious, either.

To work properly, the `Makefile` entry has to do the same things you do when you run *imake* manually. That is, it must generate an *imake* command that specifies the locations of the configuration file directory and the project root:

```
Makefile::
        imake -Iconfdir -DTOPDIR=topdir
```

This is slightly paradoxical. The configuration files generate the entry, but the entry refers to `confdir`, the location of those same files. For the value of `confdir` to be correct, the configuration files must possess self-knowledge of their own location. They cannot derive that knowledge on their own, so you must instill it yourself by informing them where they live. For instance, you could create in *Project.tmpl* a parameter `IRULESRC` that acts as a self-reference holding the name of the configuration file directory:

```
#ifndef IRuleSrc
#define IRuleSrc confdir
#endif

IRULESRC = IRuleSrc
```

Using `IRULESRC`, the `Makefile` entry becomes:

```
Makefile::
        imake -I$(IRULESRC) -DTOPDIR=topdir
```

The entry still needs to give a value to `TOPDIR`. Here we remember that the `Makefile` entry operates from within the context of a *Makefile*, and that the *Makefile* contains a parameter `TOP` indicating where the project root is. Thus, we can write the entry like this:

```
Makefile::
        imake -I$(IRULESRC) -DTOPDIR=$(TOP)
```

This is another paradox: `TOP` gets its value from `TOPDIR` when the *Makefile* is created, and `TOPDIR` gets its value from `TOP` when the *Makefile* itself creates a new *Makefile*. But how does this interplay of `TOPDIR` and `TOP` setting each other get started?

The cycle begins when you create the initial *Makefile*, e.g., with a bootstrapper. For example, if you're in the project root and the configuration files are located in *config*, the bootstrapper might generate an *imake* command something like this:

```
imake -I./config -DTOPDIR=.
```

This command defines the value of `TOPDIR`, which sets the value of `TOP` written into the the initial *Makefile*, which can then rebuild itself using the `Makefile` entry.

Where Are the Configuration Files?

I fudged on specifying a value when I wrote the preceding definition for `IRuleSrc`. There are two cases. If your files are installed in some public directory, you'd use an absolute path name:

```
#ifndef IRuleSrc
#define IRuleSrc /usr/lib/myconfdir
#endif
```

If the configuration files are installed within your project, you should specify a value relative to `TOP` so it will be correct no matter where the project is located:

```
#ifndef IRuleSrc
#define IRuleSrc $(TOP)/config
#endif
```

However, things can be more complicated: the files might be installed in both places. For instance, if you write configuration files for a particular project, it makes most sense to keep them in the project tree. If you later decide to configure other projects with them, you'd install them publicly as well, so those projects can access them.

To handle this, you specify both locations and choose one as circumstances warrant. X11 sets up its configuration files this way, selecting one location or the other based on whether or not the symbol `UseInstalled` is defined. For configuring X itself, `UseInstalled` is normally undefined, and the set of files within the project is selected. When X is installed, it copies the configuration files to a public location. Then other X-based projects outside the X source tree can select the public set of configuration files by defining `UseInstalled` when their Makefiles are built.

We can copy that idea. The following fragment (which you'd put in *Project.tmpl*) shows what you might write to indicate that a project has its own configuration files but also installs them publicly for use by other projects:

```
#ifndef ConfigDir
#define ConfigDir /usr/lib/myconfdir
#endif
#ifndef ConfigSrc
#define ConfigSrc $(TOP)/config
#endif
    CONFIGDIR = ConfigDir
    CONFIGSRC = ConfigSrc
#ifdef UseInstalled
    IRULESRC = $(CONFIGDIR)
#else
    IRULESRC = $(CONFIGSRC)
#endif
```

Now our `Makefile` entry can take two forms. If we're building a *Makefile* in the project to which the configuration files belong, we'd leave `UseInstalled` undefined and use the configuration files located in the project tree. The `Makefile` entry is therefore the same as before:

```
Makefile::
    imake -I$(IRULESRC) -DTOPDIR=$(TOP)
```

If we're building a *Makefile* for a project that's using the publicly-installed files, `UseInstalled` must be defined:

```
Makefile::
    imake -DUseInstalled -I$(IRULESRC) -DTOPDIR=$(TOP)
```

The rule that generates these entries must itself adjust properly to whether `UseInstalled` is defined or not. A rule that does so is shown below:

```
#ifndef MakefileTarget
#ifdef UseInstalled
#define MakefileTarget()                                  @@\
Makefile::                                                @@\
    imake -DUseInstalled -I$(IRULESRC) -DTOPDIR=$(TOP)
#else
#define MakefileTarget()                                  @@\
Makefile::                                                @@\
    imake -I$(IRULESRC) -DTOPDIR=$(TOP)
#endif
#endif /* MakefileTarget */
```

This rule is quite simple and, as such, has some deficiencies that should be remedied. We won't do so here, but it's worth noting what they are:

- *imake* should be parameterized and the reference to it replaced with `$(IMAKE)`.
- The rule should save any existing *Makefile* by renaming it before running *imake*. In the event that something goes wrong, it's often useful to have the old *Makefile*.

Building Makefiles Recursively

It's a great convenience to be able to use a *Makefile* to rebuild itself, but we can go further and use it to build Makefiles in subdirectories, too. This process can be made recursive so as to build a whole project tree of Makefiles.

We do this by writing a `Makefiles` target entry for generating Makefiles in subdirectories of the current directory. Then, after building the *Makefile* in the project root, we can build the rest of the Makefiles in a project with:

```
% make Makefiles
```

For each subdirectory of the current directory, the `Makefiles` entry must generate commands to:

- Move into the subdirectory
- Run *imake* to generate the *Makefile* there
- Run *make Makefiles* using the new *Makefile*, in case the subdirectory has subdirectories of its own

In practice, the `Makefiles` entry must execute all three steps as part of the same command line, something like this:

```
cd subdir ; imake args ; make Makefiles
```

The commands must be combined onto a single line because *make* spawns a new shell for each command line in a *Makefile* entry. (If the commands were on separate lines, they'd be executed by separate shells. The effect of the *cd* command would not persist into the second and third commands, and they'd execute in the wrong directory.) The effect of the *cd* terminates when the command line finishes executing, so there's no need to *cd* back up out of the subdirectory.

Let's consider what arguments the `Makefiles` entry should pass to the *imake* command. We'll still need to specify the locations of the configuration directory and the project root, and we might need to define `Use-Installed`, too. I assume in the following example that the location of the project root is specified as a relative path. If its location is specified as an absolute path, the following remarks still apply except that no path adjustment takes place.

Specifying the location of the project root is a little tricky when a *Makefile* builds a *Makefile* in a subdirectory. The *Makefile* in the parent directory has to generate an *imake* command that executes in the subdirectory, where the path to the project root is different. We have to anticipate this and compensate in advance for the difference.

If the subdirectory is one level lower in the project tree than the parent, the relative location of the project root is one level higher. To adjust the value of TOPDIR so it's correct in the subdirectory, we prepend "../" to TOP:

```
-DTOPDIR=../$(TOP)
```

If the subdirectory is two, three, etc., levels lower than the parent, the adjustment value is "../../", "../../../", etc.

If we're using configuration files located within the project, we also need to adjust how their location is specified, because it's defined in terms of TOP (IRULESRC is defined as $(CONFIGSRC), which is defined as $(TOP)/*config*). Thus the *imake* command that the *Makefile* in the parent directory generates to write a *Makefile* in a subdirectory immediately below it looks like this:

```
imake -I../$(IRULESRC) -DTOPDIR=../$(TOP)
```

If we're using configuration files that are installed publicly, Use-Installed should be defined and the *imake* command looks like this:

```
imake -DUseInstalled -I$(IRULESRC) -DTOPDIR=../$(TOP)
```

In this case, the value of IRULESRC is an absolute pathname and doesn't need any adjustment.

Now we need to implement our knowledge as a rule that generates a Makefiles target entry. Such rules are typically somewhat difficult to write. The one shown below is an exceedingly stripped-down example.*

```
/*
 * MakefileSubdirs - generate entry to build Makefiles
 * recursively
 */
#ifndef MakefileSubdirs
#define MakefileSubdirs(dirs)                          @@\
Makefiles::                                            @@\
```

---

*Even so, the rule uses some constructs that haven't been covered yet; for details, see the section "Shell Programming in Rules" in Chapter 12, *Configuration Problems and Solutions*.

```
       for i in dirs ; \                                           @@\
       do \                                                        @@\
           (cd $$i; \                                              @@\
           imake -I$(IRULESRC) -DTOPDIR=../$(TOP); \               @@\
           make Makefiles); \                                      @@\
       done
#endif /* MakefileSubdirs */
```

This rule is primitive, as recursive *Makefile*-generating rules go. And, like the `MakefileTarget()` rule shown earlier, it has some deficiencies that we simply note in passing:

- It adjusts `TOP` correctly only for subdirectories immediately below the current directory.
- It doesn't handle the case when `TOP` is an absolute path.
- It doesn't notice whether or not `UseInstalled` is defined.
- It doesn't save existing Makefiles by renaming them before running *imake*.
- It doesn't tell the user much about what it's doing or where it's executing.

As you might guess, when these problems are addressed, rules to recursively generate Makefiles tend to become marvels of intricacy.

Makefile Generation in X11

The X11 configuration files have their own versions of the `Makefile-Target()` and `MakefileSubdirs()` rules to generate `Makefile` and `Makefiles` target entries. Normally, you don't have to invoke either of these rules in your *Imakefile* because the last section of *Imake.tmpl* automatically does so for you, in a sequence that looks something like this:

```
MakefileTarget()

#ifdef IHaveSubdirs
MakefileSubdirs($(SUBDIRS))
#else
Makefiles::
#endif
```

The `MakefileTarget()` rule generates an entry containing an *imake* command that looks like this:

```
$(IMAKE_CMD) -DTOPDIR=$(TOP) -DCURDIR=$(CURRENT_DIR)
```

The two *−D* arguments communicate information about the project tree. `TOPDIR`, as already discussed, is the location of the project root, and the meaning of `-DTOPDIR=$(TOP)` should be familiar. `CURDIR` and

CURRENT_DIR specify the location of the current directory within the project. They set each other reflexively, just like TOPDIR and TOP. The X rules use CURRENT_DIR to generate messages announcing to the user where in the project tree *make* happens to be executing. This is useful feedback when you're watching the progress of a long recursive *make* operation, but has no functional significance for *Makefile*-building.

The *imake* program and the location of the configuration files aren't named explicitly in the preceding command. They're specified in the value of IMAKE_CMD, which is defined like this:

```
#ifdef UseInstalled
    IRULESRC = $(CONFIGDIR)
    IMAKE_CMD = $(IMAKE) -DUseInstalled \
                    -I$(IRULESRC) $(IMAKE_DEFINES)
#else
    IRULESRC = $(CONFIGSRC)
    IMAKE_CMD = $(NEWTOP)$(IMAKE) \
                    -I$(NEWTOP)$(IRULESRC) $(IMAKE_DEFINES)
#endif
```

IMAKE specifies the *imake* program and the *–I* argument indicates where the configuration files are.

Here's how IMAKE_CMD works:

- X can be configured using versions of the configuration files located either in a public directory (CONFIGDIR) or within the project tree (CONFIGSRC). This is determined according to whether or not the *cpp* symbol UseInstalled is defined. The default values of CONFIGDIR and CONFIGSRC are */usr/lib/X11/config* and $(TOP)/config; IRULE-SRC is set to the one that applies.

- In X, UseInstalled determines not only where the configuration files are, but also where *imake* itself is found. If UseInstalled is defined, IMAKE is simply *imake*, i.e., it's assumed to be somewhere in your search path. Otherwise, IMAKE is $(TOP)/config/imake, i.e., it's found in the X source tree; this works because the source for *imake* is bundled into the X distribution to allow you to build X even if you don't already have *imake*.

- Since the value of IMAKE_CMD is selected based on whether Use-Installed is defined (or not), each value causes UseInstalled to be defined (or not) in future *imake* commands. The value selected if UseInstalled is defined makes sure it continues to be defined by passing -DUseInstalled to *imake*, whereas the value selected if UseInstalled isn't defined continues to leave it undefined.

- `NEWTOP` is a path adjustment value to compensate for any discrepancy between the value of `TOP` in the directory in which the *imake* command is generated versus the value of `TOP` in the directory in which the command executes. If the two directories are the same (e.g., during *make Makefile*), `NEWTOP` is empty. If the two directories are different (e.g., during *make Makefiles*), `NEWTOP` adjusts paths so that within-project configuration files and *imake* are found correctly. `NEWTOP` is "`../`" for a subdirectory one level down, "`../../`" for a subdirectory two levels down, etc.

- `IMAKE_DEFINES` allows arguments to be passed to the *imake* command from the *make* command line; it's usually empty and you can ignore it.

The X11 `MakefileSubdirs()` rule generates a recursive *Makefile*-generating target entry. Conceptually, `MakefileSubdirs()` is relatively straightforward. It takes a list of directories as its argument. For each one, it determines the correct value of `NEWTOP`, changes into the directory, executes `IMAKE_CMD` to create the *Makefile* there, and runs *make Makefiles* with the new *Makefile* in case the directory has any subdirectories of its own. The implementation is quite another matter, however. If you want the full story, take a look at the X11 *Imake.rules* for full details, but don't say you weren't warned.

In this chapter:
- *Creating the Starter Project*
- *Testing the Starter Project*
- *Using the Starter Project*

8

A Configuration Starter Project

Well begun is half done.
—Aristotle, *Politics*

When you write configuration files, content depends on intent. If you want them to produce Makefiles for building programs, you write program-building rules and parameters. If you want them to produce Makefiles for document production, you write document preparation rules and parameters. But one thing configuration files should do regardless of your intent is to produce Makefiles that rebuild themselves properly. You want to be able to regenerate them easily using these commands:

```
% make Makefile
% make Makefiles
```

Chapter 7, *A Closer Look at Makefile Generation*, discusses the mechanisms by which Makefiles rebuild themselves. This chapter shows how to make sure these mechanisms operate correctly when you copy an existing set of configuration files to create another.

We'll copy the X11 files to create a starter project, denoted as SP. You can use it as a basis for other projects that provide their configuration files within the project tree. Or, if you like, you can use it to develop files to be installed in a public directory for use by other projects that don't provide their own configuration files.

The differences between the X11 and SP files will be minimal. The purpose of the starter project isn't to develop new or different configuration functionality, but to illustrate the problems relating to *Makefile* generation that crop up when we copy a set of configuration files, and to show how to solve them.

If you want to compare the X11 files with the resulting SP files as you follow this discussion, retrieve the SP distribution (see Appendix A, *Obtaining Configuration Software*).

Creating the Starter Project

To create the starter project, we must first set up the directory structure and populate the project with configuration files. Let's assume initially that we'll be developing a project containing its own private configuration files. (We'll discuss later in this chapter the changes necessary to install the files publicly.)

Configuration files are important, but they aren't the reason a project exists—the programs it builds are. We can indicate the subservient role of the configuration files by isolating them into a *config* directory under the project root rather than cluttering up the root directory with them. Depending on whether or not a project builds everything in the project root, the project tree might look like one of those shown in Figure 8–1 or Figure 8–2. However, when we consider only the configuration-related parts of the project trees that are common to both, they reduce to the one shown in Figure 8–3, and that's what we need to set up to create the starter project.

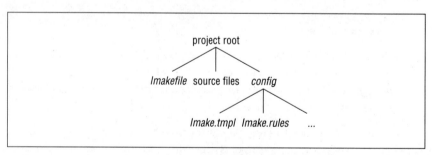

Figure 8-1: Project that builds programs in project root

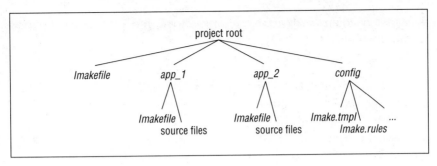

Figure 8-2: Project that builds programs in subdirectories

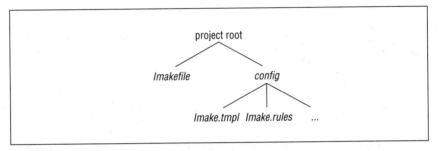

Figure 8-3: Minimal configuration-related parts of project tree

Figure 8–3 shows that we need a project root directory, as well as a *config* subdirectory to hold the configuration files. Create the initial project structure like this:

```
% mkdir SP
% cd SP
% mkdir config
```

Then populate the *config* directory with copies of the X11 configuration files:

```
% cp /usr/lib/X11/config/* config
```

The X11 files may have been installed read-only. We'll need to modify our copies, so make them writable:

```
% chmod 644 config/*      (or chmod u+w config/*)
```

We'll also need an *Imakefile* in the project root. Just create an empty one for the moment:

```
% touch Imakefile
```

Now we have enough structure to try using the configuration files to generate a *Makefile*. For programs configured with the X files, we'd normally bootstrap a *Makefile* with *xmkmf*. That does not work for the SP files because the command *xmkmf* invokes uses the original X files in */usr/lib/X11/config*, not our copies:

```
% xmkmf
imake -DUseInstalled -I/usr/lib/X11/config
```

We can mimic *xmkmf* by invoking *imake* manually and substituting the correct location of our files:

```
% imake -DUseInstalled -I./config
```

That command uses the starter project's configuration files, but the resulting *Makefile* does not regenerate itself properly:

```
% make Makefile
imake -DUseInstalled -I/usr/lib/X11/config -DTOPDIR=. -DCURDIR=.
```

This happens because our files still expect to find themselves installed in */usr/lib/X11/config*. Consequently, the `Makefile` target entry they generate looks in that directory for the configuration files, and the *Makefile* rebuilds itself using the original X files, not our copies.

Let's try bootstrapping and rebuilding the *Makefile* without defining `Use-Installed`:

```
% imake -I./config
% make Makefile
bootstrapping config/imake from Makefile.ini in ./config first...
make: Fatal error: Can't find "Makefile.ini": No such file or directory
```

That does not work, either. When we build the *Makefile* without defining `UseInstalled`, the `Makefile` target entry looks for configuration files in the *config* directory, but also assumes that's where *imake* lives and tries to build it there if it's missing. Our *config* directory contains only configuration files, so the attempt to build *imake* fails. (The same command sequence works in the X project tree because the X *config* directory contains *imake* source code.)

The preceding exercise illustrates the initial difficulties we face when we copy the X11 configuration files to create a new set:

- We need a bootstrapper that works with our files, since *xmkmf* is intended for the X11 files.

- The `Makefile` target entry generated by the configuration files does not behave correctly. When `UseInstalled` isn't defined, the entry tries to build *imake* from source. When `UseInstalled` is defined, the entry looks in the wrong place for the configuration files. The files don't know their own location (i.e., their self-reference is incorrect).

We'll defer the bootstrapping problem until Chapter 9, *Coordinating Sets of Configuration Files*, and concentrate here on `UseInstalled` and the self-reference.

In X11, `UseInstalled` has two functions, both of which at the moment have been carried over without modification into the SP files.

First, the self-reference (the location where the configuration files look for themselves) is determined by `UseInstalled`. The self-reference is *config* under the project root when `UseInstalled` isn't defined, and */usr/lib/X11/config* when it is. This allows X itself to be configured using the configuration files located in the X source tree and accommodates installing the files publicly for use by other X-based software. That's a useful mechanism to carry along into the starter project, to allow it to configure itself using the within-project files, and to optionally install the files for use by other projects.

However, we need to change the value of the self-reference if we do plan on installing the configuration files. When `UseInstalled` is defined, the self-reference still points to the location of the installed X11 files. That isn't correct for the SP files, because we can't put them in the same place as the X11 files.

Second, X11 uses `UseInstalled` to determine where to find the configuration programs *imake, makedepend*, and *mkdirhier*. They're expected to be installed in a public directory in your search path when `UseInstalled` is defined. But when `UseInstalled` is undefined, X expects to find the programs within the X source tree and builds them on the fly if necessary. That's useful in the sense that you can build X even if you didn't have the programs before. However, it does require that the source for the programs be bundled into the X distribution.

As a general practice, this second use of `UseInstalled` causes unnecessary redundancy: all projects configured along similar lines would need to include the programs within the project tree. One copy of the configuration programs is sufficient; we may as well install them once and be done with it. Then we can dissolve the connection between `UseInstalled` and the location of the programs. The changes needed to do this are shown in the following sections. They involve modifying files in the *config* directory so that *imake, makedepend,* and *mkdirhier* are always assumed to be installed publicly, not just when `UseInstalled` is defined.

Changes To Imake.tmpl

As originally written, `IMAKE_CMD` looks for *imake* in the project tree if `UseInstalled` isn't defined. If we assume *imake* is installed publicly, the definition of `IMAKE_CMD` must change. The original definition looks like this:

```
#ifdef UseInstalled
   IRULESRC = $(CONFIGDIR)   /* used in rules file */
   IMAKE_CMD = $(IMAKE) -DUseInstalled -I$(IRULESRC) $(IMAKE_DEFINES)
#else
   IRULESRC = $(CONFIGSRC)
   IMAKE_CMD = $(NEWTOP)$(IMAKE) -I$(NEWTOP)$(IRULESRC) $(IMAKE_DEFINES)
#endif
```

Remove `$(NEWTOP)` from the line before the `#endif` so the definition looks like this:

```
#ifdef UseInstalled
   IRULESRC = $(CONFIGDIR)   /* used in rules file */
   IMAKE_CMD = $(IMAKE) -DUseInstalled -I$(IRULESRC) $(IMAKE_DEFINES)
#else
   IRULESRC = $(CONFIGSRC)
   IMAKE_CMD = $(IMAKE) -I$(NEWTOP)$(IRULESRC) $(IMAKE_DEFINES)
#endif
```

`InstallCmd` needs to be changed for the same reason.

Original:

```
#ifndef InstallCmd
#if SystemV | SystemV4
#ifdef UseInstalled
#define InstallCmd $(BINDIR)/bsdinst
#else
#define InstallCmd $(SCRIPTSRC)/bsdinst.sh
#endif
```

```
#else
#define InstallCmd install
#endif
#endif
```

Change to:

```
#ifndef InstallCmd
#if SystemV || SystemV4
#define InstallCmd bsdinst
#else
#define InstallCmd install
#endif
#endif
```

Changes To Project.tmpl

The fragment of *Project.tmpl* that needs to be modified looks like this (the sections marked *other stuff* refer to some X-related parameters which are of no concern to us here):

```
#ifdef UseInstalled
        IMAKE = imake           /* assume BINDIR in path */
        DEPEND = makedepend     /* assume BINDIR in path */
    ...other stuff...
     MKDIRHIER = BourneShell $(BINDIR)/mkdirhier
#else
        IMAKE = $(IMAKESRC)/imake
        DEPEND = DependCmd
    ...other stuff...
     MKDIRHIER = BourneShell $(SCRIPTSRC)/mkdirhier.sh
#endif
```

As written above, the variables IMAKE, DEPEND, and MKDIRHIER are set to within-project paths when UseInstalled isn't defined. We need to change them so they do not depend on UseInstalled. Change the fragment (leaving the *other stuff* sections alone) so it looks like this:

```
        IMAKE = imake           /* assume publicly installed */
        DEPEND = makedepend     /* ditto */
     MKDIRHIER = mkdirhier      /* ditto */
#ifdef UseInstalled
    ...other stuff...
#else
    ...other stuff...
#endif
```

This change causes *imake, makedepend,* and *mkdirhier* to be assumed installed in a directory that's in your search path. Note that MKDIRHIER is revised so it does not depend on BINDIR, which allows you to change BINDIR without breaking the configuration files' ability to locate *mkdirhier*.

Changes to Imake.rules

The original X11 definitions of the ImakeDependency() and Depend-Dependency() rules vary according to whether or not UseInstalled is defined. If it's not, the rules check whether *imake* and *makedepend* have been built within the project tree and try to build them if they have not been. This must change, because we don't want to look for or build the programs in the project tree.

The cleanest thing to do is remove the definitions of Imake-Dependency() and DependDependency() entirely. Then eliminate the line that invokes ImakeDependency() from the definition of Build-MakefileTarget(), and eliminate the lines that invoke Depend-Dependency() from the definitions of DependTarget() and Depend-Target3().

Testing the Starter Project

The changes made so far are sufficient to allow us to use the starter project to configure itself. Verify this as follows:

- Bootstrap the *Makefile* in the project root using the files in the *config* directory:

  ```
  % imake -I./config
  ```

- Make sure that the *Makefile* rebuilds itself using the same files:

  ```
  % make Makefile
  + rm -f Makefile.bak
  + mv Makefile Makefile.bak
  imake -I./config -DTOPDIR=. -DCURDIR=.
  ```

Now you can use the starter project as a basis for configuring other projects.

Using the Starter Project

Make a copy of the starter project and move into it. For instance, assuming the starter project is located under your current directory, you can do this:

```
% cp -r SP myproj
% cd myproj
```

If your *cp* does not have a *–r* (recursive copy) option, do this instead:

```
% mkdir myproj
% cd SP
% tar cf - . | ( cd ../myproj ; tar xf - )
% cd ../myproj
```

The *Imakefile* in the project root directory is empty, because that's all we needed for getting the starter project set up. Of course, a real project needs a more extensive *Imakefile*. If the project builds all its programs in the project root, put the information for building them into the *Imakefile*, perhaps using rules like `SimpleProgramTarget()`, `Complex-ProgramTarget()`, or `NormalProgramTarget()`. If the project builds programs in subdirectories, write the *Imakefile* in the project root directory to include subdirectory support as described in Chapter 5, *Writing Imakefiles*.

Either way, once you've set up your project and written the *Imakefile* (or several Imakefiles, if you have subdirectories), run the following commands to verify that the project can configure itself:

```
% imake -I./config
% make Makefile
% make Makefiles          (if you have subdirectories)
```

As you develop your project's programs, you'll get a better idea of their unique configuration requirements and you can further modify the configuration files accordingly. This may involve adding new parameters or rules, or perhaps deleting or modifying those already present. We'll take up these and other issues in Chapters 10 through 12, which discuss configuration file writing in more detail.

Installing Your Project's Configuration Files

By default, the starter project does not install the configuration files, and neither will any copy of it you're using. That's suitable if your project has unique configuration requirements and uses its own configuration files privately within the project tree. On the other hand, it might make sense to install the configuration files publicly so other projects can use them (e.g., if you have related projects with similar configuration requirements).

To install the configuration files, three changes are necessary:

- Change the *Imakefile* in the project root so *make* operations descend into the *config* directory.

  If the *Imakefile* in the project root already contains subdirectory support, add *config* to the value of SUBDIRS. Otherwise, put the following at the beginning of the *Imakefile*:

  ```
  #define IHaveSubdirs
  #define PassCDebugFlags

  SUBDIRS = config

  MakeSubdirs($(SUBDIRS))
  DependSubdirs($(SUBDIRS))
  ```

  The modification allows the Makefile entry in the project root *Makefile* to descend into the *config* directory when recursive *make* operations are performed.

- Change the self-reference that specifies the configuration file installation directory.

  Move into the *config* directory and modify the value of ConfigDir in *Project.tmpl*. ConfigDir still points to */usr/lib/X11/config*, so if you don't change it, installing the *myproj* configuration files will wipe out the X11 files. If you want to install the files into */usr/lib/config/myproj*, for example, the definition should look like this:

  ```
  #ifndef ConfigDir
  #define ConfigDir $(USRLIBDIR)/config/myproj
  #endif
  ```

- Create an *Imakefile* in the *config* directory to direct installation of the configuration files.

  The *Imakefile* should look like this:

  ```
          FILES = *.tmpl *.rules site.def *.cf *.bac
  INSTALLFLAGS = $(INSTDATFLAGS)

  all::
  depend::

  InstallMultiple($(FILES),$(CONFIGDIR))
  ```

InstallMultiple() generates an `install` target entry to install the configuration files in CONFIGDIR. The empty `all` and `depend` entries are needed to suppress "don't know how to make XXX" complaints that would otherwise result from the following commands:

```
% make all
% make depend
```

To verify these changes, rebuild the Makefiles by running the following commands in the project root:*

```
% make Makefile
+ rm -f Makefile.bak
+ mv Makefile Makefile.bak
imake -I./config -DTOPDIR=. -DCURDIR=.
% make Makefiles
making Makefiles in ./config...
rm -f config/Makefile.bak
+ mv config/Makefile config/Makefile.bak
cd config; imake -I../.config -DTOPDIR=../. -DCURDIR=./config; \
make Makefiles
```

Then change into the *config* directory and check where the *Makefile* thinks it should install the configuration files. Use *−n* so *make* announces its intentions without actually installing anything:

```
% cd config
% make -n install
if [ -d /usr/lib/config/myproj ]; then set +x; \
else (set -x; mkdirhier /usr/lib/config/myproj); fi
case '-n' in *[i]*) set +e;; esac \
for i in *.rules *.tmpl site.def *.cf *.bac; do \
(set -x; install -c -m 0444 $i /usr/lib/config/myproj); \
done
echo "install in . done"
```

The pathname of the intended installation directory (*/usr/lib/config/myproj*) should appear in the *make* command output. If it does not, check the value of ConfigDir in *Project.tmpl*. Otherwise you can run *make install* without the *−n* option, and they'll be put in the right place.

---

*The output shown is what you should see if *config* is the only subdirectory of the project root. You'll see additional output if there are other subdirectories. Alternatively, limit the second command to the *config* directory:

```
% make Makefiles "SUBDIRS=config"
```

In this chapter:
- *Designing a General Purpose Bootstrapper*
- *Implementing imboot*
- *Cooperating with imboot*
- *Backward Compatibility*
- *Using imboot in Makefiles*

9

Coordinating Sets of Configuration Files

"Will you walk into my parlor?"
said the spider to the fly . . .
—Mary Howitt,
The Spider and the Fly

Once upon a time, the X11 configuration files were the only widely used files around. Just about everything configured with *imake* used the same set of configuration files, and life was simple. But there's nothing to stop new sets of files from being developed. For instance, in Chapter 8, *A Configuration Starter Project*, we adapt the X configuration files into a starter project that can serve as a beginning point for developing your own configuration files. And in Chapter 10, *Introduction to Configuration File Writing*, and Chapter 11, *Writing Rule Macros*, we use the starter project to do just that, to illustrate the process that gives rise to a new set of files. Each time we go through this process, another set of configuration files springs into existence. In such a world, life becomes more complex. So, instead of letting that complexity sneak up on us and catch us unawares, this chapter discusses the problems that arise from trying to coordinate multiple sets of configuration files and shows how to solve them.

The most obvious problem caused by the existence of multiple sets is location. We can't put the files from different sets in the same place; they'd collide with each other and create a big mess. So we need to place them in different locations to ensure that this doesn't happen. Then, for any given set, we need to make its location known in two places:

- **The configuration files themselves.**

  The files must know where they are so they can construct Makefiles that rebuild themselves with these commands:

  ```
  % make Makefile
  % make Makefiles
  ```

- **The bootstrapper that uses the files.**

  The `Makefile` and `Makefiles` target entries only work when you already have a working *Makefile*. When you don't, you need a bootstrapper that knows where the configuration files are so it can tell *imake* where to find them.

With respect to the proper operation of the `Makefile` and `Makefiles` target entries, the existence of multiple sets of files doesn't in itself present any special difficulties. As long as each set correctly references its own location, Makefiles build themselves using the proper set.

What about bootstrapping with multiple sets? Here we have a problem: each set of files is located in a different place and must be used with a bootstrapper that knows its location. That's not a difficulty for any particular set of files, because we can write a bootstrapper that knows where they are. But the effect of that approach over the long haul is that we end up drowning in bootstrappers.

When you develop a set of configuration files, presumably you do so for specific and unique purposes and can make a good case for its existence. That's not true of bootstrappers. They all have essentially the same purpose (to spare you the fate of typing *imake* commands manually), so multiplying bootstrappers just creates litter. It would be better to have a single one that understands how to use different sets.

Designing a General Purpose Bootstrapper

Let's consider how to avoid replicating bootstrappers by designing one that helps you work with multiple sets of configuration files easily. We'll call it *imboot,* a name that (unlike *xmkmf*) reflects its general purpose nature in being tied to *imake* rather than to a particular project.*

From a user's point of view, selecting configuration files should be as simple as naming the set we want:

```
% imboot -c X11
% imboot -c SP
% etc.
```

From an implementer's point of view, things are less simple. It's easy enough to get the name of the configuration files from the command-line arguments, but what do we do with it? A bootstrapper that works with any of several sets of files must know how to find each of them. This implies either that *imboot* knows explicitly where every set is located, or that we organize them according to some principle *imboot* can use to map names onto locations.

Both approaches have advantages and disadvantages. If we give *imboot* explicit knowledge about sets of files by hardwiring their locations into it, we have the luxury of putting them anywhere at all in the file system. For instance, in a shell script we could write a *case* statement with an entry for each set of files *imboot* should know about. The following example knows how to find the files for X11, Open Windows, and the starter project:

```
case "$name" in
    X11)    dir=/usr/lib/X11/config ;;
    OW)     dir=/usr/openwin/lib/config ;;
    SP)     dir=/usr/lib/config/SP ;;
    *)      echo "file set $name unknown" 1>&2
            exit 1
            ;;
esac
```

With this approach, *imboot* is limited strictly to the files listed, and it must be modified every time we install another set. That makes it inherently nonportable since at any given site there will be an arbitrary number of paths to hardwire into it. You might have three sets of files; I might have eight.

If an organizing principle is used instead, we can figure out the location of any set of files from its name without explicitly coding the group's location into *imboot.* A reasonable way to do this is to exploit the natural hierarchical structure of the UNIX file system. We can provide a root directory for

---

* *imkmf* might have been a better name (it's more like *xmkmf*), but the Khoros project already used it.

configuration files, */usr/lib/config*, under which we install sets of files.*
Each set gets its own subdirectory, the name of which being the name the
files are known by.

By designating a configuration root directory and installing sets of files
under it, *imboot* can find any set of files knowing just the name. This organization accommodates 200 sets just as well as it accommodates two, which
makes *imboot* implicitly extensible: no modifications to it are required
when new files are installed.

Use of a configuration root also minimizes the machine dependencies in
imboot itself. Only the root path need be parameterized, not the paths to
some arbitrary number of sets of files.

The preceding discussion of the benefits of organizing files under
/usr/lib/config may seem idyllic, but there is a downside: like any coopera-
tive agreement, the organizational scheme must be adhered to by all partic-
ipants (all sets of configuration files). The principle of arranging files by
installing them all under the configuration root implicitly assumes we can
put them all there. That assumption doesn't always hold: some existing
sets of files are not installed under */usr/lib/config*, e.g., the X11 files in
/usr/lib/X11/config.

However, backward compatibility is often easy to provide; the reach of the
configuration root directory can be extended to files installed elsewhere by
using symlinks. For the X11 files, we can do this with a single command:

```
% ln -s /usr/lib/X11/config /usr/lib/config/X11
```

The symbolic link makes the configuration root appear to have a set of files
named X11 under it and allows us to use them to bootstrap Makefiles like
this:

```
% imboot -c X11
```

Essentially, *imboot* is the spider, */usr/lib/config* is the parlor, and the symlink lures the X11 flies into it.

A special class of configuration files not installed under the configuration
root involves those not installed publicly at all, i.e., those that are stored in
the source tree of a project that uses them privately. We could handle this
with symlinks, but there's an easier way: we can consider private configuration files to be "nameless" and signify our desire to use them simply by

---

*You can use a root directory other than */usr/lib/config*, as long as you do so consistently for
all files installed on your machine.

the absence of any *−c name* option on the *imboot* command line. Of course, *imboot* needs to know where in the project to look for them. Examination of existing *imake*-configured projects suggests that the *config* directory under the project root is the closest thing to a convention available.

Implementing imboot

The information *imboot* needs is described in the list below. (The second and third points are based on the *Makefile*-generation issues discussed in Chapter 7, *A Closer Look at Makefile Generation.*)

- **The location of the configuration file directory.**

  imboot needs to tell *imake* where the configuration files are. By default, it assumes they're in the *config* directory under the project root. If a *−c name* option is present on the *imboot* command line, the directory */usr/lib/config/name* is used instead.

- **The location of the project root.**

  imboot needs to tell *imake* the location of the project root. *imboot* doesn't know where that is, though, so it must allow the location to be specified on the command line. (We could decree that *imboot* can only be used in project root directories and assume the location of the root is always ".", but there is good reason to want to use *imboot* in arbitrary project directories. For example, you might generate a corrupt *Makefile* somewhere down inside a project tree and need to bootstrap a new one. Or you might want to write a recursive *Makefile*-generating rule that uses *imboot* rather than *imake*.)

- **The location of the current directory within the project**

  It can be useful for *imboot* to tell *imake* the location of the current directory within the project (recursive rules are often written to use that information to give feedback to the user as a progress indicator). Since *imboot* doesn't know the current directory, it must allow that location to be specified on the command line.

Putting this together, *imboot* allows a *−c name* option to specify the name of a set of configuration files and one or two other arguments specifying the locations of the project root and current directory. The syntax of *imboot* is:

> **imboot** [**-c** *name*] [*topdir* [*curdir*]]

Other than the *−c* option, this syntax is similar to that of *xmkmf*.

imboot is easily implemented as a shell script:*

```
 1: #!/bin/sh
 2:
 3: configrootdir=/usr/lib/config
 4: configname=
 5: topdir=.
 6: curdir=.
 7:
 8: if [ $# -ge 2 -a "$1" = "-c" ]; then
 9:     configname="$2"
10:     shift;shift
11: fi
12:
13: if [ $# -gt 0 ]; then
14:     topdir="$1"
15:     shift
16: fi
17: if [ $# -gt 0 ]; then
18:     curdir="$1"
19: fi
20:
21: if [ "$configname" = "" ]; then
22:     useinstalled=
23:     configdir="-I$topdir/config"
24: else
25:     useinstalled=-DUseInstalled
26:     configdir="-I$configrootdir/$configname"
27: fi
28:
29: if [ -f Makefile ]; then
30:     echo mv Makefile Makefile.bak
31:     mv Makefile Makefile.bak
32: fi
33:
34: echo imake $useinstalled $configdir -DTOPDIR=$topdir -DCURDIR=$curdir
35: imake $useinstalled $configdir -DTOPDIR=$topdir -DCURDIR=$curdir
```

The first line indicates *imboot* is a Bourne shell script. (On systems that don't support the #! script-execution mechanism, change the first line to a colon.)

The next section of *imboot* sets up some default values (lines 3–6):

- The path to the configuration root directory.
- The default name of the configuration files, initially unknown.
- The default locations of the project root and current directory. By default we assume we're in the project root directory.

---

*This is a preliminary version that we'll replace with a more capable one in Chapter 14, *Designing Extensible Configuration Files*. But it will do for now.

After setting up the initial values, *imboot* examines the command arguments (lines 8–19), first determining whether any set of configuration files was named on the command line, then using any remaining arguments to override the default project root and current directory locations.

Once the arguments have been collected from the command line, *imboot* determines how to construct the *imake* command (lines 21–27). If no set of configuration files was named, we leave UseInstalled undefined and look for them within the project. Otherwise, we're using publicly-installed files, so we define UseInstalled and look for them under */usr/lib/config*.

The last section of *imboot* saves the current *Makefile* if it exists, then generates a new one (lines 29–35).

This version of *imboot* is simple, but functional. Now we need to consider how to write configuration files to cooperate with it, and how to achieve backward compatibility with configuration files that are already installed somewhere else.

Cooperating with imboot

imboot makes assumptions about the locations of the configuration files and about the meanings of UseInstalled, TOPDIR, and CURDIR. Obviously, this imposes some constraints on you as a configuration file writer. But if you keep the following guidelines in mind when you write your files, they'll be compatible with *imboot*, and you won't have to write your own bootstrapper:

- If you're going to use your files privately within a project, keep them in a directory named *config* under the project root.
- If you're going to install your files publicly, you need to do a couple of things. First, select a name for them. Remember that your files need to coexist with other sets of files. The potential exists for name clashing under */usr/lib/config*, so select a name you don't think anyone else will use. It's impossible to know in advance whether your name is sufficiently unique, of course, but names such as LOCAL or MYFILES are bound to be poor choices.

  Second, tell your files the name of the directory in which they'll be installed under the configuration root */usr/lib/config*, and install them there after you finish the other steps below. Essentially, this amounts to making sure the self- reference reference is correct. If the name of your set of files is XYZ, and the macro and variable you use to express the self-reference are `ConfigDir` and `CONFIGDIR`, write the following in *Project.tmpl*:

```
#ifndef ConfigDir
#define ConfigDir $(USRLIBDIR)/config/XYZ
#endif

CONFIGDIR = ConfigDir
```

Take a look at the starter project files for an instance of this technique.

- In your configuration files, use `UseInstalled`, `TOPDIR`, and `CURDIR` as follows:

  — Differentiate between installed and within-project versions of your configuration files based on whether or not `UseInstalled` is defined.

  — If you have parameters that signify the locations of the project root and current directory, set their values using the *cpp* macros `TOPDIR` and `CURDIR`. Here's an example showing how `TOPDIR` and `CUR-DIR` set the parameters `TOP` and `CURRENT_DIR`. `TOPDIR` and `CURDIR` are normally defined on the *imake* command line, but you still need to specify a default value in the configuration files.

  ```
  #ifndef TOPDIR
  #define TOPDIR .
  #endif
  #ifndef CURDIR
  #define CURDIR .
  #endif
          TOP = TOPDIR
  CURRENT_DIR = CURDIR
  ```

Backward Compatibility

Some configuration files violate *imboot*'s assumptions and don't provide the cooperation it requires. Nevertheless, in certain cases we can subsume noncompliant files under *imboot*'s aegis. If a set of files is already installed somewhere else than under the configuration root */usr/lib/config*, we might still be able to fit it into *imboot*'s view of the world.

The X11 Configuration Files

It's easy to make *imboot* backward-compatible with the X11 files. These files are typically installed in */usr/lib/X11/config*, but a symlink tells *imboot* how to find them:

```
% ln -s /usr/lib/X11/config /usr/lib/config/X11
```

This allows you to use *imboot* to bootstrap Makefiles using the X configuration files:

```
% imboot -c X11
```

Obviously, that command isn't as easy to type as:

```
% xmkmf
```

However, *imboot* has an important advantage over *xmkmf* in that you can use *imboot* in any directory of any X project. Just specify the location of the project root:

```
% imboot -c X11 topdir
```

xmkmf will build a *Makefile* in any X project directory, too, but TOP will be misconfigured in all directories except the project root. That doesn't matter if your project has just one directory. But if you have multiple directories and if your Imakefiles refer to various project directories in terms of TOP, you can't bootstrap a correctly configured *Makefile* with *xmkmf* anywhere but the project root.

Multiple X11 Releases

imboot helps you coordinate configuration files used for different projects. It can also help you coordinate configuration files used for different releases of the same project.

As I write, X11 is at Release 5. When X11R6 comes out there will be a period of transition during which there might be compatibility problems if Imakefiles written for R5 need some rewriting for R6. The transition can be made smoother if you can keep both sets of files online and switch between them easily. You can do this with *imboot*.

Presumably the default installation directory for the R6 configuration files will be the same as for the R5 files, so installing R6 will wipe out the R5 files (just as installing R5 wiped out the R4 files). This means you need to save the R5 files first. Create a directory */usr/lib/config/X11R5* and copy the R5 configuration files into it:

```
% cd /usr/lib/config
% mkdir X11R5
% cp /usr/lib/X11/config/* X11R5
```

In */usr/lib/config/X11R5/Project.tmpl*, find the self-reference:

```
#ifndef ConfigDir
#define ConfigDir $(LIBDIR)/config
#endif
```

Change it to this:

```
#ifndef ConfigDir
#define ConfigDir $(USRLIBDIR)/config/X11R5
#endif
```

Once you've made these modifications, you can install R6. That will put the R6 configuration files into */usr/lib/X11/config*. The symlink */usr/lib/config/X11* you created earlier that points to */usr/lib/X11/config* now points to the R6 files.

This procedure allows you to bootstrap Makefiles using either the R5 or R6 files:

```
% imboot -c X11R5
imake -DUseInstalled -I/usr/lib/config/X11R5 -DTOPDIR=. -DCURDIR=.

% imboot -c X11
imake -DUseInstalled -I/usr/lib/config/X11 -DTOPDIR=. -DCURDIR=.
```

In a similar way, you can use the R4 files if you have need to, by copying them into */usr/lib/config/X11R4*, changing the self-reference in *Project.tmpl*, and bootstrapping like this:

```
% imboot -c X11R4
```

The point of this exercise isn't to encourage you to keep old configuration files around, but to illustrate how *imboot* provides a practical solution to a real difficulty.

Kerberos V5

Kerberos (an authentication system developed at MIT) locates its configuration files in the *config* directory under the Kerberos project root. This is consonant with *imboot*'s assumptions about within-project files, so configuring Kerberos using *imboot* is trivial: leave off the −c option so *imboot* looks in the project tree for the configuration directory. In the Kerberos project root, do this to build all the Makefiles:

```
% imboot
% make Makefiles
```

Individual Makefiles anywhere within the Kerberos project can be bootstrapped like this:

```
% imboot topdir
```

Motif and Open Windows

Motif and Open Windows present special difficulties. They're closely related to X, and in fact use the X configuration files. However, each has configuration requirements that go beyond what's provided by the X files. For developers in such a situation, the temptation to tweak the X files is considerable.

The Motif developers gave in and modified the X template *Imake.tmpl* to accommodate a couple of Motif-specific configuration files, *Motif.tmpl* and *Motif.rules*. However, the X files configure an extremely large project, they're widely used, and they need to remain stable. If one development group can say, "Our project uses the X files, but they must be modified in such-and-such a manner," so can any other—and there is no mechanism to ensure that independent modifications by different groups will coexist.

In the case of Open Windows, a different approach was taken. The configuration files were left alone (although they're installed in a nonstandard location, */usr/openwin/lib/config*). The configuration programs were modified instead. Open Windows (versions 2 and 3, at least) is distributed with nonstandard versions of *imake* and *xmkmf* that have some built-in knowledge about the Open Windows directory layout. These modified programs are intended to make it simpler to configure Open Windows-based projects. Unfortunately, the modifications also make the programs Open Windows-specific so that it's difficult to use them with any other set of configuration files.

I suggest that it's preferable to use standard versions of *imake* and *xmkmf* and to make any necessary parameter modifications to independent copies of the X configuration files. Then there's no need for variant versions of the configuration programs *imake* and *xmkmf*, and changes to the configuration files are made independently for different projects, so they don't conflict.

You can try out this approach for yourself using the following procedures. They work with the standard versions of *imake* and *xmkmf*, and they leave the original X configuration files alone.

Motif (Version 1.2)

Create a directory */usr/lib/config/Motif,* move into it, and copy the X11R5 and Motif configuration files into it. Modify the template *Imake.tmpl* to add references for the Motif-specific files. Find the section that looks like this:

```
#include <Project.tmpl>
#include <Imake.rules>
```

Change it to this:

```
#include <Project.tmpl>
#include <Motif.tmpl>

#include <Imake.rules>
#include <Motif.rules>
```

Reset the self-reference in *Project.tmpl* by changing the value of ConfigDir to this:

```
#ifndef ConfigDir
#define ConfigDir $(USRLIBDIR)/config/Motif
#endif
```

These changes allow you to bootstrap Makefiles for projects based on Motif as follows:

```
% imboot -c Motif
% make Makefiles
```

Open Windows (Versions 2 and 3)

It's more difficult to use *imboot* to configure projects based on Open Windows, since the configuration files currently provided by Sun don't work as shipped. The files are stored in */usr/openwin/lib/config.** Unfortunately, they don't have any Open Windows parameters specified in them! So you need to add some. The additions shown below can be put in either *sun.cf* or *site.def* (you might need to tweak the values to reflect local differences in directory layout):

```
#ifndef OpenWinHome
#define OpenWinHome /usr/openwin
#endif

#ifndef LibDir
#define LibDir $(OPENWINHOME)/lib
#endif
```

---

*More accurately, *imake* and *xmkmf* look in ${OPENWINHOME}/*lib/config,* where OPENWINHOME is an environment variable indicating the root of the Open Windows hierarchy on your system.

```
#ifndef IncRoot
#define IncRoot $(OPENWINHOME)/include
#endif

#ifndef StandardIncludes
#define StandardIncludes -I$(INCROOT)
#endif

#ifndef DefaultCCOptions
#define DefaultCCOptions -L$(OPENWINHOME)/lib
#endif

OPENWINHOME = OpenWinHome
```

Then, tell *imboot* how to find the files by making a link under the configuration root */usr/lib/config* to the directory in which the Open Windows configuration files are stored:

```
% ln -s /usr/openwin/lib/config /usr/lib/config/OW
```

Finally, if you've been using the versions of *imake* and *xmkmf* distributed with Open Windows, you should throw them away and install standard versions instead. (If you prefer something less drastic, install standard versions in a directory that your shell searches before */usr/openwin/bin* and */usr/openwin/bin/xview*.)

This procedure allows you to bootstrap Makefiles using the Open Windows configuration files:

```
% imboot -c OW
% make Makefiles
```

Incompatible Projects

Sometimes *imboot* is too incompatible with a project to be used with it. Khoros is an example. It uses *imake* in a manner that departs significantly from the X11 architecture. For instance, configuration files are stored in several directories, and TOPDIR isn't used consistently.

Kerberos V4 is incompatible with *imboot*, too. The configuration directory within the project is *util/imake.includes* rather than *config*, and TOPDIR isn't used.

Using imboot in Makefiles

When you're developing a project, you can build the initial *Makefile* with *imboot* and use the *Makefile* to rebuild itself with *make Makefile* thereafter, as long as you're on the same machine. When you move the project to another machine, the Makefile entry in the *Makefile* becomes invalid. It generates an *imake* command containing an explicit reference to the location of the configuration file directory on the original machine. That location can vary among systems, so in general you can't expect the `Makefile` entry in a *Makefile* created on one machine to work properly on another.

You can, of course, run the bootstrapper again on the second machine to regenerate the *Makefile*, but another approach is to write a rule that generates an *imboot* command instead of an *imake* command. With *imboot*, you give the name of the configuration files you want to use, which presumably remains constant from machine to machine. Since no directory need be named on the *imboot* command, it can be invoked in a machine-independent manner.

The implication is that a *Makefile* built for one machine may be misconfigured in many or most respects for another machine, but we can get it to do at least one thing reliably—generate an *imboot* command to rebuild itself so it *is* properly configured.

We can write a `BootstrapTarget()` rule like this in *Imake.rules*:

```
#ifndef BootstrapTarget
#define BootstrapTarget()                             @@\
Bootstrap::                                           @@\
    $(IMBOOT_CMD) $(TOP) $(CURRENT_DIR)
#endif /* BootstrapTarget */
```

The rule refers to the parameter `IMBOOT_CMD`, which can be specified in *Project.tmpl* along with the parameters `IMBOOT_CMD` itself depends on. For a set of files named XYZ, the information looks like this:

```
#ifndef ConfigName
#define ConfigName XYZ
#endif
#ifndef ImbootCmd
#define ImbootCmd imboot    /* assume it's publicly installed */
#endif
    CONFIGNAME = ConfigName
        IMBOOT = ImbootCmd
#ifdef UseInstalled
    IMBOOT_CMD = $(IMBOOT) -c $(CONFIGNAME)
#else
    IMBOOT_CMD = $(IMBOOT)
#endif
```

The value of `ConfigName` should be changed appropriately for your set of configuration files, of course.

To use the rule, invoke `BootstrapTarget()` in your *Imakefile*, and build the initial *Makefile* with *imboot*. Thereafter, assuming *imboot* and the proper set of configuration files are installed on a second machine, you can move a project there and reconfigure the Makefiles like this:

```
% make Bootstrap
% make Makefiles
```

You don't need to know anything but a couple of *make* commands to reconfigure the project.

My own practice is to invoke `BootstrapTarget()` in the final section of *Imake.tmpl*, so the `Bootstrap` target is included automatically in every *Makefile*. Then I don't have to remember to invoke the rule in individual Imakefiles.

In this chapter:
- *Setting Up*
- *Deleting Information*
- *Retaining Information*
- *Adding Information*

10

Introduction to Configuration File Writing

> *Simplify, simplify.*
> —Thoreau, *Walden*

When you develop a new set of configuration files, you have essentially two choices: write everything from scratch, or copy and modify existing files. We'll take the easier path and use the starter project developed in Chapter 8, *A Configuration Starter Project*, to create a new project containing configuration files; this will allow us to write Imakefiles for building and installing C programs and libraries of moderate complexity.

The purpose of this chapter isn't to create a set of super-whiz-bang configuration files. It's to demonstrate the process you go through to develop any set of files. Thus, we'll call this the demonstration project (DP).

Even when we begin with existing files, the process by which we modify one set of files to create another involves a sustained effort. This chapter discusses how to set up the DP files—how to decide what to keep, what to throw out, and what to add. Another important aspect of configuration file development is rule writing, which is a major topic in itself and is discussed separately in Chapter 11, *Writing Rule Macros*. For discussion of other miscellaneous issues that are involved in configuration file writing but aren't specifically related to the DP files, see Chapter 12, *Configuration Problems and Solutions*.

The DP distribution is available for examination (see Appendix A, *Obtaining Configuration Software*), and I recommend that you make use of it. The files in the distribution and the SP files from which they're derived differ extensively, and for some of the types of changes we'll be making, there is space here to show representative examples only. If you want to determine in detail the full scope of the modifications involved at each stage of the derivation, the distribution contains *diff* listings you can inspect.

Setting Up

Begin by making a copy of the starter project and moving into it. Assuming the starter project is located under your curent directory, do this:

```
% cp -r SP DP
% cd DP
```

If you expect to install the files for public use, do the following:

- Create a project root *Imakefile* like the following:

```
#define IHaveSubdirs
#define PassCDebugFlags

SUBDIRS = config

MakeSubdirs($(SUBDIRS))
DependSubdirs($(SUBDIRS))
```

- Move into the *config* directory and create an *Imakefile*:

```
        FILES = *.tmpl *.rules site.def *.cf *.bac
INSTALLFLAGS = $(INSTDATFLAGS)

all::
depend::

InstallMultiple($(FILES),$(CONFIGDIR))
```

- Edit *Project.tmpl* to change the value of `ConfigDir` from `$(USRLIB-DIR)`/*config/SP* to `$(USRLIBDIR)`/*config/DP*.

- Move back up into the project root and verify that the DP project can build its own Makefiles and that it knows where to install the configuration files:

```
% cd ..
% imboot
% make Makefiles
% make -n install
```

The output of the last command should confirm that */usr/lib/config/DP* will be used as the installation directory when you're ready to install the files. (To do the installation, you repeat the *make install* command, leaving off the *–n* option.)

Now we're ready to begin surgery.

When you create new configuration files by copying existing ones, there are only a few things you can do with their contents:

- **Delete information.** Information in the original files can be removed if it's superfluous to your requirements.

- **Retain information.** If a macro, rule, or parameter variable is useful to you, keep it instead of throwing it out.

- **Add information.** When the files don't provide the capabilities you need, extend them by adding new information.

The following sections show how to modify your configuration files in these ways and discuss the issues involved when you do so. Make sure you're in the *config* directory, since that's where the files are located.

Deleting Information

We'll delete information first to make the configuration files easier to work with. To do this effectively, you need to understand your goals, so you know what result you're aiming for. You also need to understand the files you're modifying, so you can determine how the goals for which they were originally written overlap with your own and how they differ. That means you need to understand something about the X11 files, because the DP files are ultimately derived from the X files (Figure 10–1). If you're not familiar with them, the design and use of the X files is discussed in Chapter 4, *The X11 Configuration Files*, and Chapter 5, *Writing Imakefiles*.

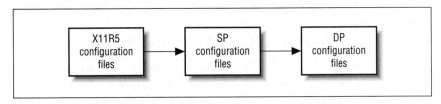

Figure 10-1: DP configuration file ancestry

Our goal is to be able to build and install moderately complex C programs and libraries. This isn't as ambitious a goal as being able to configure the X project. Consequently, our configuration files initially contain many symbols we don't need, and can thus remove, to make the files simpler. The next section covers three areas we can whittle away at: these deal with support for FORTRAN programming, the X Window System, and shared libraries.

FORTRAN Support

The configuration files provide support for FORTRAN programming in *Imake.tmpl* and *Imake.rules*. Since we're interested in C here, we can jettison the following symbols:

Macros	`HasFortran`, `FortranCmd`, `FortranFlags`, and `FortranDebugFlags`
Variables	`FC`, `FDEBUGFLAGS`, and `FCFLAGS`
Rule	`NormalFortranObjectRule()`

X Support

You'll find most of the X-specific symbols in *Project.tmpl* and *Imake.rules*. One symbol that's pretty obviously X-related and that can be safely removed is `ProjectX`:

```
#define ProjectX 5  /* do *not* change this line */
```

Throw caution to the winds, ignore the admonition in the comment, and remove the definition.

Other discardable symbols pertain to:

X libraries	`XLIB`, `DEPXLIB`, `DebugLibX`, etc.
The X server	`BuildServer`, `ConnectionFlags`, `SERVERSRC`, etc.

X utilities and auxiliary programs

> `BuildFontServer`, `InstallFSConfig`, `RGB`, `SetTty-Group`, etc.

X-related rules

> `ServerTarget()`, `FontTarget()`, `MakeFonts()`, etc.

These lists of symbols aren't exhaustive, as you'll discover when you start paring down the files. (Remember that you can retrieve the DP distribution and use the *diff* listings to determine the full extent of the changes at each step.)

Shared Library Support

Shared library development is a miasma we're going to avoid altogether, so we can delete symbols relating to it. Begin with the vendor files. Some of them contain `#include` directives that can be removed because they refer to files containing shared library rules. The files have names ending in "Lib.rules" and we can find the references to them like so:

```
% grep "include.*Lib\.rules" *.cf
att.cf:#include <sv4Lib.rules>
ibm.cf:#include <ibmLib.rules>
moto.cf:#include <sv4Lib.rules>
sgi.cf:/* #include <sgiLib.rules> */
sun.cf:#include <sunLib.rules>
x386.cf:/* #include <sv3Lib.rules> */  /* not working yet */
x386.cf:#include <sv4Lib.rules>
```

The command output tells you which lines to remove from which files. For editing, you can grab all the affected files at once as follows:

```
% vi `grep -l "include.*Lib\.rules" *.cf`
```

Each *Lib.rules* file defines symbols for building shared libraries and also defines ShLibIncludeFile as the name of a related *Lib.tmpl* file (e.g., *sunLib.rules* defines it as *sunLib.tmpl*). In turn, ShLibIncludeFile is referenced by the following section of *Project.tmpl*, which you should delete:

```
#ifndef ShLibIncludeFile
/* need this to make ANSI-style preprocessors happy */
#define ShLibIncludeFile <noop.rules>
#endif

#include ShLibIncludeFile
```

You can also remove *noop.rules* and the *Lib.rules* and *Lib.tmpl* files, since we'll not be needing them:

```
% rm -f noop.rules *Lib.rules *Lib.tmpl
```

Imake.tmpl, *Project.tmpl*, and *Library.tmpl* contain other symbols that relate to shared libraries and can be excised: HasSharedLibraries, SHARED-CODEDEF, SHLIBDEF, etc. (Many shared library symbols, such as SharedLibX, are connected with X support, so they'll already have been removed.)

If you wish, you can apply a similar procedure to remove profiling and debugging library support.

Miscellaneous Symbol Deleting Guidelines

Modifications to the configuration files should always be made in accordance with your goals. For example, since I'm not going to discuss shared libraries, I deleted support for them so I could simplify the files. You might consider it crucial to be able to develop shared libraries. If so, by all means leave in the symbols that relate to them.

Wholesale deletion of information is the quickest way to reduce the complexity of the configuration files you're working with. However, you need to temper your zeal to simplify the files against the possibility of breaking them by going too far. Keep the following principles in mind as you brandish your scimitar—they'll help you avoid making deletions you'll regret and have to undo:

- If you don't understand what a symbol is used for, it's safer to leave it in than to remove it and possibly break your configuration files. Wait until you understand the symbol's use before deciding to delete it.

- If you do understand a symbol but you're not sure if you'll need it, leave it in until you're sure you won't need it.

- If you remove a symbol, you must remove other symbols that depend on it. Stated another way, if you don't remove a symbol, you can't remove any symbols it depends on either. Consider the following definition from *Imake.tmpl*:

  ```
  #ifndef StandardCppDefines
  #define StandardCppDefines StandardDefines
  #endif
  ```

  `StandardCppDefines` depends on `StandardDefines`, so if you remove `StandardDefines`, you must also remove `StandardCpp-Defines`. Conversely, if you don't remove `StandardCppDefines`, you can't remove `StandardDefines`.

- When you're checking symbol dependencies, you may need to track down interactions involving *cpp* macros and *make* variables. Here's an example from *Project.tmpl*:

  ```
  #ifndef ManPath
  #define ManPath ManDirectoryRoot
  #endif
  #ifndef ManSourcePath
  #define ManSourcePath $(MANPATH)/man
  #endif
  MANPATH = ManPath
  ```

  This tells us that `ManSourcePath` is defined in terms of `MANPATH`, which gets its value from `ManPath`, which in turn gets its value from `ManDirectoryRoot`. The chain of dependencies means that if we delete `ManDirectoryRoot`, we must also delete `ManPath`, `MAN-PATH`, and `ManSourcePath` as well.

As you're trying to decide what can and can't be removed from your configuration files, remember that *grep* is your friend. You can use it to locate all instances of a symbol in the files, which will help you determine from context what the symbol is used for. *grep* can also help you trace through a symbol's interactions with other symbols.

While you're trimming down your template, project, and rules files by removing symbols, you can get rid of definitions in the vendor and site files that pertain to those symbols. We've already done this once by deleting from the vendor files the `#include` directives for the shared library files. You can continue the process by removing other definitions that no longer have any meaning, e.g., any definitions of `BuildServer` you find in the vendor files.

A Shocking Fact

Strictly speaking, you don't need to remove extraneous information from the configuration files. In other words, you can completely skip all the instructions I've given so far about getting rid of stuff from the DP files! And, admittedly, it's easier to leave superfluous information alone than to take the trouble to remove it.

However, if you do that, your files will contain useless details that are present simply because they were in the original files, not because they're relevant to your goals. This will be confusing later—to you after you've forgotten just why you left them in, and to others who'll be unsure why symbols with no apparent purpose are there. Remember: the more complex your files are, the harder they are to understand. If you can legitimately get rid of something (that is, you understand its purpose and know you don't need it), it's best to do so for simplicity's sake.

Retaining Information

We've removed a large portion of the original contents of our files, but there's still quite a bit left because they contain a lot of information we can keep for our own use. Some examples are:

- The definitions of `XCOMM`, `YES`, and `NO`
- The vendor blocks
- The token-pasting macros `Concat()` and `Concat3()`
- The `BootstrapCFlags`, `OSMajorVersion`, and `OSMinorVersion` macros

- The `SystemV` and `SystemV4` macros used for determining system characteristics
- Rules, macros, and parameters for:
  - Building Makefiles: `IMAKE`, `IMAKE_CMD`, `IMAKE_DEFINES`, `IRULESRC`, `CONFIGDIR`, `ConfigDir`, `CONFIGSRC`, `ConfigSrc`, `MakefileTarget()`, etc.
  - Generating header file dependencies: `UseCCMakeDepend`, `DEPEND`, `DependTarget()`, `DependTarget3()`, etc.
  - Cleaning up: `RmCmd`, `RM`, `RM_CMD`, `FilesToClean`, `Extra-FilesToClean`, `CleanTarget()`, etc.
- The final section of *Imake.tmpl* (everything past the point where the *Imakefile* is included). This section invokes several common rules automatically so you don't have to.
- The rules that allow you to perform recursive *make* operations for managing multiple directory projects. Most often these have names ending with "Subdirs", such as `CleanSubdirs()`, `Install-Subdirs()`, or `LintSubdirs()`.

Modifying Retained Information

Sometimes when we retain a construct we need to modify it slightly. `Bin-Dir` is useful for specifying the program installation directory, but its original default value is */usr/bin/X11*, which is X-specific:

```
#ifndef BinDir
#ifdef ProjectRoot
#define BinDir Concat(ProjectRoot,/bin)
#else
#define BinDir /usr/bin/X11
#endif
#endif
```

If you want a more generic value like */usr/local/bin*, change the default to this:

```
#ifndef BinDir
#ifdef ProjectRoot
#define BinDir Concat(ProjectRoot,/bin)
#else
#define BinDir /usr/local/bin
#endif
#endif
```

Simplifying Retained Information

Constructs in the original configuration files that are useful to you but unnecessarily complex can be retained but simplified. For example, the original definition of `ManDirectoryRoot` looks like this (indentation added):

```
#ifndef ManDirectoryRoot
#  ifdef ProjectRoot
#    define ManDirectoryRoot Concat(ProjectRoot,/man)
#    ifndef XmanLocalSearchPath
#      define XmanLocalSearchPath ManDirectoryRoot
#    endif
#  else
#    if SystemV4
#      define ManDirectoryRoot /usr/share/man
#    else
#      define ManDirectoryRoot /usr/man
#    endif
#  endif
#endif
```

The construct is X-related, but only partially, so instead of clobbering it altogether, we simplify it by removing the X-ism (`XmanLocalSearch-Path`):

```
#ifndef ManDirectoryRoot
#  ifdef ProjectRoot
#    define ManDirectoryRoot Concat(ProjectRoot,/man)
#  else
#    if SystemV4
#      define ManDirectoryRoot /usr/share/man
#    else
#      define ManDirectoryRoot /usr/man
#    endif
#  endif
#endif
```

The final section of the template *Imake.tmpl* automatically invokes a number of helpful rules for you to generate some commonly used targets. Two parts of it that can be simplified look like this:

```
#ifndef IHaveSpecialMakefileTarget
MakefileTarget()
#endif
    .
    .
#ifdef MakefileAdditions
MakefileAdditions()
#endif
```

If you search through the X11 distribution to determine how `IHave-SpecialMakefileTarget` and `MakefileAdditions` are used, you'll discover that ... they're not. Since neither symbol is employed anywhere in the X distribution, it's unlikely that we'll need them, either. We can remove the contingency of `MakefileTarget()` on `IHaveSpecialMakefile-Target` and dump `MakefileAdditions` completely, leaving us with only this:

```
MakefileTarget()
```

Modifications like these are relatively minor, but their cumulative effect can make your configuration files significantly easier to understand.

Some simplifications are purely structural. For instance, we're not going to change the vendor blocks at all and we can drop them out of sight so we don't have to think about them:

- Copy the section of *Imake.tmpl* that contains the vendor blocks into a file called *Imake.vb*.
- Replace the vendor block section in the template with this directive:

```
#include <Imake.vb>
```

This reorganization makes the template less complex, even though no information is discarded.

Adding Information

We've removed several types of information from our configuration files, e.g., macros, parameter variables, and rule definitions. We've also removed part of the section of the template that invokes rules for us automatically. Thus, we've reduced the bulk of our original files considerably and simplified some of what remains.

Now it's time to start adding new information, which is essentially a reversal of the process of deleting it. Adding new macros and parameters is relatively simple; so is adding new rule invocations to the end of the template. Those subjects are discussed below. By contrast, rule writing is an extensive topic and is deferred until Chapter 11, *Writing Rule Macros.*

Adding Macros and Parameter Variables

As discussed in Chapter 3, *Understanding Configuration Files*, when you need a new parameter, you usually express it using the idiom of a *make* variable that's set to the value of a *cpp* macro. The macro should be given a default value in the same file as that in which the variable assignment occurs:

```
#ifndef MacroName
#define MacroName value
#endif

VARNAME = MacroName
```

Some parameter variables are given values entirely in terms of other variables, in which case there is no corresponding *cpp* macro. CFLAGS is one of these:

```
CFLAGS = $(CDEBUGFLAGS) $(CCOPTIONS) $(ALLDEFINES)
```

Conversely, some macros have no corresponding variable. These are usually used as booleans (i.e., given a value of YES or NO) to indicate whether particular system facilities or characteristics are present, or whether or not to do something. For example, HasPutenv indicates whether the *putenv()* library function is available. RemoveTarget-ProgramByMoving indicates whether to rename *program* to *program~* when a new version is built so the old version remains available (if not, the old version is simply overwritten).

Choosing Default Macro Values

When you create a new macro, you must provide a default value. Make sure it's the best value you can come up with for the largest number of cases, and that the value isn't "dangerous." The following sections describe how to do this.

Choose defaults as well as you can

The idiom of specifying parameter variables in terms of *cpp* macros allows parameter assignments to be placed in the template or project files along with default values that can be overridden. Vendor files specify macro values for a given platform that differ from the defaults. This idiom embodies the general principle of providing a reference or baseline configuration against which it's necessary only to specify variations.

There's a lesson in this for us as configuration file writers: the more accurate we can be about guessing appropriate default values in the template and project files, the less often we'll have to override them in the vendor files.

Suppose we're specifying a parameter for the flag that tells *lint* to create a *lint* library. We could write the following in *Imake.tmpl*:

```
#ifndef LintLibFlag
#define LintLibFlag -C
#endif

LINTLIBFLAG = LintLibFlag
```

Unfortunately, that's only correct for the BSD variant of *lint*. The System V variant requires *-o* instead of *-C*. If we use the default definition given above for the DP project, we'd need to override it in more than half of the 18 vendor files. That's a lot of overriding. If we choose *-o* as the default instead, the situation is only a little better.

We can make our job easier by using the `SystemV` and `SystemV4` symbols to select the default value of `LintLibFlag`:

```
#ifndef LintLibFlag
#if SystemV || SystemV4
#define LintLibFlag -o
#else
#define LintLibFlag -C
#endif
#endif

LINTLIBFLAG = LintLibFlag
```

This does a better job of choosing the default and reduces to two the number of vendor files in which the default needs to be overridden.

Choose macro defaults conservatively

When you pick a default value for a macro that specifies how to do something, you often have to choose between two competing alternatives. For instance, there is code in the X Toolkit library that copies objects that can be larger than a byte and that can be located at arbitrary addresses. The library implements a method that's fast and efficient but depends on the CPU being able to access word and long word quantities that aren't necessarily aligned to word boundaries. Not all processors can do that, so the library also implements a byte-by-byte copy method that's slower but works on all machines.

When you provide two methods like this, you need a way to specify in the configuration files which one to use. In the case of the Xt library, the choice is between an efficient method that doesn't work on all processors and a universal method that runs more slowly. The X configuration files provide an `UnalignedReferencesAllowed` macro indicating whether the processor can perform word accesses at addresses not aligned to word boundaries. What should the default be?

Follow the principle of choosing a default that allows your programs to build and run on as many machines as possible. If an optimization is available to make a program run faster but it doesn't work universally, it's dangerous: allow it to be selected from the vendor file but don't make it the default. Err on the side of caution and choose the more conservative method that always works:

```
#ifndef UnalignedReferencesAllowed
#define UnalignedReferencesAllowed NO
#endif
```

Then, for better performance on those processors allowing arbitrary references, use the vendor file to indicate that the faster method is appropriate:

```
#ifndef UnalignedReferencesAllowed
#define UnalignedReferencesAllowed YES
#endif
```

You might wonder whether it really matters which default you choose. After all, when you develop your configuration files, you'll certainly make sure the default is overridden as necessary in all the vendor files. So it shouldn't make any difference whether you choose the more conservative value or not, right?

Wrong. You aren't necessarily the only person who'll use your configuration files. If others port your software to a machine on which it's never been built, they'll need to write a new vendor file. They won't understand your configuration files as well as you do, so minimize what someone must know about them by providing defaults that are as reasonable as possible. This way the software works with no modification, but effort spent in selecting optimizations pays a dividend.

In this context, a default value of `NO` for `UnalignedReferences-Allowed` is reasonable. The code will run on any system—more slowly than necessary on some systems, perhaps, but at least it won't crash mysteriously on others.

Sooner or later you'll write code that you know works on your own machines but won't work on certain other machines unless you plan for that in advance, i.e., unless you write it portably. It's tempting to just get the code to run locally. This mindset easily carries over into the design of configuration files: "This only needs to work at our site on our VAX and our SPARCstation;" "We only have little-endian machines;" "Our machines are all BSD-based;" etc. For instance, if all your local machines can do unaligned word accesses, it's tempting to forget about making sure your copy routines work on machines that can't do such accesses. In that case, you might not even bother to create a macro like `UnalignedRefer-encesAllowed` for expressing the machine-dependency, even though it reduces the portability of your software if you don't.

If you can safely assume that your machines are going to run forever and you'll never get different ones, and you'll never get a new job somewhere else and want to take some of your software with you, and that no one anywhere will ever want any of your programs, then fine. Go ahead and write your configuration files with limited portability in mind. Otherwise, design for a wide audience. If you assume someone else will be using your configuration files, it can make a lot of difference in your outlook on how generally you write them. This will help you write your configuration files so they won't require a lot of patching up later.

Subdirectory Support

In Chapter 5, *Writing Imakefiles*, we discussed how the X11 configuration files allow projects comprising multiple directories to be managed easily. This is done through the use of recursive rules (which the X files provide in abundance). The DP files ultimately derive from the X files, so the same rules are available to us. It's important to retain them* because recursive operations are one of the trickier things you can use *make* for, one of the most difficult to write *Makefile* entries for, and one of the easiest to get wrong. *imake* helps you with them two ways:

- *imake* lets you encapsulate recursive entries in the form of rule macros. Then you only need to figure out how to write each type of entry once. After that, you can propagate them into your Makefiles easily, simply by invoking them in your Imakefiles.

- Since *imake* provides a means for explicitly representing experience in configuring software, you can take advantage of someone else's hard-won knowledge by appropriating already-written rules from a set of configuration files in which the recursive rules are known to work. So usually you don't have to write the rules even once.

In addition to carrying over recursive rules from the X11 files to the DP files, we've also retained the final section of *Imake.tmpl*, which invokes a number of recursive rules for you to help automate their use. Thus, for

---

*Most of them, anyway. You might find that some of them are of not useful for your purposes; those you can delete, of course.

rules such as `InstallSubdirs()` and `CleanSubdirs()`, it isn't necessary to explicitly invoke them in Imakefiles. Essentially, you get recursive `install` and `clean` targets (among others) for free.

However, there are certain useful targets not generated for you by the template, in particular, `all` and `depend`. This means that unless you generate those targets yourself from within each *Imakefile* of a project, the *make all* and *make depend* commands won't work uniformly throughout the project tree.

This problem came up when we discussed multiple directory projects in Chapter 5, *Writing Imakefiles*. There we saw that if a directory has subdirectories, we need to generate recursive `all` and `depend` entries to tell *make* to descend into the directories named by `SUBDIRS`. Since this is true whenever there are subdirectories, we may as well modify the final section of the template to invoke the proper rules for us automatically. Find the part of the template that looks like this:

```
#ifdef IHaveSubdirs
XCOMM -------------------------------------------
XCOMM rules for building in SUBDIRS - do not edit
```

Change it to this:

```
#ifdef IHaveSubdirs
XCOMM ---------------------------
XCOMM rules for building in SUBDIRS

MakeSubdirs($(SUBDIRS))
DependSubdirs($(SUBDIRS))
```

This modification makes a DP *Imakefile* a little easier to write than the otherwise equivalent X11 *Imakefile*, because there are two fewer rules to invoke.

For a directory without subdirectories, it's less clear what to do about `all` and `depend` entries from within the template. We can't say with certainty what it will mean to carry out the `all` or `depend` operations for some arbitrary *Makefile*. On the other hand, entries for the `all` and `depend` operations still need to be present. Otherwise, when you try to perform those operations project-wide, they'll fail for any *Makefile* that doesn't support them. At the very least, empty `all` and `depend` entries need to be present.

Unfortunately, given our inability to predict the *Imakefile* writer's intentions, empty entries are also the most we can provide from within the template. Find the part of the template that applies when there aren't subdirectories:

```
XCOMM ----------------------------------------------------------------
XCOMM empty rules for directories that do not have SUBDIRS - do not edit
```

Change it to this:

```
XCOMM -----------------------------------------------------
XCOMM empty rules for directories that do not have SUBDIRS
all::
depend::
```

The only purpose of these entries is to prevent the `all` and `depend` operations from failing when *make* traverses the project tree. Nevertheless, these entries are empty and they don't cause any actual work to be done. In each *Imakefile*, you must still associate an `all` entry with each target you want built, and you must still invoke `DependTarget()` to generate header file dependencies if you're working with C source files.

In this chapter:
- *Rule Syntax*
- *Building the Basic Rule*
- *Making the Rule Work Harder*
- *Refining the Scope of a Target*
- *Documenting Rules*
- *Building Libraries*
- *Installation Rules*

11

Writing Rule Macros

If at first you don't succeed . . .
—Thomas Palmer,
Teacher's Manual

In Chapter 10, *Introduction to Configuration File Writing*, we began to develop a new set of configuration files called the demonstration project (DP) files. We continue that process in this chapter, focusing primarily on how to write rule macros. Since the DP files are oriented toward building and installing C programs, we'll design a small set of program development rules. (The DP rules file *Imake.rules* already contains program building rules, of course. I'm going to pretend they don't exist in order to show the process of developing a set of rules from beginning to end.)

In some cases, a configuration parameter or rule we create in this chapter has the same name as one that is already in the DP files. When this occurs, I'll say whether you can use the version already in the files, or whether you need to replace it with the version we develop here. For example, we write a rule `AllTarget()`, but it's the same as the one that is already in the DP file *Imake.rules*, so you don't actually need to add anything to *Imake.rules*. On the other hand, we write a rule `InstallManPage()` that has a different definition than the original rule with that name in *Imake.rules*. In this case, you should replace the original version with the one we write.

Rule Syntax

The following list details the syntax we use for writing rule macros:

- Rules are defined using the following form. The first line specifies the invocation sequence, those following specify the body of the rule:

```
#define rule-name(rule-parameters)                    @@\
rule-body line 1                                       @@\
...                                                    @@\
rule-body line n-1                                     @@\
rule-body line n
```

- All lines of a rule but the last end with "@@\".

- Indent lines in the rule definition body the way you want them indented in the *Makefile*. If the line you're writing will end up as a command line in a *Makefile* entry, it must be indented with a tab. If it's intended as a dependency line, do not indent it (make sure there are no leading spaces or tabs). If the line invokes another rule, generally you don't indent it. If it's a *make* variable assignment, it can be indented, but use spaces, not tabs.

- Enclose every rule definition within #ifndef/#endif pairs so the rule can be overridden or replaced:

```
#ifndef rule-name
#define rule-name(rule-parameters)                     @@\
rule-body line 1                                        @@\
...                                                     @@\
rule-body line n-1                                      @@\
rule-body line n
#endif /* rule-name */
```

For brevity, I omit the #ifndef/#endif pairs from all rules discussed in this chapter, but you should always include them in your own definitions.

- Don't terminate the #ifndef or #endif lines with "@@\".

Building the Basic Rule

Let's start by defining a rule BuildProgram() for building C programs. We'll write a simple version and go through several iterations of analyzing it, finding its limitations, and refining it. After you follow this discussion through, you'll be able to write rules effectively because you'll know what kind of functionality to design into them from the start instead of going through the revision process after you've already started using your rules in production.

As a first approximation, `BuildProgram()` can be defined like this:

```
#define BuildProgram(prog,objs)                          @@\
prog: objs                                               @@\
    cc -o prog objs
```

This definition indicates the target you want built (`prog`) and the object files from which to build it (`objs`). `BuildProgram()` as given is sufficient for building simple targets, but since we're not at the end of the chapter yet, it would be best to identify several shortcomings so we have something to talk about:

- Parameterization is lacking. What if you want to use a different C compiler, such as *gcc*? You can edit the rule to change it, but then the rule isn't correct for anyone who wants to use *cc*. We should use $(CC) in the rule body instead of a literal `cc` and select from the other configuration files the value of `CC` that's appropriate for the system on which the program is built.

- Generality is deficient. The rule can't build programs that require libraries or special linker flags, and it doesn't let us compensate for oddities such as broken "standard" libraries. For instance, some C libraries in early releases of Mips RISC/os are missing *vfprintf()*. Our rule cannot handle special cases like this.

- The rule doesn't work very hard; it produces only the final executable program. It could also generate entries for common useful operations such as a `clean` entry to remove the program after we've built and installed it.

We can address these issues one at a time through incremental revision.

Parameterizing the Rule

The definition of `BuildProgram()` will be more flexible if we refer to the C compiler using a parameter rather than by writing the name literally:

```
#define BuildProgram(prog,objs)                          @@\
prog: objs                                               @@\
    $(CC) -o prog objs
```

The system parameters section of *Imake.tmpl* must support CC, so make sure the template contains the following:*

```
#ifndef CcCmd
#define CcCmd cc
#endif
CC = CcCmd
```

The usual idiom whereby the value of a *make* variable comes from a corresponding *cpp* macro is used here. The macro CcCmd sets the variable CC. A default value for CcCmd is supplied, but it can be overridden in *site.def* or *vendor.cf* so the C compiler can be selected easily without changing any Imakefiles.

This simple change reflects an important principle: don't literally write the names of tools, utilities, etc., into your rule definitions; parameterize them to make them flexible.

To make BuildProgram() even more general by providing support for libraries, link flags, etc., we must be able to specify more information.

Link Libraries

BuildProgram() doesn't let us say whether a program needs any libraries at link time. We could specify them by writing them literally into the rule definition. For instance, to link in the math and terminal capability libraries, we could change the rule to name them on the CC command line:

```
#define BuildProgram(prog,objs)                        @@\
prog: objs                                             @@\
    $(CC) -o prog objs -lm -ltermcap
```

This is the wrong way to make a change, because the rule really isn't any more general. The libraries are hardwired in, which isn't useful unless we'll always want exactly those two libraries every time the rule is used. (Not likely!) In general, there's no way to anticipate which libraries a given program will require, so we must let the *Imakefile* writer specify them. This can be done more than one way; I'll show two.

We could rewrite BuildProgram() to refer to a *make* variable BPTLIBS to which the *Imakefile* writer can assign a value:

---

*You can use the CcCmd and CC that are already present in the DP *Imake.tmpl* file.

```
#define BuildProgram(prog,objs)                            @@\
prog: objs                                                 @@\
     $(CC) -o prog objs $(BPTLIBS)
```

To use the rule for a single program, you'd put something like this in your *Imakefile*:

```
BPTLIBS = -lm -ltermcap
BuildProgram(myprog,myprog.o)
```

Now suppose you want to build a second program *myprog2* that needs the DBM and *termlib* libraries. To make sure each program links correctly, BPTLIBS must name the libraries used by both programs:

```
BPTLIBS = -lm -ltermcap -ldbm -ltermlib
BuildProgram(myprog,myprog.o)
BuildProgram(myprog2,myprog2.o)
```

As the number of targets you build grows, so does the list of libraries named by BPTLIBS. That isn't a problem as far as *make* is concerned, because variables can have long definitions. However, the *Imakefile* becomes less informative because it isn't explicit anywhere which libraries are needed by which program. There is also the possibility of linker conflict: if two libraries happen to provide a function with the same name, you might not get the one you want. (This is not unlikely for the example just shown; the *termcap* and *termlib* libraries are quite similar in purpose.)

Alternatively, we can name libraries for a program by passing them as an argument to BuildProgram(). To do this, we must change its invocation sequence:

```
#define BuildProgram(prog,objs,libs)                       @@\
prog: objs                                                 @@\
     $(CC) -o prog objs libs
```

Now libraries can be given on a program-specific basis. That is, different libraries can be specified for each invocation of BuildProgram():

```
BuildProgram(myprog,myprog.o,-lm -ltermcap)
BuildProgram(myprog2,myprog2.o,-ldbm -ltermlib)
```

Passing Information to Rules

We happen to be discussing libraries here, but the issue we're confronting is really more general: how can information be transmitted into a rule? As we've just seen, there's more than one way to do it, each with its own characteristics.

If you specify information as the value of a *make* variable in the rule definition, the value of the variable applies *Makefile*-wide to all entries produced by invocations of the rule. If you pass the information as an argument to a rule when you invoke it, the value of the argument applies only to entries generated by that one instance of the rule.

With respect to specifying libraries, these two approaches have different implications. If you name libraries using a *make* variable that the program building rule refers to, all programs will be built using the same set of libraries. If you pass libraries as rule arguments, you have the flexibility to specify them independently for each program.

So, for libraries, which method is better? The choice depends on what you're trying to accomplish and which method's characteristics best match your goals. In the present case, `BuildProgram()` can be used to build multiple programs in the same *Imakefile*, and it's likely that different programs will use different libraries. Therefore, it's a better choice to pass libraries as a rule argument than to assign them to a *make* variable.

In general, *make* variables are not helpful for types of information that vary from target to target. When specifying such things as program name, object files, or libraries, rule arguments give you a degree of control that's difficult to achieve with a *make* variable.

On the other hand, *make* variables are a good choice when you want to specify values that should remain constant for multiple targets. For example, the preferred C compiler might vary from system to system or from project to project, but it's unlikely to vary from target to target within a project. It would just be a bother to the *Imakefile* writer if the compiler had to be named in every instance of program building rules. The name is best expressed as a parameter that can be set once in the configuration files using a *make* variable.

Libraries as Dependencies

In the definition of `BuildProgram()`, the `objs` parameter is used in the program's dependency list and in the link command that creates the executable. However, the program is just as dependent on its libraries as on its object files. Why not write the rule so it tells *make* about this dependency, too? That's easy enough to do, by naming the `libs` parameter in the dependency list:

```
#define BuildProgram(prog,objs,libs)                        @@\
prog: objs libs                                             @@\
    $(CC) -o prog objs libs
```

Unfortunately, this version of `BuildProgram()` doesn't work. If we invoke it like this:

```
BuildProgram(prog,prog.o,-lm)
```

we'll end up with this entry:

```
prog: prog.o -lm
    $(CC) -o prog prog.o -lm
```

–lm isn't a legal library specifier in a dependency list because *make* understands only filenames there. As discussed in Chapter 5, *Writing Imakefiles*, we need two kinds of library specifiers. One kind names the libraries in a form suitable for linking (using either the *–l* form or pathnames). The other kind names them in a form suitable for dependencies (as pathnames). Thus `BuildProgram()` should be written like this:

```
#define BuildProgram(prog,objs,linklibs,deplibs)           @@\
prog: objs deplibs                                          @@\
    $(CC) -o prog objs linklibs
```

Our rule now handles many more cases and is much more versatile than it was initially. `BuildProgram()` is sufficiently general that we can use it to build many kinds of programs:

```
/* program with no libraries */
BuildProgram(prog1,prog1.o,NullParameter,NullParameter)

/* program with local libraries (built within the project) */
BuildProgram(prog2,prog2.o,libmylib.a,libmylib.a)

/* program with system libraries */
BuildProgram(prog3,prog3.o,-lndbm -lm,NullParameter)

/* program with local and system libraries */
BuildProgram(prog4,prog4.o,libmylib.a -lndbm -lm,libmylib.a)
```

Implications of Parameterization

Changing the literal `cc` to the *make* variable `CC` in the definition of `Build-Program()` is a form of parameterization that changes the implementation of the rule. The modification requires cooperation from other configuration files (*Imake.tmpl* must provide a default value of `CC` in this case), but the changes can be made by the configuration file writer without involving *Imakefile* writers.

Adding `linklibs` and `deplibs` to the definition of `BuildProgram()` is a form of parameterization that changes the way you use the rule. This kind of modification is not so benign as parameterizing the C compiler, because it affects *Imakefile* writers: changing a rule's invocation sequence immediately breaks every *Imakefile* that uses the rule! People who write Imakefiles using our configuration files are not likely to appreciate our indiscretion.

It's best to think through the ways in which you'll want to use a rule as well as you can while you're designing it and before you begin using it in production. While you're still in the process of developing a rule, you have the liberty to change it as you like. Once you start using it, your options become more limited. If `BuildProgram()` was already a well known or widely used rule when we started thinking about adding library parameters, it probably would have been better to define a new rule than to break existing Imakefiles.

Special Linker Information

We still need a way to specify special linker information, such as loader prefix flags, compatibility libraries for deficient systems, and other miscellaneous low-level options that are sometimes necessary to make the linker behave itself. Before doing so, it's worthwhile to step back a little and reflect on what we've done so far. The original rule has been changed in two ways:

- Parameterization of tools used in the rule body (e.g., the C compiler) to allow them to be selected on a system- or project specific basis in the configuration files.

- Adding parameters to the rule calling sequence to allow information to be specified in rule invocations and substituted into the rule body on a target-specific basis.

Which of these two kinds of changes should we choose for specifying linker information? We could add parameters to the invocation sequence, but that's more appropriate for information that varies from program to program. Information needed to make the linker work properly tends to vary on a system or project basis. Therefore, instead of adding parameters to the calling sequence, we'll parameterize the rule body further:

```
#define BuildProgram(prog,objs,linklibs,deplibs)         @@\
prog: objs deplibs                                       @@\
    $(CC) -o prog objs $(LOADOPTS) linklibs $(LOADLIBS)
```

LOADOPTS and LOADLIBS can be defined appropriately in the configuration files as any extra flags and libraries the linker needs, respectively. The basic support for them goes in *Imake.tmpl*:

```
#ifndef LoadOpts
#define LoadOpts /* as nothing */
#endif
#ifndef LoadLibs
#define LoadLibs /* as nothing */
#endif

LOADOPTS = LoadOpts
LOADLIBS = LoadLibs
```

The default values for LOADOPTS and LOADLIBS assume no special flags or libraries are needed, but can be overridden in the vendor-specific file as necessary to adapt to particular systems. For instance, Mips RISC/os provides System V and BSD versions of system libraries, but fails to include *vfprintf()* in the BSD C library for releases of the OS prior to 4.50. That routine is found in either the *termcap* or *curses* libraries. We can use the vendor file *Mips.cf* to compensate for the deficiency like so:

```
#ifndef LoadLibs
#define LoadLibs -ltermcap
#endif
```

This works, but it's painting with a rather broad brush. We need the fix only when compiling under the BSD environment using early releases of the OS. Here's a more specific way to indicate when to use the library:

```
/*
 * vfprintf() is not in the BSD version of the C library in releases
 * of RISC/os prior to 4.50.  Link in -ltermcap to get it.
 */
#ifndef LoadLibs
#if !defined(SystemV) && !defined(SystemV4)
#if OSMajorVersion < 4 || (OSMajorVersion == 4 && OSMinorVersion < 50)
#define LoadLibs -ltermcap
#endif
#endif
#endif
```

If you were using *make* directly, a broken C library is the kind of shortcoming you typically would compensate for by editing the *Makefile*. That's ugly because you have to think about the machine-dependency of whether extra libraries need to be linked into a program that calls *vfprintf()*.

With *imake* you don't concern yourself about the problem: it's handled in the vendor file and the solution is propagated into the *Makefile* automatically. The machine-independence of the *Imakefile* is retained, and the burden on the programmer is lessened. The person who writes *Mips.cf* has to know about the problem with the C library, of course, but nobody else using the configuration files needs to. In effect, *Mips.cf* fixes a bug, silently. Programmers need not be aware of the special case the vendor file compensates for, and programs that use *vfprintf()* build correctly.

Making the Rule Work Harder

At this point, BuildProgram() is a reasonably capable rule. On a system- or project-wide basis, we can choose the C compiler and be flexible about special options needed at link time by providing that information in the configuration files. On a per-invocation basis, BuildProgram() allows us to specify the object files and libraries needed to produce the final executable.

The primary purpose of BuildProgram() is to build programs. That has now been accomplished, but we can flesh out the rule a bit to do more for us. How much? That depends on how all-encompassing we want the rule to be. For our discussion, we'll extend BuildProgram() to generate entries for clean, all, and lint targets.

The clean Target

BuildProgram() builds a program, so it might as well help us clean up afterward too, by generating a clean entry. (Logically, after you build your program, you'd install it, but we'll discuss installation rules later in their own section.) In order to avoid writing the name of the file-removing program literally into the rule, parameterization support is needed in the template *Imake.tmpl*:*

```
#ifndef RmCmd
#define RmCmd rm -f
#endif

RM = RmCmd
```

As usual, the default parameter value can be overridden in the vendor file by providing a different definition of RmCmd.

We must also consider what it is that should be "cleaned." For programs, this generally means removing the final executable image and the *.o* files created from its source files. The last section of *Imake.tmpl* automatically

---

*You can use the RmCmd and RM that are already present in the DP *Imake.tmpl* file.

provides a default `clean` entry that removes *.o* files, so the entry generated by `BuildProgram()` need only remove the final executable:

```
#define BuildProgram(prog,objs,linklibs,deplibs)          @@\
prog: objs deplibs                                        @@\
     $(CC) -o prog objs $(LOADOPTS) linklibs $(LOADLIBS)  @@\
clean::                                                   @@\
     $(RM) prog
```

The `clean` entry is written with a double colon instead of a single colon, because the `clean` target name might be associated with multiple entries (one for each invocation of `BuildProgram()` in the *Imakefile* and one for the default `clean` entry provided by *Imake.tmpl*). The double colon ensures that *make* generates and executes an RM command for each `clean` entry, instead of quitting with "inconsistent entry," "target conflict," or "too many rules for target" errors. Thus, we can remove debris for every program built by the *Makefile* by saying:

```
% make clean
```

Note that the `clean` entry is written at the end of the definition of `Build-Program()`. If you put it at the beginning, `clean` becomes the default target for your *Makefile*, and *make* with no arguments doesn't build your program, as you'd normally want—it removes it!

The result of adding a `clean` entry to `BuildProgram()` is a more functional *Makefile* with no change to the *Imakefile*. We can take advantage of the modified rule simply by rebuilding the *Makefile*. That beats editing Makefiles manually to add `clean` entries.

Since a `clean` entry is a generally useful thing, it's worthwhile to put one in other target-building rules we write, too. But let's think ahead a little bit. The path we're now traveling is to write the entry literally into the rule definition. If we do this for each rule that generates a `clean` entry, we might have problems later. Suppose we decide to change the form of our `clean` entries; having written them literally into rule definitions, we'd have to edit them all individually.

We can improve our rules and solve this problem with a level of indirection, that is, by defining another rule and invoking it to generate the `clean` entry. `CleanTarget()` is a reasonable name for the rule, but a rule with that name already exists in the rules file and has a different purpose (it generates the generic `clean` entry). We'll call our new rule `StuffTo-Clean()` instead. It looks like this:

```
#define StuffToClean(stuff)                                    @@\
clean::                                                        @@\
    $(RM) stuff
```

It's easy to revise `BuildProgram()` to use `StuffToClean()`:

```
#define BuildProgram(prog,objs,linklibs,deplibs)              @@\
prog: objs deplibs                    .                       @@\
    $(CC) -o prog objs $(LOADOPTS) linklibs $(LOADLIBS)       @@\
StuffToClean(prog)
```

By using `StuffToClean()`, we can make changes to or fix bugs in `clean` entries simply by changing the definition of `StuffToClean()`—a single modification. It's unnecessary to change every rule that uses it.

This flexibility can help you achieve portability more easily. Suppose you find that `StuffToClean()` doesn't work on a particular platform (this isn't likely to happen for such a simple rule, but humor me for this example). You can provide a working version of `StuffToClean()` in the vendor file for that platform. By doing so, you fix `BuildProgram()` and any other rules that invoke `StuffToClean()`. If you had written `clean` entries literally into those rules, you'd have to redefine every one of them in the vendor file.

Another reason to write the file-removal entry as a separate rule is that we can invoke it on its own to easily generate additional `clean` entries. Suppose you have an *Imakefile* into which you've written a `test` entry that runs a program to generate some test output:

```
BuildProgram(myprog,myprog.o,NullParameter,NullParameter)

test:: myprog
    myprog > myprog.out
```

`StuffToClean()` is useful for removing any kind of debris, not just executables, so it can help you clean up the test output. Just add it to your *Imakefile*:

```
BuildProgram(myprog,myprog.o,NullParameter,NullParameter)

test:: myprog
    myprog > myprog.out

StuffToClean(myprog.out)
```

The all Target

If an *Imakefile* contains a single invocation of `BuildProgram()`, the *Makefile* will contain an entry to build the program and a `clean` entry to clean it up. Since the program building entry is first, it's the default target and *make* with no arguments builds it. If the *Imakefile* contains several invocations of `BuildProgram()`, the *Makefile* will contain several program building entries and several `clean` entries. Now what's the default target? It's still the program building entry for the first program, so if we say:

```
% make
```

only the first program is built. Not very useful.

Neither is this:

```
% make all
make: Fatal error: Don't know how to make target "all"
```

The error occurs because there's no `all` target in the *Imakefile*.

make all should certainly build all the programs, and if we can just say *make* with no arguments to cause the same thing to happen, so much the better. But that's not what happens, which is troublesome:

* `BuildProgram()` builds Makefiles that do not behave the way we'd expect and therefore surprise the user.
* `BuildProgram()` builds Makefiles that are hard to use. To build all the targets, each one must be named explicitly on the command line.

We could "fix" the problem by writing an `all` entry at the top of our *Imakefile*:

```
all:: program1 program2 program3 ...
```

This indeed causes *make* or *make all* to build all the programs, but we have to change the `all` entry every time we add or delete an invocation of `BuildProgram()` from the *Imakefile*. That's a poor solution—we're forcing the *Imakefile* writer to work around problems that really should be handled in the configuration files.

An alternative that involves no *Imakefile* editing is to modify `Build-Program()` to produce an `all` entry. First we define a rule `All-Target()` to generate the entry:*

```
#define AllTarget(target)                                        @@\
all:: target
```

Then we invoke `AllTarget()` from within `BuildProgram()`:

```
#define BuildProgram(prog,objs,linklibs,deplibs)                 @@\
AllTarget(prog)                                                  @@\
prog: objs deplibs                                               @@\
     $(CC) -o prog objs $(LOADOPTS) linklibs $(LOADLIBS)         @@\
StuffToClean(prog)
```

Since the `all` target might be associated with multiple entries, `All-Target()` uses a double colon on the dependency line. Also, `All-Target()` appears at the beginning of `BuildProgram()`, so that an `all` entry appears first in the *Makefile*. Thus, `all` becomes the default target.

Once again, a simple change to `BuildProgram()` results in a more functional *Makefile* without changing the *Imakefile*. The modification is minor but its effect is significant:

- Our Imakefiles produce Makefiles that don't surprise people who use them. `BuildProgram()` causes *make all* to behave as we'd normally expect (it builds all the programs).

- Our Imakefiles produce Makefiles that are easier to use. Since `all` is the default target, *make* with no arguments is shorthand for *make all*. (We can still build individual programs by naming them on the *make* command line, of course.)

The lint Target

Many programmers use *lint* to check their source files for problems, so let's consider how we might extend `BuildProgram()` to help us use it. We can guess that `BuildProgram()` should look something like this:

```
#define BuildProgram(prog,objs,linklibs,deplibs)                 @@\
AllTarget(prog)                                                  @@\
prog: objs deplibs                                               @@\
     $(CC) -o prog objs $(LOADOPTS) linklibs $(LOADLIBS)         @@\
StuffToClean(prog)                                               @@\
LintSources(arguments)
```

What arguments should we pass to `LintSources()`?

---

*You can use the `AllTarget()` that is already present in the DP *Imake.rules* file.

If `BuildProgramTarget()` generates a `lint` target entry for us, then the command:

```
% make lint
```

should generate one *lint* command for each program built by the *Makefile*. Each command passes the source files for one program to *lint*. (This contrasts with *makedepend*, to which you pass all sources for all programs in the *Makefile* simultaneously.) For example, if we have two programs, *prog1* and *prog2*, this is what should happen:

```
% make lint
lint lint-flags prog1-sources
lint lint-flags prog2-sources
```

Unfortunately, *lint* needs to know the set of source files used to build a program, but that information isn't available from within `Build-Program()` at present. If `LintSources()` is invoked from within `BuildProgram()`, the latter must be changed to accept the target program source list as one of its own parameters, otherwise it can't pass the list to `LintSources()`. This change makes `BuildProgram()` more complicated to invoke.

Another possibility to consider is whether `BuildProgram()` is really the correct place to generate a `lint` entry after all. We can invoke `Lint-Sources()` independently of `BuildProgram()` if we want. If we make that choice, we don't need to change the latter at all, although we do end up with longer Imakefiles.

I'll come down on the side of adding the parameter to `BuildProgram()` and not having to remember to invoke `LintSources()` explicitly:

```
#define BuildProgram(prog,srcs,objs,linklibs,deplibs)          @@\
AllTarget(prog)                                                @@\
prog: objs deplibs                                             @@\
        $(CC) -o prog objs $(LOADOPTS) linklibs $(LOADLIBS)    @@\
StuffToClean(prog)                                             @@\
LintSources(srcs)
```

`LintSources()` might look something like this:

```
#define LintSources(srcs)                                      @@\
lint::                                                         @@\
        $(LINT) $(LINTOPTS) srcs $(LINTLIBS)
```

A double colon is in order because the `lint` target can be associated with multiple entries. The rule uses three *make* variable parameters. LINT names the *lint* program itself. LINTOPTS specifies any flags needed to get *lint* to run properly. LINTLIBS names any special *lint* libraries needed for source checking that aren't in the default set of libraries. Each of these needs to be given appropriate defaults in *Imake.tmpl*:*

```
#ifndef LintCmd
#define LintCmd lint
#endif
#ifndef LintOpts
#if SystemV || SystemV4
#define LintOpts -bh
#else
#define LintOpts -axz
#endif
#endif
#ifndef LintLibs
#define LintLibs /* as nothing */
#endif

    LINT = LintCmd
LINTOPTS = LintOpts
LINTLIBS = LintLibs
```

Refining the Scope of a Target

If you issue the following command, the source for every program in the *Imakefile* is checked by *lint*:

```
% make lint
```

That's okay when you haven't checked anything yet. But suppose you've already run *lint* on your sources and cleaned up any problems it reports. If you make some further changes to the source for a single program, you'll want to re-*lint* only that program. It's certainly overkill to *lint* every other program again, too. Unfortunately, the "granularity" of the `lint` target is insufficient to provide single-program *lint* operations.

We can modify the `LintSources()` rule to handle that by telling it the name of the program being *lint*ed:

```
#define LintSources(prog,srcs)                          @@\
lint:: lint.prog                                        @@\
lint.prog:                                              @@\
    $(LINT) $(LINTOPTS) srcs $(LINTLIBS)
```

---

*You can use the LintCmd and LINT that are already present in the DP *Imake.tmpl* file. LintOpts and LINTOPTS are already present, too, but the definition of LintOpts is incorrect; replace it. LintLibs and LINTLIBS are not present; add them.

We also need to tell `BuildProgram()` to pass the program name to the instance of `LintSources()` it contains, since the latter rule's invocation sequence has changed:

```
#define BuildProgram(prog,srcs,objs,linklibs,deplibs)          @@\
AllTarget(prog)                                                @@\
prog: objs deplibs                                             @@\
    $(CC) -o prog objs $(LOADOPTS) linklibs $(LOADLIBS)        @@\
StuffToClean(prog)                                             @@\
LintSources(prog,srcs)
```

The change to `LintSources()` interposes another target into the rule so you can say:

`% make lint.`*program*

to *lint* an individual program. As before, you can still *lint* everything with:

`% make lint`

These changes give us the flexibility to apply *lint* very specifically. Again, we achieve a more effective *Makefile* with some thought about how to design rule macros.

Documenting Rules

When you write a rule, you should think about documenting it so people who don't know how to read rules can use it more easily. Here's a comment for `BuildProgram()`. It's longer than the rule, but it will be appreciated by the uninitiated:

```
/*
 * BuildProgram() generates entries to build, remove, and
 * lint a single program.  May be invoked multiple times
 * in the same Imakefile.
 *
 * Arguments:
 * prog        program name
 * srcs        program's source files
 * objs        program's object files
 * linklibs    libraries needed to link program
 * deplibs     libraries to check as dependencies
 *             (must be given as pathnames)
 *
 * Targets produced:
 * all         build prog (and all others in Imakefile)
 * prog        build prog only
 * clean       remove all programs in Imakefile
 * lint        lint all programs in Imakefile
 * lint.prog   lint prog only
 */
```

Building Libraries

Program libraries are useful as repositories of commonly used functions that we wish to share among multiple executables. To write a rule for a library, we need to know, at minimum, the list of object files and the library's name. We could refer to a library as, for example, *libxyz.a*, but it's easier to write *xyz* and let the rule create the full name for itself using the token-pasting macro Concat():

```
Concat(lib,xyz.a)
```

The rule should generate an entry that takes the list of object files, mashes them together to create the library, and (on systems supporting it) runs the library through *ranlib*.* For good measure, the rule can also generate all and clean entries:

```
#define BuildLibrary(name,objlist)                    @@\
AllTarget(Concat(lib,name.a))                          @@\
Concat(lib,name.a): objlist                            @@\
    $(RM) $@                                           @@\
    $(AR) $@ objlist                                   @@\
    RanLibrary($@)                                     @@\
StuffToClean(Concat(lib,name.a))
```

This definition is a lightly modified copy of the X11 rule Normal-LibraryTarget(). BuildLibrary() refers to the archiving program using the variable AR and uses the RanLibrary() rule to invoke the *ranlib* program if it's available. RanLibrary() looks like this:†

```
#if DoRanlibCmd
#define RanLibrary(args) $(RANLIB) args
#else
#define RanLibrary(args) /**/
#endif
```

DoRanlibCmd is YES if *ranlib* is available on your system, NO otherwise. RANLIB is the name of the *ranlib* program.

We need support for AR, RANLIB, and DoRanlibCmd. The default values of each can be specified in *Imake.tmpl*:‡

---

* *ranlib* creates a table of contents in the library so the linker can be more efficient.

†You can use the RanLibrary() that is already present in the DP *Imake.rules* file.

‡You can use the ArCmd, AR, RanlibCmd, RANLIB, and DoRanlibCmd symbols that are already present in the DP *Imake.tmpl* file.

```
#ifndef DoRanlibCmd
#if SystemV || SystemV4
#define DoRanlibCmd NO
#else
#define DoRanlibCmd YES
#endif
#endif

#ifndef ArCmd
#define ArCmd ar cq
#endif

#ifndef RanlibCmd
#define RanlibCmd ranlib
#endif
        AR = ArCmd
#if DoRanlibCmd
    RANLIB = RanlibCmd
#endif
```

These values can be overridden in the vendor file. In particular, DoRan-libCmd should be defined as YES on any system that supports *ranlib*.

Using BuildLibrary(), an *Imakefile* to build *libxyz.a* from files *a.c, b.c,* and *c.c* might look like this:

```
SRCS = a.c b.c c.c
OBJS = a.o b.o c.o

BuildLibrary(xyz,$(OBJS))

DependTarget()
```

Installation Rules

We have not yet thought about how to install anything—a grievous over-sight, since unless we install our software, it's of dubious utility. This section describes how to write installation rules, as well as the parameter macro and variable support that undergirds them.

Several parameter and rule names used in this section are used in the DP files already. In most cases, the existing versions conflict with those we create here. To eliminate these conflicts in one fell swoop, remove the Inst*Flags macros, the INST*FLAGS variables, and all the installation rules except InstallSubdirs(), InstallManSubdirs(), the InstallMultipleDest*() rules, and InstallMultiple().*

---

*The *DP.tar.Z* distribution listed in Appendix A, *Obtaining Configuration Software*, includes a patch you can use to remove existing installation support.

For installing files, the obvious choice is the *install* program. However, there are System V and BSD variants of *install*, and they behave quite differently. For instance, the BSD variant interprets −*s* as "strip the installed image," whereas for the System V variant −*s* means "operate in silent mode."

The X11 configuration files handle this problem by assuming a BSD *install* is available and providing a compatibility script *bsdinst* for systems without one. *bsdinst* emulates BSD *install* behavior so we don't have to cope with the differences between the way the BSD and System V versions of *install* work.

I'm going to assume a BSD *install* is available as well. Installing is such a common operation that if you don't have a BSD *install*, you should install *bsdinst* in a public directory so it can be assumed available just like *imake*, *makedepend*, and *mkdirhier*. See Appendix B, *Installing Configuration Software*, if you need *bsdinst* and don't have it.

We can select the appropriate default value of the INSTALL parameter in *Imake.tmpl* based on what we know about the system type:*

```
#ifndef InstallCmd
#if SystemV || SystemV4
#define InstallCmd bsdinst
#else
#define InstallCmd install
#endif
#endif
INSTALL = InstallCmd
```

If this default doesn't happen to be correct for your system, override it in the vendor file (e.g., if you have a System V machine, but also have a BSD *install* available).

The simplest useful *install* command looks like this and installs the given file into the given directory:

```
% install -c file dir
```

The −*c* (copy) option is used because without it *install* removes the original file.†

---

*You can use the InstallCmd and INSTALL that are already present in the DP *Imake.tmpl* file.

†It takes up more room to keep the original files around, but if a multiple directory installation operation fails in the middle, you don't have to rebuild everything up to that point.

The command can be instantiated in a rule this way:

```
#define InstallTarget(file,dir)                    @@\
install:: file                                     @@\
    $(INSTALL) -c file dir
```

Unfortunately, if `dir` doesn't exist, we might run into a problem. Suppose you invoke the rule as:

```
InstallTarget(xyz,/usr/lib/abc)
```

This indicates you want *xyz* installed as */usr/lib/abc/xyz*. The problem is that if */usr/lib* exists and */usr/lib/abc* doesn't, some versions of *install* will install *xyz* as */usr/lib/abc*, i.e., as the file *abc* in the directory */usr/lib*.

Therefore, it's best to make sure the installation directory exists first. We can do the same thing the X11 installation rules do, which is to invoke another rule `MakeDir()` to create the directory if it's missing:*

```
/* if [ -d ] or [ ! -d ] causes make to fail, define this as - */
#define DirFailPrefix
#define MakeDir(dir) DirFailPrefix@if [ -d dir ]; then set +x; \    @@\
    else (set -x; $(MKDIRHIER) dir); fi
```

Define `DirFailPrefix` as "–" in your vendor file if your system doesn't perform the `-d` test properly.

Now we can rewrite `InstallTarget()` to use `MakeDir()`:

```
#define InstallTarget(file,dir)                    @@\
install:: file                                     @@\
    MakeDir(dir)                                    @@\
        $(INSTALL) -c file dir
```

Note that the body of `MakeDir()` begins on the first line of the rule definition, and that we invoke it indented in the body of another rule, rather than left-justified. These are exceptions to the usual way rules are defined and used. In general, you begin the body of a rule on the `#define` line when the purpose of the rule is to generate commands in the command section of a target entry and not to generate an entire entry.

`InstallTarget()` could use some improvement, given that it doesn't allow us to specify user and group ownership, file mode, or whether to

---

*You can use the `DirFailPrefix` and `MakeDir()` that are already present in the DP *Imake.rules* file.

strip the installed image. The way we indicate these things boils down to a choice between the usual two alternatives:

- If we specify a flag by means of a *make* variable used in the rule body, the flag applies to all targets installed by the rule. This is a good choice if we want the flag to be the same for every target we install.

- If we specify a flag by means of an argument passed to the rule when we invoke it, we can vary the flag on a per-target basis. This is a good choice if the flag differs for different targets.

The most general approach is to write a rule that supplies no flags itself but expects them all to be passed as arguments when the rule is invoked:

```
#define InstallTarget(file,dir,flags)              @@\
install:: file                                     @@\
    MakeDir(dir)                                    @@\
    $(INSTALL) -c flags file dir
```

You might use the rule like this:

```
InstallTarget(prog,$(BINDIR),-s -m 0755)
InstallTarget(prog.help,$(USRLIBDIR),-m 0444)
InstallTarget(progd,$(ETCDIR),-s -m 4755 -o root)
```

This is the most flexible way to write an installation rule because it affords the caller complete control over the installation flags. Of course, the caller also has the full burden of specifying them, so that's a mixed blessing.

We usually install files according to certain patterns, so in most cases we can make some good guesses about the proper flags for a particular type of target. Therefore, it makes sense to define other higher-level "convenience" rules that invoke `InstallTarget()` but provide best-guess flags according to the target type. Then we'd have a selection of rules to choose from to get the flags we want without specifying them all ourselves.

For instance, a rule to install binary executables is likely to install them with mode 0755 and to strip the image. Installed manual pages need to be readable by everybody, but there's no need for them to be writable; the appropriate mode is 0444. We can write rules `InstallProgram()` and `InstallManPage()` to handle these cases:

```
#define InstallProgram(file,dir)                   @@\
InstallTarget(file,dir,-s -m 0755)
```

```
#define InstallManPage(file,dir)                   @@\
InstallTarget(file,dir,-m 0444)
```

However, it's better not to write installation options literally into rules. For instance, if we don't want to strip installed programs, a literal *–s* in the rule is inconvenient. To change it, we'd have to put an override rule in *site.def.*

If instead we use a variable `INSTSTRIP`, we can define it either as *–s* or as the empty value, which gives us an easy way to modify the behavior of `InstallProgram()` without changing the rule itself.

Specifying installation options using parameters gives us a consistent symbolic means of referring to them in rules and in Imakefiles, and allows us to change them more easily in the configuration files (and therefore project-wide in Makefiles). Table 11–1 shows some installation parameters I find useful; your own set may be larger or smaller, depending on your requirements.

Table 11-1: A Set of Installation Parameters

Installation Parameters	Description
INSTSTRIP	Flag for stripping executable binaries
INSTPROGMODE	Mode for executable binaries
INSTSCRIPTMODE	Mode for executable scripts
INSTLIBMODE	Mode for libraries
INSTDATMODE	Mode for data (read-only) files
INSTMANMODE	Mode for manual pages
INSTOWNER	Owner of installed files
INSTGROUP	Group of installed files

We can parameterize the strip flag as follows:

```
#ifndef InstStrip
#define InstStrip -s
#endif
INSTSTRIP = InstStrip
```

This way, installed binary images are stripped by default, which uses less disk space. If you don't want them stripped (e.g., for debugging), you simply give `InstStrip` an empty value in *site.def*:

```
#ifndef InstStrip
#define InstStrip /**/
#endif
```

For most of the other parameters, reasonable defaults are easy to choose:

```
#ifndef InstProgMode
#define InstProgMode -m 0755
#endif
#ifndef InstScriptMode
#define InstScriptMode -m 0755
#endif
```

```
#ifndef InstLibMode
#define InstLibMode -m 0444
#endif
#ifndef InstDatMode
#define InstDatMode -m 0444
#endif
#ifndef InstManMode
#define InstManMode -m 0444
#endif
   INSTPROGMODE = InstProgMode
 INSTSCRIPTMODE = InstScriptMode
    INSTLIBMODE = InstLibMode
    INSTDATMODE = InstDatMode
    INSTMANMODE = InstManMode
```

The owner and group flags are different; we leave them empty, because there isn't any good way to guess defaults:

```
#ifndef InstOwner
#define InstOwner /* as nothing */
#endif
#ifndef InstGroup
#define InstGroup /* as nothing */
#endif
INSTOWNER = InstOwner
INSTGROUP = InstGroup
```

You can override `InstOwner` and `InstGroup` in the vendor or site file if you don't want targets installed using whatever default user and group ID your *install* program uses.

Now that we have our individual installation flags parameterized, we can define some additional parameters that give us useful combinations of flags:

```
 INSTPROGFLAGS = $(INSTOWNER) $(INSTGROUP) $(INSTSTRIP) $(INSTPROGMODE)
INSTSCRIPTFLAGS = $(INSTOWNER) $(INSTGROUP) $(INSTSCRIPTMODE)
   INSTLIBFLAGS = $(INSTOWNER) $(INSTGROUP) $(INSTLIBMODE)
   INSTDATFLAGS = $(INSTOWNER) $(INSTGROUP) $(INSTDATMODE)
   INSTMANFLAGS = $(INSTOWNER) $(INSTGROUP) $(INSTMANMODE)
```

We can rewrite the convenience rules in terms of these combination flag parameters to eliminate references to literal flags:

```
#define InstallManPage(file,dir)                      @@\
InstallTarget(file,dir,$(INSTMANFLAGS))

#define InstallProgram(file,dir)                      @@\
InstallTarget(file,dir,$(INSTPROGFLAGS))
```

Other convenience rules might look like this:

```
#define InstallScript(file,dir)                         @@\
InstallTarget(file,dir,$(INSTSCRIPTFLAGS))

#define InstallData(file,dir)                           @@\
InstallTarget(file,dir,$(INSTDATFLAGS))
```

Library installation presents a special problem because we not only need to install the library image, but to run *ranlib* again if it's available:

```
#define InstallLibrary(name,dir)                        @@\
InstallTarget(Concat(lib,name.a),dir,$(INSTLIBFLAGS))   @@\
install:: Concat(lib,name.a)                            @@\
    RanLibrary(Concat(dir/lib,name.a))
```

For targets that require special treatment, bypass the convenience rules and invoke `InstallTarget()` directly. For instance, to install a setuid-*root* program, the owner and mode must be indicated specially:

```
InstallTarget(file,dir,-o root $(INSTGROUP) $(INSTSTRIP) -m 04755)
```

Should BuildProgram( ) Generate an install Target?

We could make `BuildProgram()` more comprehensive by changing it to invoke an installation rule. Do we want to do this, or invoke the installation rule separately?

If we change `BuildProgram()` to install the program, we need either to add installation-related parameters to its invocation sequence or assume defaults for them. `BuildProgram()` already has several parameters; it's unclear that adding more is a good idea. If instead we assume default installation parameters, we'll actually limit the usefulness of `Build-Program()`. For example, if we assume an installation mode of 0755, the rule can't be used with setuid programs.

Neither alternative warrants changing `BuildProgram()`; it's best to leave it alone and invoke the appropriate installation rule separately. If you expect to install several programs exactly the same way, you can always define another rule that invokes `BuildProgram()` as well as an installation rule:

```
#define BuildAndInstallProgram(prog,srcs,objs,linklibs,deplibs) @@\
BuildProgram(prog,srcs,objs,linklibs,deplibs)                   @@\
InstallProgram(prog,$(BINDIR))
```

Refining the Scope of Installation Rules

If you say:

```
% make install
```

all targets in the *Makefile* are installed. That's okay for the initial installation because you want to install everything. But if you rebuild a single target later, do you want to install everything else along with it? No. We encountered this same kind of problem earlier with `LintSources()`, where *make lint* caused all programs in the *Makefile* to be run though *lint*, even if we wanted only to *lint* a single program.

We handled that difficulty by revising `LintSources()` to allow single-target `lint` granularity. We can do the same thing to `install` rules to allow installing at the individual target level without losing the general install-everything-in-sight result of *make install*. When you see the following in an installation rule:

```
install:: target                                         @@\
```

change it to this:

```
install:: install.target                                 @@\
install.target: target                                   @@\
```

After regenerating the *Makefile*, we can say either of the following:

```
% make install.program        Install program only
% make install                Install everything
```

In this chapter:
- *Describing Project Layout*
- *Specifying Library Names*
- *Handling Newly Discovered Nonportabilities*
- *Conditionals in Imakefiles*
- *Configuring Source Files*
- *Using make Suffix Rules*
- *Shell Programming in Rules*
- *Writing a World Target*

12

Configuration Problems and Solutions

> *You know how hard it is to get hammers these days.*
>
> —Betty MacDonald,
> *Mrs. Piggle-Wiggle*

In Chapter 10, *Introduction to Configuration File Writing*, and Chapter 11, *Writing Rule Macros*, we discuss general configuration file writing techniques in the context of modifying the starter project (SP) files to create a "product," i.e., the demonstration project (DP) files.

This chapter takes a different approach. Instead of focusing on a particular set of configuration files, several miscellaneous configuration problems are discussed, to show how *imake* helps you solve them. Because this is a problem-oriented rather than product-oriented approach, the discussion is by necessity something of a collection of odds and ends.

Describing Project Layout

In a multiple directory project it's common for an *Imakefile* in one directory to refer to files or directories located elsewhere in the project tree. Figure 12–1 shows a simple project with a root directory and subdirectories for header files, library source files, and application source files. In the context of program development, the *Imakefile* in the *lib* directory would likely refer to the *include* header file directory, and the *Imakefile* in the *app* directory would likely refer to both the *include* and *lib* directories.

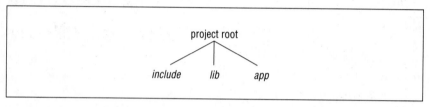

Figure 12-1: Simple project tree

One way of referring to directories is to write out pathnames literally in your Imakefiles. You can use either relative or absolute paths. If you use relative paths, the path to a given directory varies depending on your location within the project tree. Table 12–1 illustrates this variation, showing how paths to the header file and library directories change by location within the project. Because of this variation in pathnames, you have to be careful to write them correctly each time you use them. Moreover, if you rearrange the project layout, as sometimes occurs during the development process, you have to revise all the references to reflect the changes.

Table 12-1: Directory Locations Expressed Using Relative Pathnames

From . . .	Path to *include*	Path to *lib*
project root	./include	./lib
lib	../include	.
app	../include	../lib

You can write the directory references as absolute pathnames instead, but then you get pathname variation from machine to machine. If the project is installed at */usr/src/proj* on one machine and */usr/local/src/proj* on another, all the paths must be edited when the project is moved from one machine to the other.

imake allows you to use symbolic references and to propagate symbol values throughout your project, so you might as well take advantage of those capabilities. As an alternative to writing out directory references literally, we can define parameters and refer to those instead. It's most convenient to specify project directory parameters in terms of TOP, the project root location. Thus, for the header file and library directories, you'd define parameters in *Project.tmpl* like this:

```
#ifndef IncludeSrc
#define IncludeSrc $(TOP)/include
#endif
#ifndef LibSrc
#define LibSrc $(TOP)/lib
#endif
INCLUDESRC = IncludeSrc
    LIBSRC = LibSrc
```

This has two distinct advantages over literal paths:

* TOP specifies the location of the top of the project tree. *imake* ensures that TOP is correct no matter what the current directory is, so parameters defined relative to TOP (such as INCLUDESRC and LIBSRC) are automatically defined correctly in every *Makefile*. This gives you a consistent way of referring to the header file and library directories (compare Tables 12–1 and 12–2).

* Parameters make it easy to change directory references, e.g., to reconfigure your project after rearranging the source tree. Simply modify the parameter values in the configuration files to reflect layout changes, and rebuild your Makefiles to propagate the new values thoughout the project.

Table 12-2: Directory Locations Expressed Using Parameters

From . . .	Path to *include*	Path to *lib*
project root	$(INCLUDESRC)	$(LIBSRC)
lib	$(INCLUDESRC)	$(LIBSRC)
app	$(INCLUDESRC)	$(LIBSRC)

Specifying Library Names

Suppose you've written a library of useful functions that you build as *lib-useful.a* in the *lib* directory of your project. You could refer to this library in the project's Imakefiles by writing out the pathname literally, but that is subject to the problems just discussed in the previous section: the path to the library directory varies by location within the project (or from machine to machine), and the path references must be revised if you rearrange the project. An additional consideration is that if the library is really so wonderful, you'll probably decide to use it in other projects, too. If you do, you might split it out into a separate project and install it as a system library for general use. When you do that, however, references to the library from within the original project change (from pathname form to *–luseful*) and must be revised.

We can solve the problem using parameters instead of literal values. When *libuseful.a* is built within your project, define parameters for it in *Project.tmpl* like this:

```
#ifndef UsefulLib
#define UsefulLib $(TOP)/lib/libuseful.a
#endif
#ifndef DepUsefulLib
#define DepUsefulLib $(TOP)/lib/libuseful.a
#endif
    USEFULLIB = UsefulLib
DEPUSEFULLIB = DepUsefulLib
```

Then you refer to the library in your project's Imakefiles using these parameters. For example:

```
BuildProgram(prog,$(SRCS),$(OBJS),$(USEFULLIB),$(DEPUSEFULLIB))
```

If you split out *libuseful.a* into its own project and make it a system library later, the only change you need to make to the original project is to change the values of UsefulLib and DepUsefulLib in the configuration files:

```
#ifndef UsefulLib
#define UsefulLib -luseful
#endif
#ifndef DepUsefulLib
#define DepUsefulLib /**/
#endif
    USEFULLIB = UsefulLib
DEPUSEFULLIB = DepUsefulLib
```

No other changes are needed. You still refer to the library the same way in the Imakefiles ($(USEFULLIB), $(DEPUSEFULLIB)), even though the library now comes from a different source. This illustrates how parameters promote nomenclatural stability: the underlying details of library specification are buried in the configuration files so you can write Imakefiles in a consistent way.

Handling Newly Discovered Nonportabilities

Suppose you've written a project containing programs that create temporary files. You've ported the project to four different systems. On all of them */tmp* is the preferred temporary file directory, so you've done the expedient thing and written "/tmp" into your programs. Then you port the project to a fifth system and find that the temporary file directory is */var/tmp*. You've discovered a nonportability.

You might try to view this fly in the ointment as an opportunity to improve your code rather than as an annoyance, but regardless of the nature of your disposition, the system variation you've identified needs to be parameterized. TMPDIR will do for a parameter name, and we can set its value in *Project.tmpl* using the macro TmpDir.

What should the default value be? Here we use our porting experience to make a decision. The temporary file directory was the same on all systems except the most recent, so the default should be the value we've been using all along:

```
#ifndef TmpDir
#define TmpDir /tmp
#endif

TMPDIR = TmpDir
```

The default needs only to be overridden (as */var/tmp*) in the vendor file associated with the system we've most recently ported to. No overriding is necessary in the four original vendor files.

Each time you discover you've written a nonportable construct, fix it and add the discovery to your repertoire of experience. If possible, codify your knowledge by adding a mechanism to ensure portability to your configuration files (in the present case, we added the parameter TMPDIR). Instantiating your knowledge reduces your work in the future by helping to automate or formalize a configuration task. It also helps others since the nonportability is made explicit in your configuration files (and so is the solution). This gives others who use and/or study your files the benefit of your experience and increases their awareness of portability issues that may affect their own projects.

Of course, we must still fix the source code of the programs that referred directly to */tmp*, so we need a mechanism to transmit the value of TMPDIR to the programs that need it. That's a topic in its own right, and is discussed in the section "Configuring Source Files."

Conditionals in Imakefiles

It's a given that you'll use *cpp* conditionals in your configuration files, but less widely appreciated that conditionals can be used in Imakefiles, too. I'll show three applications of this fact:

- Selecting targets to build
- Selecting files or directories to process
- Selecting flags for commands

Selecting Targets to Build

You can use *cpp* conditionals in an *Imakefile* to select which programs to build. Suppose you have a project for a client-server application, and you want to build different programs depending on whether the machine is a client machine and/or server machine. If the macros ClientHost and ServerHost are defined as YES or NO, you can write the *Imakefile* like this:

```
#if ClientHost
CSRCS = client.c
COBJS = client.o
BuildProgram(client,$(CSRCS),$(COBJS),NullParameter,NullParameter)
#endif

#if ServerHost
SSRCS = server.c
SOBJS = server.o
BuildProgram(server,$(SSRCS),$(SOBJS),NullParameter,NullParameter)
#endif

 SRCS = $(CSRCS) $(SSRCS)
DependTarget()
```

The defaults for ClientHost and ServerHost can be placed in *Project.tmpl* and overidden appropriately on a per-host basis in *site.def.*

Note that if both `ClientHost` and `ServerHost` are `NO`, nothing is built. If you consider that an error, you can write the following at the beginning of the *Imakefile*:

```
#if !ClientHost && !ServerHost
all::
      @echo "Neither a client nor a server be?"
      @echo "Please define ClientHost and/or ServerHost as YES."
#endif
```

If both symbols are `NO` when the *Makefile* is generated, *make* alerts you to the problem at build time.

Selecting Files or Directories to Process

imake is designed to allow you to write machine-independent target description files, but sometimes you really do need to know what kind of machine you're running on. In such cases, it's helpful to exploit *imake*'s knowledge about your system.

Suppose you're writing a project that shares some of its source among all platforms on which the project is built, but also contains a significant amount of platform-dependent source. You can put the machine-independent source in one subdirectory, *mi*, and partition the machine-dependent source for each platform into separate subdirectories.

When you build the project, the code in *mi* is used on all platforms, so that directory should always be processed. But only one of the machine-dependent directories should be processed. How do you tell which one? *imake* helps us here. The system type is determined by the vendor blocks in the configuration files when *imake* runs, and each vendor block defines a unique architecture symbol like `UltrixArchitecture` or `Sun-Architecture`. You can test those symbols using conditionals in the *Imakefile* to select the proper machine-dependent directory.

If you've ported the project to Sun, HP, SGI, and DEC machines, for example, you can write the *Imakefile* as shown in Figure 12–2. The figure illustrates how the *Imakefile* selects the proper parts of the project tree for processing. *mi* is always included in the value of `SUBDIRS`, regardless of architecture. The directory named by `MD_DIR` is machine-dependent; the architecture symbols are used to determine its value. This organization helps you modularize your project to keep its complexity manageable: to port the program to a new system, add a new directory containing code for that system and add a new selector block to the project root *Imakefile*.

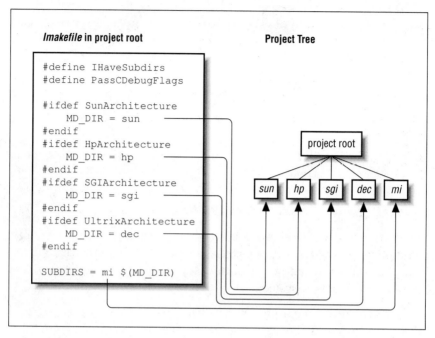

Imakefile in project root

```
#define IHaveSubdirs
#define PassCDebugFlags

#ifdef SunArchitecture
    MD_DIR = sun
#endif
#ifdef HpArchitecture
    MD_DIR = hp
#endif
#ifdef SGIArchitecture
    MD_DIR = sgi
#endif
#ifdef UltrixArchitecture
    MD_DIR = dec
#endif

SUBDIRS = mi $(MD_DIR)
```

Project Tree

Figure 12-2: Directory-selecting Imakefile

If the amount of machine-dependent code is not extensive, it may make more sense to keep it all in a single directory and select individual files rather than directories. Suppose you're writing a program that processes CPU-load information. This involves yanking CPU-time information out of the running kernel. Unfortunately, the system interface to get that information varies widely among versions of UNIX and is highly machine-dependent. Table 12–3 shows some of the differences for three types of systems.

Table 12-3: System CPU-time Interface Differences

	Ultrix	**RISC/os**	**SunOS 4.xx**
UNIX image name	*/vmunix*	*/unix*	not needed
CPU-time symbol name	*_cp_time*	*sysinfo*	*_cp_time*
function to read namelist	*nlist()*	*nlist()*	*kvm_nlist()*
function to read CPU time	*read()*	*read()*	*kvm_read()*
number of CPU states	4	5	4
link library	none	*–lmld*	*–lkvm*

All these differences add up to a fun time when you're trying to write a portable program. You could tear your hair out and give up; decide to scrap the goal of portability and make your program run on a single kind of machine; or litter its source code with an ugly rat's nest of #ifdef's that test for machine type. Or you can let *imake* help you determine the machine type, again by making use of the architecture symbols defined in the configuration files.

One way to attack the difficulty is to wedge a level of abstraction between the system calls and the main body of your program. Instead of writing your main program to know about different system interfaces, you define specifications for a standard interface. For example, you can declare that the "CPU-load interface" consists of two functions: InitCPULoad(), to do any system-specific initialization necessary, and GetCPULoad(), to return the current CPU load.

Then you write a machine-dependent source file implementing this standard interface for each system you support. Each file performs all the gyrations necessary to wrest the desired information from one particular system type and maps it onto a form suitable for the standard interface.

In the *Imakefile*, use the architecture indicator symbols defined by the vendor blocks in the configuration files to select the machine-dependent file. The *Imakefile* below generates a *Makefile* that compiles the program from *main.c* and the appropriate machine-dependent file, and links in any special library needed:

```
#ifdef SunArchitecture
    CPU_SRC = cpu-sun.c
    CPU_OBJ = cpu-sun.o
    CPU_LIB = -lkvm
#endif
#if defined(MipsBsdArchitecture) || defined(MipsSysvArchitecture)
    CPU_SRC = cpu-mips.c
    CPU_OBJ = cpu-mips.o
    CPU_LIB = -lmld
#endif
#ifdef UltrixArchitecture
    CPU_SRC = cpu-ultrix.c
    CPU_OBJ = cpu-ultrix.o
    CPU_LIB =
#endif
        SRCS = main.c $(CPU_SRC)
        OBJS = main.o $(CPU_OBJ)
BuildProgram(prog,$(SRCS),$(OBJS),$(CPU_LIB),NullParameter)
```

Selecting Flags For Commands

The X11, SP, and DP files each allow you to pass special definitions to compile commands in a given directory by assigning a value to DEFINES in the *Imakefile*.

You can set DEFINES unconditionally:

```
DEFINES = -Dflag
```

Or, if you need to pass a flag only when some condition holds, you can make the assignment conditional:

```
#if condition
    DEFINES = -Dflag
#endif
```

When you have several conditional flags, setting DEFINES becomes trickier. Suppose you have two conditional flags. You could set DEFINES by testing each combination of conditions:

```
#if condition_1
#  if condition_2
    DEFINES = -Dflag_1 -Dflag_2
#  else
    DEFINES = -Dflag_1
#  endif
#else
#  if condition_2
    DEFINES = -Dflag_2
#  else
    DEFINES =
#  endif
#endif
```

The trouble with this approach is that the number of tests grows exponentially as the number of conditions increases: for n conditions, the number of tests is 2^n, which quickly becomes unmanageable. For instance, the Kerberos V distribution has 19 such conditional flags. The number of tests needed to check every combination of conditions exceeds half a million.

A better way to attack the complexity that arises from multiple conditions is to test each one independently, record the result in an auxiliary *make* variable, and concatenate the results after all the tests are performed. Then the number of tests equals the number of conditions.

Suppose you have four conditional flags. To check every combination of conditions we'd need 16 tests. Instead we can do this to keep the number of tests at four:

```
#if condition_1
    AUXDEF_1 = -Dflag_1
#endif
#if condition_2
    AUXDEF_2 = -Dflag_2
#endif
#if condition_3
    AUXDEF_3 = -Dflag_3
#endif
#if condition_4
    AUXDEF_4 = -Dflag_4
#endif
        DEFINES = $(AUXDEF_1) $(AUXDEF_2) $(AUXDEF_3) $(AUXDEF_4)
```

Each `AUXDEF_n` variable records the result of a test. If condition n holds, the variable is set to `-Dflag_n`, otherwise it's empty.* Then `DEFINES` is set to the concatenation of the auxiliary variables. The Kerberos V distribution uses this technique for its 19 conditional flags to keep the number of tests at 19.

Configuring Source Files

imake characteristically generates Makefiles that contain values for each of your configuration parameters, represented by *make* variables. These variables are available at your fingertips for generating commands from within *Makefile* target entries. But sometimes you need the values of those variables in files other than a *Makefile*:

- A C program or shell script creates temporary files. How do the programs know where your system's temporary file directory is?

- A project installs a server program and a file that the server reads when it starts up. How does the server know where its startup file is?

- A help file needs to be edited to reflect local convention for the e-mail address to which help requests can be sent. How can that be done automatically?

- A program needs to know whether or not it can use shared memory. How can it tell?

---

*That is, the variable is not assigned any value and is therefore implicitly empty.

All these questions can be answered if we can find a way to get values of our configuration parameters into the source files we want to configure.

Let's say our files need to know the pathname of the system directory used for temporary files. We can define the parameter in *Project.tmpl*:

```
#ifndef TmpDir
#define TmpDir /tmp
#endif
TMPDIR = TmpDir
```

Makefiles generated using the configuration files will have a line in them like this:

```
TMPDIR = /tmp
```

The value of `TmpDir` can be overridden as necessary in the vendor or site file, e.g., as */usr/tmp, /var/tmp*, etc., and Makefiles are affected accordingly.

We can get this parameter value into our source files several ways. To pass the value to a single C source file, compile the file specially using `SpecialObjectRule()`, a rule discussed in Chapter 5, *Writing Imakefiles*:

```
SpecialObjectRule(src.o,src.c,'-DTMPDIR="$(TMPDIR)"')
```

This passes a definition for the macro `TMPDIR` to the command that compiles *src.c*. The value of the macro `TMPDIR` is the value of the variable `TMPDIR` from the *Makefile*. You might use its value in *src.c* like this:

```
char *tmpDir = TMPDIR;
```

If you want to provide a "best guess" default value in *src.c* (e.g., so it can be compiled by hand), write this instead:

```
#ifndef TMPDIR
#define TMPDIR "/usr/tmp"
#endif
char *tmpDir = TMPDIR;
```

The same technique can be used to compile a server program that needs to know where its startup file is. Assuming that `ETCDIR` is defined in the configuration files somewhere, you can write the *Imakefile* like this:

```
SERVCONFFILE = $(ETCDIR)/myserv.conf
        SRCS = myserv.c
        OBJS = myserv.o
BuildProgram(myserv,$(SRCS),$(OBJS),NullParameter,NullParameter)
InstallProgram(myserv,$(ETCDIR))
SpecialObjectRule(myserv.o,myserv.c,'-DSERVCONFFILE="$(SERVCONFFILE)"')
InstallData(myserv.conf,$(ETCDIR))
```

In *myserv.c*, you might access the startup file name like this:

```
if ((f = fopen (SERVCONFFILE, "r")) == (FILE *) NULL) ...
```

When you need to send a parameter value into several or all C source files in a directory, `SpecialObjectRule()` isn't very convenient since you must invoke it once for every file you want to compile. Instead, include the parameter in the value of `DEFINES`, which is passed to every compile command. For the previous examples, instead of invoking `SpecialObject-Rule()`, we could assign values to `DEFINES` like this:

```
DEFINES = '-DTMPDIR="$(TMPDIR)"'
DEFINES = '-DSERVCONFFILE="$(SERVCONFFILE)"'
```

`SpecialObjectRule()` and `DEFINES` are appropriate only for C source files. If you need to configure executable scripts, the X11 rule `Cpp-ScriptTarget()` might be helpful. To use it, create a template file containing references to the parameters you're interested in. `CppScript-Target()` generates an entry that runs the template through *cpp* to perform parameter value substitution and writes the output to the destination file. For instance, if we want to generate a shell script that needs to know the value of `TMPDIR`, we could write it as a template *script.sh* and put a line like this in it:

```
tmpdir=TMPDIR
```

To produce the script from the template, invoke `CppScriptTarget()` in the *Imakefile*:

```
CppScriptTarget(script,script.sh,'-DTMPDIR=$(TMPDIR)',NullParameter)
```

The script generated by the resulting *Makefile* target entry will have a line in it like this:

```
tmpdir=/tmp
```

A related rule is `CppFileTarget()`, which is like `CppScriptTarget()` except that the target isn't made executable.

You can specify more than one *−D* option in the last argument to `SpecialObjectRule()` or in the third argument to `CppScript-Target()` or `CppFileTarget()`, but it doesn't take very many definitions before invocations of these rules become long and unwieldy. Both rules also require that you specify a definition for every parameter you want to substitute into the template.

Configuring Source Files with *msub*

An alternative is to use *msub*, a program designed specifically to yank parameter values out of Makefiles and substitute them into templates to produce properly configured destination files.* It reads a *Makefile* and determines the values of all the parameters named in it, then reads a template file and replaces parameter references in it with the corresponding parameter values. You refer to parameter variables in *msub* templates the same way as in a *Makefile*, i.e., as `$(var)` or `${var}`. No prior arrangement is necessary to use a particular *make* variable; all of them are available on demand.

Suppose a program uses a help file that indicates the local e-mail address to which questions about the program may be sent. The address can be parameterized and given a default value in *Project.tmpl*:

```
#ifndef EMailHelpAddr
#define EMailHelpAddr help@localhost
#endif

EMAILHELPADDR = EMailHelpAddr
```

This address is likely to vary from machine to machine, but the default can be overridden in *site.def* as necessary.

To use the e-mail parameter, write the help file as an *msub* template *helpfile.msub* that contains the following:

```
    :
    :
If you have questions, send an electronic mail message
to $(EMAILHELPADDR).
    :
    :
```

To generate the help file manually, use this command:

```
% msub helpfile.msub > helpfile
```

The result, *helpfile*, looks like this:

```
    :
    :
If you have questions, send an electronic mail message
to help@localhost.
    :
    :
```

---

* *msub* is available as part of the *imake.tar.Z* distribution. See Appendix A, *Obtaining Configuration Software*.

To use *msub* with *imake*, we need a rule to produce a target entry. Here's a simple one:

```
#define MsubTarget(dest,src)                        @@\
AllTarget(dest)                                     @@\
dest: src                                           @@\
    $(MSUB) src > dest                              @@\
StuffToClean(dest)
```

This rule refers to MSUB, which we define either in the system description section of *Imake.tmpl* or in *Project.tmpl*:

```
#ifndef MsubCmd
#define MsubCmd msub
#endif
MSUB = MsubCmd
```

A target description for *helpfile* in an *Imakefile* looks like this:

```
MsubTarget(helpfile,helpfile.msub)
```

msub can also be used to produce other kinds of targets, such as executable scripts. A rule for doing this is shown below. It's similar to Msub-Target(), but it makes the target executable:

```
#define MsubProgramTarget(dest,src)                 @@\
AllTarget(dest)                                     @@\
dest: src                                           @@\
    $(MSUB) src > dest                              @@\
    chmod a+x dest                                  @@\
StuffToClean(dest)
```

Use the rule as follows. Suppose you want to write a script that formats and prints manual pages. You can write a template *prman.msub* that looks like this:

```
#!$(SHELL)
$(TROFF) $(MANMACROS) $1 | $(PRINTER)
```

The target description for *prman* in an *Imakefile* looks like this:

```
MsubProgramTarget(prman,prman.msub)
```

After generating the *Makefile* you can produce the executable script *prman*:

```
% make prman
msub prman.msub > prman
chmod a+x prman
```

What does *prman* look like? It depends on your *Makefile*. If the *Makefile* contains the following parameter assignments:

```
    TROFF = $(BINDIR)/pstroff
 MANMACROS = -man
   PRINTER = $(LPR) -P$(PSPRINTER)
       LPR = lpr
 PSPRINTER = laser1
    BINDIR = /usr/bin
     SHELL = /bin/sh
```

then *prman* will look like this:

```
#!/bin/sh
/usr/bin/pstroff -man $1 | lpr -Plaser1
```

Note that *msub* unwinds embedded variable references, e.g., TROFF is defined as $(BINDIR)/*pstroff,* but the value that's substituted into the template for TROFF is */usr/bin/pstroff.*

When *msub* is used to produce input files for script processors that allow variable references of the form ${*var*} or $(*var*), an ambiguity arises. For instance, *msub* and *sh* both recognize ${*var*} as a variable reference, so in an *msub* template does ${*var*} refer to a shell variable that you want *msub* to leave alone, or to a *make* variable for which you want *msub* to substitute the variable's value?

To avoid the ambiguity, you can make use of the fact that the shell recognizes *$var* and *msub* doesn't, whereas *msub* recognizes $(*var*) and the shell doesn't.

It's also possible to eliminate the ambiguity. You can tell *msub* to recognize variable reference delimiters other than $(. . .) and ${ . . . } using the *+R* and *–R* options.

For example, to use @< and >@ to refer to variables that you want *msub* to recognize, invoke *msub* like this:

```
% msub +R"@<" -R">@" template > output
```

It's necessary to quote the delimiters in this case because < and > are special to the shell.

An example of a script that uses these delimiters follows:

```
#!@<SHELL>@
TMPFILE=@<TMPDIR>@/xxx$$
command1 $* > ${TMPFILE}
command2 < ${TMPFILE}
@<RM>@ ${TMPFILE}
```

The references to ${TMPFILE} are unambiguous when *msub* is told to recognize only @< and @>.

The MsubProgramTarget() rule shown earlier doesn't allow any means of passing the *+R* and *−R* options to *msub*, so we need a rule with a little more flexibility:

```
#define MsubProgramTargetWithFlags(dest,src,flags)   @@\
AllTarget(dest)                                      @@\
dest: src                                            @@\
    $(MSUB) flags src > dest                         @@\
    chmod a+x dest                                   @@\
StuffToClean(dest)
```

Now we can write target descriptions like this:

```
MsubProgramTargetWithFlags(script,script.msub,+R"@<" -R">@")
```

Configuring Macro Values into Source Files

The methods we've discussed for configuring source files are all predicated on the use of parameters that are available as *make* variables. Sometimes it's necessary to configure files based on the values of *cpp* macros instead. For instance, if you're writing a program that uses shared memory when it's available and a fallback method otherwise, you can express the system's shared memory capability using a macro:

```
#ifndef HasShm
#if SystemV || SystemV4
#define HasShm YES
#else
#define HasShm NO
#endif
#endif
```

However, you can't test HasShm in C source files because it's available when the *Makefile* is generated, not when the compiler runs. But you can transmit the macro value to compiler commands by assigning it to a macro the compiler does have access to.

To do so for an individual file, use SpecialObjectRule():

```
SpecialObjectRule(src.o,src,c,-DHASSHM=HasShm)
```

To pass the value to all compiler commands, use DEFINES:

```
DEFINES = -DHASSHM=HasShm
```

Either way, the effect is to define HASSHM at compile time as either YES or NO (i.e., as either 1 or 0). Within C source files, test HASSHM to determine availability of shared memory:

```
#if HASSHM
        /* use shared-memory method */
#else
        /* use alternate method */
#endif
```

Configuring Header Files

If a programming project uses several configuration parameters in several C source files, it's tedious to write out the parameters in invocations of SpecialObjectRule() or in definitions of DEFINES, especially if you need to do so in multiple Imakefiles. It would be much easier if any source file that needed access to any of the parameter values could simply #include a header file.

We can accomplish that by generating just such a header file from an *msub* template. Suppose we want to write a template file *conf.msub* that contains the parameters we've discussed in the previous examples (temporary file directory, server startup file pathname, e-mail address, shared memory availability). TMPDIR, SERVCONFFILE, and EMAILHELPADDR can be taken directly from the *Makefile* by *msub*, since they're *make* variables. However, the availablility of shared memory is determined by a macro HasShm, not a variable which is accessible to *msub*. We need to get around this by inventing a *make* variable that corresponds to HasShm so *msub* can get at it:

```
HASSHM = HasShm
```

Now we can write *conf.msub* like this:

```
/* configuration parameter header file */
#define tmpDir          "${TMPDIR}"
#define servConfFile    "${SERVCONFFILE}"
#define emailHelpAddr   "${EMAILHELPADDR}"
#define HASSHM          ${HASSHM}
```

To produce the header file *conf.h*, invoke MsubTarget() in the *Imakefile*:

```
MsubTarget(conf.h,conf.msub)
depend:: conf.h
```

The depend entry is necessary because source files may depend on *conf.h*, and we must ensure *conf.h* exists before header file dependencies are generated. The `depend` line should precede the invocation of `Depend-Target()` in the *Imakefile*.

Using make Suffix Rules

In addition to explicit rules for building targets, *make* supports the concept of implicit rules to determine how to produce one type of file from another (e.g., how to derive object files from C source files, C source files from *lex* files, object files from FORTRAN source files). These rules are called **suffix rules** because they're driven by filename suffixes (*.c*, *.o*, *.l*, *.f*, etc.). This section describes how to use *imake* to take advantage of them.

An example suffix rule (for deriving a *.o* file from a *.c* file) follows. It specifies the source and target suffixes, as well as the command to execute to produce the target file from the source file. (`$<` signifies the file from which the target is built):

```
.c.o:
    $(CC) $(CFLAGS) -c $<
```

make has a set of built-in (default) suffix rules used to produce targets provided there are no explicit instructions otherwise. For those occasions when the built-in rules are inadequate, you can modify *make*'s behavior several ways. Some examples are:

- You can tell *make* to compile certain object files specially, but compile all others using the default rule. This is done by overriding the default suffix rules for particular targets without changing the default rules.

- You can tell *make* to compile all object files a certain way. This is done by redefining a suffix rule to change the way all object files are produced.

- You can invent new suffix rules to define new target types. For instance, you can tell *make* how to process *.abc* files to produce *.xyz* targets.

Suppose you're compiling a set of *.c* source files to produce a set of *.o* object files. By default, *make* uses its built-in rule describing the *.c→.o* transformation. To suspend use of that rule for a particular target (to turn on debugging code with *−DDEBUG*, for example), use the *Makefile* to explicitly associate the target with the commands that produce it:

```
file.o: file.c
    $(CC) $(CFLAGS) -DDEBUG -c file.c
```

This tells *make* to ignore the implicit built-in rule for *file.o*; other object files are produced with the built-in rule.

You can suspend the default for any number of individual targets:

```
file1.o: file1.c
    $(CC) $(CFLAGS) -DDEBUG -c file1.c
file2.o: file2.c
    $(CC) $(CFLAGS) -DDEBUG -c file2.c
file3.o: file3.c
    $(CC) $(CFLAGS) -DDEBUG -c file3.c
```

However, you can achieve the same result more easily with *imake* by writing a rule macro and placing it in *Imake.rules*:

```
/* compile obj from src with debugging code enabled */
#define DebugCompile(obj,src)                            @@\
obj: src                                                 @@\
    $(CC) $(CFLAGS) -DDEBUG -c src
```

Then we invoke `DebugCompile()` in the *Imakefile* once for each object file to be compiled specially:

```
DebugCompile(file1.o,file1.c)
DebugCompile(file2.o,file2.c)
DebugCompile(file3.o,file3.c)
```

This allows us to write more concise target descriptions. Using the resulting *Makefile*, *make* compiles *file1.o*, *file2.o*, and *file3.o* specially; other object files are still compiled normally.

If you want to compile every object in the *Imakefile* specially, you can invoke `DebugCompile()` for each one, but it's easier and more efficient to redefine the suffix rule itself:

```
.c.o:
    $(CC) $(CFLAGS) -DDEBUG -c $<
```

What you do with the rule depends on the extent to which you want it to propagate into your Makefiles:

- You can place the suffix rule directly in the *Imakefile*:

```
.c.o:
    $(CC) $(CFLAGS) -DDEBUG -c $<
    :
    :
    other target descriptions
    :
    :
```

This is suitable when you want the rule to apply to a single *Makefile*. However, to make the rule apply to several Makefiles throughout your project, you'd have to write it into several Imakefiles. That's a lot of work to begin with, and if you want to change the rule later, you're faced with several tedious and repetitive edits.

- You can place the suffix rule directly in *Imake.rules*:

```
.c.o:
    $(CC) $(CFLAGS) -DDEBUG -c $<
    ⋮
other rule definitions
    ⋮
```

This method is suitable when you want to override the default suffix rule project-wide. Since *Imake.rules* is used to generate all your Makefiles, centralizing the rule definition into *Imake.rules* propagates it into every *Makefile* automatically. It's unnecessary to write the rule into every *Imakefile*. This method also makes the rule easy to change; just edit *Imake.rules* and run *imake* to regenerate your Makefiles with the new definition.

However, since the method propagates the suffix rule indiscriminately into every *Makefile*, it doesn't give you much help if you want the rule to apply only to certain Makefiles.

- You can place the suffix rule in *Imake.rules* as a rule macro instead of writing it directly:

```
#define DebugCompileRule()                  @@\
.c.o:                                       @@\
    $(CC) $(CFLAGS) -DDEBUG -c $<
    ⋮
other rule definitions
    ⋮
```

In this case, you invoke the macro (once) in each *Imakefile* to which you want the suffix rule to apply:

```
DebugCompileRule()
    ⋮
other target descriptions
    ⋮
```

Again the definition is centralized in *Imake.rules*, so it's written only once and it's easy to change. In addition, you have complete control over propagation of the suffix rule: if you invoke `DebugCompile-Rule()` in the *Imakefile*, the modified suffix rule applies to the corresponding *Makefile*; if you do not invoke it, the default rule applies.

Defining New Target Types

You can write new suffix rules to define new target types. To do so, write the rule and use the methods just described to propagate it into your Makefiles. The only difference is that in addition to providing a definition for the suffix rule, you must also supply a `.SUFFIXES` line to inform *make* of the new suffixes.

For example, suppose you have a project that runs *.abc* files through a filter to produce *.xyz* files. You might write a suffix rule like this (`$@` signifies the target to be built):

```
.SUFFIXES: .abc .xyz
.abc.xyz:
    filter $< > $@
```

As before, you can put this suffix rule in an *Imakefile* to propagate it into an individual *Makefile*, or in *Imake.rules* to propagate it into all Makefiles. Or, if you want the rule to apply selectively only to certain Makefiles, write it as a rule macro:

```
#define AbcXyzSuffixRule ()          @@\
.SUFFIXES: .abc .xyz                  @@\
.abc.xyz:                             @@\
    filter $< > $@
```

Then invoke `AbcXyzSuffixRule()` once in each *Imakefile* to which you want the suffix rule to apply.

Shell Programming in Rules

This section discusses some ways to use shell programming constructs in *imake* rules. It's sometimes necessary to use these constructs to circumvent some of *make*'s limitations. For example, *make* support for programming facilities such as conditionals or loops is meager, but you can get around this with a little creative use of the shell in *Makefile* entries.

Multiple Line Constructs

The shell allows you to write command sequences that execute over the course of several lines. Here's an example:

```
set +x
for i in a b c; do
    echo $i
done
```

Multiple-line sequences like this that you might put in a shell script don't work the same way in a *Makefile* target entry. We must make several changes:

- *make* and the shell both treat *$* specially, so *$i* is not sufficient to indicate a shell variable reference. To tell *make* to pass a *$* to the shell, you must double it.

- *make* spawns a new shell for each command line of a *Makefile* entry, which causes two problems:

  — Shell flag and variable settings don't carry over from one line to another. The effect of *set +x* vanishes as soon as the *set* command finishes executing. Similarly, the shell variable *i* only retains its value through the end of the line on which it's set; by the time the *echo* command is executed, *i* has no value.

  — You lose the continuity necessary for multiple-line statements. A *for* loop only makes sense when executed by a single shell. In the previous entry, the loop is executed by multiple shells, the continuity is lost, and you get syntax errors.

  Both problems can be corrected by treating multiple-line constructs as a single command line. To do this, introduce semicolons between commands and backslash continuation characters at the ends of line as necessary.

When we double the *$*-signs and add semicolons and backslashes, the target entry looks like this:

```
target:
    set +x;                 \
    for i in a b c; do  \
        echo $$i;           \
    done
```

To convert a multiple-line construct in a *Makefile* entry that contains multiple-line constructs for use as an *imake* rule, we add the usual *imake*

continuation sequence @@\ at the ends of rule lines. Thus, the preceding
target entry looks like this in a rule definition:

```
#define SomeRule()                           @@\
target:                                      @@\
    set +x;                      \           @@\
    for i in a b c; do  \                    @@\
        echo $$i;            \               @@\
    done
```

The syntax is ugly, but constructs like this are indispensible for carrying out
complex tasks such as multiple-file or recursive operations.

Directory Changes

Sometimes it's necessary to write a rule that changes directory, e.g., to process files in subdirectories. You can use *cd* in a target entry, but the commands the *cd* applies to must be part of the same command line so they're
all executed by the same shell:

```
#define SomeRule(dir)                        @@\
target:                                      @@\
    cd dir;              \                   @@\
    command1;            \                   @@\
    command2
```

A complication is that if a *cd* should apply to only some of the commands
on a command line, its effect must be isolated. For example, a loop that
processes subdirectories might need to change into each subdirectory, run
some commands, then return to the parent directory before the next pass
through the loop. Restoration of the parent directory can be accomplished
by executing the *cd* and the commands associated with it in a subshell.
This is done by surrounding them with parentheses:

```
#define SomeRule(dirs)                       @@\
target::                                     @@\
    for i in dirs; do            \           @@\
        (cd $$i; commands);      \           @@\
    done
```

It is incorrect to *cd* into a directory and then *cd* back up. If a subdirectory
is a symlink, the second *cd* command won't change back into the original
parent directory. So don't write the rule like this:

```
#define IncorrectRule(dirs)                  @@\
target::                                     @@\
    for i in dirs; do                \       @@\
        cd $$i; commands; cd ..;     \       @@\
    done
```

Command Echoing

make normally echoes commands before it executes them; an @-prefix on a command suppresses echoing. However, in a multiple-command sequence, you can't use @ as a prefix on any but the first command since *make* doesn't recognize @ in the middle of command lines. If you want to suppress echoing of some commands within a sequence but not others, use @ at the beginning of the sequence and adopt one of the following approaches:

- Use *echo* explicitly to echo those commands you deem important to announce:

```
#define SomeRule(args)              @@\
target:                            @@\
    @for a in args;        \       @@\
    do                     \       @@\
        echo "command 1";  \       @@\
        command 1;         \       @@\
        command 2;         \       @@\
    done
```

- Use *set −x* to invoke the shell's own echoing facilities. It's also useful to enclose within parentheses the commands you want echoed so that echoing terminates when the subshell finishes:

```
#define SomeRule(args)                   @@\
target:                                 @@\
    @for a in args;             \       @@\
    do                          \       @@\
        (set -x; command 1);    \       @@\
        command 2;              \       @@\
    done
```

Error Processing in Rules

make normally quits when a command terminates in error, but you can specify *−i* on the command line to tell *make* to ignore errors and continue processing. A related flag is *−k*. When a target depends on multiple prerequisites, *−k* tells *make* to build as many prerequisites as possible, even if the attempts to build some of them fail.

The *−i* and *−k* flags both cause *make* to execute commands more aggressively than usual in the face of error. However, a command line in a target entry that consists of multiple commands can subvert the intent of these options. (If any command in the line fails, the shell exits early without executing the rest of the line.) If you want all commands to execute in partially failed multiple-command lines, too, you can use *set +e* to turn off the shell's early termination behavior.

Within a target entry, you can use the following construct to execute *set +e* conditionally according to the presence or absence of *−i*:

```
case '${MFLAGS}' in *[i]*) set +e;; esac
```

Use the construct by prepending it to the command sequence to which it should apply. Here's an example (a rule that installs several files one at a time):

```
#define InstallFiles(files,dir,flags)              @@\
install:: files                                    @@\
    MakeDir(dir)                                    @@\
    @case '${MFLAGS}' in *[i]*) set +e;; esac;    \ @@\
    for i in files; do                            \ @@\
        (set -x; $(INSTALL) -c flags $$i dir);    \ @@\
    done
```

In a recursive rule you may want to test for both *−i* and *−k*. This example runs *make clean* in each of a set of directories:

```
#define RecursiveClean(dirs)                       @@\
clean::                                            @@\
    @case '${MFLAGS}' in *[ik]*) set +e;; esac;   \ @@\
    for i in dirs ;                               \ @@\
    do                                            \ @@\
        (cd $$i;                                  \ @@\
        echo "cleaning in $(CURRENT_DIR)/$$i...";  \ @@\
        $(MAKE) $(MFLAGS) clean);                  \ @@\
    done
```

Writing a World Target

The commands to build a project from start to finish might look something like this:

```
% make Makefile
% make Makefiles
% make clean
% make depend
% make
```

It's convenient to have a `World` target in the project root *Makefile* that allows you to do the same thing with one command:

```
% make World
```

The easiest way to write a `World` target entry in the *Makefile* is to concatenate the commands you run by hand:

```
World:
        $(MAKE) $(MFLAGS) Makefile
        $(MAKE) $(MFLAGS) Makefiles
        $(MAKE) $(MFLAGS) clean
        $(MAKE) $(MFLAGS) depend
        $(MAKE) $(MFLAGS)
```

`World` entries tend to vary enough from project to project that it's not worth it to write a rule to generate them. Just put the `World` entry directly in the *Imakefile*.

Note that when you move the project to another machine, you'll likely need to bootstrap the top-level *Makefile* before the `World` operation can be performed. Be sure to include instructions in your documentation. (No manual bootstrapping should be necessary if you use *imboot* and begin the `World` entry with *make Bootstrap* instead of *make Makefile*. See Chapter 9, *Coordinating Sets of Configuration Files*, for further details on writing a `Bootstrap` rule.)

In this chapter:
- *Three Simple Rule Syntax Errors*
- *Extraneous Spaces in Rule Definitions*
- *Unbalanced Conditionals*
- *Malformed Conditionals*
- *Missing Default Values*
- *Troublemaker make Comments*
- *Incorrect Version Number Tests*
- *Missing Template*
- *Nonportable cpp or make Constructs*
- *Insufficient Wariness of cpp*

13

Troubleshooting Configuration Files

> *Double, double, toil and trouble;*
> *Fire burn and cauldron bubble.*
> —Shakespeare, *Macbeth*

This chapter describes how to court disaster as you write or otherwise modify configuration files, i.e., various ways you can break them. You should also read Chapter 6, *Imakefile Troubleshooting*, because many of the problems that occur in Imakefiles can also occur in configuration files.

Three Simple Rule Syntax Errors

Suppose you have a rule that looks like this:

```
#define RuleName(param1,param2)                    @@\
line a                                             @@\
line b                                             @@\
line c
```

If you edit this rule's definition, there are several mistakes that are particularly easy to make.

- You add a line in the middle of the rule and forget the trailing "@@\":

```
#define RuleName(param1,param2)              @@\
line a                                       @@\
new line
line b                                       @@\
line c
```

The new definition won't include line b or line c.

- You add a line at the end of the rule and forget to add @@\ to the end of the preceding line:

```
#define RuleName(param1,param2)              @@\
line a                                       @@\
line b                                       @@\
line c
new line
```

The new definition won't include new line.

- You delete the last line of the rule and forget to drop the @@\ from the end of the preceding line:

```
#define RuleName(param1,param2)              @@\
line a                                       @@\
line b                                       @@\
```

The new definition will, but shouldn't, include the line following line b, whatever it might be.

Beware of making any of these errors—and suspect one of them immediately if you edit a rule and your Makefiles are broken after you rebuild them.

It is prudent while developing configuration files periodically to run *make Makefile* twice in a row as a sanity check on your modifications. The first time builds a *Makefile* that incorporates the changes you've made; the second time verifies that the changes didn't break the new *Makefile*.

Extraneous Spaces in Rule Definitions

Rules should be defined with no space between the rule name and the parameter list:

```
/* correct */
#define Rule(paramlist) ...
/* incorrect */
#define Rule (paramlist) ...
```

In the second case, *cpp* defines `Rule` as a parameterless macro with value (`paramlist`). If you invoke `Rule()` in an *Imakefile*, it causes two errors. First, you get an "argument mismatch" error from *cpp* when you generate the *Makefile*. Second, when you use the *Makefile*, you discover it's malformed:

```
make: line nnn: syntax error
```

At line *nnn* of the *Makefile*, you'll find (`paramlist`), because `Rule()` wasn't expanded properly.* Get rid of that extra space and all will be well.

Unbalanced Conditionals

Conditional constructs begin with `#if`, `#ifdef`, or `#ifndef`, and end with `#endif`. If you're missing either the beginning or the end, *cpp* complains:

```
cpp: If-less endif        (Beginning of conditional missing)
cpp: missing endif        (End of conditional missing)
```

These errors usually occur if you forget to do the whole job when you're adding or removing a conditional construct. They're sometimes pernicious and difficult to find, since *cpp* may not alert you until it's far away from the source of the problem. (For instance, *cpp* doesn't detect or announce a missing `#endif` until it sees "end of file" on the input stream.) Another reason a missing beginning or ending might be hard to spot, even if you have some idea where the problem might be, is that it can be embedded in a morass of other conditionals. The following construct (modified from part of X11's *Imake.tmpl*) illustrates this. Do you see the problem?

```
#ifndef UsrLibDir
#ifdef ProjectRoot
#define UsrLibDir Concat(ProjectRoot,/lib)
#ifndef AlternateUsrLibDir
#define AlternateUsrLibDir YES
#endif
#else
#define UsrLibDir /usr/lib
#ifndef AlternateUsrLibDir
#define AlternateUsrLibDir NO
#endif
#else
#ifndef AlternateUsrLibDir
#define AlternateUsrLibDir YES
```

---

*Actually, "expanded properly" depends on your point of view. *cpp* did what you told it, after all. But not what you expected.

```
#endif
#endif
```

The error is a missing #endif after the tenth line.

Before resigning yourself to some careful detective work, you might try using *imdent*, a utility that shows *cpp* conditional levels by adding indentation based on #if (#ifdef, #ifndef) nesting.* *imdent* often gives a strong visual clue as to the location of imbalances.

Malformed Conditionals

Some *cpp* macros are used in boolean fashion and are defined as either YES or NO. Others are "existence" macros; they're "turned off" by being left undefined and "turned on" by being defined. These two types of macros are defined and tested differently, as summarized in Table 13–1.

Table 13-1: Macro Types

Macro use	How to define	How to test
Boolean	#define *macro* YES #define *macro* NO	#if *macro* #if !*macro*
Existence	#define *macro*	#ifdef *macro* #ifndef *macro*

Failure to distinquish the sense in which each type of macro is used leads to problems.

Error #1: Failure to test boolean macros properly. If a macro has a value of YES or NO and you test it with #ifdef, the test always succeeds since the macro is defined in either case. Use #if instead.

Error #2: Failure to test existence macros properly. Such a macro is defined with an empty value:

```
#define macro /* as nothing */
```

---

* *imdent* is available as part of the *imake.tar.Z* distribution. See Appendix A, *Obtaining Configuration Software.*

Suppose you test it like this:

```
#if macro
```

When *macro* is replaced by its value (i.e., nothing), the test turns into this:

```
#if
```

Since that's not a legal conditional, *cpp* complains about it:

```
cpp: line nnn: syntax error
```

Always use `#ifdef` and `#ifndef` to test existence macros.

Error #3: Overriding a macro with a value of the wrong type. Suppose a macro is defined as a `YES/NO` boolean in the template or project file, and you override the default in the site file by defining it as an existence macro:

```
#define macro /* as nothing */
```

Your definition takes precedence, but now tests of the macro in the configuration files won't work correctly because you've given *macro* the wrong type of value.

Similarly, if a macro is normally defined as an existence value, and you override the default by defining it as though it were a boolean (e.g., by giving it the value NO), you'll sabotage your configuration files. The test:

```
#ifdef macro
```

succeeds, even if *macro*'s value is NO.

Missing Default Values

When a *make* variable is equated to the value of a *cpp* macro, the macro must be defined somewhere. Otherwise the *make* variable is set to the literal macro name.

Suppose you create a parameter for the *awk* program so you can refer to it symbolically. To do this, you put a new parameter assignment in your configuration files:

```
AWK = AwkCmd
```

After you regenerate the *Makefile*, you set about building a target that's produced using *awk*:

```
% make awk-thing
AwkCmd file > output
sh: AwkCmd: not found
*** Error code 1
make: Fatal error: Command failed for target "awk-thing"
```

When you look through your *Makefile*, you find that the parameter assignment is exactly as you specified in the configuration files:

```
AWK = AwkCmd
```

No macro substitution occurred for `AwkCmd`. That's because you forgot to provide a default value for it. Without it, *cpp* thinks `AwkCmd` is a literal value, not a macro name. You need to provide a default:

```
#ifndef AwkCmd
#define AwkCmd awk
#endif
AWK = AwkCmd
```

Now after you rebuild the *Makefile*, *awk-thing* will build properly:

```
% make awk-thing
awk file > output
```

Troublemaker make Comments

make comments that follow other information on the same line are problematic. Suppose you define three parameters in your configuration files this way:

```
ABC = x # some comment about ABC
DEF = y
GHI = $(ABC)/$(DEF)
```

When putting a comment at the end of a line, it's quite natural (and more readable) to separate it from the preceding information by whitespace. Unfortunately, for some versions of *make*, that whitespace becomes part of the definition. All versions of *make* strip off the comment, but only some strip whitespace at the end of variable definitions.

Thus, if you expect the value of $(GHI) to be x/y, you'll be unpleasantly surprised to find that some versions of *make* set it to x /y instead (that is, with a space in the middle). The difference can be significant. To take an extreme example, consider what happens if x is /usr, y is lib/mystuff, and you use GHI in a command such as:

```
rm -rf $(GHI)
```

Depending on how *make* behaves, this command expands in one of the following two ways:

```
rm -rf /usr/lib/mystuff
rm -rf /usr /lib/mystuff
```

The latter command has serious consequences, particularly if executed as *root*. It's safer to write this instead:

```
# some comment about ABC
ABC = x
DEF = y
GHI = $(ABC)/$(DEF)
```

Incorrect Version Number Tests

Vendor files often make adjustments to parameter values depending on the version of the operating system (e.g., to compensate for deficiencies of older releases or to take advantage of new facilities in more recent releases). It's easy to write these so they appear correct but aren't quite. X11's *bsd.cf* contains the following example. It correctly distinguishes 4.2BSD from 4.3BSD and 4.4BSD, but the `OSMinorVersion` clause of the test will fail if a 5.0BSD distribution is ever released:

```
#if OSMajorVersion >= 4 && OSMinorVersion >= 3
#define SetTtyGroup YES
#endif
```

The test should be written like this instead:

```
#if OSMajorVersion > 4 || (OSMajorVersion == 4 && OSMinorVersion >= 3)
#define SetTtyGroup YES
#endif
```

Missing Template

If the self-reference in your configuration files is incorrect, you'll end up with misconfigured rules for generating `Makefile` target entries. The result is that *imake* commands generated by them won't specify the correct location of the configuration directory. This causes the *Makefile* generation process to fail at a very early stage because the template cannot be found. You'll see the following error from *cpp*:

```
Can't find include file Imake.tmpl
```

See Chapter 7, *A Closer Look at Makefile Generation*, for instructions on making sure the self-reference is correct.

Another possibility is that you're using software from a vendor that ships broken versions of the bootstrapper and/or *imake*. You may have better luck with configuration software from a standard distribution (see Appendix B, *Installing Configuration Software*).

Nonportable cpp or make Constructs

Configuration files should be written assuming as little as possible about *cpp* because use of nonuniversal extensions reduces portability of those files. For instance, the following construct might work fine on your system:

```
#if Something
    /* stuff */
#elif SomethingElse
    /* more stuff */
#else
    /* yet more stuff */
#endif
```

However, many *cpp*'s don't recognize #elif. It's mandated by the ANSI standard, but that's certainly no guarantee of portability. Other directives to avoid are #import and #pragma. Using them reduces the portability of your configuration files.

Don't put comment text after #else or #endif narratives without protecting it in comment markers; older versions of *cpp* allow such comments, but the ANSI standard forbids them:

```
Incorrect:  #endif end of test
Correct:    #endif /* end of test */
```

Just as you shouldn't write nonportable *cpp* constructs in your configuration files, those files shouldn't generate *Makefile* constructs that rely on extensions made to different versions of *make*. Doing so reduces the portability of the *Makefile* produced by your configuration files. Avoid, for instance, the VPATH variable, the use of null suffixes in suffix rules, and dependencies that specify individual files within a library.

Insufficient Wariness of cpp

Sometimes *cpp* bites you in ways that are very difficult to catch. For instance, what's wrong with the following rule?

```
#define CleanDir(dir)                    @@\
clean::                                  @@\
    $(RM) dir/*.o
```

Give up?

The problem is that `dir/*.o` contains an instance of "`/*`", the C begin-comment sequence. From *cpp*'s perspective, this looks like a comment that's missing a terminator.

In this chapter:
- *Reusing Configuration Files*
- *Are the X11 Configuration Files Reusable?*
- *Methods of Reusing Configuration Files*
- *Implementing Extensible Configuration Files*
- *Does This Architecture Really Work?*

14

Designing Extensible Configuration Files

> *Various authors have tackled bits and pieces of imake, but they fail to separate the tool's general use from the eccentricities of its employment in the distribution of the X Window System.*
>
> —Oram and Talbott,
> *Managing Projects with make*

To use *imake* to configure a project, we need a set of configuration files to use for building the Makefiles. However, we want to avoid writing configuration files for every project. Developing software that way makes the *imake* cure worse than the nonportability disease.

One way to minimize the cost of configuring new projects is to reuse the configuration files from an existing project. This chapter is the first of three that cover the design and use of general purpose configuration files that can be used again and again to configure multiple, possibly unrelated projects. It presents the necessary background and discusses implementation problems. Chapter 15, *Creating Extensible Configuration Files*, presents the implementation in cookbook form as a procedure you can apply to a set of existing configuration files to convert them for multiple-project use. Chapter 16, *Using Extensible Configuration Files*, shows how to use the files once you've created them.

Reusing Configuration Files

We don't rewrite *imake* when we start a new project, so why should we create new configuration files? Why not just reuse existing files over and over? Those are reasonable questions—but just what does it mean to "reuse" configuration files?

Reusability is related to portability. Thus far we've discussed portability as it applies to software projects. For configuration files, portability and reusability are somewhat different.

Software	Configuration Files
Written to run on a system.	Written to configure a project.
If portable, can be reused without a lot of rewriting to run on different systems.	If portable, can be reused without a lot of rewriting to configure different projects.

It's clear that *imake* has been used successfully to achieve software portability. X is evidence of that—it runs on zillions of systems. It's not so clear whether configuration file portability has been achieved. This is reflected in our language: we speak of "the X configuration files," "the Kerberos files," etc., identifying them according to the project for which they were designed and revealing our expectation that they will be put to a particular use.

The issues pertaining to this project specificity that we'll examine here are:

* Can we use configuration files written specifically for a given project to configure a different project?

* Are there difficulties we're likely to encounter in doing so? If there are, what alternatives are available?

We'll consider these questions in relation to the X11 configuration files. X has been widely and successfully deployed. The fact that X runs on so many different systems attests to the portability of the X software, the success of *imake* in configuring it, and how well-suited the X files are to configuring the X distribution. The X configuration files are sufficiently well-written that if any set of files might be expected to be reusable, they're it.

Are the X11 Configuration Files Reusable?

We can determine whether the X11 files are usable for projects other than X itself by inspecting existing software. For instance, the *contrib* software adjunct to the X core distribution and the Usenet newsgroup *comp.sources.x* are both sources of projects configured using the X files. This shows that the X files can indeed configure other programs—quite a few of them, in fact! But these projects do not tell us much about how generally the X files can be applied. After all, *contrib* and *comp.sources.x* projects are closely related to X itself, and they use the same sort of information: X libraries, X header files, X toolkits, X utilities, X this, X that.

If instead we want to configure a project that isn't based on X and hence doesn't use the same configuration information, we begin to run into difficulties. These arise principally from two somewhat contradictory properties of the X configuration files:

- **Too much information**.

  The X files contain a striking amount of information, which will be irrelevant to our project—this is extra bulk and complexity that we could do without.* Parameters used to specify the names and locations of X libraries, header files, and utility programs are of no use to non-X programs. For instance, it's not likely we'll have a use for this particular bit of information, assuming we even know what it means:

  ```
  #ifndef BDFTOSNFFILT
  #define BDFTOSNFFILT -DBDFTOSNFFILT=\"$(BINDIR)/bdftosnf\"
  #endif
  ```

- **Too little information**.

  The X files are tuned to X and not to our project, so we may need configuration information that's missing from them. If we need to find header files located in a nonstandard place, we must specify where they are. If we need to build a type of target not covered by the X rules, we need to define a new rule. If the project is built using programs not used to build X, we need to specify configuration parameters for those programs and any options they might take.

---

*And the amount of information isn't likely to decrease any time soon, if the historical evidence means anything. The number of configuration parameters has increased steadily from R1 through R5.

These two properties of the X files mean that they may not be the best match for the requirements of our project. Can we adapt them for our purposes? In theory we could go into */usr/lib/X11/config* and modify the X files directly, but in practice we're not supposed to do that. (Witness the "Don't modify these files!" warnings they contain.) Of course, no one could stop us if we really wanted to make changes, but the warnings aren't there for nothing. In a very real sense the X files are "owned" by the X project: making arbitrary changes to them is definitely the wrong way to adapt them for other projects.

You can't simplify the X configuration files by deleting information your project doesn't need, since you can't just decide *ex cathedra* that information is superfluous to your project and that you'll therefore remove it; you'll break existing X-based projects. It's not especially safe to add anything to the files, either. You'd better understand them pretty thoroughly before you put anything else in them, or again you run the risk of breaking existing X projects. Also, you must check any new symbols you define to be sure they really are new, and it isn't sufficient to check only the configuration files—you also need to check every *Imakefile* in the entire X distribution. For example, if you were thinking about using the symbol `Other-Sources`, be aware that although it isn't used anywhere in the installed configuration files, it is used under the server part of the source tree. You don't want to define it and possibly mess up server configuration, do you? The phrase "fraught with peril" comes to mind and takes on a new and frightening immediacy in this context.

Instead of modifying the configuration files we can add information to the *Imakefile*. When we need to access header files found in a nonstandard place, we can tell the C compiler where to look by adding a line like this:

```
INCLUDES = -I/extra/include/dir/path
```

Similarly, to add special symbol definitions, a line like this will do:

```
DEFINES = -Ddef1 -Ddef2 ...
```

The degree to which this kind of tweaking is reasonable depends on how extensive it needs to be. If we only have to add information to a single *Imakefile*, it might be acceptable. But if your project spans multiple directories and you need to add a nontrivial amount of project specific configuration information to each *Imakefile*, this process gets ugly, tedious, and error prone very quickly. The misery associated with this kind of exercise is one of the things *imake* is supposed to help us avoid! We begin to suspect that the *i* in *imake* stands not for "include," as we were taught in the days of our youth, but for "invidious."

The feasibility of using the X configuration files for a new project is a direct function of the degree to which the project's configuration requirements are a subset of the requirements of X. If you have a project not related to X, you can probably *force* the X files to work, given enough effort and ingenuity, but you'll feel like Procrustes, trying to shoehorn configuration information into a framework not meant for it.

I'm not trying to pick on the X files. They are very good indeed at the task for which they were designed. They're simply not generally applicable outside of the X world. Limitations on reusability aren't inherent to X only: any set of files designed specifically for a particular project will be useful for that project and other closely related ones, but often unsuitable otherwise.

This phenomenon of configuration file project specificity reveals something of a paradox. *imake* helps us widen our view of software development beyond the limited scope of a single system or platform. But in our effort to write code to run on a wide variety of machines, we can become so focused on the requirements of our project that our configuration files become very special purpose and oriented only toward that particular project. As our code is freed from the confines of a single platform, our configuration files become bound to a single project. And if we can't take a set of files developed for one project and easily configure another project with them, they're not very reusable. *imake* helps us write portable code that can easily be moved around to various systems, but it doesn't in itself help us to write portable configuration files.

I'm not saying configuration files should automatically be considered deficient if they're not reusable. That may not have been the goal in writing them. If their purpose is to make a single project portable to different systems, and they alleviate the need to do a lot of ugly reconfiguring by hand when the project is moved around from machine to machine, then they achieve their purpose. What I'm suggesting is that our purpose can be more far-reaching: our overall effort can be reduced by minimizing the work involved when we're configuring several projects rather than just one. When we have that goal in mind, configuration files oriented toward a particular project are limiting.

Methods of Reusing Configuration Files

This section discusses how to develop configuration files that can be shared among (and thus be portable between) several projects, even if those projects aren't necessarily strongly related. I'll show three ways of attempting to do this. The first two fail to achieve the goal of providing general purpose configuration files, but in so doing illustrate design traps to avoid and point the way to a third method that's not subject to the same pitfalls.

Method 1: Copy and Modify Existing Configuration Files

One way to reuse configuration files is to keep a set of prototypes. These could be the X11 files, the SP files, the DP files, whatever. When we start a new project, we create a *config* directory under its top-level directory, copy the prototypes there, and modify the copies appropriately. For example, to use the X11 files as the prototypes, we'd do something like this:

```
% mkdir myproject
% cd myproject
% mkdir config
% cp /usr/lib/X11/config/* config
% cd config
% vi Imake.tmpl Project.tmpl site.def ...
```

Since we're working with copies, not the original files "owned" by X, we're not constrained to leave them alone. This affords complete control over a project's configuration and allows us to make any kind of change we wish. We can hack out what we don't need and add in whatever we like.

The primary drawback of this approach is that we may end up with many sets of configuration files. It's possible to switch between multiple sets of files easily (Chapter 9, *Coordinating Sets of Configuration Files*), but whether they can be maintained easily is another matter. The sets of files share a common "ancestor" (the prototype files), but as projects develop, the files used to configure them develop, too, and each set of files begins to take on individual characteristics. In effect, they form separate lineages on a family tree.

The resulting proliferation of file sets, each slightly different from the others, creates maintenance difficulties. Suppose you discover a bug in one of your rules. Was the bug present in the prototype files? If so, you need to fix the prototypes and then go look through each project using them to see if its configuration files have the same bug. If instead it's a bug you introduced during a modification to one of the copies of the prototypes, you need to look through each project in which you may have made a similar modification. Your labors begin to bear a striking resemblance to the task confronting Heracles at the Augean stables. Do you really want to maintain independent sets of configuration files for each project this way? What a headache!*

imake is supposed to reduce, not multiply, software maintenance chores, so this result is discouraging, and suggests that the copy/modify approach might be suitable on a limited basis for a small number of projects, but not for long term software development involving a significant number of projects. The method doesn't really solve the problem of reusing files, either— they're not really being shared among projects, simply replicated. What have we actually gained? Yet more sets of single-project files. So the copy/modify method merely perpetuates the syndrome of project specific configuration files.

Method 2: Share Comprehensive Configuration Files

Instead of copying configuration files for each new project, we could try to create a single set of files that will do everything and use it for all our projects. That is, for each configuration situation that arises, we put into the files the information necessary to handle it—the "everything but the kitchen sink" method. This minimizes the number of files that have to be maintained, unlike the copy/modify method, and there's no problem of sets of files getting out of sync with each other, since there's only one set. The disadvantages are that files constructed along these lines become unstable and tend inevitably to greater and greater complexity:

- Instability occurs because do-everything files must continually be changed to accommodate special requirements of new projects they're called on to configure. Any set of configuration files changes somewhat over time, but the kitchen-sink method accelerates the process.

- Complexity increases as we find new configuration situations not handled and that need to be incorporated into the files as new parameters. A library here, a header file there, a new rule or two, and soon we find ourselves overwhelmed—led by our method into a slow death of

---

*Worse than a headache, really. Eventually you reach the point where you lay awake at night with thoughts of all those sets of files running through your head. They begin to take on a life of their own, clamoring incessantly for your attention, raising a racket, preying on your insecurities, cackling hideously: "Have you changed *that* set of files, but not changed *me*? You know I'll exact revenge on you sooner or later if you haven't!" O *cruel files—A pox! A pox on imake!* you cry, exhausted and weary, wracked with doubt and uncertainty. The next day, seeking less stressful work, you quit your job to become a flight controller.

asphyxiation from information overload. The investment necessary to "speak *imake*" fluently becomes greatly increased. The creator of such files might understand them, but it will be difficult for anyone else to.

Backward compatibility can be difficult to maintain in the face of instability and increasing complexity. Suppose you develop projects A, B, C, etc., making changes to the configuration files to handle the requirements of each project as you go along. Several months (and projects) later, you decide to return to project A to do some further work on it. You'd better hope none of the changes you've made to the configuration files are incompatible with the way they worked when you originally developed the project. There's an irony here: the files can't get out of sync with themselves, but they might get out of sync with the projects they're supposed to configure!

Consider also what happens if other people decide to use your configuration files as a basis for their own work. Modifications they make to the files will be independent of your own changes, effectively resulting in a new set of files floating around, despite the effort to keep the number of sets at one. These multiple sets will exhibit the same kinds of divergence that plagued the copy/modify method. The lesson suggested by this observation is that multiplication of file sets is something we simply can't prevent entirely. Instead of trying to prohibit replication and divergence, we should simply try to minimize the need for that to happen, whenever possible, and provide a mechanism for managing its occurrence in an orderly fashion otherwise.

We already have the mechanism for managing several sets of configuration files. In Chapter 9, *Coordinating Sets of Configuration Files*, I discussed how to coordinate multiple sets as they spring up. I said there that the method for doing so "accommodates 200 sets just as well as it accommodates two." Nevertheless, I take it as a given that two sets are preferable to 200. To help keep the number of sets to a minimum, we must reduce the need to develop new sets, and we haven't achieved that yet.

Method 3: Share Extensible Configuration Files

The basic problem of the copy/modify method is that the number of configuration files we need to maintain is a function of the number of projects—one set for each project. The result is a spreading contagion of configuration files as we create new projects. The kitchen sink method attempts to solve this problem by combining all sets into one and sharing it among all projects. But because they have to do everything, the files quickly become complex, and unstable due to frequent change.

These are not trivial problems, but we can discover something about how to avoid them if we simply step back, forget about *imake* for the moment, and consider the nature of our work.

Suppose you develop several projects (by any method), then stop to reflect on how you went about it. You'll recognize two things: you use certain habits, and you diverge from your habits.

- You use habits because projects are not all completely different and they share some common elements: if you're building C programs, you use the same C compiler most of the time; you usually install public programs in the same directory; you put frequently-used functions in a library rather than multiply instances of identical source code; you use the same set of formatting tools to process documentation.

- You diverge from your habits because, although projects have similarities, they're not completely similar: one project requires ANSI C rather than K&R C; another builds a program that must be linked in a special way; another requires a non standard installation directory.

Projects are neither completely different nor completely similar, and you work accordingly. You take the requirements presented to you by the projects you work on and adapt to them.

Now let's come back to *imake*. Can these observations be applied to the problem of designing reusable configuration files? Yes—if we change our thinking a bit. *imake* is usually used to express the requirements of a project so it can be adapted to multiple platforms. The question we need to ask is whether we can use *imake* to reflect our development patterns and help us apply them to multiple projects. This is a change of focus.

Rather than designing configuration files specifically for a particular project, consider several projects you've worked on and the patterns you recognize to be typical of your efforts as you've gone about developing them. Each project can be characterized in terms of how much it has in common with other projects, and how much it requires its own unique (project specific) treatment. For configuration files to facilitate this kind of characterization and allow us to avoid the problems of the copy/modify and kitchen sink methods, they need to be designed with certain goals in mind:

- **Minimize the number of files to be maintained**.

  We should recognize patterns by identifying common elements in configuration requirements of different projects and in the way we develop them. This redundancy and overlap should be used to form a baseline level of configuration functionality. The files providing this functionality should be shared among projects rather than replicated unnecessarily for each project.

- **Allow for extensibility.**

  We must be able to address the special configuration needs of individual projects. When a project's requirements differ from the baseline, we must be able to override a general pattern with a more specific one or to specify something entirely new instead. This will reduce the need to multiply sets of files unnecessarily. If a project can supply its own extensions to a baseline configuration, there is less incentive for developers to go off and write a whole new set of files.

- **Keep files simple.**

  Complexity increases when we try to specify too much in configuration files, as with the kitchen sink method. Therefore, information that's specific to individual projects should be separated from information that's shared among multiple projects.

These goals can be met using a two-directory strategy. First, we provide a public directory containing standard (baseline) configuration files. This is a public directory; its files are shared among the set of projects that use them. Next, we allow each project to designate a directory in which it provides configuration information that applies only to itself. Files in this directory are private, or project specific. Finally, we tell *imake* to give files in the project specific directory precedence over those in the public directory, thus allowing private information to override shared information.

Implementing Extensible Configuration Files

It's anathema to write configuration files from scratch, so we'll implement the two-directory strategy—how else?—by starting with an existing set and modifying it to create reusable files. We'll begin with the starter project (SP) files created in Chapter 8, *A Configuration Starter Project*, and turn them into a project containing extensible architecture (EA) files. If you want to see the configuration files we'll end up with, so you can follow along in them while reading this discussion, retrieve the EA distribution (see Appendix A, *Obtaining Configuration Software*). For the remainder of the present chapter, we'll focus on architecture design and the problem of

Makefile generation. Chapter 15, *Creating Extensible Configuration Files*, shows the conversion process from start to finish in recipe form.

There are a number of aspects to the conversion process, but there are three principal issues we must address if we're to have any hope of making things work:

- Modifying the architecture of the template file *Imake.tmpl* to allow coordination of access to shared and project specific information.

- Deciding where to put the directories containing the shared and project specific configuration files.

- Making sure we have a bootstrapper and *Makefile*-building commands that know about the shared and project specific configuration file directories.

Step 1: Modify Imake.tmpl

The SP files we're using here were developed from the X11 files, and both sets have the same basic architecture (Figure 14–1). Recall that `Macro-IncludeFile` refers to the vendor-specific file and `INCLUDE_IMAKE-FILE` refers to the *Imakefile*.

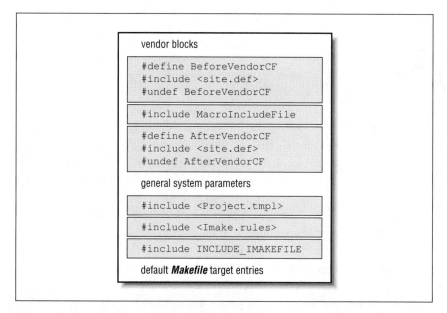

Figure 14-1: X11R5/SP template architecture

To allow a project to specify its own unique requirements, the template must refer to additional files that the project can supply. The modified *Imake.tmpl* is shown in Figure 14–2; new files are shown in boldface.

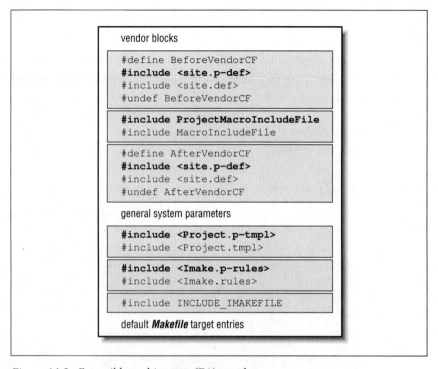

```
  vendor blocks

      #define BeforeVendorCF
      #include <site.p-def>
      #include <site.def>
      #undef BeforeVendorCF

      #include ProjectMacroIncludeFile
      #include MacroIncludeFile

      #define AfterVendorCF
      #include <site.p-def>
      #include <site.def>
      #undef AfterVendorCF

  general system parameters

      #include <Project.p-tmpl>
      #include <Project.tmpl>

      #include <Imake.p-rules>
      #include <Imake.rules>

      #include INCLUDE_IMAKEFILE

  default Makefile target entries
```

Figure 14-2: Extensible architecture (EA) template

The modified architecture has the following characteristics:

- The template refers to *vendor.cf, site.def, Project.tmpl,* and *Imake.rules.* These are shared files that describe the baseline configuration; they're taken from the public directory. The template now also refers to project specific files *vendor.p-cf, site.p-def, Project.p-tmpl,* and *Imake.p-rules,* which are taken from a project's private directory. (*Project.tmpl* now applies to multiple projects, but we leave the name alone for compatibility with existing files.)

- Each project specific file is included immediately before the shared file to which it's related (*site.p-def* before *site.def,* etc.), so that private information takes precedence over public information.

- The vendor blocks define the name of the vendor file. Since there's a project specific vendor file in the architecture now, each vendor block must be modified to define the name of that file. For instance, the modifications to the Sun vendor block look like this:

Original:

```
#ifdef sun
#define MacroIncludeFile <sun.cf>
#define MacroFile sun.cf
#undef sun
#define SunArchitecture
#endif /* sun */
```

Extra crispy:

```
#ifdef sun
#define ProjectMacroIncludeFile <sun.p-cf>
#define ProjectMacroFile sun.p-cf
#define MacroIncludeFile <sun.cf>
#define MacroFile sun.cf
#undef sun
#define SunArchitecture
#endif /* sun */
```

By expressing a project's individual requirements in the project specific files, developers have latitude to override or extend the contents of the shared files. Since each project has its own private configuration directory, it can tailor files in that directory to its own requirements without regard to those of any other project, and without need to have any changes made to the shared files.

But what if a project doesn't need any project specific information? In that case, the shared files are entirely sufficient. This presents us with a dilemma. We don't want to require a project to supply private files if it has no need for them, but they do need to be somewhere, or *cpp* will issue rude "file not found" file-inclusion errors.

One simple solution is to create dummy versions of the project specific files and put them in the shared configuration directory. The dummy files should be empty—all we care about is that they exist, to keep *cpp* happy when a project doesn't provide its own versions. The contents of the shared directory therefore consist of two kinds of files:

Shared baseline files	*Dummy project specific files*
site.def	site.p-def
Project.tmpl	Project.p-tmpl
Imake.rules	Imake.p-rules
generic.cf, sun.cf, ...	generic.p-cf, sun.p-cf, ...

The following examples illustrate how the EA files provide an additional degree of flexibility and extensibility compared to the standard X11/SP architecture:

- **Greater flexibility in specifying parameter values.**

  Sites often have a directory for locally installed programs, but the location of that directory is quite likely to vary from site to site, and sometimes from project to project at a given site. The value of a parameter that names that directory is therefore likely to vary also. The way to handle this is with the shared files *Project.tmpl* and *site.def,* and the project specific file *site.p-def. Project.tmpl* should contain a *cpp* macro BinDir supplying a best-guess value for the installation directory, and setting the *make* variable BINDIR to that macro:

  ```
  #ifndef BinDir
  #define BinDir /usr/local/bin
  #endif

  BINDIR = BinDir
  ```

  When you install the shared configuration files on a given machine, you check whether the default value in *Project.tmpl* is appropriate for local convention. If not, you supply the correct value in *site.def.* For instance, if programs are installed in */usr/local* instead of */usr/local/bin,* *site.def* should contain the following definition to override the default:

  ```
  #ifndef BinDir
  #define BinDir /usr/local
  #endif
  ```

  Projects that want programs installed in the "usual" directory simply refer to BINDIR in their Imakefiles; the site default is sufficient and need not be overridden. To use an alternate directory for a particular project instead, you specify an override value for BinDir in *site.p-def.* For example, if I'm developing a project which builds programs for my own use only, and I want to install them in my own *bin* directory, I create a version of *site.p-def* in the project's private directory and specify the value of BinDir there:

  ```
  #ifndef BinDir
  #define BinDir /u/dubois/bin
  #endif
  ```

  This overrides the default value in the shared configuration files and allows my project to put programs where it wants without requiring any changes to the shared files and without infringing on the configuration requirements of any other projects.

- **Extensibility of the baseline configuration.**

  Project specific files may be used to specify configuration parameters or
  rule macros not appearing at all in the shared files. For instance, if you
  want to install some of a project's programs in BINDIR, and others in a
  private directory, you can write *Project.p-tmpl* to provide a new parameter PROJBINDIR for the latter purpose. In this case, you're not just
  overriding the value of an existing parameter. You're inventing a new
  one, so you must provide a *make* variable to hold the parameter value,
  in addition to the *cpp* macro specifying the default value:

  ```
  #ifndef ProjBinDir
  #define ProjBinDir /usr/myproject/bin
  #endif

  PROJBINDIR = ProjBinDir
  ```

  If you override the default value of this new parameter in *site.p-def,* you
  do so by supplying the macro definition only (not another *make* variable assignment).

The extensible architecture has a few drawbacks: *Imake.tmpl* is more complex because it references more files; each vendor block must be modified;
and the shared directory must be populated with dummy *vendor.p-cf,*
site.p-def, Project.p-tmpl, and *Imake.p-rules* files. But *Imake.tmpl* need only
be modified once to add the extra #include directives and change the
vendor blocks, and it's easy to create the dummy files since they're all
empty:

```
% touch Project.p-tmpl
% touch Imake.p-rules
% touch site.p-def
% touch generic.p-cf
% touch sun.p-cf
% ...
```

Step 2: Determine Configuration File Directory Locations

If we're going to use public configuration files in a shared directory and private files in a project specific directory, where exactly should those directories be located? The organizational principles adopted to arrange configuration file directories in Chapter 9, *Coordinating Sets of Configuration
Files,* are directly applicable here:

- Project specific configuration files are in a directory *config* under the
  project root.

- Publicly installed configuration files are in a directory under the configuration root */usr/lib/config.*

These principles were originally developed to handle projects configured with either private or public files, and to select files from one directory or the other. The extensible architecture allows us to configure projects with private and public files, selecting files from each directory as we please. The simplest thing to do is adopt the same organizational principles but use the within-project and public directories conjunctively rather than disjunctively, looking under the project root as well as under the configuration root.

Step 3: Modify Makefile Building Commands

We need to figure out how to construct *imake* commands that use the extensible files and the project specific files. If the EA files weren't extensible, we'd only look in one directory for them, and the *imake* command to build a *Makefile* would look something like this:

```
% imake -DUseInstalled -I/usr/lib/config/EA -DTOPDIR=.
```

But since we need to tell *imake* to look in a project's private configuration file directory as well as in the shared directory, the *imake* command is slightly more complex. The private directory is always *config* under the project root, and the public directory is *EA* under the configuration root */usr/lib/config.* We have to search the project specific directory first so that files in the project's private directory take precedence. This prevents the dummy versions in the public directory from overriding them.

In the root directory of a project we build the *Makefile* like this:

```
% imake -DUseInstalled -I./config -I/usr/lib/config/EA -DTOPDIR=.
```

The general command to build the *Makefile* in an arbitrary directory of a project configured with the EA files looks like this, where `topdir` denotes the location of the project root:

```
% imake -DUseInstalled -Itopdir/config -I/usr/lib/config/EA \
    -DTOPDIR=topdir
```

It's a nuisance to type such long commands manually, though. *imboot* and the `Makefile` and `Makefiles` target entries should generate *imake* commands for us. *imboot* is discussed in Chapter 9, *Coordinating Sets of Configuration Files,* and the *Makefile*-generating target entries are discussed in Chapter 7, *A Closer Look at Makefile Generation.* However, none of the *Makefile*-building methods described in these chapters work with the extensible architecture because they all assume the configuration files are found in a single directory. We need to adapt our methods to construct *imake* commands appropriately for a two-directory architecture.

Bootstrapping a makefile

imboot as developed in Chapter 9 passed to *imake* either the directory *config* under the project root or, if a *–c name* argument was given, the directory */usr/lib/config/name*. Now we want to be able to tell it to pass both. This can be done by using *–C* instead of *–c* and defining *–C name* to mean that the project specific directory should be used in addition to the public directory */usr/lib/config/name*.

This EA-compatible version of *imboot* differs from the one developed in Chapter 9 only in that if we use *–C* instead of *–c*, it looks in the private and public directories, not just in the public directory.* To use it in a project root directory, bootstrap the *Makefile* like this:

```
% imboot -C EA
```

Otherwise, specify the location of the project root:

```
% imboot -C EA topdir
```

Makefile generation revisited

We can bootstrap a *Makefile* with *imboot,* but we also need to make sure that we can use an existing *Makefile* to rebuild itself or Makefiles in sub-directories with these commands:

```
% make Makefile
% make Makefiles
```

The rules that generate the `Makefile` and `Makefiles` entries are `Make-fileTarget()` and `MakefileSubdirs()`, but all they do is supply the correct values of `TOPDIR` and `CURDIR` to the *imake* command specified by the `IMAKE_CMD` variable. Thus, we need to change `IMAKE_CMD` to understand the extensible architecture.

---

*I don't show the listing of the new version of *imboot* here. You can examine it by retrieving the *imake.tar.Z* distribution of which it is a part. See Appendix A, *Obtaining Configuration Software,* for more information.

Here's the definition of `IMAKE_CMD` from the starter project *Imake.tmpl*:

```
#ifdef UseInstalled
    IRULESRC = $(CONFIGDIR)
    IMAKE_CMD = $(IMAKE) -DUseInstalled \
                -I$(IRULESRC) $(IMAKE_DEFINES)
#else
    IRULESRC = $(CONFIGSRC)
    IMAKE_CMD = $(IMAKE) \
                -I$(NEWTOP)$(IRULESRC) $(IMAKE_DEFINES)
#endif
```

Here, `IMAKE_CMD` specifies only one directory in which to look for configuration files. We must change it for the EA files to look in two directories. Before we do that, though, some additional parameters in *Project.tmpl* will be helpful:

CONFIGROOTDIR   The root directory for installed configuration files. It should be an absolute pathname.

CONFIGNAME   The name of the configuration file set. This is the name of the directory under `CONFIGROOTDIR` that holds the shared configuration files.

PUBCONFIGDIR   The pathname of the directory that holds the shared files. Its value is constructed from `CONFIGROOTDIR` and `CONFIGNAME`.

PRIVCONFIGDIR   The private, project specific configuration directory. It's located within the project tree and thus is defined relative to the top of the tree.

The values of these variables are specified using the usual macro/variable idiom:

```
#ifndef ConfigRootDir
#define ConfigRootDir $(USRLIBDIR)/config
#endif

#ifndef ConfigName
#define ConfigName EA
#endif

#ifndef PubConfigDir
#define PubConfigDir $(CONFIGROOTDIR)/$(CONFIGNAME)
#endif

#ifndef PrivConfigDir
#define PrivConfigDir $(TOP)/config
#endif

CONFIGROOTDIR = ConfigRootDir
   CONFIGNAME = ConfigName
 PUBCONFIGDIR = PubConfigDir
PRIVCONFIGDIR = PrivConfigDir
```

With this parameter support in *Project.tmpl*, IMAKE_CMD becomes:

```
#ifdef UseInstalled
    IMAKE_CMD = $(IMAKE) -DUseInstalled \
                -I$(NEWTOP)$(PRIVCONFIGDIR) -I$(PUBCONFIGDIR) \
                $(IMAKE_DEFINES)
#else
    IMAKE_CMD = $(IMAKE) \
                -I$(NEWTOP)$(PRIVCONFIGDIR) -I$(PUBCONFIGDIR) \
                $(IMAKE_DEFINES)
#endif
```

Note that these changes make IRULESRC, CONFIGDIR, and CONFIGSRC obsolete.

Does This Architecture Really Work?

Now we need to ask an important question: do the architectural changes just described in fact satisfy the three goals listed earlier in this chapter? Let's revisit each goal in turn.

- **Minimize the number of files to be maintained**.

  The multiple-project version of *Imake.tmpl* references more configuration files than the X11 template does. However, when we're developing multiple projects, the total number of files to be maintained is much lower than if individual projects have their own complete set. By recognizing patterns in our project development habits and in the configuration requirements of our projects, we can factor out common information and centralize it in the shared files *Imake.tmpl*, *vendor.cf*, *site.def*, *Project.tmpl*, and *Imake.rules*. Since these files are located in the public directory, multiple projects may use them cooperatively. We don't need a full set for each project, thus avoiding the problem of the copy/modify method where we end up with a huge mess of configuration files multiplying without limit.

- **Allow for extensibility**.

  The shared files describe a standard baseline configuration held in common by all projects that use them. A project can extend or override information in the shared files if necessary, using project specific files *vendor.p-cf*, *site.p-def*, *Project.p-tmpl*, and *Imake.p-rules* in a private configuration directory. But a project isn't forced to provide private files if the shared files are sufficient for its needs, because dummy versions of the project specific files are provided in the shared directory. Private override files need be supplied only to the extent that a project's requirements differ from the baseline.

By providing for private configuration files, the extensible architecture gives us the flexibility to make changes to the configuration of one project without affecting other projects. The architecture also promotes stability of the shared files, because private override files minimize the need to modify them. This differs from the kitchen sink approach, where the files are modified each time we make any change to the configuration requirements for any project.

By designing configuration files so they can be shared by (i.e., be portable between) different projects, it's less work to begin a new project. The ability to use private files to extend a set of shared files means you don't need to find a set of shared files that supplies every last detail of your configuration requirements—just one that handles a reasonable subset of them. That way, you're more likely to be able to build on an existing set of files and less likely to need to write a new set.

- **Keep files simple**.

  The architecture provides a means for gathering common elements of the configuration requirements of a group of projects, while splitting out project specific elements. This allows us to make the shared files simpler, since project specific information can be kept out of them. They're also more accessible to people who didn't write them since simpler files are easier to understand and use. This contrasts with the tendency toward unbounded complexity characterizing files constructed by the kitchen sink method.

This configuration architecture satisfies the design goals by exploiting redundancy among project configurations while allowing project specific information to be specified in a way that doesn't affect other projects. Furthermore, using the arrangement discussed in Chapter 9, *Coordinating Sets of Configuration Files*, multiple sets of configuration files can peacefully coexist on a single machine.

In this chapter:
- *Preliminaries*
- *Setting Up*
- *Modify the Architecture*
- *Make the Files Self-aware*
- *Generalize File Contents*
- *Install the Files*

15

Creating Extensible Configuration Files

Q.E.D.
—Euclid,
Elements

The reason for writing extensible configuration files is simple: to avoid work! Extensible files can easily be used and extended by multiple, possibly unrelated projects. This allows us to avoid much of the cost of setting up new projects. There is, of course, the question of how to get extensible files in the first place. The answer is to create them by modifying a set of project-specific files. After all, we certainly don't want to expend any more effort than necessary. By taking advantage of existing work, we don't have to write the files from scratch.

As in Chapter 14, *Designing Extensible Configuration Files*, we'll use the starter project (SP) files to produce a set of extensible architecture (EA) files. By necessity, the discussion repeats certain points from that chapter, but the emphasis is different. Chapter 14 focuses on general background information. This chapter is more pragmatic and "recipe-oriented." It provides step by step guidelines for converting project-specific configuration files to be extensible.

Preliminaries

I'll assume availability of the general purpose *Makefile*-bootstrapper *imboot* on your machine, and develop the extensible files in accordance with its organizational conventions. Specifically, *imboot* uses a configuration root directory under which all directories used to hold shared configuration files are located. I'll assume the configuration root is */usr/lib/config* in this discussion; modify the instructions below appropriately if the root path is different on your machine.

Setting Up

There are a few things we need to do to get ready to create extensible configuration files.

1. Select a name for your configuration files. Ultimately, the files will be installed in a directory with that name under the configuration root, and projects that use your shared files will expect to find them there. Since that directory needs to coexist with others, you should try to select a unique name.

   For this discussion, we'll use the name EA; the installation directory is therefore */usr/lib/config/EA.*

2. Create a "configuration project" in which to work. For example, if the starter project is located under your current directory, do this to make a copy of it:

   ```
   % cp -r SP EA
   ```

   You could just create the installation directory */usr/lib/config/EA*, install the configuration files into it, and do all your work right there, but I recommend against it. Any improvements you make to files in the public directory are immediately available to any project that uses them, but so are any bugs.* It's better to use a separate development directory in which to work. That way you can work on your files and install them only after you've tested them to be sure any changes you make are correct, without inflicting the results of your experiments on other people.

Modify the Architecture

Now we can convert the configuration files so they're extensible.

1. Make sure you're in the directory containing the configuration files:

   ```
   % cd EA/config
   ```

2. Examine the template to see where it references other configuration files. For each instance of an #include directive, precede it with an #include for a related project-specific file. This process was

---

*Not that you'd ever introduce a bug, of course.

described for the starter project files in Chapter 14, *Designing Extensible Configuration Files.* You should end up with a template that looks like the one shown in Figure 15–1 (the new files are shown in boldface).

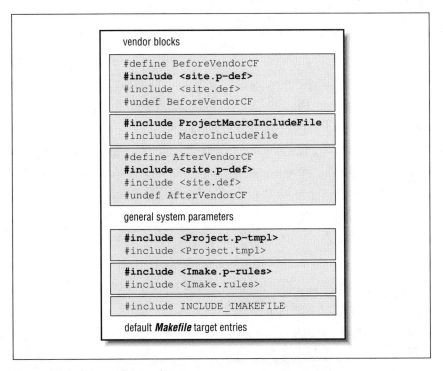

Figure 15-1: EA template architecture

3. Change the vendor blocks in the template so each one defines symbols for the project-specific vendor files. If a vendor block looks like this:

```
#ifdef trigger
#define MacroIncludeFile <vendor.cf>
#define MacroFile vendor.cf
#undef trigger
#define VendorArchitecture
#endif
```

Change it to this:

```
#ifdef trigger
#define ProjectMacroIncludeFile <vendor.p-cf>
#define ProjectMacroFile vendor.p-cf
#define MacroIncludeFile <vendor.cf>
#define MacroFile vendor.cf
#undef trigger
```

```
#define VendorArchitecture
#endif
```

4. Create dummy project-specific files:

```
% touch site.p-def
% touch Project.p-tmpl
% touch Imake.p-rules
% touch `ls *.cf|sed 's/\.cf$/.p-cf/'`
```

The last command creates an empty *vendor.p-cf* file for each *vendor.cf* file. (Or just create all the *vendor.p-cf* files manually.)

Make the Files Self-aware

1. Add the following to *Project.tmpl* to indicate the name of the configuration files, the path to the configuration root, and the path to the public (shared) configuration directory used to hold the files:

```
#ifndef ConfigName
#define ConfigName EA
#endif
#ifndef ConfigRootDir
#define ConfigRootDir $(USRLIBDIR)/config
#endif
#ifndef PubConfigDir
#define PubConfigDir $(CONFIGROOTDIR)/$(CONFIGNAME)
#endif
    CONFIGNAME = ConfigName
 CONFIGROOTDIR = ConfigRootDir
  PUBCONFIGDIR = PubConfigDir
```

Make sure the configuration root `ConfigRootDir` has the same value that *imboot* uses.

2. In *Project.tmpl*, indicate the location of the project-specific configuration directory. This is where *imake* will look for any private configuration files a project might supply. *imboot* assumes they're in *config* under the project root; I recommend using the same value in the absence of a compelling reason to do otherwise:

```
#ifndef
#define PrivConfigDir $(TOP)/config
#endif
PRIVCONFIGDIR = PrivConfigDir
```

3. In *Imake.tmpl*, change `IMAKE_CMD` to reference two configuration directories instead of just one. This command must refer to `PUBCON-FIGDIR` and `PRIVCONFIGDIR`, the public and private directory parameters you just created. The modification to `IMAKE_CMD` is as follows.

Original:

```
#ifdef UseInstalled
    IRULESRC = $(CONFIGDIR)
    IMAKE_CMD = $(IMAKE) -DUseInstalled \
                -I$(IRULESRC) $(IMAKE_DEFINES)
#else
    IRULESRC = $(CONFIGSRC)
    IMAKE_CMD = $(IMAKE) \
                -I$(NEWTOP)$(IRULESRC) $(IMAKE_DEFINES)
#endif
```

Change to:

```
#ifdef UseInstalled
    IMAKE_CMD = $(IMAKE) -DUseInstalled \
                -I$(NEWTOP)$(PRIVCONFIGDIR) -I$(PUBCONFIGDIR) \
                $(IMAKE_DEFINES)
#else
    IMAKE_CMD = $(IMAKE) \
                -I$(NEWTOP)$(PRIVCONFIGDIR) -I$(PUBCONFIGDIR) \
                $(IMAKE_DEFINES)
#endif
```

As discussed in Chapter 14, *Designing Extensible Configuration Files*, this modification makes IRULESRC obsolete.

4. By default, the starter project doesn't install the configuration files any-where, nor do any copies of it. The EA project is just such a copy, and we must add installation support because we're developing public files that must be installed to be useful.

— Create an *Imakefile* in the EA project root that looks like this:

```
#define IHaveSubdirs
#define PassCDebugFlags

SUBDIRS = config

MakeSubdirs($(SUBDIRS))
DependSubdirs($(SUBDIRS))
```

— Create an *Imakefile* in the *config* directory:

```
FILES = *.rules *.p-rules *.tmpl *.p-tmpl \
        site.def site.p-def *.cf *.p-cf *.bac
INSTALLFLAGS = $(INSTDATFLAGS)

all::
depend::

InstallMultiple($(FILES),$(PUBCONFIGDIR))
```

Generalize File Contents

Look for extraneous symbols that can be dropped, such as parameters specific to the project for which the files were originally designed, and for which you don't anticipate any use in a more general purpose setting. Remove these symbols to reduce noise and simplify your files.

When you delete a symbol from configuration files, exercise caution (and *grep*) to make sure the symbol isn't used somewhere else in the configuration files. If you're not confident you understand the configuration files, it's better to leave a symbol in than to remove it and suffer the potential consequences.

The choice of what to delete depends on your goals. For instance, the EA files trace their ancestry through the SP files to the X11 files, and still contain all the X parameters. If you want to use the EA files to configure X-based projects more easily (e.g., to allow projects to supply additional parameters in the private project-specific files), you wouldn't remove any X parameters. On the other hand, you'd treat the files quite differently if you want to use them for projects unrelated to X; in that case, you'd excise X-specific symbols. (The latter course is the one we took in Chapter 10, *Introduction to Configuration File Writing*, when we developed the DP files.)

After you've removed irrelevant configuration information, generalize all constructs that are written in such a way that you can't override them easily. These come in two forms: *cpp* macro definitions that aren't enclosed within #ifndef/#endif, and *make* variables that are set to literal values rather than to *cpp* macros or other *make* variables.

- Look for *cpp* symbol definitions that aren't enclosed within #ifndef/#endif blocks. They're a problem since you might want to override them in project-specific files. Vendor files are common offenders in this regard; they usually appear so early in the sequence of files referenced by the template that configuration file writers often assume that any macros defined in the vendor file will not have already been defined. In an environment where *vendor.p-cf* is included before *vendor.cf* that assumption becomes invalid. For example, *moto.cf* defines a couple of search path macros:

```
#define DefaultUserPath :/bin:/usr/bin:$(BINDIR)
#define DefaultSystemPath /etc:/bin:/usr/bin:$(BINDIR)
```

Definitions like this cause trouble in a multiple-project environment; a project built on a Motorola system that wanted to change these paths in a project-specific *moto.p-cf* would be out of luck. The definitions should be rewritten like this:

```
#ifndef DefaultUserPath
#define DefaultUserPath :/bin:/usr/bin:$(BINDIR)
#endif
#ifndef DefaultSystemPath
#define DefaultSystemPath /etc:/bin:/usr/bin:$(BINDIR)
#endif
```

cpp macro definitions in configuration files should always be written so they can be overridden. This includes definitions you think will never need to be changed because they occur in files processed early in the configuration process. Somewhere down the road you might modify your configuration file architecture and have a need to override things in ways you don't now anticipate.

- Look for *make* variables (parameters) that are assigned literal or partly-literal values. Directly assigning parameters like this works in a single-project environment, but not in a shared environment where different projects might want to give different values to a given parameter. We need to make sure parameters get their values from *cpp* macros that can be overridden or from other *make* variables.

  For example, due to their X11 heritage, the EA configuration files contain several *SRC variables in *Project.tmpl*:

```
   DOCSRC = $(TOP)/doc
INCLUDESRC = $(TOP)/X11
   LIBSRC = $(TOP)/lib
```

  These are used to designate various parts of the X distribution within the project tree. Since the layout of the X project doesn't change from system to system, the X configuration files don't provide any way of overriding the locations of these directories. This causes a problem in the context of extensible configuration files. You want the variables to reflect the structure of the project you're configuring, not that of the X tree. To work in a multi-project environment where projects organize their directories differently, assignments like those just shown must be rewritten so they can be overridden.

Usually, this is fairly easy. For example, instead of directly setting DOCSRC to $(TOP)/*doc*, introduce a macro DocSrc and use $(TOP)/*doc* for its default value. Then set DOCSRC to DocSrc:

```
#ifndef DocSrc
#define DocSrc $(TOP)/doc
#endif

DOCSRC = DocSrc
```

Individual projects can redefine DocSrc as necessary in *Project.p-tmpl*.

It's less clear how to change INCLUDESRC, because $(TOP)/*X11* is not an especially good general purpose default value. Here you need to be guided by your own experience. I tend to use a directory named *h* near the top of the project tree to hold project-specific header files. You might use a different name, such as *include*. Select a default that reflects your habits:

```
#ifndef IncludeSrc
#define IncludeSrc $(TOP)/include
#endif

INCLUDESRC = IncludeSrc
```

The important thing is that whether you choose $(TOP)/*h*, $(TOP)/*include*, or something else entirely, individual projects can override the default by providing the appropriate value in their own *Project.p-tmpl*.

- Not all parameter assignments need to be modified so they can be overridden, as the following example shows. VAR1 and VAR2 are already written entirely in terms of macros that can be overridden. VAR3 is not, but it needs no rewriting since you can change its value by overriding Macro1, Macro2, or Macro3:

  ```
  #ifndef Macro1
  #define Macro1 value1
  #endif
  #ifndef Macro2
  #define Macro2 value2
  #endif
  #ifndef Macro3
  #define Macro3 value3
  #endif

  VAR1 = Macro1
  VAR2 = Macro2
  VAR3 = $(VAR1) $(VAR2)/Macro3
  ```

In general, if a parameter is assigned a value entirely in terms of *make* variables and/or *cpp* macros, you need not rewrite it: if part or all of a parameter's value is literal, you do.

Install the Files

We can configure the Makefiles for the EA project itself by executing the following commands in the EA root directory:

```
% imboot
imake -I./config -DTOPDIR=. -DCURDIR=.
% make Makefiles
making Makefiles in ./config...
rm -f config/Makefile.bak
+ mv config/Makefile config/Makefile.bak
cd config; imake -I../././config -I/usr/lib/config/EA \
    -DTOPDIR=../. -DCURDIR=./config; \
    make Makefiles
```

The *make* command generates an *imake* command that looks for configuration files in $(TOP)/*config* as well as in */usr/lib/config/EA.* There won't be anything in the latter directory until the files are installed, but that doesn't matter because $(TOP)/*config* contains all the files we need. (That's where the files in */usr/lib/config/EA* will come from, anyway!)

After building the Makefiles, change into the *config* directory and verify that the *Makefile* there will install the configuration files in the right place:

```
% cd config
% make -n install
if [ -d /usr/lib/config/EA ]; then set +x; \
else (set -x; mkdirhier /usr/lib/config/EA); fi
case '-n' in *[i]*) set +e;; esac; \
for i in *.rules *.tmpl site.def *.cf *.bac; do \
(set -x; install -c -m 0444 $i /usr/lib/config/EA); \
done
echo "install in ./config done"
```

The *−n* option is used so we can see what *make* will do. If the output seems okay (look for */usr/lib/config/EA* as the installation directory), repeat the command without the *−n* to actually perform the installation.

We're finished. Quite Easily Done.

In this chapter:
- *Starting Your Project*
- *Override and Extension Principles*
- *Project Layout*
- *Installation Directories*
- *Project-specific Rules*
- *Libraries*
- *System Characteristics*
- *The Site-specific File*
- *Configuration File Experimentation*
- *Distributing Software Configured with Extensible Files*
- *Creating a New Set of Extensible Files*

16

Using Extensible Configuration Files

Let us, then, be up and doing.
—Longfellow,
A Psalm of Life

In Chapter 15, *Creating Extensible Configuration Files*, we convert a group of project-specific configuration files to produce extensible architecture (EA) files that can be shared among and extended by multiple projects. Here we discuss how to take advantage of the flexibility extensible files provide when you configure projects with them. First, I'll describe how to set up such a project and the principles by which you use the project's private configuration files to override or extend the information in the shared files. Then I'll present some examples which will show you how to put the principles to work in practice.

Starting Your Project

Before you can do anything else, you need to set up some minimal project structure. You can create a blank "skeleton" project as follows:

```
% mkdir myproj        Create project directory
% cd myproj           Move into it
% mkdir config        Create directory for private configuration information
% touch Imakefile     Create Imakefile
% imboot -C EA        Boot initial Makefile from Imakefile
```

Once you have a blank project, you can elaborate it by creating the rest of the project tree, other Imakefiles, and your source files.

If the project root is your only source directory, there isn't much project tree to create. Otherwise, you're dealing with a multiple directory project and more complexity. (For general information on managing multiple directory projects, see Chapter 5, *Writing Imakefiles*, and Chapter 10, *Introduction to Configuration File Writing*.) At the very least, the root *Imakefile* must define IHaveSubdirs and PassCDebugFlags and assign a value to SUBDIRS:

```
#define IHaveSubdirs
#define PassCDebugFlags
SUBDIRS = subdirectory-list
```

The *config* directory need not be listed in the value of SUBDIRS, since operations such as clean and install don't need to be done there. *config* is used only as a repository for project-specific configuration information. You provide this information when you create private configuration files *Project.p-tmpl*, *Imake.p-rules*, *site.p-def*, or *vendor.p-cf*.

Override and Extension Principles

When you configure a project using extensible files, you use a set of shared files installed in a public directory, and optionally some project-specific files stored in the private *config* directory under the project root. The private configuration files function to override the values of parameters that are present in the shared files, and to extend the shared files by defining new parameters that aren't present in them. Three principles govern the specifics of what you put in the private files:

- If a parameter is present in the shared files and its specified value is appropriate for your project, you need not put any information for that parameter in the private files.

- If a parameter is present in the shared files but its value isn't appropriate for your project, override the value in the private files.

- If you need a parameter that isn't present at all in the shared files, create a new parameter in the private files.

These principles can be applied in various ways, as illustrated by the examples in the following sections.

Project Layout

In Chapter 12, *Configuration Problems and Solutions*, we discussed how to specify the layout of your project using parameter variables in *Project.tmpl*. Some advantages of using variables instead of literal pathnames are:

- You can refer to project directories in terms of TOP (the location of the project root) and let *imake* figure out the value of TOP that's correct in each directory.

- You can refer to directories in a consistent symbolic way.

- You can rearrange the project easily, since you need only change the variable values once in the configuration files and then rebuild the Makefiles. It's unnecessary to edit all the Makefiles individually.

But what if *Project.tmpl* is shared by different projects that don't all have the same layout? Not all projects have the same set of directories, nor do they always arrange them the same way. The values of the layout parameters vary from project to project—variation that's hard to deal with if you put the layout parameters in a single file shared among several projects.

You can handle this problem easily using extensible configuration files. One way is to move the layout specification from the shared files to the private files. That is, instead of putting the layout parameters in the shared *Project.tmpl*, put them in the private *Project.p-tmpl* of the project to which they apply. This works well if your projects tend to have unique layouts.*

On the other hand, maybe you really do tend to use a similar layout over and over. In that case, you can leave the layout specification in the shared *Project.tmpl* to exploit the redundancy between projects. The specification can be considered a prototype, but one you have the flexibility to modify as necessary. This allows you to take advantage of common structural ele-

---

*TOP should always remain in the shared files; the fact that it names the top of the project tree must be invariant across all projects.

ments among projects, yet still be able to specify differences between them.

If your typical layout is that shown in Figure 16–1, specify it like this in *Project.tmpl*:

```
#ifndef IncludeSrc
#define IncludeSrc $(TOP)/include
#endif
#ifndef LibSrc
#define LibSrc $(TOP)/lib
#endif
#ifndef ApplSrc
#define ApplSrc $(TOP)/appl
#endif
#ifndef ManSrc
#define ManSrc $(TOP)/man
#endif
#ifndef DocSrc
#define DocSrc $(TOP)/doc
#endif

INCLUDESRC = IncludeSrc
    LIBSRC = LibSrc
   APPLSRC = ApplSrc
   MANSRC = ManSrc
   DOCSRC = DocSrc
```

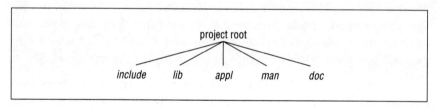

Figure 16-1: Prototype project layout

When a project conforms to the prototype, it's unnecessary to specify any layout information for it in the project's private configuration files. When a project differs, use *Project.p-tmpl* to say how.

Suppose a project uses *h* rather than *include* for its header file directory and has an *examples* directory not appearing at all in the prototype layout (Figure 16–2). Specify how this layout differs from the prototype in *Project.p-tmpl* as follows:

```
#ifndef IncludeSrc
#define IncludeSrc $(TOP)/h
#endif
#ifndef ExampleSrc
```

```
#define ExampleSrc $(TOP)/examples
#endif
EXAMPLESRC = ExampleSrc
```

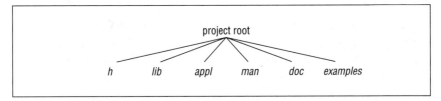

Figure 16-2: Project with layout differing from prototype

There is already a parameter for the header file directory location in the shared files, so we need only to override the value of IncludeSrc. For the *examples* directory, there is no parameter, so we must provide not only the macro definition but the variable assignment.

Installation Directories

Specifying installation directories is the inverse of specifying project layout: you're indicating where files should go rather than where they come from. However, the principles by which you specify the parameters are the same.

If you tend to use a particular installation directory frequently, you can provide the usual value as a parameter BINDIR set from the macro BinDir in the shared configuration files. If all of a project's files are installed in BINDIR and the value of BINDIR supplied in the shared configuration files is appropriate, you don't specify anything in the project's private files. If the value of BINDIR is incorrect for a project, override it by defining the macro BinDir in *Project.p-tmpl*. If a project's files are not all installed in a single directory, create new parameters. For example, if you want to install some files in */usr/etc* and others in a library directory */usr/lib/mylib*, put this in *Project.p-tmpl*:

```
#ifndef EtcDir
#define EtcDir /usr/etc
#endif
#ifndef ProjLibDir
#define ProjLibDir $(USRLIBDIR)/mylib
#endif
    ETCDIR = EtcDir
PROJLIBDIR = ProjLibDir
```

Then refer to `ETCDIR` and `PROJLIBDIR` when you invoke installation rules.

Project-specific Rules

The extension and override principles apply to rules, too. If a rule in the shared file *Imake.rules* is suitable, use it as is. If a rule in *Imake.rules* isn't suitable, override it in *Imake.p-rules* with a different version. And if you need a rule for your project that's not present in the shared rules file, define it in *Imake.p-rules*.

Libraries

Use the shared files to define parameters for libraries you tend to use commonly in project after project. Thus, if you use the math library a lot and you want to refer to it symbolically, put this in *Project.tmpl*:

```
#ifndef MathLib
#define MathLib -lm
#endif

MATHLIB = MathLib
```

Use the private file *Project.p-tmpl* to define parameters for libraries you don't use commonly, but need for a given project. These are usually libraries that are built within and used by only that project, or system libraries used on a more specialized basis only by a few projects:

```
/* within-project library */
#ifndef ProjLib
#define ProjLib $(TOP)/lib/libproj.a
#endif

/* rarely used system library */
#ifndef RareLib
#define RareLib -lrare
#endif

PROJLIB = ProjLib
RARELIB = RareLib
```

System Characteristics

In Chapter 10, *Introduction to Configuration File Writing*, we discussed the mechanism of using *cpp* macros to indicate the presence or absence of system features. Typically you define defaults for these macros in the template or project files, and override them as necessary on a platform-specific basis in the vendor files.

You can write your configuration files to provide symbols for any system feature you want: `HasVFork`, `HasShm`, `HasMmap`, `HasBlueEyes`, etc. The danger when you're writing configuration files shared among many different projects is that each project's need for particular feature symbols contributes additional complexity to the files. You can end up with quite a large set of symbols if the configuration file architecture doesn't provide any way of keeping less commonly used symbols out of the shared files.

We can better partition these symbols using an extensible configuration file architecture. The shared files hold symbols for the most commonly needed features only, thus those symbols are centralized instead of being unnecessarily duplicated in the private files of several individual projects. Conversely, infrequently used feature symbols are defined in the private configuration files of specific projects, which reduces clutter in the shared files. Table 16–1 summarizes where you define the default and override values for symbols, depending on how extensively you need to refer to them.

Table 16-1: Defining Feature Symbol Default and Override Values

Feature Symbol Type	Define Default In . . .	Override Default In . . .
Commonly used	*Imake.tmpl, Project.tmpl*	*vendor.cf*
Infrequently used	*Project.p-tmpl*	*vendor.p-cf*

The Site-specific File

The site-specific file *site.def* in the X11 files (and in the SP, DP, and EA files) is split into two sections that are selected depending on which of the two macros `BeforeVendorCF` and `AfterVendorCF` is defined. If your configuration files use a shared *site.def* that follows the same pattern, any private *site.p-def* in a project's *config* directory should follow it, too. Site-specific definitions should be placed in the appropriate half of *site.p-def*:

```
#ifdef BeforeVendorCF
    /* site-specific definitions needed by vendor files */
#endif
#ifdef AfterVendorCF
    /* other site-specific definitions */
#endif
```

If a project has already been installed and you want to do some further work on it but leave the original installation alone, you can use *site.p-def* to help build a parallel project release. Specify a set of alternate installation directories in *site.p-def* (e.g., directories under your own account) and install everything into them. When you're satisfied with your modifications, remove the alternate definitions from *site.p-def*, reconfigure and rebuild the project, and reinstall it into the real destination directories.

Configuration File Experimentation

The extensible architecture allows you to test the effect of modifying information in the shared files without actually making any changes to those files, by copying information from them into private configuration files of a test project. For example, if you want to try out different versions of a rule that's in *Imake.rules*, copy the rule into your project's *Imake.p-rules* file. By modifying the copy, you can see how your changes work without disturbing the shared files or other projects that use the shared files. If you decide the modified version is an improvement worth installing, put it back into *Imake.rules*.

Distributing Software Configured with Extensible Files

When you distribute a project configured with extensible files, you should include any private configuration files in the project distribution. Of course, the project is dependent on the shared configuration files, too, so the shared files need to be made available as well. In the documentation for your project, you should note its dependency on the shared configuration files and indicate how to get them.

Creating a New Set of Extensible Files

The nature of extensible configuration files is such that you can develop an arbitrary number of projects with them, even if the files don't match exactly the configuration requirements of any particular project. This reduces the need to create new sets of configuration files. Nevertheless, at some point you might find you need to develop some projects with requirements significantly different than those you've been writing.

For instance, you may have a set of extensible files oriented toward program development. If you need to develop projects oriented toward database management, for example, you'll be producing different kinds of targets (report generators, canned queries, etc.). You may well decide to write another set of shared configuration files for use with this grou, projects.

To create a new set of extensible configuration files, use the following procedure:

- Select a name for your files and copy an existing set of extensible files. If the EA project is located under your current directory, create a copy of it like this:

  ```
  % cp -r EA NEW-EA
  ```

- Change the self-reference by editing *config/Project.tmpl* to indicate the name of the new set of files:

  ```
  #ifndef ConfigName
  #define ConfigName NEW-EA
  #endif
  ```

- Make any other modifications you need. The specifics of this step vary according to the purposes you have in mind for the new files, of course.

- In the NEW-EA project root, build the Makefiles and install the configuration files:

  ```
  % imboot
  % make Makefiles
  % make -n install
  ```

  In the last command, we use *−n* to see where *make* thinks it should install the files. If the directory is correct in the output, repeat the command without the *−n*.

Now you can develop projects using the NEW-EA files. Bootstrap Makefiles in such projects like this:

```
% imboot -C NEW-EA
% make Makefiles
```

Obtaining Configuration Software

This appendix describes how to obtain the software discussed in this book. All distributions listed below are available as compressed *tar* files.

imake.tar.Z The configuration software described in this book. The distribution contains *imake, xmkmf, imboot, makedepend, mkdirhier, msub, bsdinst, imdent,* the X11 configuration files, and some other miscellaneous utilities. Instructions for building and installing this distribution are given in Appendix B, *Installing Configuration Software.*

TOUR.tar.Z The examples in Chapter 2, *A Tour of imake,* are based on the X11 configuration files. *TOUR.tar.Z* contains an alternate set of configuration files that can be used for the examples. They're similar to the X files, but simplified to be easier to understand.

SP.tar.Z The starter project files described in Chapter 8, *A Configuration Starter Project.*

DP.tar.Z The demonstration project files developed in Chapter 10, *Introduction to Configuration File Writing,* and Chapter 11, *Writing Rule Macros.*

EA.tar.Z The configuration files implementing the extensible architecture described in Chapter 14, *Designing Extensible Configuration Files,* and Chapter 15, *Creating Extensible Configuration Files.*

mouse-cpp.tar.Z

DECUS-cpp.tar.Z

> Two alternative implementations of *cpp*. You might find them useful if your C preprocessor doesn't work with *imake*.

bookcf.tar.Z   The configuration files used in connection with the writing of *Software Portability with imake*.

Errata.tar.Z   Last and, I hope, least, the current list of known errors in this book.

Obtaining the Distributions

The software is available electronically in a number of ways: by FTP, GOPHER, FTPMAIL, BITFTP, and UUCP. The cheapest, fastest, and easiest ways are listed first. The first one that works for you is probably the best. Use FTP or GOPHER if you are directly on the Internet. Use FTPMAIL if you are not on the Internet but can send and receive electronic mail to Internet sites (this includes CompuServe users). Use BITFTP if you send electronic mail via BITNET. Use UUCP if none of the above works.

FTP

To use FTP, you need a machine with direct access to the Internet. The software may be obtained from any of the hosts below. (The last host is likely to have the most up-to-date distributions.)

Machine	Directory
ftp.uu.net	*/published/oreilly/nutshell/imake*
ftp.ora.com	*/pub/nutshell/imake*
ftp.primate.wisc.edu	*/pub/imake-book*

A sample session is shown, with what you should type in boldface:

```
% ftp ftp.uu.net
Connected to ftp.uu.net.
220 FTP server (Version 6.21 Tue Mar 10 22:09:55 EST 1992) ready.
Name (ftp.uu.net:kismet): anonymous
331 Guest login OK, send domain style e-mail address as password.
Password: kismet@ora.com (Use your user name and host here)
230 Guest login OK, access restrictions apply.
ftp> cd /published/oreilly/nutshell/imake
250 CWD command successful.
ftp> binary (Very important! You must specify binary transfer for compressed files.)
```

```
200 Type set to I.
ftp> get imake.tar.Z
200 PORT command successful.
150 Opening BINARY mode data connection for imake.tar.Z.
226 Transfer complete.
ftp> quit
221 Goodbye.
%
```

Once you obtain a distribution, extract the files from it by typing:

```
% zcat imake.tar.Z | tar xf -
```

System V systems require the following *tar* command instead:

```
% zcat imake.tar.Z | tar xof -
```

If *zcat* is not available on your system, use separate *uncompress* and *tar* commands:

```
% uncompress imake.tar.Z
% tar xf imake.tar.Z        (or tar xof imake.tar.Z)
```

GOPHER

To retrieve the software using GOPHER, connect to *gopher.- primate.wisc.edu*, selecting "Primate Center Software Archives" from the main menu, then selecting the "imake-book" item, and then select the distribution you want.

GOPHER clients vary considerably; consult your local documentation for specific instructions.

Once you've got the desired distribution, extract the files from it by following the directions under FTP.

FTPMAIL

FTPMAIL is a mail server available to anyone who can send and receive electronic mail to and from Internet sites. This includes most workstations that have an e-mail connection to the outside world, and CompuServe users. You do not need to be directly on the Internet. Here's how to do it.

You send mail to *ftpmail@decwrl.dec.com*. In the message body, give the name of the anonymous FTP host and the FTP commands you want to run. The server will run anonymous FTP for you and mail the files back to you. To get a complete help file, send a message with no subject and the single word "help" in the body. The following is an example mail session that should get you a listing of the files in the selected directory and the file *imake.tar.Z.* The listing is useful in case there are other files you may be interested in.

```
% mail ftpmail@decwrl.dec.com
Subject:
reply alan@ora.com                    (where you want files mailed)
connect ftp.uu.net
cd /published/oreilly/nutshell/imake
dir
binary
uuencode                              (or btoa if you have it)
get imake.tar.Z
quit
%
```

A signature at the end of the message is acceptable as long as it appears after "quit."

All retrieved files will be split into 60KB chunks and mailed to you. You then remove the mail headers and concatenate them into one file, and then *uudecode* or *atob* it. Once you've got the desired distribution, extract the files from it by following the directions under FTP.

BITFTP

BITFTP is a mail server for BITNET users. You send it electronic mail messages requesting files, and it sends you back the files by electronic mail. BITFTP currently serves only users who send it mail from nodes that are directly on BITNET, EARN, or NetNorth. BITFTP is a public service of Princeton University. Here's how it works.

To use BITFTP, send mail containing your FTP commands to *BITFTP@PUCC.* For a complete help file, send HELP as the message body.

The following is the message body you should send to BITFTP:

```
FTP  ftp.uu.net  NETDATA
USER  anonymous
PASS your Internet e-mail address (not your bitnet address)
CD  /published/oreilly/nutshell/imake
DIR
BINARY
GET  imake.tar.Z
QUIT
```

Once you've got the desired distribution, extract the files from it by following the directions under FTP.

Questions about BITFTP can be directed to *MAINT@PUCC* on BITNET.

UUCP

UUCP is standard on virtually all UNIX systems. The software is available by UUCP via modem from UUNET; UUNET's connect-time charges apply.

You can get the software from UUNET whether you have an account or not. If you or your company has an account with UUNET, you will have a system with a direct UUCP connection to UUNET. Find that system, and type the following command (type everything on one line):

```
uucp uunet\!~/published/oreilly/nutshell/imake/imake.tar.Z
    yourhost\!~/yourname/
```

The backslashes can be omitted if you use the Bourne shell (*sh*) instead of *csh*. The file should appear some time later (up to a day or more) in the directory */usr/spool/uucppublic/yourname.* If you don't have an account but would like one so that you can get electronic mail, then contact UUNET at 703-204-8000.

If you don't have a UUNET account, you can set up a UUCP connection to UUNET using the phone number 1-900-468-7727. As of this writing, the cost is 50 cents per minute. The charges will appear on your next telephone bill. The login name is "uucp" with no password. For example, an *L.sys/Systems* entry might look like:

```
uunet Any ACU 19200 1-900-468-7727 ogin:--ogin: uucp
```

Your entry may vary depending on your UUCP configuration. If you have a PEP-capable modem, make sure s50=255s111=30 is set before calling.

Try to get the file */published/oreilly/nutshell/imake/ls-lR.Z* as a short test file containing the filenames and sizes of all the files in the directory.

Once you've got the desired distribution, extract the files from it by following the directions under FTP.

B

Installing Configuration Software

This appendix describes how to build and install *imake* and related configuration software if you do not already have it on your machine. The software (referred to here as "the distribution") is available as *imake.tar.Z* from the archive sites listed in Appendix A, *Obtaining Configuration Software*.

The essential programs you will need for working your way through this book are:

imake	*Makefile* generator
xmkmf	Bootstrapper that uses the X11 configuration files
imboot	General purpose bootstrapper
makedepend	Header file dependency generator
mkdirhier	Directory creation tool

Some of these may be new to you, particularly if you are looking at this appendix without reading the rest of the book first. *imake*, of course, is discussed throughout the book. *xmkmf*, *makedepend*, and *mkdirhier* are discussed in Chapter 2, *A Tour of imake*. *imboot* is discussed in Chapter 9, *Coordinating Sets of Configuration Files*, and Chapter 14, *Designing Extensible Configuration Files*.

The distribution also includes the X11 configuration files and some miscellaneous programs like *msub* and *imdent*.

Most of the distribution is based on the current release of X11 (X11R5, patchlevel 24 at the time of writing), but some programs are not part of the standard X distribution, e.g., *imboot*, *msub*, and *imdent*.

Distribution Layout

The software is distributed as a compressed *tar* file *imake.tar.Z.* Retrieve and unpack it according to the instructions in Appendix A. This will create the project tree shown in Figure B–1 (an *imake* directory and several sub-directories).

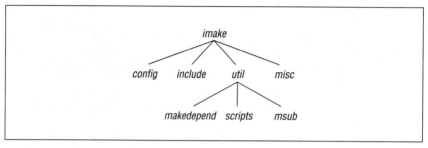

Figure B-1: imake distribution project tree

You should then familiarize yourself with the distribution's structure and contents. Move into the distribution root so you can look around:

```
% cd imake
```

The distribution root directory contains these subdirectories:

config   The X11 configuration files and source for *imake.*

include   The header file *Xosdefs.h,* needed to compile *imake* and *makedepend.*

util   Parent of utility directories.

misc   Miscellaneous bits and pieces: portions of the X11 Release Notes that pertain to *imake;* any errors that have been found in these instructions since publication; troubleshooting information too detailed or specialized to be included in this appendix; reader-contributed notes about porting *imake* to systems not covered by the distribution, etc.

The *util* directory contains a number of subdirectories:

makedepend   Source for the C version of *makedepend.* Several programs go by this name; the version included here is intended for use with *imake* and is written by Todd Brunhoff, *imake's* author.

scripts   Source for *xmkmf, mkdirhier, imboot,* and *bsdinst,* and some other miscellaneous scripts, such as *imdent, which,* and a script version of *makedepend* (if you can't get the C version to work).

msub   Source for *msub.*

Find Out What You Already Have

Survey the landscape of your system, since some or all of the software may already be present on your machine. For instance, if you are using a workstation running X, there is a good chance the configuration files and some of the programs are already installed, because X itself is configured with *imake.*

To find programs, use the *which* command. It will tell you either where a program is located, or, if it couldn't find it, which directories it looked in (usually the directories named in your PATH variable).* Here, *which* tells you that *imake* is installed in */usr/local/bin:*

```
% which imake
/usr/local/bin/imake
```

On the other hand, if *which* can't find *imake,* you will get a result like this:

```
% which imake
no imake in . /usr/local/bin /usr/bin/X11 /usr/ucb /bin /usr/bin
```

In most instances, if you discover that a program included in the distribution is already installed, you do not need to install it. However, you should make exceptions when you have out-of-date or broken versions of programs:

- Current versions of *makedepend* and *xmkmf* each understand an *−a* option. Older versions distributed prior to X11R5 do not. Install the versions in the distribution to update your system.

- If you are running Open Windows, be aware that the versions of *imake* and *xmkmf* distributed with it are difficult to work with. See the section "*imake* versus Open Windows" later in this appendix.

---

*If you do not have *which,* you can use either of the scripts *which.sh* or *which.csh* supplied in the *scripts* directory. Alternatively, use *find* or poke around by hand looking for programs in system directories like */usr/local/bin, /usr/bin, /usr/bin/X11,* etc.

In addition to the programs, you need a copy of the X11 configuration files, because many examples throughout this book assume they are available to play with. The default location for the X files is */usr/lib/X11/config*. If they are not there, and you have *xmkmf* installed, look at it to see where it expects to find the X11 files.

Prepare to Install the Distribution

Before building the distribution you must decide where you will install the software to avoid misconfiguring the programs. Some installation locations are built in. The defaults are:

/usr/bin/X11	Location of programs
/usr/lib/X11/config	Location of the X11 configuration files
/usr/lib/config	Location of the *imboot* configuration root directory

You can change the default installation locations if you like. If you do, then whenever you see the defaults in examples elsewhere in this book, you must substitute the locations you have chosen.

Suppose you want to install programs in */usr/local/bin* and the X11 configuration files in */var/X11R5/lib/config*, and that you want to use */var/lib/config* for the *imboot* configuration root. Make the changes as follows:

- To change the program installation directory, add the following to the second half of *config/site.def*:

      #ifndef BinDir
      #define BinDir /usr/local/bin
      #endif

- To change the X11 configuration file installation directory, add the following to the second half of *config/site.def*:

      #ifndef ConfigDir
      #define ConfigDir /var/X11R5/lib/config
      #endif

- To change the configuration root directory used by *imboot*, edit this line in *util/scripts/Imakefile*:

      CONFIGROOTDIR = $(USRLIBDIR)/config

  Change it to this:

```
CONFIGROOTDIR = /var/lib/config
```

Installing with Limited Privileges

If you have insufficient privileges to install software on your machine wherever you like, try to convince a sympathetic site administrator to install files that need to go in system directories.* If that is not possible, install everything under your own account (use the instructions just given for changing the default locations). If the path to your home directory is */u/you*, I suggest the following installation directories:

/u/you/bin	Location of programs
/u/you/lib/X11/config	Location of the X11 configuration files
/u/you/lib/config	Location of the *imboot* configuration root directory

Build the Distribution— Quick Instructions

This section contains quick instructions for building the distribution. If they do not work, read the section "Detailed Instructions."

Change into the *config* directory and look around; you will see the configuration files and the source code for *imake*:

```
% cd config
% ls
DGUX.cf        Server.tmpl    ibm.cf         noop.rules     sunLib.rules
Imake.rules    apollo.cf      ibmLib.rules   oldlib.rules   sunLib.tmpl
Imake.tmpl     att.cf         ibmLib.tmpl    pegasus.cf     sv4Lib.rules
Imakefile      bsd.cf         imake.c        rtcchack.bac   sv4Lib.tmpl
Library.tmpl   ccimake.c      imake.man      sgi.cf         ultrix.cf
Makefile.ini   convex.cf      imakemdep.h    sgiLib.rules   x386.cf
Mips.cf        cray.cf        luna.cf        site.def
Project.tmpl   generic.cf     macII.cf       sony.cf
README         hp.cf          moto.cf        sun.cf
```

Find a vendor-specific configuration file that applies to your machine. This will be one of the files named with a *.cf* suffix. For Sun machines, use *sun.cf*, for Silicon Graphics machines, use *sgi.cf*, etc. If you do not find a vendor file for your system, you may need to write one using the detailed instructions. (First look in the *misc* directory, though. It contains instructions for some systems that aren't supported in the standard X11

---

*Yes, I know that "sympathetic site administrator" is oxymoronic.

distribution.)

Find the definitions of `OSMajorVersion` and `OSMinorVersion` in the
vendor file. They represent the major and minor release numbers for your
operating system. Check that they are correct, and change them if they are
not. Suppose *ultrix.cf* specifies Ultrix 4.2:

```
#define OSMajorVersion 4
#define OSMinorVersion 2
```

If you are running Ultrix 4.1, the major number is correct, but you must
change the minor number to 1:

```
#define OSMajorVersion 4
#define OSMinorVersion 1
```

Look over *site.def* to see whether you want to change anything. In particular, to use *gcc* as your C compiler, define `HasGcc` as `YES` by uncomment-
ing the `#define` that is already there.

Look in Table B–1 and find the bootstrap flags for your system. If the value
is *varies*, several values are possible and you must look through the vendor file and figure out which value is appropriate for your machine. If your
system is not listed, the distribution hasn't been ported to it and you need
to use the detailed instructions.

Table B-1: Bootstrap Flags for Various Systems

Vendor File	Bootstrap Flags	Remark
DGUX.cf	-DDGUX	
Mips.cf	-DMips	
apollo.cf	-Dapollo	
att.cf	-Datt	
bsd.cf	-DNOSTDHDRS	
convex.cf	-D__convex__ -tm c1	
cray.cf	-DCRAY	
hp.cf	-Dhpux	
ibm.cf	*varies*	Will include -Dibm
luna.cf	-Dluna	
macII.cf	-DmacII	
moto.cf	-DMOTOROLA -DSVR4	If SVR4 conformant
	-DMOTOROLA -DSYSV	If not SVR4 conformant
pegasus.cf	-DM4310 -DUTEK	
sgi.cf	-Dsgi	
sony.cf	-Dsony	

Table B.1: Bootstrap Flags for Various Systems (continued)

Vendor File	Bootstrap Flags	Remark
sun.cf	`-Dsun`	For SunOS 4.1 and up
	`-Dsun -DNOSTDHDRS`	For SunOS before 4.1
ultrix.cf	`-Dultrix`	
x386.cf	`varies`	Will include `-DSYSV386`

Look in the *misc* directory under the distribution root to see if there are any files pertaining to your system. Some patches to make the distribution build on older releases of OS'es are contained there, and you may need to apply one of them.

In the distribution root (the *imake* directory) execute the following command, replacing *flags* with the appropriate bootstrap flags for your system:*

```
% make World BOOTSTRAPCFLAGS="flags" >& make.world
```

Examples:

```
% make World BOOTSTRAPCFLAGS="-Dsun" >& make.world
% make World BOOTSTRAPCFLAGS="-Dhpux" >& make.world
% make World BOOTSTRAPCFLAGS="-DMOTOROLA -DSVR4" >& make.world
```

When the command terminates, take a look through *make.world* to see whether or not the `World` operation completed without error. If it failed, use the detailed instructions to build the distribution. Otherwise, go ahead and install the software.

Install the Software

If you want to install everything, use the following command in the distribution root directory:

```
% make install
```

Otherwise, change into individual directories and install only those files in which you are interested. The instructions below show how to do this; leave out the parts for the files you do not want to install.

---

*The command uses *csh* output redirection. If you are using *sh*, use this command instead:

```
$ make World BOOTSTRAPCFLAGS="flags" > make.world 2>&1
```

In *config*—install *imake* and the X11 configuration files:

```
% make install.imake
% make install.cffiles
```

Do not install *ccimake*; it is only needed for compiling *imake*.

In *util/makedepend*—if you built the compiled version of *makedepend* (the default on most systems) install it:

```
% make install.makedepend
```

If you did not build the compiled version, the script version will be installed from *util/scripts*.

In *util/scripts*—install gobs of stuff:

```
% make install.xmkmf
% make install.mkdirhier
% make install.imboot
% make install.imdent
```

If you have a System V version of *install* instead of a BSD-compatible one, the distribution contains a script *bsdinst* you can use instead (you need to install *bsdinst* if the installation commands you have just been executing used it):

```
% make install.bsdinst
```

If you built the script version of *makedepend*, install it:

```
% make install.makedepend
```

In *util/msub*—install *msub*:

```
% make install.msub
```

Detailed Instructions

This section contains detailed instructions for building *imake*. You're probably reading it either because *imake* hasn't been ported to your type of system, or because the quick instructions did not work on your machine. In the first case, you need to modify your copy of the distribution according to the following instructions. In the second case, you should look for discrepancies between what the distribution already says about your system and what these instructions indicate it should say. Make sure you have read through the quick instructions first because they contains information you will need here. You might also find it helpful to read Chapter 3,

Understanding Configuration Files, to get some idea of how *imake* works. That will help you understand the result you are trying to produce.

When *imake* runs, it invokes *cpp* to process the configuration files. Default values for most configuration parameters are defined in *Imake.tmpl*, *Project.tmpl*, etc. Also included among the configuration files are many vendor files, each of which contains parameter values that override any defaults that are inappropriate for a particular vendor's systems. Since there are several different vendor files from which to choose, *cpp* has to figure out which is the right one for the machine you are actually using. *cpp* does this by checking various symbols known to identify different types of systems. The one that is defined determines the current system type.

The symbol that identifies your system can come from a couple of sources. Some vendors ship a *cpp* that predefines a symbol unique to that vendor's systems. For instance, on Ultrix, *cpp* predefines `ultrix`, which makes it easy to ascertain the system type:

```
#ifdef ultrix
    /* it's Ultrix, all right... */
#endif
```

Unfortunately, some vendor-supplied symbols aren't useful for system identification because they are ambiguous (or have become so). For instance, at one time (in X11R3) the `mips` symbol unambiguously indicated a true Mips Computers, Inc. machine, but the symbol later became ambiguous when several other OS's written to run on Mips processors also defined `mips` (Ultrix, NEWS OS, IRIX, etc.). In the absence of a unique predefined vendor symbol, it is necessary to make up an identifier symbol and to tell *imake* to define it when starting up *cpp*. Thus, to signify true Mips machines, the "artificial" symbol `Mips` is now used.

It might even be that your preprocessor predefines no useful system-indicating symbols at all. ANSI C takes a dim view of most predefined symbols, and the trend in preprocessors as the ANSI juggernaut rolls on is toward fewer predefinitions. Here, too, you invent an identifier symbol and make sure *imake* defines it so *cpp* can determine which vendor file to use.

Thus, to port *imake* to your machine, there are three requirements you must satisfy:

1. You need a vendor file that describes your system and contains any information needed to override default values of parameters specified in the other configuration files.

2. The configuration files must contain a block of code that "recognizes" your system type and selects the correct vendor file. The block is called the **vendor block** and the system-identifier symbol that activates it is called the **trigger** symbol. In the X11 configuration files, the vendor blocks are located near the beginning of *Imake.tmpl*.

3. *imake* must make sure the trigger symbol is defined when *cpp* starts up if *cpp* does not predefine it.

We'll discuss how to meet these requirements by porting *imake* to systems built by the hypothetical vendor Brand XYZ, as well as what to look for if *imake* has already been ported to your type of system but you can't get it to work on your machine.

Write the Vendor File

For a new port of *imake*, you have to write the vendor file from scratch. For Brand XYZ systems, we will write a file *brandxyz.cf.* If there is already a vendor file for your system type, you need to fix the vendor file you do have.

There are a few symbols you must define in the vendor file:

- Define the major and minor release numbers for your operating system. For instance, if your OS is at release 3.41, write this:

  ```
  #define OSMajorVersion 3
  #define OSMinorVersion 41
  ```

  The OS numbers are used when you need to select parameter values that vary for different releases of the system. Define them even if you do not use them anywhere else in the vendor file because *Imakefile* writers sometimes need to know the release numbers.

- If your system is based on System V Release 2 or 3, define `SystemV`:

  ```
  #define SystemV YES
  ```

  If your system is based on System V Release 4, define `SystemV4`:

  ```
  #define SystemV4 YES
  ```

  If your system is not based on System V, do not define either symbol.

The remaining contents of the vendor file are largely determined by whether the default parameter values provided in the template and project files are appropriate for your system. Provide override values in the vendor file for those that are not.

To some extent, you find out which defaults to override by trial and error: write the vendor file and try to build the distribution. If the build fails because a parameter value is incorrect, put the correct value in the vendor file and try again. However, you can minimize trial and error by taking advantage of the experience of those who've gone before you. Existing vendor files serve as a guide to help you figure out what should go in your own vendor file by giving you some idea of the parameters most likely to need special treatment (especially if any existing files are for OS's similar to yours).

Write the Vendor Block

The vendor block for your system goes in the vendor block section of *Imake.tmpl* and is activated by the trigger symbol. The SunOS and Ultrix blocks are shown below. Use them as a guide for writing your own block.

```
#ifdef sun
#define MacroIncludeFile <sun.cf>
#define MacroFile sun.cf
#undef sun
#define SunArchitecture
#endif /* sun */

#ifdef ultrix
#define MacroIncludeFile <ultrix.cf>
#define MacroFile ultrix.cf
#ifdef vax
#undef vax
#define VaxArchitecture
#endif
#ifdef mips
#undef mips
#define MipsArchitecture
#endif
#undef ultrix
#define UltrixArchitecture
#endif
```

The first line of each block tests the trigger symbol. If it is not defined, the block is skipped. Otherwise, the block does three things:

1. It defines the name of the vendor file. The name is defined two different ways because it is used in different contexts later.

2. It undefines the trigger symbol and any other OS- or processor-specific symbols that *cpp* might have predefined.

3. It defines a vendor-specific OS architecture symbol. If the OS runs on more than one type of processor, a processor-specific architecture symbol is usually defined, too (e.g., `VaxArchitecture`,

MipsArchitecture in the Ultrix vendor block). Architecture symbols are useful in Imakefiles when it is necessary to know the OS or hardware type.

Following this model, you can write the vendor block for Brand XYZ systems using brandxyz as the trigger symbol and BrandXYZ-Architecture as the architecture symbol:

```
#ifdef brandxyz
#define MacroIncludeFile <brandxyz.cf>
#define MacroFile brandxyz.cf
#undef brandxyz
#define BrandXYZArchitecture
#endif
```

After you write the vendor block, document the trigger symbol that identifies your system type by putting a definition for BootstrapCFlags in your vendor file. The following line goes in *brandxyz.cf*:

```
#define BootstrapCFlags -Dbrandxyz
```

You now have the vendor file and the vendor block written; all you need is *imake*.

Configure imake

imake is compiled using a minimal hand-written file *Makefile.ini*. You want the *Makefile.ini* that is in the *config* directory, not the one in the distribution root directory. (If you see a *Makefile* in the directory in which you are building *imake*, ignore it, as it was not configured on your machine.)

Makefile.ini builds *imake* in two steps because some systems require special flags to ensure proper compilation of all but the most trivial programs. *imake* is not especially complex, but it is not trivial, either, so a small helper program *ccimake* is compiled first. *ccimake* is designed to be simple enough to compile with no special treatment, and it figures out any extra flags needed to get *imake* to compile without error on your platform. Those flags are added to the *imake*-building command.

To build *ccimake* and *imake*, you run the following *make* command (do not do this yet; we won't be ready for a few pages):

```
% make -f Makefile.ini BOOTSTRAPCFLAGS="flags"
$(CC) -o ccimake $(CFLAGS) ccimake.c
$(CC) -c $(CFLAGS) `./ccimake` imake.c
$(CC) -o imake imake.o
```

The trigger is specified in the value of BOOTSTRAPCFLAGS.* For existing ports, determine *flags* from Table B–1. For new ports, use *–Dtrigger* (e.g., *–Dbrandxyz* for Brand XYZ systems).

Makefile.ini incorporates the value of BOOTSTRAPCFLAGS into CFLAGS and generates the three commands just shown. The first compiles *ccimake*. The second invokes *ccimake* and includes the result in the arguments passed to the command that compiles *imake.o*. The third produces the *imake* executable.

The trigger symbol passed in through BOOTSTRAPCFLAGS is used to determine the platform type, but in different ways for each program. The key to understanding trigger use is *imakemdep.h*. This header file is included by the source for *ccimake* and *imake* and has one part for each. (It has also used by *makedepend* and has a third part for that program; we will get to that shortly.)

The contents of *imakemdep.h* are organized like this:

```
#ifdef CCIMAKE
        /* part 1 (for ccimake) */
#else
#    ifndef MAKEDEPEND
        /* part 2 (for imake) */
#    else
        /* part 3 (for makedepend) */
#    endif
#endif
```

The source for *ccimake* defines CCIMAKE before including *imakemdep.h*, so that part 1 is processed. *makedepend* source defines MAKEDEPEND, so that part 3 is processed. *imake* source does not define either symbol, so part 2 is processed.

For a new port of *imake*, you must add the proper information for your system to each part of *imakemdep.h*. For existing ports you need to verify that the information already there is correct, and fix it if it is not. The following discussion shows how to set up each part of *imakemdep.h*.

---

*If your *cpp* predefines the trigger, BOOTSTRAPCFLAGS can be empty:

```
% make -f Makefile.ini BOOTSTRAPCFLAGS=""
```

However, it does not hurt to specify the trigger explicitly.

imakemdep.h—Part 1 (for ccimake)

The first part of *imakemdep.h* consists of a bunch of #ifdef/#endif blocks. Each of them defines imake_ccflags as a string containing the flags needed to get *imake* to compile on a particular platform. The proper definition is selected according to the trigger symbol that is defined when *ccimake* is compiled.

Some flags commonly specified in the definition of imake_ccflags are -DSYSV (System V, Release 2 or 3), -DSVR4 (System V, Release 4), or -DUSG to indicate USG systems. For instance, if Brand XYZ systems are System V-based, specify the following:

```
#ifdef brandxyz
#define imake_ccflags "-DSYSV"
#endif
```

You might need more than one flag (see the hpux block for a particularly unpleasant example). Note that all flags are specified in a single string.

If no special flags are necessary to compile *imake*, there need not be any block for your system, and imake_ccflags is given a default definition (currently -O).

If you do not know whether *ccimake* needs to produce any special flags or not, experiment by trying to compile *imake* by hand. Once you figure out how to do it, make your knowledge explicit by defining imake_ccflags appropriately in *imakemdep.h*.

imakemdep.h—Part 2 (for imake)

The second part of *imakemdep.h* contains four sections. Each of them poses a question:

- Do you have a working *dup2()* system call? If not, define a work-around for it.

- Does your *cpp* collapse tabs in macro expansions? If not, define FIX-UP_CPP_WHITESPACE or your Makefiles will not have tabs where necessary and the @@\ sequences will not be stripped out properly.

- Do you want to use the default preprocessor */lib/cpp?* If not, choose an alternate by defining DEFAULT_CPP. The value of DEFAULT_CPP must be a full pathname and only a pathname (no arguments). You can specify an alternate preprocessor at *imake* runtime by setting the IMAKECPP environment variable, but it is better to compile it in using DEFAULT_CPP so *imake* knows the correct value automatically. This may sound nonportable, and it is, because on your machine you want *imake* to know where *cpp* is so you do not have to tell it.

- Are there arguments you want *imake* to pass to *cpp* automatically? This section initializes a string array `cpp_argv[]` with those arguments. The most important entry is a definition for the trigger symbol used to select the correct vendor block in *Imake.tmpl*, but other entries may be necessary, too.

Of the four sections of *imakemdep.h* that apply to *imake*, the one that sets up the string array `cpp_argv[]` is the most complex. It contains a set of `#ifdef/#endif` blocks that adds entries to the array. The most common construction looks like this:

```
#ifdef trigger
    "-Dtrigger",
#endif
```

If `trigger` is defined when *imake* is compiled, it causes a definition of itself to be passed to *cpp* when *imake* executes. (If your *cpp* predefines the trigger, you may not see an instance of this construction for your system, but there is no harm in adding one explicitly.)

For Brand XYZ systems, add the following entry to `cpp_argv[]`:

```
#ifdef brandxyz
    "-Dbrandxyz",
#endif
```

This causes *imake* to pass *–Dbrandxyz* to *cpp*, allowing *cpp* to select the Brand XYZ vendor block as it processes the configuration files.

If you need to pass more than one argument to *cpp*, add the definitions for each argument as separate strings:

```
#ifdef brandxyz
    "-Dbrandxyz",
    "-DSYSV",
#endif
```

imakemdep.h—Part 3 (for makedepend)

The third part of *imakemdep.h* applies to the compiled version of *make-depend*. (This has nothing to do with compiling *imake*, but since we're talking about *imakemdep.h*, we might as well cover it here.)

This part of *imakemdep.h* puts entries in the `predefs[]` string array based on which of various system- and compiler-related definitions are predefined by *cpp*. *makedepend* uses this information to be smart about which header files to pay attention to when it generates header file dependencies. Consider the following C program fragment:

```
#ifdef ultrix
#include "inca.h"
#else
#include "incb.h"
#endif
```

makedepend knows to generate a dependency for *inca.h* and not *incb.h* if `ultrix` is defined, and the other way around if it is undefined; a dumb dependency generator has to assume dependencies on both files in either case.

For existing ports, you can leave this part of *imakemdep.h* alone. For a new port, add symbols appropriate for your system if they are not already listed among the `predefs[]` initializers. First, find the lines that end the `predefs[]` initialization:

```
/* add any additional symbols before this line */
{NULL, NULL}
```

Then add new entries before those lines for any symbols predefined by your *cpp*:

```
#ifdef sym1
    {"sym1", "1"},
#endif
#ifdef sym2
    {"sym2", "1"},
#endif
    /* add any additional symbols before this line */
    {NULL, NULL}
```

Build imake

You're ready to build *imake*. This should be simple if you have set up the vendor file, vendor block, and *imakemdep.h* correctly. First remove the remains of any previous failed build attempts:

```
% make -f Makefile.ini clean
rm -f ccimake imake.o imake
rm -f *.CKP *.ln *.BAK *.bak *.o core errs ,* *~ *.a \
    tags TAGS make.log \#*
```

Then build *ccimake* and *imake*, substituting the bootstrap flags for your system into the following command:

```
% make -f Makefile.ini BOOTSTRAPCFLAGS="flags"
```

For Brand XYZ, the command looks like this:

```
% make -f Makefile.ini BOOTSTRAPCFLAGS="-Dbrandxyz"
making imake with BOOTSTRAPCFLAGS=-Dbrandxyz
cc -o ccimake -Dbrandxyz -O -I../include ccimake.c
cc -c -Dbrandxyz -O -I../include `./ccimake` imake.c
cc -o imake imake.o
```

After you build *imake*, test whether it is configured correctly, using *imake*'s –*v* option to tell it to echo the *cpp* command it executes. The normal input and output is of no interest here, so we also use –*T/dev/null* to provide an empty input template, and –*s/dev/null* to throw away the output:

```
% imake -v -T/dev/null -s/dev/null
cpp -I. -Uunix -Dbrandxyz
```

If you see a definition for your trigger symbol in the *cpp* command echoed by *imake* (–*Dbrandxyz* in the example above), *imake* is properly configured. If you do not see the definition, *imake* should still be okay if *cpp* predefines the trigger. Use the following command to check whether that is so (assuming the preprocessor *imake* uses is */lib/cpp*):

```
% echo "trigger" | /lib/cpp
```

If the trigger does not appear in the output or turns into "1", *cpp* predefines it. If you see the trigger string literally in the output, *cpp* does not predefine it, and you need to reconfigure *imake* to pass –*Dtrigger to cpp* explicitly.

Build the Rest of the Distribution

Now that you have the configuration files properly set up to build *imake*, you should be able to execute the World operation. In the distribution root directory, run this command:

```
% make World BOOTSTRAPCFLAGS="flags" >& make.world
```

This will rebuild *imake* and also build the rest of the distribution. After it finishes, see the section "Install the Software" for installation instructions.

If you can build *imake* but *make World* still fails, try building the distribution in stages to get an idea of where the problem lies. First, build the Makefiles:

```
% ./config/imake -I./config
% make Makefiles
```

If that works, try the following:

```
% make clean
% make depend
% make
```

If *make depend* fails while trying to compile *makedepend*, skip it and try the following step. You can go back later and try to figure out why *make-depend* does not build.

If you can't get any of this to work, read *misc/Porting* to see if it contains any helpful advice.

If you have to modify the distribution to build it on your system, please send your changes to me at *dubois@primate.wisc.edu.*

imake versus Open Windows

The versions of *imake* and *xmkmf* distributed with Open Windows (versions 2 and 3, at least) are nonstandard versions modified specially for use with Open Windows. If the pathnames for your versions of *imake* and *xmkmf* have *openwin* in them (e.g., */usr/openwin/bin/imake*), you are better off installing the standard versions because the versions distributed with Open Windows do not work very well to configure non-Open Windows software.

There are three difficulties:

- The Open Windows modification to *xmkmf* is not correct (as evidenced by the periodic requests on the net for the patch to the patch).

- The Open Windows version of *imake* is particularly obdurate: when the environment variable OPENWINHOME is set, *imake* assumes the configuration files are in ${OPENWINHOME}/*lib/config* and looks for them there before looking in any directory specified on the command line. This means the Open Windows configuration files take precedence over any others you might be trying to use. You can defeat this behavior by setting the environment variable IMAKEINCLUDE to *−Ipath* (where *path* is the directory in which you keep your configuration files). But that is undesirable because using IMAKEINCLUDE makes successful configuration activities depend on something hidden in your environment, rather than something explicit in the configuration files. It is also difficult to switch between different sets of files when you use IMAKE-INCLUDE because you must keep changing its value.

- The configuration files distributed with Open Windows contain no information about the location of Open Windows header files, libraries, etc.

It may be that these problems have been rectified by the time you read this. If not, you can work around them as follows:

- Throw away the Open Windows versions of *imake* and *xmkmf*.

- Follow the instructions in Chapter 9, *Coordinating Sets of Configuration Files*, for adding Open Windows-specific parameter values to the configuration files to create a set of configuration files that is Open Windows aware.

- Use the standard version of *imake* and the bootstrapper *imboot* to bootstrap Makefiles using the Open Windows configuration files.

- Use the standard version of *xmkmf* to bootstrap Makefiles using the X11 configuration files.

C

Configuration Programs: A Quick Reference

This appendix briefly documents the programs *imake, imboot, imdent, makedepend, mkdirhier, msub,* and *xmkmf.* The information here is similar, but not identical to what may be found in the manual pages for these programs. Generally the descriptions here are more condensed, e.g., to eliminate mention of obscure or rarely used options.

Several manual pages on which parts of this appendix are based were written by Todd Brunhoff and Jim Fulton.

imake

NAME

imake – generate a *Makefile* from an *Imakefile* and a set of configuration files.

SYNOPSIS

```
imake [ options ]
```

DESCRIPTION

imake generates a *Makefile* by running *cpp* to process an *Imakefile* and a set of configuration files. One of the configuration files is a template that directs the order in which the files are processed. The template tells *cpp* to read other configuration files containing machine- and site-dependent configuration parameters, rules for generating *Makefile* target entries, and, finally, the *Imakefile*. The *Imakefile* contains descriptions of targets to be built, written as calls to *cpp* macros. *imake* takes care of expanding the macros into the corresponding *Makefile* target entries. The entries are properly configured for the current machine using the machine dependencies specified in the configuration files. This allows machine-specific information (such as compiler options, alternate command names, and special *make* rules) to be kept separate from the descriptions of the various items to be built.

OPTIONS

imake understands the following options:

–Dname, –Dname=value, –Idir

These options are passed directly to *cpp*. The *–D* options are typically used to set directory-specific variables, such as TOPDIR and CURDIR to indicate the top of the project and the current directory within the project. The *–I* option is used to indicate where to find the configuration files.

–Ttemplate   This option specifies the name of the template. The default is *Imake.tmpl*.

–ffilename   This option specifies the name of the per-directory input file. The default is *Imakefile*.

–sfilename   This option specifies the name of the output file. The default is *Makefile*.

−e   This option tells *imake* to execute the generated *Makefile*. The default is not to do so.

−v   This option tells *imake* to print the *cpp* command line that it is using to generate the *Makefile*.

ENVIRONMENT VARIABLES

imake uses the following environment variables if they are defined. Their use is not recommended, as they introduce dependencies that are not readily apparent when *imake* is run:

IMAKEINCLUDE

This variable may be defined as a *−Idir* argument to indicate the directory in which to look for configuration files, e.g., *−I/usr/include/local*. Actually, any *cpp* arguments are allowed in IMAKEINCLUDE, but the first one must begin with *−I* or *imake* will reject it.

IMAKECPP

By default, *imake* uses */lib/cpp* as the preprocessor program. IMAKECPP may be defined to specify the path of an alternate preprocessor, e.g., */usr/local/cpp*.

IMAKEMAKE

By default, *imake* uses whatever *make* program is found first in your search path. IMAKEMAKE may be defined to specify the path of an alternative *make*, e.g., */bin/s5make*. IMAKEMAKE has no effect unless *−e* is specified on the command line.

imboot

NAME

imboot – bootstrap a *Makefile* from an *Imakefile*.

SYNOPSIS

`imboot [ options ] [ topdir [ curdir ] ]`

DESCRIPTION

imboot bootstraps a *Makefile* from an *Imakefile* by generating an *imake* command. By default, *imboot* looks for configuration files in the *config* directory under the project root directory. The –c (or –C) option may be given to tell *imboot* to use a set of publicly-installed configuration files instead of (or in addition to) any files in the project's *config* directory.

The `topdir` argument specifies the location of the project root. The default is "." and thus may be omitted if the current directory is the project root. Otherwise it may be specified as an absolute pathname or as a path relative to the current directory. `curdir`, if given, specifies the name of the current directory, relative to the project root. `curdir` is usually omitted.

OPTIONS

imboot understands the following options:

–c *name*   Use the named set of configuration files instead of the files in the project's *config* directory. The files are assumed to be installed in the *name* directory under */usr/lib/config*.

–C *name*   Use the named set of configuration files in addition to the files in the project's *config* directory. The files are assumed to be installed in the *name* directory under */usr/lib/config*. They are also assumed to use an extensible architecture so that individual projects can provide project specific configuration information that extends or overrides information in the public files. *imboot* tells *imake* to look in the *config* directory under the project root before */usr/lib/config/name* when searching for configuration files.

NAME

imdent – indent *cpp* directives to show nesting level.

SYNOPSIS

```
imdent [ options ] [ file ] ...
```

DESCRIPTION

imdent reads the named input files, or the standard input if no files are named, and adds indentation to *cpp* directives based on the nesting level of conditional directives. This shows the nesting visually as an aid to finding malformed conditional constructs, and can be helpful when debugging *imake* configuration files.

Example: given the following input:

```
#ifndef LintLibFlag
#if SystemV || SystemV4
#define LintLibFlag -o
#else
#define LintLibFlag -C
#endif
#endif
```

imdent produces the following output:

```
#ifndef LintLibFlag
#   if SystemV || SystemV4
#     define LintLibFlag -o
#   else
#     define LintLibFlag -C
#   endif
#endif
```

OPTION

imdent understands the following option:

−*n*   Specify indentation increment per nesting level. *n* is a number. The default is 2 spaces. −*0* removes all indentation.

makedepend

NAME

makedepend – create header-file dependencies in Makefiles.

SYNOPSIS

makedepend [*options*] *file* . . .

DESCRIPTION

Every file that a source file references via an #include directive is what *makedepend* calls a "dependency." For example, if the source file *main.c* includes *defs.h*, which in turn includes *conf.h*, then the object file *main.o* depends on both *def.h* and *conf.h*. This is expressed in a *Makefile* as:

```
main.o: defs.h conf.h
```

makedepend reads the named input source files in sequence and parses them to process #include, #define, #undef, #ifdef, #ifndef, #endif, #if, and #else directives so that it can tell which #include directives would be used in a compilation. Any #include directives can reference files having other #include directives, and parsing occurs in those files as well. *makedepend* determines the dependencies and writes them to the *Makefile* so that *make* knows which object files must be recompiled when a dependency has changed.

makedepend first searches the *Makefile* for the line:

```
# DO NOT DELETE THIS LINE -- make depend depends on it.
```

If *makedepend* finds this line, it deletes everything following it to the end of the *Makefile* and writes the dependencies after it. If it doesn't find the line, *makedepend* appends it to the end of the *Makefile* before writing the dependencies.

By default, *makedepend* writes its output to *makefile* if it exists, or to *Makefile* if it does not. An alternate *Makefile* may be specified with the *–f* option.

To use *makedepend* with *imake*, set the variable SRCS to the names of the source files to be checked and invoke DependTarget() in the *Imakefile*:

```
SRCS = main.c aux.c funcs.c io.c
DependTarget()
```

After generating the *Makefile*, generate dependencies by typing *make depend*.

OPTIONS

makedepend ignores any option it does not understand so that you may use the same arguments you would use for *cc*. *makedepend* understands the following options:

−Dname=value, −Dname

>Define *name* with the given value (first form) or with value 1 (second form).

−Idir

>By default, *makedepend* searches only */usr/include* to find files named on #include directives. This option tells *makedepend* to prepend *dir* to the list of directories it searches.

−a

>Append dependencies to any that already exist in the *Makefile* instead of replacing them.

−ffilename

>Write dependencies to *filename* instead of to *makefile* or *Makefile*.

−− options −−

>When *makedepend* encounters a double hyphen (−−) in the argument list, any unrecognized argument following it is silently ignored; a second double hyphen terminates this special treatment. In this way, *makedepend* can be made to safely ignore esoteric compiler arguments. All options that *makedepend* recognizes that appear between the pair of double hyphens are processed normally.

mkdirhier

NAME

mkdirhier – make a directory hierarchy.

SYNOPSIS

mkdirhier *dir*

DESCRIPTION

mkdirhier creates the specified directory and any missing parent directories. Suppose you execute the following command:

```
% mkdirhier /usr/local/lib/myproj
```

If any of the directories */usr*, */usr/local*, or */usr/local/lib* do not exist, *mkdirhier* creates them before creating */usr/local/lib/myproj*. This differs from *mkdir*, which fails if any parent directories are missing.

NAME

msub – substitute *make* variables into a template to produce a script.

SYNOPSIS

```
msub [ options ] [ file ] . . .
```

DESCRIPTION

msub allows targets to be produced easily from templates that contain references to the variables found in a *Makefile*.

First *msub* reads the *Makefile* in the current directory to find all variable definition lines of the form "*var* = *value*". Then it reads any files named on the command line (or the standard input if none), searches through them for references to the *Makefile* variables, and replaces the references with the corresponding variable values. References to undefined variables are replaced by the empty string. The result is written to the standard output.

OPTIONS

msub understands the following options:

–f file   By default, variable values are extracted from *Makefile* (or *makefile* if *Makefile* is missing) in the current directory. If the –*f* option is given, variable values are extracted from *file* instead.

+Rstr, –Rstr   The default variable reference indicators within templates are the same as those used by *make*, i.e., $(and), and ${ and }. These can be changed with the +*R* and –*R* options, which must be specified in pairs. +*R* specifies the string that initiates a variable reference and –*R* specifies the string that terminates it. Multiple pairs of reference indicators may be given.

NAME

xmkmf – bootstrap a *Makefile* from an *Imakefile*.

SYNOPSIS

xmkmf [*options*] [*topdir* [*curdir*]]

DESCRIPTION

When invoked with no arguments in a directory containing an *Imakefile,* *xmkmf* runs *imake* with arguments appropriate to use the publicly-installed X11 configuration files to generate a *Makefile*.

If you specify a *topdir* argument to indicate the root directory of your project, *xmkmf* does not use the installed configuration files. Instead, it looks for the files in the *config* directory under the project root.

curdir may be specified as a relative pathname from the top of the build tree to the current directory. *curdir* is usually omitted.

OPTION

xmkmf understands the following option:

−a   The command *xmkmf -a* is equivalent to the following command sequence:

```
% xmkmf
% make Makefiles
% make includes
% make depend
```

D

Generating Makefiles:
A Quick Reference

The command you use to build a *Makefile* from an *Imakefile* depends on the configuration files you're using and where they're located:

% *xmkmf*   Bootstrap a *Makefile* using the X11 configuration files.

% *imboot*[`topdir`]

> Bootstrap a *Makefile* using configuration files stored in the *config* directory under the project root. `topdir` is the path from your current directory to the project root directory; it's optional if you're in the root.

% *imboot -c name* [`topdir`]

> Bootstrap a *Makefile* using installed configuration files named *name.*

% *imboot -C name* [`topdir`]

> Bootstrap a *Makefile* using installed extensible configuration files named *name.*

% *make Makefile*

> Rebuild a *Makefile* using an existing *Makefile* built by any of the above methods.

% *make Makefiles*

> Build Makefiles in subdirectories (you must build the *Makefile* in the current directory first).

% *make Makefiles "SUBDIRS=a b c"*

> Build Makefiles only in subdirectories *a*, *b*, and *c*.

% *make depend*

> Append header file dependencies to the *Makefile*, should be
> done after any bootstrapping command, *make Makefile*, or
> *make Makefiles*.

Whenever you modify an *Imakefile*, rebuild the *Makefile* so your changes
take effect. Also, when you first install a project on your machine, rebuild
its Makefiles to configure them properly.

For background information on the *Makefile*-generation process, see Chapter 7, *A Closer Look at Makefile Generation*; Chapter 9, *Coordinating Sets of Configuration Files*; and Chapter 14, *Designing Extensible Configuration Files*.

Writing Imakefiles: A Quick Reference

This appendix discusses rule invocation etiquette and some X11 rules commonly used to write Imakefiles.

- To invoke a rule, you simply name it and pass any arguments necessary:

  ```
  RuleName(arguments)
  ```

- Some rules have no arguments, some have one, some have many:

  ```
  DependTarget()
  SimpleProgramTarget(myprog)
  CppScriptTarget(scrpt,scrpt.cpp,-D'LIBDIR="$(LIBDIR)"',Makefile)
  ```

- Don't put any spaces before or after arguments, or the rule may not expand properly in the *Makefile*:

  ```
  InstallLibrary( mylib,$(USRLIBDIR))      /* incorrect */
  InstallLibrary(mylib ,$(USRLIBDIR))      /* incorrect */
  InstallLibrary( mylib , $(USRLIBDIR) )   /* VERY incorrect */
  InstallLibrary(mylib,$(USRLIBDIR))       /* correct */
  ```

- However, an argument may contain spaces internally when it comprises a list of items such as filenames, libraries, or flags:

  ```
  NormalLibraryTarget(mylib,a.o b.o c.o)
  ComplexProgramTarget_1(myprog,$(XMULIB) $(XLIB),-ly -lm)
  SpecialObjectRule(file.o,file.c,-DFLAG1 -DFLAG2)
  ```

- Specify empty arguments using a macro defined as nothing. The X11 configuration files provide `NullParameter` for this purpose:

  ```
  ComplexProgramTarget_1(myprog,NullParameter,NullParameter)
  ```

Subdirectory Support

To write an *Imakefile* that generates target entries for processing subdirectories, begin by putting in the following three lines:

```
#define IHaveSubdirs
#define PassCDebugFlags
SUBDIRS = subdirectory-list
```

The value assigned to SUBDIRS consists of the names of the subdirectories in which you want *make* to run, in the order you want them processed.

The presence of the IHaveSubdirs, PassCDebugFlags, and SUBDIRS lines tells the configuration files to generate certain default target entries for processing subdirectories recursively. The particular set of entries depends on the configuration files you're using:

- The X11 files generate install, install.man, clean, tags, Makefiles, and includes entries. They don't automatically generate recursive all or depend target entries; you need to invoke Make-Subdirs() and DependSubdirs() yourself:

  ```
  #define IHaveSubdirs
  #define PassCDebugFlags
  SUBDIRS = subdirectory-list

  MakeSubdirs($(SUBDIRS))
  DependSubdirs($(SUBDIRS))
  ```

- The DP configuration files developed in Chapters 10 and 11 generate recursive all and depend entries for you automatically, so you don't need to invoke MakeSubdirs() or DependSubdirs().

To determine what entries your configuration files generate for you, check the tail end of the template file *Imake.tmpl*.

If you want to pass debugging flags to *make* operations in subdirectories, don't give PassCDebugFlags an empty value; define it like this instead:

```
#define PassCDebugFlags 'CDEBUGFLAGS=$(CDEBUGFLAGS)'
```

Then you can specify debugging flags from the *make* command line, e.g.:

```
% make "CDEBUGFLAGS=-g"
```

For more information on writing Imakefiles that cause *make* operations to be performed in subdirectories, see Chapter 5, *Writing Imakefiles*, and Chapter 10, *Introduction to Configuration File Writing*.

Some common X11 rules are described on the following pages. If you're using different configuration files, they might contain similar rules. For more information, see Chapter 4, *The X11 Configuration Files*, and Chapter 5, *Writing Imakefiles*.

NAME

SimpleProgramTarget()

SYNOPSIS

Build a single program from a single source file.

SYNTAX

SimpleProgramTarget(*prog*)

prog is the name of the program.

DESCRIPTION

SimpleProgramTarget() is the simplest program building rule:

- You tell it only the name of your program, which must consist of a single source file *prog.c.*

- SimpleProgramTarget() generates a target entry *prog* for building your program, as well as all, install, install.man, depend, lint, and clean entries.

- If you need to link libraries into your program, you set certain *make* variables in the *Imakefile*. Use LOCAL_LIBRARIES for local libraries or X libraries. Specify local libraries built within the project using pathnames. Specify X libraries using the variables XLIB, XMULIB, XTOOL-LIB, etc. Use SYS_LIBRARIES for system link libraries, specified using −*lname* syntax.

- To indicate libraries for dependency-checking, assign a value to the variable DEPLIBS. (Asssign the empty value if there are no dependency libraries.) Dependency libraries must be given in pathname form. Specify local within-project libraries just as for LOCAL_LIBRAR-IES. Specify X libraries using the variables DEPXLIB, DEPXMULIB, DEPXTOOLLIB, etc. But don't specify system libraries, since, in general, there's no portable pathname form for them.

EXAMPLE

```
LOCAL_LIBRARIES = $(TOP)/lib/libmylib.a $(XMULIB) $(XLIB)
  SYS_LIBRARIES = -lm
        DEPLIBS = $(TOP)/lib/libmylib.a $(DEPXMULIB) $(DEPXLIB)
SimpleProgramTarget(myprog)
```

CAVEAT

`SimpleProgramTarget()` can be invoked only once per *Imakefile*.

ComplexProgramTarget

NAME

ComplexProgramTarget()

SYNOPSIS

Build a single program from multiple source files.

SYNTAX

ComplexProgramTarget(*prog*)

prog is the name of the program.

DESCRIPTION

ComplexProgramTarget() is much like SimpleProgramTarget(), but the program can be built from an arbitrary number of files:

* ComplexProgramTarget() makes no assumptions about the names of the files, so you must set the *make* variables SRCS and OBJS to the names of the source files and object files.

* ComplexProgramTarget() generates the same target entries as SimpleProgramTarget().

* Libraries are specified the same way for ComplexProgramTarget() as for SimpleProgramTarget().

EXAMPLE

```
            SRCS = myproga.c myprogb.c myprogc.c
            OBJS = myproga.o myprogb.o myprogc.o
LOCAL_LIBRARIES = $(XLIB)
  SYS_LIBRARIES =
        DEPLIBS = $(DEPXLIB)
ComplexProgramTarget(myprog)
```

CAVEAT

ComplexProgramTarget() can be invoked only once per *Imakefile*.

NAME

```
ComplexProgramTarget_1()
ComplexProgramTarget_2()
ComplexProgramTarget_3()
```

SYNOPSIS

Build two or three programs; each may consist of multiple source files.

SYNTAX

```
ComplexProgramTarget_1(prog, loclibs, syslibs)
ComplexProgramTarget_2(prog, loclibs, syslibs)
ComplexProgramTarget_3(prog, loclibs, syslibs)
```

prog is the name of the program; *loclibs* and *syslibs* name local and system link libraries. *loclibs* and *syslibs* are analogous to LOCAL_LIBRARIES and SYS_LIBRARIES, except that you specify them as rule arguments rather than as *make* variables.

DESCRIPTION

To use any of the ComplexProgramTarget_n() rules:

- Set the *make* variable PROGRAMS to the names of the programs you wish to build.

- Set the variables SRCSn and OBJSn to the source and object files for program *n* and invoke the corresponding rule.

- To specify dependency libraries for program *n*, assign a value to DEP-LIBSn (asssign the empty value if there are no dependency libraries).

- The ComplexProgramTarget_n() rules generate a target entry for each program to be built, as well as all, install, install.man, depend, lint, and clean entries.

EXAMPLE

```
PROGRAMS = prog1 prog2 prog3
   SRCS1 = prog1a.c prog1b.c
   OBJS1 = prog1a.o prog1b.o
DEPLIBS1 = $(DEPXLIB)
   SRCS2 = prog2a.c
   OBJS2 = prog2a.o
```

```
DEPLIBS2 =
    SRCS3 = prog3a.c prog3b.c prog3c.c
    OBJS3 = prog3a.o prog3b.o prog3c.o
DEPLIBS3 = $(DEPXTOOLLIB) $(DEPXLIB)
ComplexProgramTarget_1(prog1,$(XLIB),NullParameter)
ComplexProgramTarget_2(prog2,NullParameter,-lm)
ComplexProgramTarget_3(prog3,$(XTOOLLIB) $(XLIB),NullParameter)
```

CAVEAT

Each rule can be invoked only once in an *Imakefile*. The second and third rules cannot be invoked without the first.

NAME

NormalProgramTarget()

SYNOPSIS

Build an arbitrary number of programs.

SYNTAX

NormalProgramTarget(*prog*, *objs*, *deplibs*, *loclibs*, *syslibs*)

prog is the name of the program; *objs* names the object files from which to build the program; *deplibs* names the dependency libraries; *loclibs* and *syslibs* name the local and system link libraries.

DESCRIPTION

NormalProgramTarget() provides a general purpose interface for program building:

- You can invoke NormalProgramTarget() any number of times in an *Imakefile* to build any number of programs.

- However, NormalProgramTarget() generates only two entries (a *prog* entry to build the program, and a clean entry to remove it), so you must invoke additional rules to generate all, install, install.man, depend, or lint entries. Thus, each use of Normal-ProgramTarget() is normally preceded by AllTarget() to generate an all entry and followed by installation rules to generate install and install.man entries.

- In addition, to generate depend and lint entries, set SRCS to the names of all the source files for all the programs and invoke Depend-Target() and LintTarget() once each at the end of the *Imakefile*.

EXAMPLE

```
SRCS1 = prog1a.c prog1b.c
OBJS1 = prog1a.o prog1b.o

SRCS2 = prog2a.c prog2b.c prog2c.c prog2d.c
OBJS2 = prog2a.o prog2b.o prog2c.o prog2d.o
    .
    .
    .
SRCSn = progna.c prognb.c
OBJSn = progna.o prognb.o
 SRCS = $(SRCS1) $(SRCS2) ... $(SRCSn)
```

```
AllTarget(prog1)
NormalProgramTarget(prog1,$(OBJS1),$(DEPXLIB),$(XLIB),NullParameter)
InstallProgram(prog1,$(BINDIR))
InstallManPage(prog1,$(MANDIR))

AllTarget(prog2)
NormalProgramTarget(prog2,$(OBJS2),$(DEPXLIB),$(XLIB),-lm)
InstallProgram(prog2,$(BINDIR))
InstallManPage(prog2,$(MANDIR))
    .
    .
    .
AllTarget(progn)
NormalProgramTarget(progn,$(OBJSn),$(DEPXLIB),$(XLIB),-ly)
InstallProgram(progn,$(BINDIR))
InstallManPage(progn,$(MANDIR))

DependTarget()
LintTarget()
```

The second argument to `InstallProgram()` and `InstallManPage()` is the installation directory for the program and manual page. The first argument to `InstallManPage()` is the name of the program to which the page applies, but the manual page file itself should be named *prog.man*.

NAME

NormalLibraryTarget()

SYNOPSIS

Build a library.

SYNTAX

NormalLibraryTarget(*name,objs*)

name is the basename of the library (e.g., for *libmylib.a*, *name* should be mylib); *objs* names the object files from which to build the library.

DESCRIPTION

NormalLibraryTarget() builds a library:

- You should precede it with an invocation of NormalLibrary-
  ObjectRule() so the configuration files can set up some additional
  library-building machinery.

- For a library with basename mylib, NormalLibraryTarget() generates a libmylib.a target entry and an all entry.

- NormalLibraryTarget() doesn't generate depend or lint targets, so you should also set SRCS and invoke DependTarget() and
  LintTarget().

- If you intend to install the library, invoke InstallLibrary() to generate an install entry.

- No explicit clean entry is necessary; the X11 configuration files provide a default clean entry that removes *.a* files.

EXAMPLE

```
SRCS = file1.c file2.c file3.c ... filen.c
OBJS = file1.o file2.o file3.o ... filen.o
NormalLibraryObjectRule()
NormalLibraryTarget(mylib,$(OBJS))
InstallLibrary(mylib,$(USRLIBDIR))
DependTarget()
LintTarget()
```

The second argument to InstallLibrary() is the installation directory.

CAVEAT

Building shared, profiled, or debugging libraries is more complicated. See Chapter 5, *Writing Imakefiles*, for more details.

F

Writing Configuration Files: A Quick Reference

Specifics for developing configuration files are given in Chapter 10, *Introduction to Configuration File Writing*; Chapter 11, *Writing Rule Macros*; and Chapter 12, *Configuration Problems and Solutions*. If you're writing a set of extensible configuration files, see also Chapter 15, *Creating Extensible Configuration Files*.

Here are some general guidelines for creating configuration files:

- To avoid writing everything from scratch, copy an existing set of files. For instance, you can start with the SP files discussed in Chapter 8, *A Configuration Starter Project*, or the EA files discussed in Chapter 15, *Creating Extensible Configuration Files*, depending on whether you want nonextensible or extensible files.

- Simplify the files you're starting with by deleting information from them that's superfluous to your configuration requirements. But make sure you understand the purpose of the symbols you remove so you know you really can get rid of them, and don't remove a symbol if other symbols you retain depend on it.

- Add configuration information you need that wasn't in the original configuration files.

- If you intend to install the configuration files publicly, modify the self-reference by changing the value of `ConfigDir` in *Project.tmpl* to point to the installation location. If the files are extensible, set `ConfigName` to the name of your set of files instead, and make sure `ConfigRoot-Dir` is set to the configuration root directory *imboot* uses on your machine.

Parameter Settings and Feature Symbols

Parameter settings and feature symbols go in *Imake.tmpl* or *Project.tmpl*, depending on whether they describe the system or the project. Choose default values that reflect the likely choice on the widest variety of machines, and use the vendor files to override the defaults as necessary.

To create new parameters, use *make* variables, define default values using *cpp* macros, and set the values of the parameter variables using the macros:

```
#ifndef LexCmd
#define LexCmd lex
#endif
#ifndef LexLib
#define LexLib -ll
#endif
    LEX = LexCmd
 LEXLIB = LexLib
```

Feature symbols are similar except that there's no corresponding *make* variable:

```
#ifndef HasPutenv
#define HasPutenv NO
#endif
```

In either case, you can override the macro value if necessary in the site or vendor file:

```
#ifndef LexCmd
#define LexCmd flex /* use GNU flex instead */
#endif
#ifndef LexLib
#define LexLib -lfl /* use GNU flex library instead */
#endif

#ifndef HasPutenv
#define HasPutenv YES
#endif
```

Rule Syntax

This section briefly discusses rule syntax and the various parts of a rule. For more information, see Chapter 11, *Writing Rule Macros.*

New rules go in *Imake.rules*, defined as *cpp* macros. Following is a simple example that illustrates some basic rule-writing principles.

```
 1: /*
 2:     BuildProgram() builds the program "prog" from the
 3:     given object files and libraries.  It may be
 4:     invoked multiple times in the same Imakefile to
 5:     build several different programs.
 6:
 7:     Arguments:
 8:     prog    program name
 9:     objs    object files from which program is built
10:     libs    libraries needed to link program
11:
12:     Targets produced:
13:     prog    build this program
14:     all     build prog (and any others in Imakefile)
15:     clean   remove program (and others in Imakefile)
16: */
17:
18: #ifndef BuildProgram
19: #define BuildProgram(prog,objs,libs)              @@\
20: all:: prog                                        @@\
21: prog: objs                                        @@\
22:     $(CC) -o prog objs $(LDOPTS) libs $(LDLIBS)   @@\
23: StuffToClean(prog)
24: #endif /* BuildProgram */
```

Lines   Meaning

1–16   Comment describing the purpose of the rule. Especially helpful to those unfamiliar with rule syntax.

19–23   Rule definition. All lines of the definition but the last are terminated by "@@\", a special sequence signifying that the rule definition continues onto the next line.

19   The rule begins with a `#define` directive specifying the rule name and parameter list. There should be no spaces from the beginning of the rule name to the end of the parameter list. Separate multiple parameters by commas.

20–23   The body of the rule. This determines what the rule expands to. Parameter values passed to a rule when it's invoked are substituted into the body of the rule as it's expanded, and apply to that invocation only.

21–22   Main target entry built by rule (the entry named after the program).

- Line 21 specifies that `prog` depends on its object files. The target name is followed by a single colon. To allow a target name to be associated with multiple entries in a *Makefile*, use a double colon instead. (`all`, `clean`, and `install` targets are likely candidates for double colons.)

- Line 22 specifies the command used to perform the final link step.

  Command lines must be indented by a tab, not spaces.

  CC, LDOPTS, and LDLIBS are configuration parameters—*make* variables defined elsewhere in the configuration files. The values of these variables apply to all invocations of the rule.

18,24 #ifndef and #endif directives to protect the definition given on lines 19–23 so the definition can be overridden by one occurring earlier in configuration file processing.

- All rule definitions should be surrounded by #ifndef and #endif.

- The #ifndef and #endif lines are not part of the macro definition and do not end with "@@\".

- The #endif is followed by a comment repeating the name of the rule. This is not required, but sometimes helpful in finding the end of a complex rule.

20 This line generates an all target entry.

- all is dependent on prog, so *make all* builds the program.

- The all target entry precedes the prog entry so all (not prog) becomes the default target when BuildProgram() is the first rule invoked in the *Imakefile*.

- A double colon is used so multiple entries may be associated with the all target. For instance, if you invoke Build-Program() several times in the *Imakefile*, each invocation generates an all entry.

23 Rule definitions can invoke other rules, which are expanded in turn to generate additional target entries. In this case, StuffTo-Clean() generates a clean target entry to remove the final executable.

If you want to use shell programming constructs in a rule there are additional considerations. Here's a simple rule that removes .o files from directories named by the dirs parameter:

```
 1: /*
 2:     Remove object files from the named directories
 3: */
 4:
 5: #ifndef CleanObjects
 6: #define CleanObjects(dirs)                                    @@\
 7: cleanobjs::                                                   @@\
 8:     for i in dirs ;                             \             @@\
 9:     do                                          \             @@\
10:         echo "removing object files in $$i..." ;  \           @@\
11:         (cd $$i; $(RM) *.o) ;                   \             @@\
12:     done
13: #endif /* CleanObjects */
```

The rule illustrates the following conventions to be aware of:

- Refer to shell variables using two $-signs (e.g., $$i on lines 10,11).

- Multiple-command constructs require special care:

  — Multiple commands in a command sequence should be separated by semicolons as necessary to keep the shell from running them together.

  — Command sequences that continue over several lines should be joined by backslashes placed after all but the last line. The backslashes go after the commands on the line but before the @@\ marker.

  — The cd and $(RM) commands on line 11 are enclosed within (and) to force them to execute in a subshell. This isolates the effect of the cd so the current directory is restored after the subshell terminates.

G

Basics of make and cpp

This appendix is a brief introduction to some basic concepts of *make* and *cpp* that will help you understand *imake*. Since *imake* produces Makefiles, you need to understand a little about *make*. *imake* uses *cpp* to do most of its work, so you should also understand something about *cpp*.

For more information on either program, see the references suggested in Appendix I, *Related Documents*.

Basics of make

make operates by reading a file named *Makefile* that functions as a kind of script specifying how to build targets you're interested in, such as programs or libraries. The *Makefile* contains entries that provide specifics for target-building. The form of an entry is:

```
target: dependencies
        commands
```

`target` is the thing you want to build. `dependencies` lists the things that target depends on. For example, if the object file *src.o* is built from the source file *src.c*, *src.o* depends on *src.c*. *make* uses dependencies to determine whether it needs to do anything. If a target is newer than all its dependencies (as determined from the last modified time of each), the target is assumed to be up-to-date. If the target is older than any of its dependencies (or if the target doesn't exist), it needs to be rebuilt. When *make* determines that a target is out of date, it executes the `commands` part of the entry to bring the target up-to-date. `commands` may contain more than one line; each line must be indented with a tab.

For example, if a program *prog* is built from source files *a.c* and *b.c*, the target entry might look like this:

```
prog: a.o b.o
    cc -o prog a.o b.o
```

This specifies that *prog* is the target, that the object files *a.o* and *b.o* are the dependencies, and that to build the program we run the C compiler to link it from the object files.

There are some dependencies here we haven't specified: *a.o* and *b.o* are built from *a.c* and *b.c* and therefore depend on them. We don't need to list those dependencies explicitly because *make* has built-in knowledge about the relationship between *.c* files and *.o* files, and how to compile the former to produce the latter.

If you write a lot of program building entries in a *Makefile*, you'll have many instances of the C compiler's name. To substitute another C compiler like *gcc*, you have to edit each instance. *make* allows you to use variables to alleviate this difficulty. So, you could use the variable CC, and assign it a value like this:

```
CC = cc
```

Then you refer to it either as $ (CC) or ${CC}. The two forms are equivalent, although this book always uses the first form. A revised *Makefile* using the variable looks like this:

```
CC = cc
prog: a.o b.o
    $(CC) -o prog a.o b.o
```

To change the C compiler, you just change the value assigned to CC.

Note that what I'm calling *make* variables are sometimes referred to in other *make* documentation as *make* macros. *cpp* has macros, too; to avoid confusion, in this book the word macro always means a *cpp* macro, not a *make* macro.

It's not an error to refer to a variable that hasn't been assigned a value. Undefined variables implicitly have an empty value.

When you invoke *make*, you can specify particular targets you want built. If you don't name any, it just builds the first target listed in the *Makefile*.

In addition to target names, you can specify options on the command line. One that's especially useful is –*n*, which tells *make* to show you the commands it would execute to bring the targets named on the command line up-to-date, without actually executing those commands.

make is picky about where you put tabs and spaces. Do not indent command lines in a target entry with spaces (use tabs). Do not indent variable assignments with tabs (use spaces).

Comments may be placed in a *Makefile*; they begin with a # character and continue until the end of the line:

```
# This is a comment
```

Basics of cpp

The C preprocessor *cpp* performs several operations on its input that are important for *imake's* purposes, such as macro definition, file inclusion, and conditional testing. All of these operations are triggered by lines beginning with # followed by a keyword. These are called preprocessing directives.

Macro Definition

cpp allows a macro to be defined and given a value such that further instances of the macro name in the input are replaced by the macro value in the output. For example, given the following definition:

```
#define BinDir /usr/local/bin
```

then the input:

```
BinDir/program
```

is transformed to this in the output:

```
/usr/local/bin/program
```

Macros may be defined in terms of other macros:

```
#define YES 1
#define OUI YES
```

Given these definitions, the value of OUI is 1.

Macros may be defined with parameters. When the macro is invoked later, the arguments in the invocation are substituted for the parameters in the definition. Thus the following input:

```
#define Append(a,b) cat a >> b
Append(current,archive)
```

produces this output:

```
cat current >> archive
```

Macros may be defined with the empty value:

```
#define EmptyMacro
```

This is useful in conjunction with conditional tests for which you only need to know whether or not a symbol is defined.

Long macro definitions may be spread across lines by using backslashes to indicate continuation:

```
#define LongMacro This\
is\
a\
long\
value
```

There is no backslash on the last line. The backslashes and the newlines following them are deleted when the definition is processed. For the preceding example, the value of `LongMacro` is `Thisisalongvalue`.

Although you can split a macro definition across lines, you cannot split a macro invocation. The following invocations are unlikely to produce a useful result, if indeed your *cpp* doesn't simply consider them illegal:

```
Long\
Macro

Append(current,\
archive)
```

Macros may be undefined:

```
#undef MacroName
```

Macros may be defined or undefined from the *cpp* command line with the *−D* and *−U* options. The following command defines *DEBUG*, defines *TMPDIR* with a value of */usr/tmp*, and makes sure *unix* is undefined (some *cpp*'s predefine it by default):

```
% cpp -DDEBUG -D'TMPDIR="/usr/tmp"' -Uunix
```

File Inclusion

When *cpp* encounters a directive that takes either of the following forms, it inserts the contents of `filename` into the input stream:

```
#include <filename>
#include "filename"
```

If *filename* is surrounded by angle brackets (< and >), *cpp* looks for the file in the include-file directories named on the *cpp* command line using *–I* arguments (and in a list of standard directories). For instance, if *cpp* is invoked like this:

```
% cpp -I/usr/include -I/var/include
```

it will first look in */usr/include*, then in */var/include*, and then in the standard directories.

If *filename* is surrounded by double quotes rather than angle brackets, *cpp* looks in the current directory first before searching the other directories.

A directive of the form:

```
#include MacroName
```

interpolates the file named by `MacroName` if its value is of the form *<filename> or "filename"*.

Conditional Testing

cpp allows a primitive form of flow control using conditional constructs:

```
1)  #if condition       2)  #ifdef symbol       3)  #ifndef symbol
        stuff                   stuff                   stuff
    #endif                  #endif                  #endif
```

In the first form, when *condition* is true (non-zero), *stuff* is processed (and ignored otherwise). In the second form, *stuff* is processed if *symbol* has previously been defined in a `#define` statement. The third form is like the second, but *stuff* is processed if *symbol* is not defined.

Conditionals may have an `#else` clause:

```
#if condition
    stuff
#else
    other-stuff
#endif
```

If *condition* is true, *stuff* is processed, otherwise *other-stuff* is processed.

The following two constructs are equivalent:

```
#ifdef symbol
#if defined(symbol)
```

So are these:

```
#ifndef symbol
#if !defined(symbol)
```

Comments may be written by surrounding them with /* and */:

```
/* this is a comment */
```

A comment doesn't have to begin and end on the same line:

```
/*
 * this is a 3-line comment
 */
```

H

A Little History

imake is often thought to have been developed for the X Window System. It's true that the two have been closely associated through all releases of X11, but that's not how *imake* came into being.

Todd Brunhoff wrote *imake* at the Tektronix Research Labs about 1982–1984 while developing operating systems for a research platform called Magnolia. This was a 68010-based, dual-processor computer with 40MB disk, 2MB memory, a 19-inch black-and-white display, and a proprietary window system. *imake* was first used to help port Berkeley UNIX to this machine. Writing correct Makefiles by hand was difficult and time-consuming, but it was relatively simple to generate them using *imake*.

Later, during development of X11R1 at MIT, Brunhoff rewrote *imake* to support multiple platforms (the design it retains today), and engineered the first X11 configuration files. The rewrite was intended to allow R1 to be configured more easily, but acceptance of *imake* was far from automatic: "Most everyone was incredulous about the usefulness of this cryptic software beast, and getting everyone to buy into it was very difficult."

Nevertheless, *imake* proved its worth. X11R1 became the first publicly available project configured with it, and later releases continued to use *imake*. Jim Fulton wrote *xmkmf* and maintained the configuration files from X11R2 through X11R4. Bob Scheifler took over from Fulton as Keeper of the Files after X11R4, and retains the major oversight for them today.

When asked to comment on the preceding account, Fulton said, "I'd almost be tempted to mention that Brunhoff and Fulton now disclaim all knowledge of *imake* and stare blankly when asked about it."

Joining in this sentiment, Brunhoff added, "Fulton and Brunhoff have suffered terribly from their intimate association with *imake* and are known to display various nervous tics when the subject is broached. They now can only find employment with regional traveling carnivals, but do maintain their email addresses."

I

Related Documents

The references listed below serve as useful sources of information for *make*, *cpp*, and the X11 configuration files.

- *Managing Projects with make*, Andrew Oram and Steve Talbott. O'Reilly & Associates, Inc., 1991. The standard reference for *make*.

- *The C Programming Language* (2nd. edition), Brian W. Kernighan and Dennis M. Ritchie. Prentice Hall, 1988. The standard reference for the C language. Includes information on *cpp*.

- *Configuration Management in the X Window System*, Jim Fulton. A general description of *imake* as used for X. This paper is included in the X11R5 distribution in *mit/doc/config/usenixws/paper.ms*.

- *Using Imake to Configure the X Window System*, Paul DuBois. The main body of the paper has been superceded (by this book), but the appendix contains a catalog of rules provided by the X11 configuration files. Written for X11R4 but most of the information is still current. Available via anonymous FTP on *ftp.primate.wisc.edu*, in the */pub/imake-stuff* directory, or by connecting via GOPHER to *gopher.primate.wisc.edu*.

In this appendix:
- *Changes to the X11 Project Tree Layout*
- *Changes to imake*
- *Changes to the Configuration Files*
- *Changes to Other Configuration Utilities*
- *Coexistence Between X11 Releases*

J

X11R6

The X distribution was at X11R5, patchlevel 24 when *Software Portability with imake* was written. Since the book's initial publication, X11R6 has been released. This appendix serves as a brief guide to the differences between R5 and R6. It focuses on changes in four aspects of X11R6:

- The X11 project tree layout
- The *imake* program itself
- The configuration files
- Other configuration utilities

Throughout, I've tried to point out difficulties or incompatibilities you may experience if you're moving from R5 to R6 or if you want to maintain both releases online simultaneously.

You should read the R6 release notes, of course, particularly sections 1, 2.3.1, 3.3, 3.4, 3.5, 3.8, and 4.13.

Changes to the X11 Project Tree Layout

The R5 source root is named *mit* and the configuration related files and programs are found in two locations under the root:

mit/config   This directory contains the source for *imake* and the configuration files.

mit/util   This directory is something of a miscellany. Its subdirectories contain the source for several configuration utilities such as *makedepend, xmkmf,* and *lndir*, but it's also the location of non-configuration utilities such as *patch* and *compress*.

The source tree has been reorganized for R6. The root is named *xc*, and the tree is structured to place all configuration files and programs under the *config* directory. *config* consists of four subdirectories with the following contents:

xc/config/cf	The configuration files.
xc/config/imake	The source for the *imake* program.
xc/config/makedepend	The source for the *makedepend* program.
xc/config/util	The source for other configuration-related utilities such as *xmkmf* and *mkshadow*.

Note that the path from the source root to the configuration files has changed from *./config* in R5 to *./config/cf* in R6.

Non-configuration utilities such as *patch* and *compress* are still included, but they're located under *xc/config*.

Installation Directories

The default installation directories are located under `ProjectRoot`, which has a default value of */usr/X11R6*. In R5, `ProjectRoot` is by default undefined; if you define it, the suggested value is */usr/X11R5*.

If you built R5 with `ProjectRoot` undefined, undefining `ProjectRoot` when you build R6 will wipe out your R5 installation, because the install directories are the same for both releases when `ProjectRoot` is undefined (Table J–1).

Table J-1: R5 and R6 Install Directories

	`ProjectRoot` defined		`ProjectRoot` undefined
	X11R5	X11R6[*]	X11R5,[*] X11R6
binaries	*/usr/X11R5/bin*	*/usr/X11R6/bin*	*/usr/bin/X11*
include files	*/usr/X11R5/include*	*/usr/X11R6/include*	*/usr/include/X11*
libraries	*/usr/X11R5/lib*	*/usr/X11R6/lib*	*/usr/lib*
manual pages	*/usr/X11R5/man*	*/usr/X11R6/man*	*/usr/man*

[*] The default for each release.

If you use shared libraries and you install R6 into a different location than R5, you may need to run *ldconfig* after performing the installation so the loader can find the new versions of the libraries. Alternatively, you can make links from the old names to the new.

Changes to imake

imake has been modified in some important ways to allow it to work on more systems, including Windows NT, a non-UNIX system. Some of the NT-related changes are that *imake* looks for carriage returns in line endings, not just linefeeds, and it allows rule macros to be written that generate *make* variables that are "local" to individual invocations of the rules.

imake is also more tolerant of cranky preprocessors now. For one thing, *imake* no longer writes to *cpp* standard input. Versions of *imake* in releases up through R5 cause the configuration files to be processed by generating the following three-line sequence, defining the template file and description file names, and feeding it into *cpp*'s standard input:

```
#define IMAKE_TEMPLATE "template-name"
#define INCLUDE_IMAKEFILE <Imakefile-name>
#include IMAKE_TEMPLATE
```

However, *cpp* on some systems will process only named files and won't accept input on *stdin*. This makes it difficult to compile prior releases on such systems unless you use a different version of *cpp*. (The problem occurs under some versions of OSF/1, for example.) To deal with this difficulty, R6 *imake* provides *cpp* with a named file by writing the three-line sequence to a temporary file, *Imakefile.c*, passing that file to *cpp*, and removing it when *cpp* finishes.

Another preprocessor-related change concerns the handling of XCOMM, the symbol used for writing comments into Makefiles. XCOMM is defined in *Imake.tmpl* like this:

```
#define XCOMM #
```

However, some ANSI preprocessors interpret the second # as the "convert to string" operator and therefore fail to generate comments properly. (See the section "Commenting" in Chapter 4, *The X11 Configuration Files.*)

R6 solves this problem by shifting the burden of XCOMM processing from *cpp* to *imake*. XCOMM is no longer defined as a macro in *Imake.tmpl*. Instead, *imake* itself translates XCOMM to # as part of the postprocessing it does on *cpp* output. Since XCOMM isn't a macro, *cpp* doesn't try to interpret it as anything special, and thus avoids the conflict with ANSI preprocessors.

The shifting of XCOMM processing responsibility causes a problem if you use R5 *imake* with R6 configuration files. *imake* will expect *cpp* to handle XCOMM, but the configuration files will expect *imake* to handle it. The result is that no one handles it, and you end up with XCOMM lines in your Makefiles. This problem can occur if you have an older version of *imake* installed in a directory that your shell searches before the directory where the R6 *imake* is located. Try the following command to determine the location of the *imake* your shell finds first:

```
% which imake
```

If it's the wrong (older) one, remove it from your system or at least change your search path so the R6 *imake* is found first.

By the way, the R6 release notes now explicitly discourage use of # for writing comments in Imakefiles. Sometimes you can get away with that because *imake* looks through the *Imakefile* and protects any leading # character not followed by a valid preprocessor directive keyword (#if, #ifdef, etc.) However, this mechanism has never been completely fool-proof, so you shouldn't rely on it. You should get into the habit of using XCOMM for all comments—not just in configuration files, but in Imakefiles as well.

Changes to the Configuration Files

The R5 and R6 configuration file architectures are not very different: the template includes a few more files, and the rules file *Imake.rules* is referenced at a different point in the inclusion order. By contrast, the contents of the configuration files have been modified and extended considerably. For example, more systems are recognized, new system capabilities are parameterized, C++ support is provided, and library-related variables are produced using generator macros that can be defined on a system-specific basis.

Configuration File Architecture

Figure J–1 shows a comparison of the R5 and R6 *Imake.tmpl* files. The primary architectural changes in R6 are:

- The vendor blocks that select the proper vendor file have been moved out of the template into a separate file *Imake.cf.* (This file has the same function as *Imake.vb* in Chapter 3, *Understanding Configuration Files.*)

- The system parameter settings have been split into two sections. The first section contains those parameters necessary for proper processing of *Imake.rules*; the second section contains all other parameters.

- The rules file *Imake.rules* is included by the template earlier, between the two system parameters sections. In relation to their positions in the R5 template, *Project.tmpl* and *Imake.rules* have switched places.

- Two extra files, `LocalRulesFile` and `LocalTmplFile`, can be included at your discretion. By default they are both defined as the empty file *noop.rules*, but you can redefine `LocalRulesFile` and `LocalTmplFile` in *site.def*. This allows you to extend the template to include information beyond that provided by the X11 files. This is important because without changing any of the X11 configuration files other than *site.def*, you can use them to configure a wider variety of projects than in the past.

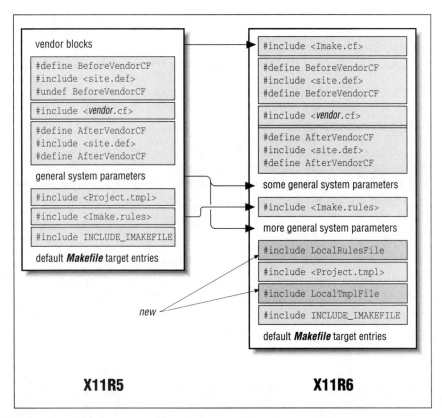

Figure J-1: Architecture of X11 configuration file template Imake.tmpl

For example, Motif 1.2, when used with R5, requires that you modify *Imake.tmpl* to add references for the Motif-specific files, *Motif.rules* and *Motif.tmpl*. With the R6 template this is no longer necessary. Instead, you install the two Motif files in the directory where you installed the R6 configuration files and add the following to *site.def*:

```
#define LocalRulesFile <Motif.rules>
#define LocalTmplFile <Motif.tmpl>
```

Configuration File Contents

The following sections describe some of the changes to the contents of individual configuration files.

Imake.tmpl

The template file contains many new macros for parameterizing additional system characteristics: the presence or absence of BSD 4.4 sockets, DECnet, the *poll()* system call, streams I/O, GNU *gcc* 2.x, CodeCenter, TestCenter, CenterLine C and C++ compilers, Sentinel, Purify, and Kerberos.

C++ support is present, provided through the *Cplusplus* macros and the *CXX* *make* variables.

Filename parameterization is improved. The object file suffix is parameterized as the macro Osuf, making it possible to build software on systems that use a suffix other than *.o*. The CCsuf macro parameterizes the C++ input file suffix to accommodate systems that don't use the default of *.cxx*.

Imake.cf and Vendor Files

Imake.cf is a new configuration file. It contains the vendor blocks that used to be in *Imake.tmpl* and that determine the proper vendor file. *Imake.tmpl* is more stable as a result: there is no longer any reason to modify it, not even to add support for a new platform. Instead, you supply an appropriate vendor file and add a new vendor block that recognizes the system to *Imake.cf*.

Compared to R5, more vendor files (and the accompanying vendor blocks in *Imake.cf*) are provided.

The following vendor files are new:

Amoeba.cf	*Oki.cf*	*fujitsu.cf*	*nec.cf*	*svr4.cf*
FreeBSD.cf	*Win32.cf*	*linux.cf*	*osf1.cf*	*usl.cf*
NetBSD.cf	*bsdi.cf*	*ncr.cf*	*sequent.cf*	*xfree86.cf*

Amoeba.cf is known to require work.

One vendor file, *att.cf*, is no longer included in the distribution.

Imake.rules

X-specific rules have been moved from *Imake.rules* into *Project.tmpl*. This makes *Imake.rules* more generic, further continuing the process begun in R4/R5 of collecting X-related information into *Project.tmpl*.

The family of token concatenation macros has grown, and the macros have been relocated and generalized:

- `Concat()` and `Concat3()` have a new sibling, `Concat4()`, that concatentates four arguments.
- The `Concat*()` macro definitions have been moved from *Imake.tmpl* to *Imake.rules*. (That's one reason *Imake.rules* is included earlier than in R5. These macros are heavily used, so the definitions for them must be seen early.)
- The definitions have been redesigned to function properly on more kinds of systems. In R5, the definitions test `__STDC__` to determine whether to concatenate tokens using empty C comments (`/**/`) or using the ANSI token pasting operator (`##`). On systems where the ANSI method is chosen incorrectly, you can define the macro `UnixCpp` to force concatenation using empty comments. But on systems where the empty comment method is chosen incorrectly, R5 provided no way to force ANSI token pasting. In R6, this is no longer a limitation because you can define the new macro `AnsiCpp` to force ANSI concatenation.

Rules for processing *lex* and *yacc* files are provided.

C++ support is present, provided through the `*Cplusplus*` rules.

The final (link) step in program building is now performed using `CCLINK` rather than `CC`. The difference is that `CCLINK` is defined on systems that need it to set the environment variable `LD_RUN_PATH` before invoking the C compiler.

The rules for building libraries have been revised substantially.

Project.tmpl

The R6 distribution builds a number of new libraries, so there are several yards of new terrain in *Project.tmpl* containing yet more library macro and variable definitions.

Macros associated with some of the libraries have been renamed. The *LibX, *OldLibX, and *LibXinput macros now have names of the forms *LibX11, *OldX, and *LibXi. The *LibXArchive macros have disappeared.

Library-related variables (*XXXLIB*, *DEPXXXLIB*) are produced in *Project.tmpl* using the generator macros UnsharedLibReferences(), SharedLibReferences(), and SharedDSLibReferences(). These macros are given default values in *Imake.rules* but may be overridden on a system-specific basis in the *Lib.rules* files. The macros bring some rationality to a complex problem that has long been difficult due to differing procedures and conventions among systems.

The last section of *Project.tmpl* contains X-specific rules that were in *Imake.rules*.

Shared Library Files (*Lib.tmpl and *Lib.rules)

Shared library support has been extended to cover these additional systems: FreeBSD/NetBSD, Fujitsu, HP, Linux, NEC, Oki, OSF/1, SGI, Sony, and Windows NT. The definition of SharedLibraryTarget() in the Linux rules file *lnxLib.rules* is a stunning entry into the competition for "Most Complicated *imake* Rule Ever."

host.def

host.def is a new configuration file that can be used as a means of setting parameters that vary from host to host within a given site. By default, *host.def* is unused. It's included by *site.def* rather than by *Imake.tmpl*, so if you want to use it, look in *site.def* for the lines that reference *host.def* and uncomment them.

host.def is used when the configuration files are stored on a master host and shared by other hosts using shadow link trees. Suppose a host needs to modify definitions to supply values that apply only to itself. The link to the default *host.def* (an empty file) is replaced on that host with a real file containing the definitions. This allows per-host modifications without affecting other machines at the site.

Changes to Other Configuration Utilities

- *xmkmf*

  The path to the configuration files from the source root directory is now *./config/cf* rather than *./config*, so the R5 and R6 versions of *xmkmf* work only with their respective X11 releases when bootstrapping Makefiles using the configuration files located within the source tree. See "Coexistence Between X11 Releases" later in this appendix for more details.

- *makedepend*

  makedepend has some new options. For instance, *-osuf* sets the object suffix to *suf*, allowing production of dependencies on systems which use a suffix other than *.o*. Warnings about multiple inclusion of a given header file are no longer issued unless you specify the *-m* option.

  Expressions in conditional directives (`#if`, `#ifdef`, `#ifndef`) are parsed more completely. This revision provides better discrimination of what should and should not be processed between a conditional and its corresponding `#endif`, and, thus, it provides more accurate dependency lists.

- *mkshadow*

  This is a new program that provides an alternative to *lndir* for creating shadow link trees.

Coexistence Between X11 Releases

The R6 utilities and configuration files represent an advance over their R5 counterparts, but of course they're intended to help you build software for R6, not for earlier releases. What do you do if you still have R5-based projects, or if you still want to keep the R5 tree online? This section discusses problems you may encounter and how to deal with them.

The R6 files provide a superset of the functionality offered by the R5 files, so perhaps the easiest way to find out if a given R5-based project can be built with R6 is simply to try it. If it works, you're home free. But that approach certainly won't work for building within R5 itself, and there are bound to be other R5-based projects that can't be configured properly with the R6 files.

Most of the symbols that have changed names or disappeared between R5 and R6 appear to be intended primarily for internal use by the configuration files and not by Imakefiles. However, if an *Imakefile* does refer to any of these symbols, it is incompatible with R6. For instance, some Imakefiles refer to HasSaberC, so they aren't directly usable with the R6 configuration files. (HasSaberC has been replaced by HasCodeCenter in R6.)

The existence of release-dependent Imakefiles means you need to be able to select between the R5 and R6 configuration files. In practice this means you need to choose which version of *xmkmf* you'll use, since each version selects a different set of files.

Of course, it doesn't help matters that both versions have the same name. One way to deal with this is to rename the R5 version to *xmkmf5*. Then you can choose the set of configuration files you want by invoking the bootstrapper with the appropriate name:

```
% xmkmf5 /path/to/mit      Bootstrap using within-project R5 configuration files
% xmkmf5                   Bootstrap using installed R5 configuration files
% xmkmf /path/to/xc        Bootstrap using within-project R6 configuration files
% xmkmf                    Bootstrap using installed R6 configuration files
```

Another solution is to use *imboot*, which allows you to select either set of configuration files, as well as whether you want the installed files or the ones located within the source tree. (This requires *imboot* 1.02; earlier versions don't know the location of the configuration file directory in R6.)

To select a set of configuration files located within an X11 project tree, provide an argument specifying the path to the project root:

```
% imboot /path/to/mit      Bootstrap using R5 configuration files
% imboot /path/to/xc       Bootstrap using R6 configuration files
```

To bootstrap with the installed R5 or R6 configuration files, you need to make *imboot* aware of them by creating links under the *imboot* configuration root. Assume that the R5 and R6 configuration files are installed in */usr/X11R5/lib/X11/config* and */usr/X11R6/lib/X11/config*, and that the configuration root is */usr/lib/config*. First, create a link to the R5 configuration files if one doesn't already exist (you may have already created this link in Chapter 9, *Coordinating Sets of Configuration Files*):

```
% ln -s /usr/X11R5/lib/X11/config /usr/lib/config/X11R5
```

Then create a link to the R6 configuration files:

```
% ln -s /usr/X11R6/lib/X11/config /usr/lib/config/X11R6
```

With these links in place, you can use the *−c* option to select the set of files you want to use:

```
% imboot -c X11R5
% imboot -c X11R6
```

If for some reason you plan to install your R6 configuration files where your R5 files are already installed (e.g., if you plan to use */usr/lib/X11/config* for both installs), you need to copy the R5 files somewhere else first. The procedure for doing this is described in Chapter 9.

Index

:: (double colon), in target entries, 35
@@, 40

A

AfterVendorCF, 74
all targets, 201-202

B

BeforeVendorCF, 74
BITFTP, 296
Bootstrap target, including automatically in Makefiles, 171
bootstrappers, 17
    designing a general purpose, 158-161
    imboot, 123
    using in Makefiles, 169-171
    xmkmf, 123
bootstrapping, Makefiles, 269, 329
    with multiple sets of configuration files, 158
building, multiple programs, 95-102
    single programs, 87-90;
        multiple source files, 88-90;
        one source file, 87-88

C

C comments, in configuration files and in Imakefiles, 79
clean targets, 198-200
commands, echoing, 239
    selecting flags for, 224-227
comments, broken, 126-127
    in configuration and Imakefiles, 79-81
    make, 81
conditionals, imake support for, 236
    in Imakefiles, 220-225
    malformed, 246-247
    selecting files and directories with, 221-223
    selecting targets with, 220-221
    unbalanced, 245-246
configuration files, 63
    architecture of, 33-60
    bootstrapping sets of, 158
    comments in, 79-81
    comprehensive, 259
    coordinating sets of, 157-171
    default values in, 183
    deleting symbols from, 278
    determining file directory location, 267

configuration files (cont'd)
  extensible; creating new sets of,
    290;
    designing, 253-281;
    distributing software with, 290;
    implementing, 262-271;
    installation directories, 287;
    libraries, 288;
    overriding parameters, 284;
    project-specific rules, 288;
    sharing, 260-262;
    site-specific files, 289;
    system characteristics, 288;
    testing, 290;
    using, 283-291
  for FORTRAN support, 176
  for X support, 176
  information; adding to, 182-188;
    deleting from, 175-179;
    retaining from, 179-182
  keeping prototypes, 258
  Kerberos, 166-167
  location, 137-139;
    directory, 132-134;
    within-project, 132
  macros, adding to, 182-186
  modifying, 175-188, 258-259
  Motif, 167-169
  Open Windows, 167-169
  parameter variables, adding to,
    182-186
  reusing, 254-262;
    methods of, 258-262;
    vs. porting, 254
  shared library support, 176
  starter project, 145-155
  troubleshooting, 243-251;
    cpp problems, 250;
    incorrect version numbers, 249;
    make comments, 248-249;
    missing default values, 247-248;
    missing templates, 249-250;
    nonportable cpp or make con-
    structs, 250;
    rule syntax errors, 243-244;
    spaces in rule definitions,
    244-245;
    unbalanced conditionals,
    245-246, 246-247
  writing, 173-188, 343-347
  X11, 61-81, 164-165
configuration problems, solving,
  215-241
configuration programs, 319-328
configuration software, obtaining, 293
configuring, header files, 232-233
  source files, 225-233
cpp, 16, 37
  basics of, 349-354
  constructs, nonportable, 250
  in troubleshooting configuration
    files, 250
  macro types, 246
CPU time, allowing for interface differences, 222

D

debugging, specifying debugging
  flags, 111
default targets, 27, 75
default values, missing, 247-248
DEFINES, 111
dependency libraries, 91-92
DEPLIBS, 90-91
description files, machine-independent, 35-41
directories, locating by parameters,
  217
  locating by pathnames, 216
  managing multiple, 107
  subdirectory support, 186-188
  using conditionals to select,
    221-223
directory-specific targets, in X11, 75

E

echoing commands, 239
empty rule arguments, 86
error messages, Can't find include file
  Imake.tmpl, 249
error processing, in rules, 239-240
errors, diagnosing, 122-123

errors (cont'd)
    misspelled rules and macros, 125
    spelling, 126
extensible configuration files, 253-281,
        283-291
    creating new sets of, 290
    designing, 253-272
    distributing software with, 290
    installation directories, 287
    libraries, 288
    overriding parameters, 284
    project-specific rules, 288
    site-specific files, 289
    system characteristics, 288
    testing, 290

F

-f option, 42
flags, for commands, 224-227

H

HasGcc, 74
header file dependencies, generating,
        25, 180
header files, configuring, 232-233

I

imake, advantages of, 11
    definition, 320
    getting started, 16
    history of, 355
    how it works, 8-10
    related documents, 357
    running from a Makefile, 136-141
    versus Open Windows, 316
imake rules, (see rules)
imake template, figure of, 58
IMAKE variable, 67
IMAKE_CMD, 67
Imakefiles, 42
    bootstrapping Makefiles from, 16
    comments in, 79-81
    conditionals, 220-225

    for different versions of X11,
        165-166
    organizing source and object file
        lists, 102-103
    specifying libraries, 90
    troubleshooting, 121-130;
        broken comments, 126-127;
        diagnosing errors, 122-123;
        errors of omission, 130;
        incorrect library dependency
        specifications, 128;
        incorrect variable assignments,
        129;
        misspelled rules and macros,
        125;
        rule arguments, 124
    writing, 83-119, 331-342;
        exercise for, 17
Imake.params, 46, 48
    in template file, 46
    installation directory in, 47
Imake.rules, 43, 344
    and X11, 68
    providing FORTRAN support in,
        176
    providing X support in, 176
Imake.tmpl, 42, 44, 56, 150, 344
    and shared libraries, 177
    and vendor blocks, 69
    configuration defaults, 64
    configuration files included in, 58
    converting to different projects, 263
    figure of, 58
    for multiple projects, 271
    in X11, 62
    information contained in, 63
    modifying, 263
    Motif configuration files, 167
    parameter file in, 46
    parameterization support, 198
    providing FORTRAN support in,
        176
    specifying directory-specific targets
        in, 75

Imake.tmpl (cont'd)
  specifying machine-specifics in, 68
  specifying site-specifics in, 74
  specifying target entries in, 75
  system parameters in, 64-65, 191
  token pasting, 77
Imake.vb, 50, 58, 69, 182
imboot, 123, 322
imdent, 323
INCLUDES, 111
incompatible projects, 169
INSTALL, 208
install program, 208
InstallAppDefaults(), 107
installation commands, in Imakefiles,
  30
installation directories, extensible
  files, 287
installation rules, 106, 207-214
InstallLibrary(), 107
InstallManPage(), 106
InstallNonExecFile(), 107
InstallProgram(), 106
IRULESRC, 67

K

Kerberos, configuration files, 166-167

L

libraries, and extensible files, 288
  as dependencies, 194-195
  Athena (Xaw), 94
  building, 103-105, 206-207
  dependency, 91-92
  link, 90
    and dependency specifiers, 95
    writing into rules, 192-193
  locating with parameters, 218
  mixing types of, 95
  names, specifying, 218
  passing as rules arguments,
    193-194
  program-specific, 193
  shared library support, 176
  shared, 177

  specifying, 90
  system, 92-93
  within-project, 92
  writing rules for, 206-207
  X, 93-95
library specifications, incorrect, 128
link libraries, 90, 192-193
linkers, in rules, 196-198
LINT, 203
lint, and building multiple programs,
  102
  invoking in Imakefiles, 29
  targets, 202-204
LINTLIBS, 203
LINTOPTS, 203
local conventions, 55-57
LOCAL_LIBRARIES, 90
loops, imake support for, 236

M

m4, 37
machine specifics, specifying in template file, 68
machine-independent description files,
  35-41
MacroIncludeFile, 69
macros, adding to configuration files,
  182-186
  chosing default, 183-186
  for building Makefiles, 180
  names, 130
  naming, 37
  processors, 37
  rule (see rules)
  token pasting, 179
  types, 246
  writing, 38-41
make, basics of, 349-354
  comments, troubleshooting,
    248-249;
    in configuration files and in
    Imakefiles, 80
  constructs, nonportable, 250
  portability of, 6
  suffix rules, using with imake,
    233-236
  variable parameters, 203

make (cont'd)
  variables, 45, 111-113
make Makefile(s) command(s), 131
  for X libraries, 93
makedepend, 16
  definition, 324
Makefiles, bootstrapping, 16-17, 269, 329
  building, 180
  building recursively, 139-141
  contents of, 21
  generating, 131-143, 269, 329-330;
    in X11, 141;
  configuration file directory, 132-134;
    exercise for, 17;
    project root location, 134-135
  on different systems, 24
  producing, 38
  regenerating, 123
  running imake from, 136-141
  target entries, default, 75
  using bootstrappers in, 169-171
mkdirhier, 16, 326
Motif, configuration files, 167-169
  template file, 167
Motif.rules, 167
Motif.tmpl, 167
msub, 228-231
  definition, 327
multiple directories, managing, 107
multiple line constructs, 237

O

object files, compiling specially, 105-106
Open Windows, configuration files, 167-169
  versus imake, 316

P

parameter variables, adding to configuration files, 182-186
parameters, 44-55
  and library names, 218
  and rules, 191-192, 195-196
  for building Makefiles, 180
  Imake.params, 48
  locating directories with, 217
  make, 203
  vendor-specific files, 49
  (see also Imake.params.)
PassCDebugFlags, specifying debugging flags, 111
pathnames, directory, 216
portability, 1-13, 219-220
  vs. reusability, 254
  with make, 6
program building entries, prototype, 36
programs, building multiple, 95-102
  building single, 87-90;
    multiple source files, 88-90;
    one source file, 87-88
project root, 134
projects, building, 240-241
  incompatible, 169
  sample layout, 216-217
Project.tmpl, 65, 276, 344
  providing X support in, 176

R

recursive entries, 186-188
recursive rules, 126, 186, 186-188
rule arguments, 86
  empty, 86
  troubleshooting, 124
rule macros, (see rules)
rule syntax, 190
  errors, 243-244
rules, 202
  and links, 196-198
  arguments (see rule arguments)
  building basic, 190-198
  definition of, 37
  definitions, file included in, 43;
    spaces in, 244-245
  documenting, 205-206
  error processing in, 239-240
  for building libraries, 103
  for building Makefiles, 180
  installation, 106, 207-214

rules (cont'd)
  invoking, 86-87
  libraries as dependencies, 194-195
  parameterizing, 191-192;
    implications of, 195-196
  passing information through,
    193-194
  project-specific, 288
  purpose of, 41
  recursive, 126, 186, 186-188
  replaceable, 57
  shell programming in, 236-240
  syntax (see rule syntax)
  to change directories, 238
  writing, 38-41, 189-214
  writing link libraries into, 192-193
  X11, 68
  (see also targets.)

S

shared libraries, in template files, 177
  symbols, 177
  support, 176
shell programming, in rules, 236-240
  changing directories, 238
  multiple line constructs, 237
SimpleProgramTarget, 87
site files, 56-57
site.def, 56
  and extensible files, 289
  and vendor files, 74
  X11, 69, 74
site-specifics, specifying in
  Imake.tmpl, 74
software, in this book, obtaining, 293
  portability (see portability)
source code, allowing for different
  platforms, 221
source files, configuring, 225-233;
    with macro values, 231-232;
    with msub, 228-231
subdirectory support, 186-188
SUBDIRS, constraints on, 110-111
suffix rules, defining new target types,
  236
  using with imake, 233-236
symbol dependencies, 178

symbols, deleting from configuration
  files, 177-179, 278
  shared library, 177
SYS_LIBRARIES, 90, 92
system libraries, 92-93

T

-T option, 42
target entries, Makefile, 75
  specifying in Imake.tmpl, 75
  X11, 75
target-building patterns, 35-38
targets, all, 201-202
  clean, 198-200
  default, 27
  directory-specific, 75
  entries, 35-38
  lint, 202-204
  using conditionals to select,
    220-221
template files, 42
  Motif, 167
  shared libraries in, 177
  (see also Imake.tmpl)
templates, in X11, 62-63
  missing, 249-250
  figure of, 58
token concatenation, 76-79
token pasting, macros, 179
TOP variable, 66, 92, 134
trigger symbols, 71
  and vendor blocks, 71
troubleshooting configuration files,
  243-251
  cpp, 250
  incorrect version numbers, 249
  make comments, 248-249
  missing default values, 247-248
  missing templates, 249-250
  nonportable cpp or make con-
    structs, 250
  rule syntax errors, 243-244
  spaces in rule definitions, 244-245

troubleshooting configuration files (cont'd)
unbalanced conditionals, 245-246,
246-247
troubleshooting rule arguments, 124

U

uucp command, 297

V

values, default, in configuration files,
183
variable assignments, troubleshooting,
129-130
variables, 45
adding to configuration files,
182-186
names, 130
vendor blocks, 264, 267
and trigger symbols, 71
changing for extensible configuration files, 275
in configuration files, 50, 58
in X11, 69
vendor files, 48-55
and shared library support, 176
and site def., 74
X11, 69
vendor.blocks, 182
vendor.cf, X11, 69
vendor-specific parameter files, (see
vendor files)
version numbers, incorrect, 249

W

within-project configuration files,
location of, 132
World target, 240-241

X

X Window System, (see X11)
X11, and Imake.rules, 68
configuration files, 61-81, 164-165;
for X-specific symbols, 176
reusing, 255-257;
troubleshooting, 121-130
default Makefile target entries, 75
directory-specific targets, 75
directory locations, 65
generating Makefiles, 141
Imakefile, 75
Imake.tmpl, 62
machine-specific information, 68
make variables for X libraries, 93
Motif configuration files, 167
multiple releases, 165-166
parameters, 64-68
rules, 68
site.def, 69, 74
site-specific definitions, 74
template, 62-63
token concatenation, 76-79
trigger symbols, 71
vendor blocks, 69
vendor files, 69
vendor.cf, 69
X libraries, 93-95
Xaw widget library, 94
XCOMM, 81
Xext library, 95
xmkmf, 16-17, 123
definition, 328

About the Author

Paul DuBois is a programmer at the Wisconsin Regional Primate Research Center at the University of Wisconsin-Madison. He leads a quiet life with few interests outside of family, church, and programming.

Colophon

Our look is the result of reader comments, our own experimentation, and feedback from distribution channels.

Distinctive covers complement our distinctive approach to technical topics, breathing personality and life into potentially dry subjects. UNIX and its attendant programs can be unruly beasts. Nutshell Handbooks help you tame them.

The animal featured on the cover of *Software Portability with imake* is the boa constrictor, a snake of the Boidae family. Boa constrictors are typically grey or silver with a series of brown or deep red saddles along their backs. They are found in the warmest parts of America, from Mexico to Argentina, and can reach lengths up to eighteen feet. Their young are born live, an average brood consisting of thirty to fifty one-foot snakes. The Boids, which include boas, anacondas, and pythons, are the giants of the snake world (anacondas can reach lengths of thirty feet and can weigh over three hundred pounds).

Boas feed on birds, reptiles, and mammals. A constrictor will seize prey with its mouth, swiftly coil around it, and tighten the grip so that the victim cannot expand its chest to breathe. Contrary to popular rumor or belief, boa constrictors pose little threat to humans. When a boa perceives danger, it will usually flee or threaten by hissing with a sound that can be heard over one hundred feet away.

Edie Freedman designed this cover and the entire UNIX bestiary that appears on other Nutshell Handbooks. The beasts themselves are adapted from 19th-century engravings from the Dover Pictorial Archive. The cover layout was produced with Quark XPress 3.1 using the ITC Garamond font.

The inside layout was formatted in sqtroff by Lenny Muellner using ITC Garamond Light and ITC Garamond Book fonts, and was designed by Edie Freedman. The figures were created in Aldus Freehand 3.1 by Jeff Robbins.

Programming

UNIX, C and MULTI-PLATFORM

Books from O'Reilly & Associates, Inc.

Fall/Winter 1994-95

Fortran/Scientific Computing

Migrating to Fortran 90

By James F. Kerrigan
1st Edition November 1993
389 pages, ISBN 1-56592-049-X

Many Fortran programmers do not know where to start with Fortran 90. What is new about the language? How can it help them? How does a programmer with old habits learn new strategies?

This book is a practical guide to Fortran 90 for the current Fortran programmer. It provides a complete overview of the new features that Fortran 90 has brought to the Fortran standard, with examples and suggestions for use. The book discusses older ways of solving problems—both in FORTRAN 77 and in common tricks or extensions—and contrasts them with the new ways provided by Fortran 90.

The book has a practical focus, with the goal of getting the current Fortran programmer up to speed quickly. Two dozen examples of full programs are interspersed within the text, which includes over 4,000 lines of working code.

Topics include array sections, modules, file handling, allocatable arrays and pointers, and numeric precision. Two dozen examples of full programs are interspersed within the text, which includes over 4,000 lines of working code.

"This is a book that all Fortran programmers eager to take advantage of the excellent feature of Fortran 90 will want to have on their desk."
—*FORTRAN Journal*

High Performance Computing

By Kevin Dowd
1st Edition June 1993
398 pages, ISBN 1-56592-032-5

High Performance Computing makes sense of the newest generation of workstations for application programmers and purchasing managers. It covers everything, from the basics of modern workstation architecture, to structuring benchmarks, to squeezing more performance out of critical applications. It also explains what a good compiler can do—and what you have to do yourself. The book closes with a look at the high-performance future: parallel computers and the more "garden variety" shared memory processors that are appearing on people's desktops.

UNIX for FORTRAN Programmers

By Mike Loukides
1st Edition August 1990
264 pages, ISBN 0-937175-51-X

This handbook lowers the UNIX entry barrier by providing the serious scientific programmer with an introduction to the UNIX operating system and its tools. It familiarizes readers with the most important tools so they can be productive as quickly as possible. Assumes some knowledge of FORTRAN, none of UNIX or C.

C Programming Libraries

POSIX.4

By Bill Gallmeister
1st Edition Winter 1994-95 (est.)
400 pages (est.), ISBN 1-56592-074-0

A general introduction to real-time programming and real-time issues, this book covers the POSIX.4 standard and how to use it to solve "real-world" problems. If you're at all interested in real-time applications— which include just about everything from telemetry to transation processing—this book is for you. An essential reference.

POSIX Programmer's Guide

By Donald Lewine
1st Edition April 1991
640 pages, ISBN 0-937175-73-0

Most UNIX systems today are POSIX compliant because the Federal government requires it for its purchases. Given the manufacturer's documentation, however, it can be difficult to distinguish system-specific features from those features defined by POSIX. The *POSIX Programmer's Guide*, intended as an explanation of the POSIX standard and as a reference for the POSIX.1 programming library, helps you write more portable programs.

"If you are an intermediate to advanced C programmer and are interested in having your programs compile first time on anything from a Sun to a VMS system to an MSDOS system, then this book must be thoroughly recommended." —*Sun UK User*

Understanding and Using COFF

By Gintaras R. Gircys
1st Edition November 1988
196 pages, ISBN 0-937175-31-5

COFF—Common Object File Format—is the formal definition for the structure of machine code files in the UNIX System V environment. All machine code files are COFF files. This handbook explains COFF data structure and its manipulation.

Using C on the UNIX System

By Dave Curry
1st Edition January 1989
250 pages, ISBN 0-937175-23-4

This is the book for intermediate to experienced C programmers who want to become UNIX system programmers. It explains system calls and special library routines available on the UNIX system. It is impossible to write UNIX utilities of any sophistication without understanding the material in this book.

"A gem of a book.... The author's aim is to provide a guide to system programming, and he succeeds admirably. His balance is steady between System V and BSD-based systems, so readers come away knowing both." —*SUN Expert*

Practical C Programming

By Steve Oualline
2nd Edition January 1993
396 pages, ISBN 1-56592-035-X

C programming is more than just getting the syntax right. Style and debugging also play a tremendous part in creating programs that run well. *Practical C Programming* teaches you not only the mechanics of programming, but also how to create programs that are easy to read, maintain, and debug. There are lots of introductory C books, but this is the Nutshell Handbook®! In this edition, programs conform to ANSI C.

Programming with curses

By John Strang
1st Edition 1986
76 pages, ISBN 0-937175-02-1

Curses is a UNIX library of functions for controlling a terminal's display screen from a C program. This handbook helps you make use of the curses library. Describes the original Berkeley version of curses.

C Programming Tools

Software Portability with imake

By Paul DuBois
1st Edition July 1993
390 pages, ISBN 1-56592-055-4

imake is a utility that works with *make* to enable code to be compiled and installed on different UNIX machines. *imake* makes possible the wide portability of the X Window System code and is widely considered an X tool, but it's also useful for any software project that needs to be ported to many UNIX systems.

This Nutshell Handbook®—the only book available on *imake*—is ideal for X and UNIX programmers who want their software to be portable. The book is divided into two sections. The first section is a general explanation of *imake*, X configuration files, and how to write and debug an *Imakefile*. The second section describes how to write configuration files and presents a configuration file architecture that allows development of coexisting sets of configuration files. Several sample sets of configuration files are described and are available free over the Net.

Managing Projects with make

By Andrew Oram & Steve Talbott
2nd Edition October 1991
152 pages, ISBN 0-937175-90-0

make is one of UNIX's greatest contributions to software development, and this book is the clearest description of *make* ever written. It describes all the basic features of make and provides guidelines on meeting the needs of large, modern projects. Also contains a description of free products that contain major enhancements to *make*.

"I use *make* very frequently in my day to day work and thought I knew everything that I needed to know about it. After reading this book I realized that I was wrong! —Rob Henley, Siemens-Nixdorf

"If you can't pick up your system's *yp Makefile*, read every line, and make sense of it, you need this book." —*Root Journal*

Checking C Programs with lint

By Ian F. Darwin
1st Edition October 1988
84 pages, ISBN 0-937175-30-7

The *lint* program checker has proven time and again to be one of the best tools for finding portability problems and certain types of coding errors in C programs. *lint* verifies a program or program segments against standard libraries, checks the code for common portability errors, and tests the programming against some tried and true guidelines. *Linting* your code is a necessary (though not sufficient) step in writing clean, portable, effective programs. This book introduces you to *lint*, guides you through running it on your programs, and helps you interpret *lint's* output.

lex & yacc

By John Levine, Tony Mason & Doug Brown
2nd Edition October 1992
366 pages, ISBN 1-56592-000-7

Shows programmers how to use two UNIX utilities, *lex* and *yacc*, in program development. The second edition contains completely revised tutorial sections for novice users and reference sections for advanced users. This edition is twice the size of the first, has an expanded index, and now covers Bison and Flex.

Power Programming with RPC

By John Bloomer
1st Edition February 1992
522 pages, ISBN 0-937175-77-3

RPC, or remote procedure calling, is the ability to distribute the execution of functions on remote computers. Written from a programmer's perspective, this book shows what you can do with RPCs, like Sun RPC, the de facto standard on UNIX systems. It covers related programming topics for Sun and other UNIX systems and teaches through examples.

Multi-Platform Programming

Guide to Writing DCE Applications

By John Shirley, Wei Hu & David Magid
2nd Edition May 1994
462 pages, ISBN 1-56592-045-7

A hands-on programming guide to OSF's Distributed Computing Environment (DCE) for first-time DCE application programmers. This book is designed to help new DCE users make the transition from conventional, non-distributed applications programming to distributed DCE programming. In addition to basic RPC (remote procedure calls), this edition covers object UUIDs and basic security (authentication and authorization). Also includes practical programming examples.

Distributing Applications Across DCE and Windows NT

By Ward Rosenberry & Jim Teague
1st Edition November 1993
302 pages, ISBN 1-56592-047-3

This book links together two exciting technologies in distributed computing by showing how to develop an application that simultaneously runs on DCE and Microsoft systems through remote procedure calls (RPC). Covers the writing of portable applications and the complete differences between RPC support in the two environments.

Understanding DCE

By Ward Rosenberry, David Kenney & Gerry Fisher
1st Edition October 1992
266 pages, ISBN 1-56592-005-8

A technical and conceptual overview of OSF's Distributed Computing Environment (DCE) for programmers, technical managers, and marketing and sales people. Unlike many O'Reilly & Associates books, Understanding DCE has no hands-on programming elements. Instead, the book focuses on how DCE can be used to accomplish typical programming tasks and provides explanations to help the reader understand all the parts of DCE.

Encyclopedia of Graphics File Formats

By James D. Murray & William vanRyper
1st Edition July 1994
928 pages (CD-ROM included), ISBN 1-56592-058-9

The computer graphics world is a veritable alphabet soup of acronyms; BMP, DXF, EPS, GIF, MPEG, PCX, PIC, RIFF, RTF, TGA, and TIFF are only a few of the many different formats in which graphics images can be stored. *The Encyclopedia of Graphics File Formats* is the definitive work on file formats—the book that will become a classic for graphics programmers and everyone else who deals with the low-level technical details of graphics files. It includes technical information on nearly 100 file formats, as well as chapters on graphics and file format basics, bitmap and vector files, metafiles, scene description, animation and multimedia formats, and file compression methods. Best of all, this book comes with a CD-ROM that collects many hard-to-find resources. We've assembled original vendor file format specification documents, along with test images and code examples, and a variety of software packages for MS-DOS, Windows, OS/2, UNIX, and the Macintosh that will let you convert, view, and manipulate graphics files and images.

Multi-Platform Code Management

By Kevin Jameson
1st Edition August 1994
354 pages (two diskettes included), ISBN 1-56592-059-7

For any programmer or team struggling with builds and maintenance, this book—and its accompanying software (available for fifteen platforms, including MS-DOS and various UNIX systems)—can save dozens of errors and hours of effort. A "one-stop-shopping" solution for code management problems, it shows you how to structure a large project and keep your files and builds under control over many releases and platforms. The building blocks are simple: common-sense strategies, public-domain tools that you can obtain on a variety of systems, and special utilities developed by the author. The book also includes two diskettes that provide a complete system for managing source files and builds.

Understanding Japanese Information Processing

By Ken Lunde
1st Edition September 1993
470 pages, ISBN 1-56592-043-0

Understanding Japanese Information Processing provides detailed information on all aspects of handling Japanese text on computer systems. It brings all of the relevant information together in a single book and covers everything from the origins of modern-day Japanese to the latest information on specific emerging computer encoding standards. Appendices provide additional reference material, such as a code conversion table, character set tables, mapping tables, an extensive list of software sources, a glossary, and more.

"Ken Lunde's book is an essential reference for everyone developing or adapting software for handling Japanese text. It is a goldmine of useful and relevant information on fonts, encoding systems and standards."
—Professor Jim Breen, Monash Univ., Australia

Business

Building a Successful Software Business

By Dave Radin
1st Edition April 1994
394 pages, ISBN 1-56592-064-3

This handbook is for the new software entrepreneur and the old hand alike. If you're thinking of starting a company around a program you've written—and there's no better time than the present—this book will guide you toward success. If you're an old hand in the software industry, it will help you sharpen your skills or will provide a refresher course. It covers the basics of product planning, marketing, customer support, finance, and operations.

"A marvelous guide through the complexities of marketing high-tech products. Its range of topics, and Radin's insights, make the book valuable to the novice marketeer as well as the seasoned veteran. It is the Swiss Army Knife of high-tech marketing."
—Jerry Keane, Universal Analytics Inc.

Database

ORACLE Performance Tuning

By Peter Corrigan & Mark Gurry
1st Edition September 1993
642 pages, ISBN 1-56592-048-1

The ORACLE relational database management system is the most popular database system in use today. Organizations, ranging from government agencies to small businesses, from large financial institutions to universities, use ORACLE on computers as diverse as mainframes, minicomputers, workstations, PCs, and Macintoshes.

ORACLE offers tremendous power and flexibility, but at some cost. Demands for fast response, particularly in online transaction processing systems, make performance a major issue. With more organizations downsizing and adopting client-server and distributed database approaches, performance tuning has become all the more vital.

Whether you're a manager, a designer, a programmer, or an administrator, there's a lot you can do on your own to dramatically increase the performance of your existing ORACLE system. Whether you are running RDBMS Version 6 or Version 7, you may find that this book can save you the cost of a new machine; at the very least, it will save you a lot of headaches.

"This book is one of the best books on ORACLE that I have ever read.... [It] discloses many Oracle Tips that DBA's and Developers have locked in their brains and in their planners.... I recommend this book for any person who works with ORACLE, from managers to developers. In fact, I have to keep [it] under lock and key, because of the popularity of it."
—Mike Gangler

O'Reilly & Associates—
GLOBAL NETWORK NAVIGATOR™

The Global Network Navigator (GNN)™ is a unique kind of information service that makes the Internet easy and enjoyable to use. We organize access to the vast information resources of the Internet so that you can find what you want. We also help you understand the Internet and the many ways you can explore it.

In GNN you'll find:

Navigating the Net with GNN

 The *Whole Internet Catalog* contains a descriptive listing of the most useful Net resources and services with live links to those resources.

 The *GNN Business Pages* are where you'll learn about companies who have established a presence on the Internet and use its worldwide reach to help educate consumers.

 The *Internet Help Desk* helps folks who are new to the Net orient themselves and gets them started on the road to Internet exploration.

News

 NetNews is a weekly publication that reports on the news of the Internet, with weekly feature articles that focus on Internet trends and special events. The Sports, Weather, and Comix Pages round out the news.

Special Interest Publications

 Whether you're planning a trip or are just interested in reading about the journeys of others, you'll find that the *Travelers' Center* contains a rich collection of feature articles and ongoing columns about travel. In the *Travelers' Center*, you can link to many helpful and informative travel-related Internet resources.

 The *Personal Finance Center* is the place to go for information about money management and investment on the Internet. Whether you're an old pro at playing the market or are thinking about investing for the first time, you'll read articles and discover Internet resources that will help you to think of the Internet as a personal finance information tool.

All in all, GNN helps you get more value for the time you spend on the Internet.

 The Best of the Web

GNN received "Honorable Mention" for "**Best Overall Site**," "**Best Entertainment Service**," and "**Most Important Service Concept**."

The *GNN NetNews* received "Honorable Mention" for "**Best Document Design**."

Subscribe Today

GNN is available over the Internet as a subscription service. To get complete information about subscribing to GNN, send email to **info@gnn.com**. If you have access to a World Wide Web browser such as Mosaic or Lynx, you can use the following URL to register online: `http://gnn.com/`

If you use a browser that does not support online forms, you can retrieve an email version of the registration form automatically by sending email to **form@gnn.com**. Fill this form out and send it back to us by email, and we will confirm your registration.

O'Reilly on the Net—
ONLINE PROGRAM GUIDE

O'Reilly & Associates offers extensive information through our online resources. If you've got Internet access, we invite you to come and explore our little neck-of-the-woods.

Online Resource Center

Most comprehensive among our online offerings is the O'Reilly Resource Center. Here, you'll find detailed information and descriptions on all O'Reilly products: titles, prices, tables of contents, indexes, author bios, software contents, reviews...you can even view images of the products themselves. We also supply helpful ordering information: how to contact us, how to order online, distributors and bookstores world wide, discounts, upgrades, etc. In addition, we provide informative literature in the field: articles, interviews, and bibliographies that help you stay informed and abreast.

 The Best of the Web

The *O'Reilly Resource Center* was voted "**Best Commercial Site**" by users participating in "Best of the Web '94."

To access ORA's Online Resource Center:

Point your Web browser (e.g., `mosaic` or `lynx`) to:
`http://gnn.com/ora/`

For the plaintext version, `telnet` or `gopher` to:
`gopher.ora.com`
(telnet login: `gopher`)

FTP

The example files and programs in many of our books are available electronically via FTP.

To obtain example files and programs from O'Reilly texts:

`ftp` to:
`ftp.ora.com`
or
`ftp.uu.net`
`cd published/oreilly`

Ora-news

An easy way to stay informed of the latest projects and products from O'Reilly & Associates is to subscribe to "ora-news," our electronic news service. Subscribers receive email as soon as the information breaks.

To subscribe to "ora-news":

Send email to:
listproc@online.ora.com

and put the following information on the first line of your message (not in "Subject"):
subscribe ora-news "your name" **of** "your company"

For example:
subscribe ora-news Jim Dandy of Mighty Fine Enterprises

Email

Many customer services are provided via email. Here's a few of the most popular and useful.

nuts@ora.com
    For general questions and information.
bookquestions@ora.com
    For technical questions, or corrections, concerning book contents.
order@ora.com
    To order books online and for ordering questions.
catalog@ora.com
    To receive a free copy of our magazine/catalog, "ora.com" (please include a postal address).

Snailmail and phones

O'Reilly & Associates, Inc.
103A Morris Street, Sebastopol, CA 95472
Inquiries: **707-829-0515, 800-998-9938**
Credit card orders: **800-889-8969**
    (Weekdays 6a.m.- 6p.m. PST)
FAX: **707-829-0104**

O'Reilly & Associates—
LISTING OF TITLES

INTERNET

!%@:: A Directory of Electronic Mail
   Addressing & Networks
Connecting to the Internet:
   An O'Reilly Buyer's Guide
Internet In A Box
The Mosaic Handbook for Microsoft Windows
The Mosaic Handbook for the Macintosh
The Mosaic Handbook for the
   X Window System
Smileys
The Whole Internet User's Guide & Catalog

SYSTEM ADMINISTRATION

Computer Security Basics
DNS and BIND
Essential System Administration
Linux Network Administrator's Guide
   (Winter '94-95 est.)
Managing Internet Information Services
Managing NFS and NIS
Managing UUCP and Usenet
sendmail
Practical UNIX Security
PGP: Pretty Good Privacy (Winter '94-95 est.)
System Performance Tuning
TCP/IP Network Administration
termcap & terminfo
X Window System Administrator's Guide:
   Volume 8
X Window System, R6, Companion CD
   (Winter '94-95 est.)

USING UNIX AND X

BASICS
Learning GNU Emacs
Learning the Korn Shell
Learning the UNIX Operating System
Learning the vi Editor
MH & xmh: E-mail for Users & Programmers
SCO UNIX in a Nutshell
The USENET Handbook (Winter '94-95 est.)
Using UUCP and Usenet
UNIX in a Nutshell: System V Edition
The X Window System in a Nutshell
X Window System User's Guide: Volume 3
X Window System User's Guide, Motif Ed.:
   Volume 3M
X User Tools

ADVANCED
Exploring Expect (Winter '94-95 est.)
The Frame Handbook
Learning Perl
Making TeX Work
Programming perl
sed & awk
UNIX Power Tools (with CD-ROM)

PROGRAMMING UNIX, C, AND MULTI-PLATFORM

FORTRAN/SCIENTIFIC COMPUTING
High Performance Computing
Migrating to Fortran 90
UNIX for FORTRAN Programmers

C PROGRAMMING LIBRARIES
Practical C Programming
POSIX Programmer's Guide
POSIX.4: Programming for the Real World
   (Winter '94-95 est.)
Programming with curses
Understanding and Using COFF
Using C on the UNIX System

C PROGRAMMING TOOLS
Checking C Programs with lint
lex & yacc
Managing Projects with make
Power Programming with RPC
Software Portability with imake

MULTI-PLATFORM PROGRAMMING
Encyclopedia of Graphics File Formats
Distributing Applications Across DCE and
   Windows NT
Guide to Writing DCE Applications
ORACLE Performance Tuning
Multi-Platform Code Management
Understanding DCE
Understanding Japanese Information
   Processing

BERKELEY 4.4 SOFTWARE DISTRIBUTION

4.4BSD System Manager's Manual
4.4BSD User's Reference Manual
4.4BSD User's Supplementary Documents
4.4BSD Programmer's Reference Manual
4.4BSD Programmer's Supplementary
   Documents
4.4BSD-Lite CD Companion
4.4BSD-Lite CD Companion:
   International Version

X PROGRAMMING

Motif Programming Manual: Volume 6A
Motif Reference Manual: Volume 6B
Motif Tools
PEXlib Programming Manual
PEXlib Reference Manual
PHIGS Programming Manual
   (soft or hard cover)
PHIGS Reference Manual
Programmer's Supplement for Release 6
   (Winter '94-95 est.)
Xlib Programming Manual: Volume 1
Xlib Reference Manual: Volume 2
X Protocol Reference Manual, R5: Vol. 0
X Protocol Reference Manual, R6: Vol. 0
   (Winter '94-95 est.)
X Toolkit Intrinsics Programming Manual:
   Volume 4
X Toolkit Intrinsics Programming Manual,
   Motif Edition: Volume 4M
X Toolkit Intrinsics Reference Manual: Vol.5
XView Programming Manual: Volume 7A
XView Reference Manual: Volume 7B

THE X RESOURCE

A QUARTERLY WORKING JOURNAL FOR X PROGRAMMERS
The X Resource: Issues 0 through 13
   (Issue 13 available 1/95)

BUSINESS/CAREER

Building a Successful Software Business
Love Your Job!

TRAVEL

Travelers' Tales Thailand
Travelers' Tales Mexico
Travelers' Tales India (Winter '94-95 est.)

AUDIOTAPES

INTERNET TALK RADIO'S "GEEK OF THE WEEK" INTERVIEWS
The Future of the Internet Protocol, 4 hrs.
Global Network Operations, 2 hours
Mobile IP Networking, 1 hour
Networked Information and
   Online Libraries, 1 hour
Security and Networks, 1 hour
European Networking, 1 hour

NOTABLE SPEECHES OF THE INFORMATION AGE
John Perry Barlow, 1.5 hours

O'Reilly & Associates—
INTERNATIONAL DISTRIBUTORS

Customers outside North America can now order O'Reilly & Associates books through the following distributors. They offer our international customers faster order processing, more bookstores, increased representation at tradeshows worldwide, and the high-quality, responsive service our customers have come to expect.

EUROPE, MIDDLE EAST, AND AFRICA
(except Germany, Switzerland, and Austria)

INQUIRIES
International Thomson Publishing Europe
Berkshire House
168-173 High Holborn
London WC1V 7AA
United Kingdom
Telephone: 44-71-497-1422
Fax: 44-71-497-1426
Email: ora.orders@itpuk.co.uk

ORDERS
International Thomson Publishing Services, Ltd.
Cheriton House, North Way
Andover, Hampshire SP10 5BE
United Kingdom
Telephone: 44-264-342-832 (UK orders)
Telephone: 44-264-342-806 (outside UK)
Fax: 44-264-364418 (UK orders)
Fax: 44-264-342761 (outside UK)

GERMANY, SWITZERLAND, AND AUSTRIA
International Thomson Publishing GmbH
O'Reilly-International Thomson Verlag
Attn: Mr. G. Miske
Königswinterer Strasse 418
53227 Bonn
Germany
Telephone: 49-228-970240
Fax: 49-228-441342
Email: anfragen@orade.ora.com

ASIA
(except Japan)

INQUIRIES
International Thomson Publishing Asia
221 Henderson Road
#05 10 Henderson Building
Singapore 0315
Telephone: 65-272-6496
Fax: 65-272-6498

ORDERS
Telephone: 65-268-7867
Fax: 65-268-6727

AUSTRALIA
WoodsLane Pty. Ltd.
Unit 8, 101 Darley Street (P.O. Box 935)
Mona Vale NSW 2103
Australia
Telephone: 61-2-979-5944
Fax: 61-2-997-3348
Email: woods@tmx.mhs.oz.au

NEW ZEALAND
WoodsLane New Zealand Ltd.
21 Cooks Street (P.O. Box 575)
Wanganui, New Zealand
Telephone: 64-6-347-6543
Fax: 64-6-345-4840
Email: woods@tmx.mhs.oz.au

THE AMERICAS, JAPAN, AND OCEANIA
O'Reilly & Associates, Inc.
103A Morris Street
Sebastopol, CA 95472 U.S.A.
Telephone: 707-829-0515
Telephone: 800-998-9938 (U.S. & Canada)
Fax: 707-829-0104
Email: order@ora.com